THE ENDURANCE OF

Frankenstein

Essays on Mary Shelley's Novel

Edited by George Levine
and U. C. Knoepflmacher

University of California Press
Berkeley, Los Angeles, London

University of California Press
Berkeley and Los Angeles, California

University of California Press, Ltd.
London, England

Copyright © 1979 by
The Regents of the University of California

First Paperback Printing 1982
ISBN 0-520-04640-4
Library of Congress Catalog Card Number: 77-20325
Printed in the United States of America

Book design by Wolfgang Lederer
Vignettes in the text by U. C. Knoepflmacher

Printed in the United States of America

08   07   06   05   04   03   02   01   00
9   8   7   6   5   4   3

The paper used in this publication meets the minimum
requirements of ANSI/NISO Z39.48-1992 (R 1997)
(*Permanence of Paper*). ∞

The Endurance of *Frankenstein*

For the Progeny:
David, Rachel, Julie,
Paul, and Daniel

Contents

Illustrations

Preface

No familiar shapes
Remained, no pleasant images of trees,
Of sea or sky, no colours of green fields;
But huge and mighty forms, that do not live
Like living men, moved slowly through the mind
By day, and were a trouble to my dreams.
—Wordsworth, *The Prelude*

M ARY SHELLEY'S *Frankenstein; or, The Modern Prometheus* grew
out of a parlor game and a nightmare vision. The story of the
book's origin is a famous one, first told in the introduction Mary
Shelley wrote for the 1831 edition of the novel. The two Shelleys,
Byron, Mary's stepsister Claire Clairmont, and John William Polidori (Byron's physician) spent a "wet, ungenial summer in the Swiss
Alps." Byron suggested that "each write a ghost story." If one is to
trust Mary Shelley's account (and James Rieger has shown the un-
trustworthiness of its chronology and particulars), only she and
"poor Polidori" took the contest seriously. The two "illustrious
poets," according to her, "annoyed by the platitude of prose,
speedily relinquished their uncongenial task." Polidori, too, is
made to seem careless, unable to handle his story of a "skull-headed
lady." Though Mary Shelley is just as deprecating when she speaks
of her own "tiresome unlucky ghost story," she also suggests that
its sources went deeper. Her truant muse became active as soon as
she fastened on the "idea" of "making only a transcript of the grim
terrors of my waking dream": "'I have found it! What terrified me
will terrify others.'"

The twelve essays in this collection attest to the endurance of
Mary Shelley's "waking dream." Appropriately, though less roman-
tically, this book also grew out of a playful conversation at a party.
When several of us discovered that we were all closet aficionados
of Mary Shelley's novel, we suggested, half-jokingly, that a book

might be written in which each contributor-contestant might try to account for the persistent hold that *Frankenstein* continues to exercise on the popular imagination. Within a few months, two films—Warhol's *Frankenstein* and Mel Brooks's *Young Frankenstein*—and the Hall-Landau and Isherwood-Bachardy television versions of the novel appeared to remind us of our blunted purpose. We took these manifestations as an auspicious sign.

Beyond this sign, of course, were earlier ones. James Rieger, Robert Kiely, Masao Miyoshi, Ellen Moers, George Levine, L. J. Swingle, and Irving Massey all had written essays conclusively showing that *Frankenstein* was a novel that could not be put aside with the conventional highbrow dismissals of popular culture. And Christopher Small had devoted an entire book, *Mary Shelley's Frankenstein: Tracing the Myth* (Pittsburgh, 1973), to the tale's Romantic and scientific origins and to its survival into modern technological times. (Brian Aldiss's science-fiction fantasy *Frankenstein Unbound*, which also appeared in 1973, similarly linked the "Frankenstein mentality" to the rise of Western "organized science" and a diseased "technological society.") We felt reassured by these precedents that our own sense of the durability and power of the novel was not idiosyncratic.

Nonetheless, our eagerness to approach *Frankenstein* with the "high seriousness" of the Arnoldian literary critic was not without obvious risks. Might not a *Frankenstein* "perplex" be met with the same mixture of amusement and disbelief always shown by students toward a book assumed to contain nothing more than a story about an awkward and poorly sutured monster? Just as *Frankenstein* lends itself to parodies that belie Mary Shelley's earnest intentions, would not our own collection be received as a self-parody of the solemnity of academic criticism? Our undertaking, we also realized, might raise questions even among those more serious readers who would not have to be convinced that *Frankenstein* is much more than an adolescent flight that has somehow managed to cash in clumsily on popular traditions. Do not the stunning ambivalences of the novel defy analysis? How much of the book's complexity is actually the result of Mary Shelley's self-conscious art and how much is merely the product of the happy circumstances of subject, moment, milieu? The novel intimates that it knows little about its implications (although it seems clear enough about its literary sources in Milton, Gothic fiction, and Romantic poetry). Are not its energies, therefore, un-self-conscious and accidental?

Such questions are valid, and each contributor to this volume indirectly provides his or her own answers. *Frankenstein* continues to be read, the book's sales periodically increased by its latest popular manifestation in film or television. The essays gathered here try to account for our fascination with its rich store of fantasy. No single essay is sufficient. Together, however, the contributors suggest that *Frankenstein* resists the overly simple—sometimes simpleminded—adaptations our culture has provided. When we return to the text—whether it be the 1818 or the 1831 version—we invariably find that it is larger, infinitely more complicated and suggestive than any of its progeny. If popular culture has adapted it, no part of culture can ignore it. Its key images and the central structure of the narrative itself enter both our private and culturally shared store of dream, fantasy, and myth. The Monster, we are startled to discover, is more frightening than we had imagined, precisely because he does not stumble or speak in monosyllables, because he can speak more rationally and more feelingly than we and his creator do, because his destructiveness is not separate from us but an aspect of ourselves, our responsibility. After a century and a half, *Frankenstein* begins to look both inexhaustible and inexplicable.

The inexhaustible quality of the "story" that terrified its nineteen-year-old creator justifies the admittedly partial explications attempted in this collection. Refusing to dissipate itself into mere escapist excitement or to harden into clear and rational meaning, the novel belongs to a prophetic tradition open only, one would have thought, to mature literary imaginations, to a tradition that might include *Faust*, *Prometheus Unbound*, *The Brothers Karamazov*, and *Middlemarch*. Working from a parlor game ghost story contest, out of a mind cluttered with an extraordinary profusion of serious reading, with the political philosophy she derived from her father and from her dead mother's writings, the science she learned from Shelley, the moral ideas she adopted from all three, Mary Wollstonecraft Godwin Shelley fashioned a loving and passive Prometheus, destroyed by his ambition, destructive in his love, ambivalent about both.

The essays in this volume address many of the possibilities of meaning implied in this unusual creation. Taken together, they, too, cohere into a stitchwork of disparates. In attempting to come to terms with the text and with that text's impact on other imaginations, they are, like Victor Frankenstein and Mary Shelley, forced to create something new, to isolate the many myths—hovering dreamlike in the novel—that have helped keep Mary Shelley's creation alive. Literary tradition, Gothicism, religion, female psychology, sociology, revolution, language, the nature of the grotesque, the metaphor of animation adopted by film narrative, these are some of the coordinates that can help us understand the awkward instability and miraculous power of *Frankenstein*. Although the readings occasionally contradict each other, they are live alternatives that stem from the ambivalence of the text itself. *Frankenstein* invites, even requires, alternative readings because its mythic core is so flexible, polymorphous, and dependent on antithetical possibilities. Key passages—Victor's dream, the murder of little William, the destruction of the female monster—need to be discussed in different contexts.

The arrangement of the essays requires little explanation. The three writers in the first part are concerned with placing *Frankenstein* into a wider literary continuum. George Levine examines the pervasiveness of the metaphor "Frankenstein" in nineteenth- and twentieth-century fiction and shows, paradoxically, that this irrational romance contains the seeds of "the myth of realism." Judith Wilt looks at the novel's antecedents in Gothic fiction—a fiction which, she argues, enacts the religious patterns it seems so self-consciously to reject. Andrew Griffin fastens on the novel's images of ice and fire to investigate its kinship with later romances such as *Jane Eyre*.

The two essays grouped in the second part turn to biographical explanations for the novel's unusual vitality. Ellen Moers (whose essay is the only one not specifically written for this volume) links the book to Mary Shelley's own experience as a mother and sees it, consequently, as a specifically feminine birth-myth. U. C. Knoepflmacher, on the other hand, stresses Mary Shelley's motherless childhood and her ambivalent reaction to her philosopher-father as a key to her double impulse of empathy with, and rejection of, the increasingly aggressive monster.

The three essays in the third part enlarge the frame of reference. Kate Ellis reads *Frankenstein* as an antibourgeois fiction in which Mary Shelley relies on her mother's *A Vindication of the Rights of Woman* to dramatize the radical failure of family structures at a time when home and production have become separated. Lee Sterrenburg explores the political dimensions of the monster-metaphor used in both revolutionary and antirevolutionary writings and shows how later in the century "Frankenstein's monster" became a political trope for the Victorians. Peter Dale Scott, on the other hand, considers the novel against the background of Percy Shelley's Promethean politics and poetry and shows how Mary Shelley enlisted her reading in Dante and Volney to broaden and humanize her husband's vision.

In the fourth part Peter Brooks and Philip Stevick return to the text itself. Brooks considers the opposition between language and nature dramatized in *Frankenstein* and the implications that this clash holds for the social contract broken in the novel. Stevick locates *Frankenstein* among fictions that are simultaneously serious and comical in their mediation between irrational sources and their conscious or "secondary" elaborations.

The two essays in the fifth and final part turn to the popular adaptations of the myth. Albert LaValley provides a brief survey of the "progeny" of *Frankenstein* on the comic stage and in film and in television. William Nestrick rounds out the volume by explaining why the novel's central concern with animation should have been so eagerly adopted by the filmmaker. Both essays provide (along with many striking illustrations) new insights into our culture's persistent fascination with monstrosity and creation.

In writing their essays, the contributors worked in awareness of each other's contributions. Internal cross-references are therefore plentiful, in the nature of both agreements and disagreements. One disagreement the editors refused to settle was about the text. There are two excellent modern editions of *Frankenstein*: one edited by M. K. Joseph for Oxford University Press (1971), the other edited by James Rieger for the Bobbs-Merrill Company (1974). Rieger's volume provides all known variants, yet uses the 1818 edition as the basic text. Since several essayists deemed the 1831 edition to be the superior one, they preferred to rely on Joseph's edition of the later version. We saw no point in making the contributors conform to one text or the other. We were ourselves divided on this issue, and hence "neither of us possessed the slightest pre-eminence over the other" (chapter 1, 1818 version), but were "possessed by the very spirit of kindness and indulgence" (chapter 2, 1831 version)—the parental spirit of Alphonse and Catherine Frankenstein.

G. L.
U. C. K.

Mary Wollstonecraft Godwin Shelley and *Frankenstein*: A Chronology

PETER DALE SCOTT

1797

August 30. Mary born to William and his wife, Mary Wollstonecraft Godwin, who dies from postpartum hemorrhage September 10.

1801

December 21. William Godwin remarries a widow, Mary Jane Clairmont, who brings to the Godwin family her children Charles, aged seven, and Jane (later known as Claire), aged four.

1812

November 11. Mary's first meeting with Percy Bysshe Shelley. Mary resides with Baxter family in Dundee, 1812–14.

1814

May 5. Renewed contact in London with Percy Bysshe Shelley.

July 28. Percy Shelley elopes with Mary and Claire Clairmont from the Godwin household to France and Switzerland.

August 27. Two days after renting a house for six months at Brunnen, Lake of Lucerne, the Shelley ménage abruptly depart for England.

September 13. Return to London. Percy beleaguered by creditors and bailiffs.

November 30. Harriet, Percy's wife, gives birth to her second child, Charles.

1815

January. Erotic correspondence and involvement between Mary and T. J. Hogg.

February 22. Mary gives birth to premature female child, which dies March 6.

March 19. (Mary's Journal) "Dream that my little baby came to life again; that it had only been cold, and that we rubbed it before the fire, and it lived."

August. Mary and Percy, without Claire, settle at Bishopsgate, Windsor.

1816

January 24. A son William is born to Mary and Percy.

May 3. Percy and Mary, with Claire, leave for Switzerland, arriving ten days later at Geneva, where they meet up with Byron and Polidori.

June 15-16. Probable dates of discussion "of the principle of life," and of Byron's proposal for a story-telling competition, after which Mary, in a waking dream, sees "the pale student of unhallowed arts."

July 21-27. Shelley ménage visit Mont Blanc and the Mer de Glace at Montanvert.

July 24. (Mary's Journal) "Write my story." First journal reference to *Frankenstein*.

August 29-September 8. Shelley ménage return to England, where they settle at Bath September 10.

October 9. Fanny Imlay, Mary's half-sister, commits suicide.

December 5. (Mary's Letters) "Finished the 4 Chap of Frankenstein."

December 6-9. Mary reads Wollstonecraft's *Rights of Woman*.

December 10. Body of Harriet Shelley found drowned in Serpentine, Hyde Park.

December 30. Percy and Mary married, London.

1817

March 18. Shelleys, with Claire and her child Allegra by Byron, occupy their house at Marlow.

March 27. Lord Eldon in Court of Chancery denies Shelley custody of his two children by Harriet.

April 10-17. (Mary's Journal) "Correct 'Frankenstein.'"

April 18-May 13. Mary transcribes *Frankenstein*.

May 22-23. Shelleys to London to arrange for *Frankenstein*'s publication.

June 18. John Murray, Byron's publisher, rejects *Frankenstein*.
August 3. Percy sends *Frankenstein* to his publisher Charles Ollier,
who rejects it.
August 22. Percy contracts for publication of *Frankenstein* with
Lackington, Allen, & Co.
September 2. The Shelleys' daughter Clara born.
September 23. Percy to London to correct proofs of *Frankenstein*
and to arrange publication of *Revolt of Islam*.
October 22. (Mary's Journal) "Transcribe 'Frankenstein.'"
October 28. Percy sends Lackington from Marlow last corrections
of proofs by post.
November 8–19. Mary joins Percy in London to oversee publica-
tion of *History of a Six Weeks' Tour*, while Percy handles *Revolt of
Islam*.
December 3. Percy forwards dedication of *Frankenstein* from Mar-
low to Lackington & Co.

1818

January. *Frankenstein* published anonymously (London: Printed for
Lackington, Hughes, Harding, Mavor & Jones, Finsbury Square,
1818). Percy forwards presentation volumes to Sir Walter Scott
January 2.
January 15. (Letter from Percy to Charles Ollier) "Do you hear
anything said of 'Frankenstein'?"
February 10. Shelleys leave Marlow for literary scene of London.
March 12. Shelleys leave England permanently for Italy.
September 24. Death in Venice of Clara Shelley.
December 20. (Mary's Journal) "Correct 'Frankenstein.'"

1819

June 7. Death in Rome of William Shelley.
November 9. Date of revised manuscript of Mary's autobiographi-
cal novel *Mathilda*.
November 12. Birth of Mary's only child to survive, Percy Florence.

1822

June 16. A miscarriage almost costs Mary her life.
July 8. Percy Bysshe Shelley drowned in Gulf of Spezia.

1823

July 28. Peake's melodrama, "Presumption; or, The Fate of Frankenstein" performed at English Opera House. This is followed by second edition of *Frankenstein* (London: printed for G. W. B. Whittaker, Ave Maria Lane, 1823), 2 vol.

August 25. Mary returns to England.

Publication of Mary's novel *Valperga*, followed by *The Last Man* (1826), *Perkin Warbeck* (1830), *Lodore* (1835), and *Falkner* (1837).

1831

October 15. Date of Mary's Introduction to third edition of *Frankenstein* (London: Henry Colburn and Richard Bentley, 1831), Standard Novels.

1836

April 7. Death of William Godwin.

1851

February 1. Mary Shelley dies.

PART
ONE

TRADITIONS:

*Looking Forwards
and Backwards*

The Ambiguous Heritage
of *Frankenstein*

GEORGE LEVINE

I

IT'S A COMMONPLACE NOW, that everybody talks about *Frankenstein*, but nobody reads it. That depends on what is meant by "nobody." It is possible, of course, that "Frankenstein" became an entry in every serious recent dictionary by way of the variations—dramas, films, television versions—through which Mary Shelley's monster and his creator most obviously survive. But while *Frankenstein* is a phenomenon of popular culture, it is so because it has tapped into the center of Western feeling and imagination: we can hear echoes of it, not only in Gothic fiction, science fiction, and fantasies of all sorts, but in far more "respectable" works, written before the glut of popular cinematic distortions. *Frankenstein* has become a metaphor for our own cultural crises, and survives even yet in high literary culture whose professors may have seen Boris Karloff stumbling through the fog, hands outstretched, at least once too often.

Of course, *Frankenstein* is a "minor" novel, radically flawed by its sensationalism, by the inflexibly public and oratorical nature of even its most intimate passages. But it is, arguably, the most important minor novel in English. If we return to the text for a check on Boris Karloff, or, recently, Mel Brooks, or for some further light on Percy Shelley, invariably we find that the book is larger and richer than any of its progeny and too complex to serve as mere background. Even in our dictionaries, "Frankenstein" has become a vital metaphor, peculiarly appropriate to a culture dominated by a consumer technology, neurotically obsessed with "getting in touch" with its authentic self and frightened at what it is discovering: "a work, or agency that proves troublesomely uncontrollable,

3

esp. to its creator."[1] Latent in the metaphor are some of the fundamental dualisms, the social, moral, political and metaphysical crises of Western history since the French Revolution. It may well appear that the metaphorical implications are far more serious than the novel that gave birth to them, but that novel has qualities that allow it to exfoliate as creatively and endlessly as any important myth; if it threatens to lapse into banality and bathos, it yet lives through unforgettable dreamlike images—of the kind explored elsewhere in this volume by Philip Stevick.

Frankenstein echoes the old stories of Faust and Prometheus, exploring the limits of ambition and rebelliousness and their moral implications; but it is also the tale of a *"modern Prometheus,"* and as such it is a secular myth, with no metaphysical machinery, no gods: the creation is from mortal bodies with the assistance of electricity, not spirit; and the deaths are not pursued beyond the grave. The dream vision out of which the work grows—Mary Shelley's vision embodied in that "dreary night in November"—is echoed by Victor Frankenstein's dream vision within the novel proper, of worms and shrouds, not of angels or of devils. The dreams emerge from the complex experiences that placed the young Mary Shelley, both personally and intellectually, at a point of crisis in our modern culture, where idealism, faith in human perfectibility, and revolutionary energy were counterbalanced by the moral egotism of her radical father, the potential infidelity of her ideal husband, the cynical diabolism of Byron, the felt reality of her own pregnancy, and a great deal more. Peter Scott and U. C. Knoepflmacher discuss elsewhere in this volume what the circumstances were. But the text itself announces clearly, as only dream can make clear, the terms of our modern crises.

The distinctiveness of the Frankenstein metaphor, its peculiar appropriateness to the developing cultures of nineteenth- and twentieth-century England and America, can be usefully clarified by remarking briefly on Percy Shelley's relation to the novel. In the introduction to his excellent edition of the text, James Rieger has shown that Percy watched closely over the development of Mary's manuscript in all of its stages, and received "carte blanche" from

1. This definition is from *Webster's Third New International Dictionary* (1971). *The American Heritage Dictionary* (1969) defines it similarly: "Any agency or creation that slips from the control of and ultimately destroys its creator."

4

her to revise it as he would.[2] More than editor, Percy was, in Rieger's view, "a minor collaborator" (p. xliv). Yet, despite his involvement in many details of the writing, despite the persistence of Shelleyan images and parallels between Victor's and Percy Shelley's education,[3] the central imagination is certainly Mary's alone. Under Percy's eyes, perhaps without his fully knowing it (perhaps without fully knowing it herself), Mary created a narrative that put her husband himself to the test—that juxtaposed an ideal vision against the banalities and corruption of ordinary physical and social life in ways that, as I have described them elsewhere,[4] anticipated the preoccupations of the Victorian novel, and through it, of the culture itself. Shortly after *Frankenstein*, Percy Shelley was to create his own Prometheus, a figure who triumphs by renouncing revenge for a visionary love and generative passivity. The Spirit of the Hours, describing the effect of the fall of the tyrant Jupiter, provides us with a Shelleyan vision of man redeemed:

> The loathsome mask has fallen, the Man remains,—
> Sceptreless, free, uncircumscribed,—but Man:
> Equal, unclassed, tribeless and nationless,
> Exempt from awe, worship, degree, the King
> Over himself; just, gentle, wise; but man
> Passionless? no: yet free from guilt or pain,
> Which were, for his will made, or suffered them
> Not yet exempt, tho' ruling them like slaves,
> From chance, and death, and mutability,
> The clogs of that which else might oversoar
> The loftiest star of unascended heaven,
> Pinnacled dim in the intense inane.[5]

But *Frankenstein*, of course, denies love its triumph. Men and monster are anything but rulers over guilt and pain: Walton's nar-

2. James Rieger, ed., *Frankenstein; or, The Modern Prometheus* (the 1818 text) (Indianapolis, 1974). All quotations from *Frankenstein* will be from this edition; references will be incorporated into the text.

3. Joan Baum, of York College, CUNY, has pointed out to me several very interesting parallels between Victor Frankenstein's scientific training and Percy Shelley's.

4. "Frankenstein and the Tradition of Realism," *Novel* VII, no. 1 (1973): 517–29.

5. *Prometheus Unbound*, act III, scene 4, lines 193–204.

rative ends in the frustration of his enterprise; Victor's ends in a death caused by his creature or, more precisely, by his own vengeful pursuit of it; the Monster, with no relation consummated except through murder, goes off to self-immolation. Early on, Frankenstein tells Walton that "a human being in perfection ought always to preserve a calm and peaceful mind, and never to allow passion or a transitory desire to disturb his tranquillity" (p. 51). But the novel refuses to allow human beings to remain "in perfection." Percy Shelley's "loftiest star" may resemble Walton's or Victor's aspirations, yet the novel itself is located, with the weight of earthly gravity, in the material world. The weight is a continuing comment on Victor's ambition, as the obscene flesh of the charnel house is the imaged irony of Victor's attempt to create life out of matter. To attempt to transcend time, chance, death, and mutability by means of matter—the materials of time—is literally chimerical.

Yet the novel offers us no other means. The passivity and acquiescence of Percy Shelley's Prometheus, by which he triumphs over Jupiter, has its analogue in Victor Frankenstein's unwilled obsession with creating life. Victor falls into a "trance," so driven by his creative energy that even what is loathsome becomes possible to him. In his "work-shop of filthy creation" he loses "all soul or sensation" (p. 50) (and the equation of the two is itself interesting). But it is almost a parody of the loss of self in the Christian ideal, or the Shelleyan one. And the trance of the laboratory is echoed in the various trances by which Victor lapses out of action and overt responsibility throughout the narrative. Such trances are obviously not Promethean triumphs of the spirit, but physical, material, time-bound effects of the very passion that man "in perfection" ought not allow to disturb him. *Frankenstein* rejects the conception of man's spirit unanchored in flesh. In contrast to Percy Shelley's exploration and celebration of at least the dream of the power of spirit to fold "over the world its healing wings," Mary Shelley's novel can be seen as an exploration of the powerlessness of love to control the passions that are hidden deep in our being, that are sure to find physical expression, and, finally, that are unimaginable without pain or guilt.

Ironically, then, *Frankenstein*'s mysterious power derives from a thoroughly earthy, practical, and unideal vision of human nature and possibility. Its modernity lies in its transformation of fantasy and traditional Christian and pagan myths into unremitting secularity, into the myth of mankind as it must work within the limits of the visible, physical world. The novel echoes, for example, with the language and the narrative of *Paradise Lost*, but it is *Paradise Lost* without angels, or devils, or God. When the Monster invokes the analogy between himself and Adam or Satan, we are obviously invited to think of Frankenstein as God. Yet, we know that the Monster is a double of Victor himself, and that as he acts out his satanic impulses he is acting out another aspect of Victor's creation of him. God, however, cannot be a rebel; nor can he be Adam or Satan's "double." He cannot be complicit in his creature's weaknesses, cannot be destroyed by what he creates. The whole narrative of *Frankenstein* is, indeed, acted out in the absence of God. The grand gestures of *Frankenstein* may suggest a world of fantasy that has acquired a profound escapist appeal in modern culture, but they take place in a framework that necessarily makes an ironic commentary on them, even while our sympathies are drawn to dreams of the more than human the narrative will not allow.

This characteristic tension between an impinging, conditional, and time-bound world and a dream of something freer and better makes the central subject matter and form of the nineteenth-century novel and, ironically, of nineteenth-century science as well. The old myths enter nineteenth-century fiction, but they do so in the mode of realism (which Northrop Frye, in another context, has described as an "ironic mode"[6]). Thus, though it would be absurd to claim Mary Shelley as a direct "influence" on the dominant literary and scientific forms of the century, we can see that in her secularization of the creation myth she invented a metaphor that was irresistible to the culture as a whole. As George Eliot turned to Feuerbach to allow her to transform Christianity into a humanism with all the emotional power of religion, so the novel itself, as a genre, put its faith in a material world of fact that, as Matthew Arnold pointed out, had failed us. In writers as central and various as Feuerbach, Comte, Darwin, Marx, Frazer, and Freud we can find Victor Frankenstein's activity: the attempt to discover in matter what we had previously attributed to spirit, the bestowing *on* matter (or history, or society, or nature) the values once given to God.

6. Northrop Frye, *Anatomy of Criticism* (Princeton, 1957), p. 134 and *passim*.

This argument puts Mary Shelley in some rather remarkable company, but, of course, the point is not to equate the achievement of her little "ghost story" with that of the great thinkers named. The claim is simply that Mary Shelley did, indeed, create an image, with the authenticity of dream vision, that became prophetic; that the image articulates powerfully the dominant currents of her culture and ours; and that it is for these reasons that *Frankenstein* has survived its own adolescent clumsiness and its later distortions.

The pervasiveness of the Frankenstein metaphor in modern consciousness testifies to the richness and variousness of its implications. The dictionary definition focuses only on the uncontrollable nature of the thing created; but the image of the created Monster, emerging from the isolated workshop of the obsessed but otherwise gentle scientist, unfolds into more possibilities than I can describe. Serious readings of the novel, of the sort that follow in this volume, will work out in greater detail some of these possibilities, all of which are related to the way the myth is anchored in a newly secular reading of experience. Even Judith Wilt's evocative exploration of how Mary Shelley's narrative, reflecting a negative trinity, arches back toward a traditional religious form, reenforces the sense that *Frankenstein* offers us a metaphor that expresses the central dualities and tensions of our time by positing a world without God. At the risk of arbitrary exclusions and of belaboring what may seem obvious, I want to outline some of the major implications of the Frankenstein metaphor in contemporary consciousness, and as they have their sources in the novel proper.

II

1. *Birth and Creation.* In *Frankenstein* we are confronted immediately by the displacement of God and woman from the acts of conception and birth. Where Victor imagines himself embarked on the creation of a new race that would bless him, he behaves, even before his creation proves a monster, as though he is engaged in unnatural, shameful activity. Neither of the two attitudes is entirely undercut by the narrative, even though the dream of the new race is, of course, exploded. The image of Frankenstein in his laboratory is not only of an unnatural act, but also one of an heroic dream, and the novel's insistence, even through Walton and the Monster, on Victor's heroic nature, implies that the creation

without God, without woman, need not be taken as an unequivocal evil.

The displacement of woman obviously reflects a fear of birth and Mary Shelley's own ambivalence about childbearing (a subject explored below by Ellen Moers and U. C. Knoepflmacher); the Monster's presence on the wedding night becomes a permanent image of the horror of sexuality as opposed to the ideal and nonsexual love of the cousins, Victor and Elizabeth. The image of the Monster lurking ominously in the background, with Elizabeth sprawled on the bed, is one of the dominant icons of the film versions. Obviously, the image is profoundly phallic and profoundly violent, an unacceptable alternative to and consequence of the act of conception in the laboratory. Indeed, in the novel itself (as I shall point out later) the two scenes precisely echo each other. In both cases, there is an association that runs as constant ground-motif through the novel.

Sexuality and birth, imagination and creation are, in this heavily material world, reverse images of death and destruction. Frankenstein and his creature come to represent, in part, an alternative to the violence of sexuality, on the one hand, and to the sheer spirituality of divine creation, on the other. Victor and his Monster hover between, leaning away from the flesh alive (ironically, only to dabble in dead flesh), imitating the divine rather than the human sexual act.

2. *The Overreacher.* The aspiration to divine creative activity (akin to Romantic notions of the poet) places Victor Frankenstein in the tradition of Faustian overreachers. Frankenstein the creator is also Frankenstein the modern Prometheus, full of the great Romantic dream—concretized for a moment in the French Revolution—of a rebirth of mankind. True, Victor is seeking a kind of immortality, but, as Ellen Moers points out, Mary Shelley works the Faust tradition in an unusual (and, I might again add, secularizing) way by having Victor seek immortality not directly for himself but in the creation of offspring. If we detect the stirrings of selfishness in Victor's desire to have a whole species that would bless him, the text still insists on the profundity of his moral character and the conscious morality of all of his choices save the fatal one. Indeed (by a strategy that other novelists would have to adopt[7]), Franken-

7. The figure of the passive hero in Scott's novels is described carefully

stein is removed from direct personal responsibility even for his own ambitions: for the most part he is described as passively consumed by energies larger than himself or as quite literally unconscious and ill when his being conscious might have changed the course of the narrative.

The theme of the overreacher is largely complicated by the evidence that Victor's worst sin is not the creation of the Monster but his refusal to take responsibility for it. It is as though God had withdrawn from his creation. Characteristically, in the secularizing myth, Mary Shelley has imagined the responsibilities of God shifted to mankind. The burden is too great to allow us an easy moral placing of Victor. The theme of the overreacher in this context brings us to the kind of impasse that *Frankenstein* itself reaches in the mutual destruction of creator and created. That is, we see that the ambition is heroic and admirable, yet deadly because humans are incapable of fulfilling their dreams in material reality, or, paradoxically, of bearing the responsibility for them should they succeed.

When Victor refuses to tell Walton the secrets of infusing dead matter with life, we find the fullest justification of the popular antiintellectual interpretation of the Faustian theme. Early, Victor warns Walton: "Learn from me, if not by my precepts, at least by my example, how dangerous is the acquirement of knowledge, and how much happier that man is who believes his native town to be the world, than he who aspires to become greater than his nature will allow" (p. 48). Victor puts himself forth as a living parable of the dangers of overreaching, yet by the end he refuses to deny the validity of his undertaking and cries, "Yet another may succeed." The novel will not resolve the issue.

3. *Rebellion and Moral Isolation.* Obviously, these aspects of the myth are related to "overreaching." Yet it is important to note that they apply not only to Victor but to the Monster as well, whose ambition is really limited to the longing for domestic affection. Victor himself is not quite imagined as a rebel, except perhaps in his pursuit of alchemical knowledge after his father ridicules him

---

in Alexander Welsh, *The Hero of the Waverly Novels* (New York, 1968). This figure recurs with extraordinary persistence in Victorian fiction, most obviously in Dickens (cf. Oliver Twist himself), and all the way from Dobbin to Daniel Deronda.

for reading Paracelsus. In any case, unlike the Monster, he does not consciously rebel against authority. Yet, "animated by an almost supernatural enthusiasm," Victor takes up an intellectual pursuit (whence did the "principle of life proceed") that places him outside the traditional Christian world, and that ought to make him, like Adam eating the apple, a rebel against God. The context, however, is quietly un-Christian. Victor speaks in a scientific or at least naturalistic language that assumes a natural material answer to what was once a religious and metaphysical question. "One of the phenomena which had peculiarly attracted my attention was the structure of the human frame, and, indeed, any animal endued with life" (p. 46). And though he concedes that "some miracle might have produced" the discovery, "the stages of the discovery were distinct and probable" (p. 47). Such passages, in their insistence on the merely human credibility of the extraordinary narrative, are characteristic; and although we can recognize here that Victor has stepped over the limits of safe human behavior, and that his success will be blighted, the rhetoric of scientific probability is never seriously undercut in the book.

The moral isolation into which Victor sinks is, in effect, chosen for him by his obsession. Like Raskolnikov plotting murder, like Dimmesdale guilty of adultery, Victor lives with a secret that we understand, without explanation, must be kept from public knowledge. Here the residue of metaphysical shame works its effects, but social and psychological explanations offer themselves immediately. In any case, the activity separates Victor from normal life as fully as a direct act of murder would. He works in a solitary chamber, or cell, "at the top of the house" (p. 50). After analyzing "all the minutiae of causation," he wonders why "among so many men of genius, who had directed their inquiries towards the same science, . . . I alone should be reserved to discover so astonishing a secret" (p. 47). This humble pride echoes the tone of the peaceful Frankenstein household in Geneva; but its association with Victor's obsession with "filthy" work makes even the humility of the scientific quest an act of rebellion against the enclosed harmony of that household.

The Monster's isolation derives not so much from his actions as from his hideousness. Where Victor moves from domestic bliss to the garret, the Monster leaves the garret to seek that bliss. Victor's revolutionary action causes his isolation; the Monster's isolation causes his revolutionary action. "Believe me, Frankenstein," he says, "I was benevolent; my soul glowed with love and humanity; but am I not alone, miserably alone?" (p. 95). Unless Victor creates a companion for him, he warns, he will not again be "virtuous"; "I will glut the maw of death until it be satiated with the blood of your remaining friends" (p. 94).

Despite the apparent moral simplicity of most modern versions of *Frankenstein*, the Frankenstein metaphor implies great ambiguity about where the burden of good and evil rests. Both Victor and the Monster imply resistance to the established order. Lee Sterrenburg points out how the iconography of the monster is clearly connected with Bonaparte and political revolution. In early Romantic literature, of course, rebellion is more likely to be a virtue than a sin, and the Monster makes a strong case against social injustice. Even Walton, though warned by Victor, is instinctively convinced of the justice of the Monster's arguments.

The constantly shifting moral perspective of the narrative results from the fact that each of its major figures—Walton, Victor, the Monster—is at once victimizer and victim; and this tradition is even continued in modern movie versions. In novel and films, any singularity is punished by the community, either by forcing isolation or by literal imprisonment. The three major figures and Felix De Lacey variously challenge the established order and acquire dignity by virtue of the challenge and of the punishment that ensues. Thus the novel, which might be taken as a parable of the necessity of limits in an entirely secular world, may also be taken as a parable of the necessity for revolutionary reprisal (at whatever cost) because of the social and political limits that frustrate the noblest elements of the human spirit.

4. *The Unjust Society.* After the execution of the innocent Justine, Elizabeth Lavenza, the vessel of domestic purity, tells Victor that "men appear to me as monsters thirsting for each other's blood" (p. 88). Even if she retracts immediately ("Yet I am certainly unjust"), the notion that the world of men is itself "monstrous" is a constant motif of the novel. Even in the most conventional of the modern Frankenstein films, the motif emerges when, in the obligatory misty night, the villagers turn out as a maddened lynch mob and transform Frankenstein and the Monster into victims of an overwhelming attack on the castle. In almost every film, the townspeople are almost comically banal, the burgomeisters and gendar-

merie officious and totally without sensibility. Absurd though these figures may be (Cedric Hardwicke's wooden arm is transformed in *Dr. Strangelove* and *Young Frankenstein* into appropriately grotesque and comic parodies), they echo the essentially shallow ambitions and dreams of security that fill the background of the novel.

There the motif is handled subtly enough to make the monstrous problematic. Elizabeth's sense that "men are monsters" recurs in the monster's ingenious hectoring of Victor in a fine Godwinian rational discourse. Moreover, the De Lacey story is a continuing narrative of injustice, on all sides. And in his last speech to Walton, the Monster makes clear once more that his own monstrousness is not really different from that of the world that condemns him. Of Victor, he says:

For whilst I destroyed his hopes, I did not satisfy my own desires. They were for ever ardent and craving; still I desired love and fellowship, and I was still spurned. Was there no injustice in this? Am I to be thought the only criminal, when all human kind sinned against me? Why do you not hate Felix, who drove his friend from his door with contumely? Why do you not execrate the rustic who sought to destroy the saviour of his child? Nay, these are virtuous and immaculate beings. I, the miserable and the abandoned, am an abortion to be spurned at, and kicked, and trampled on. Even now my blood boils at the recollection of this injustice. [P. 219]

The novel has taught us to distrust the evenhandedness of the law that Victor's father praises before Justine is executed; we understand with the Monster that greed is a commonplace of social activity. Not even the family unit—Frankenstein's and the Monster's ideal—escapes the contamination that almost makes rebellion necessary and that makes Victor's escape to his laboratory from Geneva seem psychologically and socially explicable.

5. *The Defects of Domesticity.* The theme of the overreacher and the rebel—the Promethean theme—is the other side of the theme of ideal domesticity. Percy Shelley, in the preface he wrote—in the guise of Mary—for the 1818 edition, insisted that *Frankenstein*'s chief concern is "the exhibition of the amiableness of domestic affection, and the excellence of universal virtue" (p. 7). Although this assertion is more than a devious defense of a possibly offensive story, it is only part of the truth. Kate Ellis shows elsewhere in this volume that Mary Shelley treats "domestic affection" in such a way as to make it possible to read *Frankenstein* as an attack on the

13

very traditions of bourgeois society it purports to be celebrating. Certainly, as we have seen, "the amiableness of domestic affection" does nothing to satisfy Victor Frankenstein's ambitions, or to prevent the monstrous creation; nor, in the tale of the Monster's wanderings, does it extend to anything outside itself to allow for the domestication of the Monster's loving energies. "Domestic affection" is, in a way, defined by its exclusion of energy and by its resistance to the larger community. The Monster instinctively believes in the rhetoric of domesticity and the need for community; it is psychologically and dramatically appropriate that he should exhaust himself in the total destruction of ostensibly ideal domesticity when he discovers that he is excluded from it, and that the ideal is false.

The dream of moving beyond the ideal prison of domesticity and the warning that such dreaming is deadly are among the staple patterns of nineteenth-century realistic fiction. Realism tends to remove the spirit, the ideal vision, the angel, from the Miltonic worldscape to the bourgeois household. The final reduction of the religious to the secular is perhaps most evident in the way the home is imagined as a temple. In the idealized Elizabeth Lavenza, in Frankenstein's self-sacrificing mother, in selfless Justine, we have foreshadowings of the Victorian angel in the house. None of the angels survive: the monstrous (which turns out to be at least partly sexual, the creation of human energy exerted on matter) intrudes on the angelic world. The threat of such intrusion is central to the meaning of the Frankenstein metaphor, and brings us to the edge of the conception of civilization and its discontents. Even domestic affection is imprisoning, a weight on individual freedom, and it may be only less disastrous than the energy required to break free. Either way one turns, to a defective society or a rampant individualism, there is no peace without the sort of frustrated compromise Walton makes and that the Victorian novel will insist on.

6. *The Double*. Almost every critic of *Frankenstein* has noted that Victor and his Monster are doubles.[8] The doubleness even enters some of the popular versions and is un-self-consciously accepted by everyone who casually calls the Monster "Frankenstein." The motif of the *Doppelgänger* was certainly in Mary's mind during the writ-

8. See, for example, Masao Miyoshi, *The Divided Self* (New York, 1969), and Robert Kiely, *The Romantic Novel in England* (Cambridge, Mass., 1972), esp. pp. 170–73.

ing, as it was a part of the Gothic tradition in which she wrote; moreover, it is one with which she would have been intimately connected through Shelley himself, as in "Alastor" and "Epipsychidion." So pervasive has been the recognition that the Monster and Frankenstein are two aspects of the same being that the writers in this volume assume rather than argue it. The narrative requires us to see that the doubling extends beyond the two major narrators: Walton is obviously another aspect of Frankenstein, and Clerval yet another; Elizabeth can be paired with Victor's mother, with Justine, and with the unfinished "bride" of the Monster. U. C. Knoepflmacher brilliantly argues further that the Monster and Elizabeth are really one. (In the film *The Bride of Frankenstein*, as Albert LaValley reminds us, Elsa Lanchester plays both Mary Shelley and the monstrous bride; and in the recent Warhol *Frankenstein*, Victor's wife is also, and accurately, his sister.) Such doublings and triplings, with reverberations in and out of the novel in Mary Shelley's own life and in modern psychological theory, suggest again the instability and ambivalence of the book's "meanings."

They point centrally to the way "Frankenstein" as a modern metaphor implies a conception of the divided self, the creator and his work at odds. The civilized man or woman contains within the self a monstrous, destructive, and self-destructive energy. The angel in the house entails a demon outside it, the Monster leering through the window at the horrified Victor and the murdered Elizabeth. Here, in particular, we can watch the specially secularized versions of traditional mythology. The devil and the angel of the morality play are replaced by a modern pre-Freudian psychology that removes the moral issue from the metaphysical context—the traditional concepts of good and evil—and places it entirely within the self. Morality is, as it were, replaced by schizophrenia. Frankenstein's longing for domesticity is echoed in the Monster's (and in Walton's expression of loneliness in the opening pages); Frankenstein's obsession with science is echoed in the monster's obsession with destruction. The two characters haunt and hunt each other through the novel, each evoking from us sympathy for their sufferings, revulsion from their cruelties.

The echoes force themselves on us with a persistence and intensity that override the mere narrative and even enter into popular versions that are not intrinsically concerned with doubling. The book creates a psychomachia, an internal war that has its own authenticity despite the grotesqueness of the external action. If the characters seem shallow as novelistic figures within the conventions of realism we have come to assume are natural to nineteenth-century fiction, it is partly because they are imagined from the start as incomplete (a notion explored in Peter Brooks's essay). They can be seen, indeed, as fragments of a mind in conflict with itself, extremes unreconciled, striving to make themselves whole. Ambition and passivity, hate and love, the need to procreate and the need to destroy are seen, in *Frankenstein*, as symbiotic: the destruction of one is, through various narrative strategies, the destruction of the other.

7. *Technology, Entropy, and the Monstrous*. Perhaps the most obvious and continuing application of the word "Frankenstein" in modern society is to technological advances. This is altogether appropriate to Mary Shelley's original conception of the novel since Victor's discovery of the secret of life is fundamentally scientific; and he talks of his "animation" of the Monster's body as a mere trick of technology. Modern science fiction and modern industry are full of such "animated" beings, the products of computer technology; with the discovery of DNA, biologists even seem on the verge of simulating the natural process of creation of life. But both of these developments are part of the same imagination as Mary Shelley gives us with her Monster: that life is not "spirit" but matter imbued with energy, itself another form of matter.

Martin Tropp has noted that "when Mary Shelley gave her intended 'ghost story' a scientific context, she linked the Gothic concept of the double with technology."[9] Her fears of the creation of life by mere mechanisms, Tropp notes, resulted from her awareness that "technology can never be more than a magnified image of the self" (p. 55). And when that self is engaged in a psychomachia, the result can only be large-scale disaster. In a psychic world of the divided self, in a social world in which domesticity and ambition are seen as incompatible poles, the self expressed in technology can only be what our original dictionary definition tells us, "troublesomely uncontrollable, esp. to its creator," i.e., monstrous. The nightmare quality of the novel depends on this projection of the self into an objectively existing, independent reality over which one

9. Martin Tropp, *Mary Shelley's Monster* (Boston, 1976), p. 52.

necessarily loses control as it acts out one's own monstrous passions. Here all the battery of Freudian equipment comes neatly or, perhaps, explosively into play. All the elements of moral isolation, the grubbing in filthy flesh, the obsessed and inhuman energies that went into the creation of the Monster, can be seen acting themselves out in the destruction they really imply—in the incestuous destructiveness of Victor's ostensibly ideal relation to Elizabeth, in the fraternal hostility buried in his love for poor William, in the hatred of his mother implied in his failure to save Justine (who has adopted Mrs. Frankenstein's very way of life). Such implications are explored in a great deal of criticism of the novel. But the point here is that technology becomes the means by which these buried aspects of the self are enacted. The "work or agency" does not rebel against the creator but actually accomplishes what the creator wants. It is only in his "mental consciousness," as D. H. Lawrence would have called it, that the creator does not know what he wants. The uncontrolled technological creation is particularly frightening and obsessively attractive to modern consciousness because it forces a confrontation with our buried selves. It promises to reveal to us our deepest and most powerful desires, and to enact them. The Monster demands our sympathetic engagement while our social consciousness must be an act of will—almost like Walton's when he finds himself irresistibly attracted by the Monster's talk—reject him.

The duality of our relationship to creator and creature is an echo of our relationship to the technology that we worship even as we recognize that it is close to destroying us. Another way to express the duality, in technological terms, is through the idea of entropy. Victor's overreaching is an attempt to create *new* life. He fails to recognize the necessary secular–scientific myth of entropy: that in any closed system, the new energy generated will be less than the energy expended in its creation, and that ultimately the system will run down. It took a great deal of death to make the new life; the making of the Monster is at the expense of all of Victor's immediate world—brother, father, bride, friend. The world of mere matter is both finite and corrupted. Without the incalculable presence of divine spirit, creation can only entail destruction larger than itself. It is, ultimately, this nightmare image that the Monster represents to our culture.

III

These seven elements of the Frankenstein metaphor are, of course, arbitrarily chosen; each of them has further implications that remain alive for us in the idea of Frankenstein and that have sources in the novel itself. The creator-monster dualism, for example, is also the traditional dualism of mind and body, another form of schizophrenia. The novel has achieved its special place in modern consciousness through its extraordinary resistance to simple resolutions and its almost inexhaustible possibilities of significance.

The echoes of the form and implications of the novel are pervasive through the following century. This is not to deny that it is a radically uneven and awkward work, or to claim that every echo is a direct reference. Yet in the face of its remarkable participation in the central myths of developing industrial cultures, its obvious literary deficiencies become merely curious in a work so much larger than its failings. As we listen to some of the echoes, we ought not to forget that a reasonable formal case can be made for the novel.

Unlike many of its Gothic predecessors, for example, *Frankenstein* has a tight structure, a pervasively self-contained set of relevancies. The nightmarish and anarchic energies of its subjects are restrained formally and within a language inherited from a rationalist literary tradition; and the restraint can itself be seen as evidence of the authenticity of the experience. Northrop Frye, for example, identifies the special quality of genuine romance as just such formal tightness as we find in the Chinese-box-like structure of the narratives, and in the echoes and parallels that bind them together. Walton, imagining himself a scientific explorer who will do wonders for mankind, is, of course, a potential Frankenstein. The whole story is told through his letters to his sister, and Frankenstein's narrative to him is both a series of moral connections and a potentially redeeming example. Frankenstein's relation to Walton is similar to the relation of the Monster to Frankenstein himself. Volume II of *Frankenstein* is largely given over to the report of the Monster's story (which also includes *his* report of the De Lacey story); it is not clear that any of the three learn from the stories they hear.

The only other English nineteenth-century novel with so successfully tight and complicated a narrative structure is Emily Brontë's

Wuthering Heights. *Wuthering Heights*, too, juxtaposes the demonic with the domestic, the story of Heathcliff and Cathy being enclosed in the narrative of the imperceptive Lockwood, relating the story as Nelly Dean tells it. But, as Robert Dusenberry has argued in an as yet unpublished essay, the narrative of *Wuthering Heights* encloses a second generation freed from the incestuously self-destructive energies of its protagonists. Thus, Emily Brontë moves her narrative from the world of romance and nightmare into that of comic (and natural) regeneration. The comparison makes the case of *Frankenstein* all the more perplexing.

While *Wuthering Heights* achieves, in its prose and wonderful control and transcendence of Gothic traditions, an unequivocal greatness and maturity, *Frankenstein* remains in nightmare and constantly threatens to lapse into absurdity. In *Wuthering Heights* everything is dramatically embodied, and the language is precise and free from the merely assertive emotionalism of the Gothic tradition. In *Frankenstein* there is far more telling and talking, far less dramatic realization. One of the surest signs of the frailty of the language is the frequency with which Victor fails to describe his feelings. He is always telling Walton that he "cannot describe" his emotion, or that "no one can conceive" the horror. The writer too often attempts to horrify without being horrific. The great moments tend to be enacted through melodramatic gestures, appropriate to the stage. Although the "psychology" of *Frankenstein* is impressive, the book has no language for the internal processes of mind. Its method is always a public rhetoric, like that Peter Brooks points to in the language of the Monster. Everything internal is transformed into large public gesture or high rhetorical argument. Or, equally significant, motives are unexplored, as Victor, at every crucial moment, faints, sleeps, or dreams.

But this weakness of the language is the other side of the psychological intensity of sharply perceived images. The external world carries, mysteriously, the internal significances. The nightmare into which Victor lapses after he has brought the Monster to life, though full of conventional images, has a resonance that echoes through the book. In that dream Elizabeth is transformed into "the corpse of my dead mother": a "shroud enveloped her form, and I saw the grave-worms crawling in the folds of the flannel." The nightmare vision is followed by the waking vision that conflates remarkably with Elizabeth, Victor's mother, and the Monster.

The Monster appears "by the dim and yellow light of the moon," the same light that will later fall on the Monster when Victor sees him after the murder of Elizabeth: "He held up the curtain of the bed; and his eyes, if eyes they may be called, were fixed on me. His jaws opened, and he muttered some inarticulate sound, while a grin wrinkled his cheeks." His "yellow" skin "scarcely covered the work of muscles and arteries beneath" (pp. 52–53). However close to absurdity, such grisly moments are part of the still living metaphor of Frankenstein.

In fact, the Gothic trappings are essential to the book's power. *Frankenstein* is, as I have suggested in describing it as a psychomachia, a psychological novel, but certainly not in the sense that would mean anything to readers of George Eliot or Henry James. Psychological analysis in fiction tends to depend on the assumption that the workings of the human mind, if mysterious seeming, are nevertheless comprehensible within the terms of our language. And criticism, attempting to "understand" characters, tends to seek explanations that make the irrational rational. This is the peculiar strength of George Eliot, who did more to develop psychological analysis in English fiction than any English nineteenth-century writer. But the "psychology" of *Frankenstein* is essentially a psychology without explanation. To be sure, the book is full of the appearance of explanation, but its apparent absurdity is precisely its strength. The elaborate formal rhetoric actually tends to disguise the absence of explanation. In traditional psychological terms, the explanations for all the crucial events in the novel (except, ironically, the Monster's decision to make evil his good) are totally inadequate. Yet, in the long run, they are entirely credible. It is not possible, for example, to understand why Victor goes to the "filthy" lengths he does in handling corpses to create his Monster; or to explain, first, why he immediately assumes that the Monster is guilty of William's murder; second, why Justine confesses; and third, why, being so sure of her innocence, Victor does not defend her. And why does he fail to credit the Monster's threat to be with him on his wedding night? Obviously, no single set of explanations will do; yet nobody, I think, would have the action work out otherwise. The intense moments are there, without what Philip Stevick calls "secondary elaboration." The inadequacy of Mary Shelley's explanatory language is almost precisely the point—rational discourse cannot fully account for the experience, which comes to us with the authenticity of irrational dreams.

IV

That authenticity is especially confirmed by the reverberations of *Frankenstein* through the subsequent literature, even where no direct allusion is intended. The nineteenth-century English novel, as a whole, saw itself as realistic, and self-consciously rejected the kinds of excess that make the very substance of *Frankenstein*. Yet frequently it seems a kind of mirror image of Mary Shelley's story, emphasizing the particularities of domesticity but struggling to create heroes—Promethean creators—out of its protagonists, and bringing forth monsters—if domesticated ones.

One of the most interesting mirror images is in Dickens's *Great Expectations*, where the plight of Magwitch, the monstrous-seeming convict who is full of violence and the capacity to love, strangely mirrors the story of the Monster in *Frankenstein*. Like Mary Shelley's Monster, Magwitch has an autobiographical narrative that implies the Monster's theme: if society would make him happy, he would "again be virtuous." Magwitch makes clear that he was provoked to evil by social and human injustice, and though he terrifies Pip with his battered ugliness and his tale of a wicked "friend," we sympathize with him in his pain and suffering.

But if he is like the Monster in one way, he is like Victor in another. To redeem his thwarted life, he creates a gentleman—Pip. When Magwitch returns from Australia, Pip instinctively withdraws from him. Pip has become a moral monster. Magwitch's generous and grateful impulses have transformed a naive boy into a guilty, snobbish, and metaphorically murderous young man; and those generous impulses are almost as destructive as Victor's—though on a smaller scale. The motif of the *Doppelgänger*, as Julian Moynahan long ago pointed out, is at the structural and psychological center of *Great Expectations*.[10] Moynahan shows how Orlick acts out (as the Monster does for Victor) hostilities that Pip, his psychological double, is not allowed to face or even to imagine. Pip

10. Julian Moynahan, "The Hero's Guilt: The Case of *Great Expectations*," *Essays in Criticism* X, no. 1 (1960): 60–78.

may only resent his sister; Orlick brains her. Pip wishes Magwitch were not his benefactor; Orlick brings the police to cart the convict away. As in *Frankenstein*, where the relations between Victor and Monster will spread to the other characters, monsters can destroy what we are culturally required to love or respect.

The analogy between *Frankenstein* and *Great Expectations* clearly did not escape Dickens. After Pip hears the returned Magwitch's explanation of his role as provider and creator of Pip's identity as a "young gentleman," Pip recoils and remembers Mary Shelley's novel: "The imaginary student pursued by this misshapen creature he had impiously made, was not more wretched than I, pursued by the creature who had made me, and recoiling from him with a stronger repulsion, the more he admired me and the fonder he was of me" (*Great Expectations*, chapter 40). Dickens brilliantly exploits the analogy. Pip refuses to see that he, albeit a gentleman, is a created monster. He identifies with Victor, "the imaginary student," not with the "misshapen creature" who has, in the shape of Magwitch, come to haunt him. And in his repulsion of the creature who stretches out his hand towards him—just as the Monster had "stretched out" its hand—he *is* emulating Victor Frankenstein's "horror" and lack of fellow-feeling.

Dickens had resorted to *Frankenstein* earlier. As U. C. Knoepflmacher has pointed out, *The Haunted Man* (1848) inverts and exorcises the specter of monstrosity. Like Victor Frankenstein, Dickens's Redlaw is a lonely scientist, a "learned man in chemistry" who possesses the powers to "uncombine" and reconstitute "component parts." His abode is a place of ice and death, "where no sun had straggled for a hundred years," the realm of blankness that Andrew Griffin, in his essay below, identifies with the death-in-life presented in both *Frankenstein* and *Jane Eyre*. Mary Shelley has Victor deny the Monster the warmth and nurture he had himself enjoyed; only by becoming himself a victim, dispossessed of friends and mate, can Victor be brought to acknowledge his oneness with his creation. *The Haunted Man* begins with that acknowledgment. Dickens's Redlaw does not flee from but is arrested by the "uplifted hand" of the grisly Phantom who is his double. Redlaw accepts his kinship with "this awful likeness" of himself: "living man, and the animated image of himself dead" stare at each other. And he obeys the Phantom's exhortation to destroy all other kinship. He finds another analogue of himself in the "baby savage" deposited at his doorstep, "a young monster, a child who had never been a child" (*The Haunted Man*, chapter 2).

Still, *The Haunted Man* is a Christmas Book. Both Redlaw and the monster-child can be reclaimed through the ministrations of the angelic Milly Swidger, an Elizabeth-like figure who is immune to male cruelty. The Phantom itself, though as "terrible" an "instructor" as the Spirit of Christmas Future in *A Christmas Carol*, effects a beneficent transformation and teaches the humanized Redlaw to care for others. The deserted child becomes an emblem for remediable social conditions. "Woe, tenfold, to the nation that shall count its monsters such as this, lying here, by hundreds, and by thousands!" (chapter 2).

Both *Great Expectations* and *The Haunted Man* are fables, manifestations of Dickens's lifelong concern with the exorcism of private and social monstrosity. In his last complete novel, *Our Mutual Friend* (1865), Dickens animates an entire world composed of disjointed and inorganic "component parts," a world introduced by the floating cadaver in the opening chapter, and epitomized by the dust heaps and the disjointed parts of human beings in Mr. Venus's shop. Dickens resisted the specter of monstrosity, the denial of relation, which is indulged in later Victorian fantasies such as *Dr. Jekyll and Mr. Hyde* and *The Picture of Dorian Gray*.

Even in the central achievement of the Victorian realistic novel, *Middlemarch*, the *Frankenstein* metaphor emerges. Dr. Lydgate, with enormous faith in the power of biological science, seeks to discover the primitive tissue that is the source of all life. Fifteen years before *Middlemarch*, George Eliot had acknowledged her kinship with Mary Shelley in her anonymous short story, "The Lifted Veil."[11] But in *Middlemarch*, the Gothic horrors that were openly presented in "The Lifted Veil" lurk beneath the ironic fabric of allusion. Lydgate, who yearns for the "monster" preserved in Mr. Farebrother's makeshift laboratory, who identifies with that Andreas Vesalius who rifled graves, in Frankenstein fashion, to study the anatomy of cadavers and was defamed as "a poisonous monster," is himself a new Prometheus whose quest will lead to disaster.

In one of the best essays written on *Middlemarch*, David R. Carroll characterizes Lydgate as

11. For a discussion of connections between "The Lifted Veil" and *Frankenstein*, see pp. 139–43 in U. C. Knoepflmacher, *George Eliot's Early Novels* (Berkeley and Los Angeles, 1968).

pursuing the interaction of mind and matter to the apotheosis—the discovery of mind in matter—where their separateness will be resolved and paradise will eventually be regained.[12]

This Promethean dream—again, like Victor's, couched in the terms of science and invested with the forms of religion—is a more sophisticated way to imagine Victor's quest. What Victor seeks is the principle of life *in* matter, the transformation of it from brute externality to that which is compatible with humanity and the human dream. Yet with Lydgate, too, the activity is separated from the surrounding community, which regards Lydgate superstitiously—so separated, indeed, that Lydgate cannot imagine marriage as compatible with his work. Because of its realist, ironic mode, *Middlemarch* cannot allow Lydgate even preliminary success.

But again there is a remarkable transference between science and sexuality. The failure in the laboratory ostensibly results from a marriage. Incomplete and insufficiently self-aware in his great ambition, Lydgate frees in his drawing room another kind of monster—his destructive "torpedo" of a wife, Rosamond, who, instead of being a pretty, anonymous support and comforter, as Lydgate dreamed, manifests an independent will more powerful than his own. Lydgate's dream of domesticity, because it is entirely separate from his ambitions in the laboratory, ends with his being imprisoned by the dream house and the cuddly dream wife. Rosamond becomes to Lydgate what the Monster is to Victor, his own "vampire" (*Frankenstein*, p. 72).

Once again, Carroll's essay clarifies the connection, already established in *Frankenstein*, between science and vampirism. Following a convincing analysis of the vampiric relation between Bulstrode and Raffles, Carroll articulates the activity of *Middlemarch* in terms that apply directly to Mary Shelley's novel:

Now all this, especially the glimpse of vampires feeding off each other, may seem a long way from the exact functioning of a scientific hypothesis. But I suggest that one leads to the other, that George Eliot's scientific conceits (those unliterary devices paraded in *Middlemarch*) lead logically to these monsters, vampires, and assorted succubi (the stock in trade of Gothic fiction) who live a sub-

12. David Carroll, "*Middlemarch* and the Externality of Fact," in *This Particular Web: Essays on "Middlemarch,"* ed. Ian Adam (Toronto, 1975), p. 77.

terranean metaphoric life beneath the provincial surface of the novel. The mind in its pride seeks to redeem by fiat the fallen world in which it lives, but instead turns it into an inferno where it is hunted down by monsters of its own creating. [P. 84]

The people of Middlemarch believe Lydgate has resuscitated a dead body, a clinching bit of evidence for Carroll's reading of the novel in terms of the Frankenstein metaphor.

The heritage of *Frankenstein* is yet more direct and extensive than these allusions and metaphorical elaborations can suggest. Even those verbal and melodramatic elements of *Frankenstein* which can seem absurd to us now have their echoes in later literature, echoes that suggest an uncanny rightness in the adolescent's dream vision. What, we might ask, do we make of a book whose initial dramatic moment is of a man in a dog sled on an ice floe in the frozen Arctic, who pauses to look up at the captain of a ship and says, as Frankenstein does, with drawing room politeness: "Before I come on board your vessel . . . will you have the kindness to inform me whither you are bound?" (p. 18). Yet in *The Secret Sharer*, in which Joseph Conrad takes up several of the motifs of *Frankenstein*—especially that of the *Doppelgänger*—the first dramatic scene duplicates, with new literary sophistication, the opening of Mary Shelley's novel. Miles from shore, Conrad's captain-double looks over the side of his ship and asks of the man swimming by, "in my ordinary tones," "'What's the matter?'" And the escaped murderer Leggatt looks up, casually, to answer, "Cramp."[13] Both scenes blend the astonishing with the commonplace in ways that mark their mutual Romantic heritage. Both books assume and enact in their language the discontinuity and incompleteness of conventional moral life.

In *The Secret Sharer* there is no amiableness of domestic affection, but there is the same moral entropy we have seen in *Frankenstein*. This too is a fiction about birth, the rescue and delivery of Leggatt from the ship, the moral birth of the captain himself. Again we see that the expense of life is death; the mark of Leggatt's living is his killing of the mate of the *Sephora*, and the captain himself can only be "born" by risking his ship and coming close to strangling his own mate.

13. "The Secret Sharer," *Complete Works of Joseph Conrad* (London and Toronto, 1923), XIX: 98.

Just as the images and patterns of the novel recur in fiction, so they are enacted in the progress of science through the nineteenth century. Through the motif of the double, which can be transformed, as we have seen, into the motif of the vampire, we come to recognize our own potential monstrousness. At the end of the century, Freud reveals it to us with a scientific dispassion that turns it into the dominant myth of the twentieth century. We speak easily now of superego, ego, and id, of the civilized self and deepening levels of animality and instinct. Obviously, Frankenstein's Monster, though it aspires to be an ego, resolves itself into an id: certainly it is a metaphor for an uncontrollable and destructive energy. And again, no image works better than that of the figure of Elizabeth on the bed with the Monster leering through the window. Yet the particular Freudian connection with the novel comes not through the Gothic, but through the association of the Gothic with science, and with a secular vision that translates spirit into natural energy.

In an appendix to this volume, U. C. Knoepflmacher briefly analyzes a work by T. H. Huxley, *Man's Place in Nature*, which, he shows, not only works out in ways remarkably analogous to *Frankenstein*, but whose whole strategy seems to be to force on its Victorian readership the recognition that in the images of the apes, illustrations of which, front and rear view, sprinkle the text, they are —*hypocrite lecteur, mon semblable*—seeing themselves. From this perspective the entire furor over Darwinian theory can be seen as a real cultural enactment of the implied fiction of *Frankenstein*. Science, penetrating to the sources of life, finds our animal selves, our own uncontrollable instincts for life and death.

Frankenstein as metaphor has assimilated itself to all of these intellectual and scientific developments that have transformed the way we imagine our lives. The continuity and importance of this metaphor in modern English literature might be best illustrated by concluding with its rather amusing appearance in D. H. Lawrence's *The Rainbow*, where it again comes alive, in the surprisingly offhand way Lawrence can use, located in precisely that secularizing, despiritualizing focus on matter that I have taken as the specially modern quality of Mary Shelley's myth.

Who should turn up in the college laboratory where Ursula Brangwen is studying the structure of the human cell, but Dr.

Frankstone? With a delightful twist, Lawrence makes Frankstone a woman, allowing the masculine mask of Victor Frankenstein to fall away and reveal the feminine spirit of his creator. In her one major speech, she in fact articulates the assumptions implicit in Victor's creation of the Monster—the transformation of spirit into mere matter:

I don't see why we should attribute some special mystery to life— do you? We don't understand it as we understand electricity, even, but that doesn't warrant our saying it is something special, something different in kind and distinct from everything else in the universe—do you think it does? May it not be that life consists in a complexity of physical and chemical activities we already know in science? I don't see, really, why we should imagine there is a special order of life, and life alone—[14]

The Monster is, in some ways, the imaged articulation of the idea that there is nothing special about life, and Lawrence turns directly to the metaphor of Frankenstein for his image of that modern tendency to substitute mechanism for life. In the passage that follows this one, Ursula rejects such a vision while at the same time bringing to her examination of the cell the sort of passionate intensity we have already seen in both Victor and Lydgate; and in her questioning of what she sees she brings science and religious forms together.

Was she herself an impersonal force, or conjunction of forces, like one of these? She looked still at the unicellular shadow that lay within the field of light, under the microscope. It was alive. She saw it move—she saw the bright mist of its ciliary activity, she saw the gleam of its nucleus, as it slid across the plane of light. What then was its will? If it was a conjunction of forces, physical and chemical, what held these forces unified, and for what purpose were they unified? [P. 441]

Ursula here turns the narrative of *Frankenstein* on its head. Lawrence is clearly taking that narrative as the image of the domination of mental consciousness over the mystic vitality of the whole human organism. The "sweet mystery of life" about which Mel Brooks's Elizabeth uproariously sings in *Young Frankenstein* is precisely what is missing in *Frankenstein*. And Ursula makes the true discovery in

14. D. H. Lawrence, *The Rainbow* (New York, 1961), p. 440.

a Lawrencian religious vision, a discovery which, had Victor Frankenstein made it, would have sent him back to a sexual union with Elizabeth rather than on to the manufacture of his animated being, the Monster:

> She could not understand what it all was. She only knew that it was not limited mechanical energy, nor mere purpose of self-preservation and self-assertion. It was a consummation, a being infinite. She was a oneness with the infinite. To be oneself was supreme, gleaming triumph of infinity. [P. 441]

At this point Ursula feels a deep "dread of the material world" and turns to "the new life, the reality," which is her relation with Skrebensky.

Lawrence provides us with a creative reading of *Frankenstein*. With the rest of the culture, Lawrence sees the Monster as horrifying, but because he associates mere mental consciousness with mechanism and matter, he helps us understand why the Monster is not—in the novel—imagined as the raging id he is usually portrayed to be on the screen. In Lawrence's vision, the Monster is precisely the objective image of mental consciousness, which despiritualizes matter and establishes a fatal dualism between mind and matter, that psychological and moral schizophrenia that is the source of the self-destructiveness of our culture. In turning Ursula, through the vision of the "consummation" that comes to her via the microscope, from mental consciousness to sexual life, Lawrence provides yet another commentary both on Victor's moral isolation and on the Monster's murder of Elizabeth on the night and in the place where the sexual relation was to be consummated.

In his original essay on Benjamin Franklin,[15] Lawrence further elaborates his reading of *Frankenstein*. He sees with uncanny sureness that "Mary Shelley, in the midst of the idealists, gives the dark side to the ideal being, showing us Frankenstein's monster" (p. 34). Whatever the ambiguity of Mary Shelley's narrative, the idea of Frankenstein could only have emerged from a culture that had imagined the perfectibility of humanity, rationalist or apocalyptic, or both, as in the French Revolution. And that notion of perfectibility was, as Lawrence suggests, allied to the fresh sense of the

15. D. H. Lawrence, *The Symbolic Meaning*, ed. Armin Arnold (New York, 1964), pp. 34–47. This is the original version of the essay revised for *Studies in Classic American Literature*.

power of man to shape men: "The ideal being was man created by man. And so was the supreme monster" (p. 34).

The dark side to the ideal being is a rationalist, a Godwinian, and Lawrence talks about Franklin as though he *were* the Monster: "if on the one hand Benjamin Franklin is the perfect human being of Godwin, on the other hand he is a monster, not exactly as the monster in *Frankenstein*, but for the same reason, viz., that he is the production of fabrication of the human will, which projects itself upon a living being and automatises that being according to a given precept." The true monstrousness is not, then, the raging id (which Lawrence translates into the "creative mystery"), but the attempt of consciousness to impose itself on the world, either in the form of morality or science.

The brilliance of Lawrence's "reading" of *Frankenstein* is not, for my purposes, as important as the fact that he thinks he finds in the Frankenstein image the materials for a radical critique of his culture. And that image works, as I have suggested, because Mary Shelley brought together in it the central dualities of a culture in which reason and science were displacing religion as centers of value. She does so without lapsing into moralism, through the simple technique of filtering the narrative through voices not her own—in a manner that Browning used some decades later.[16] By "animating" her narrative with many voices, she escaped the narrowness of the conventional first person Gothic romance, and was released from a single perspective that might have forced her into the morally conventional.

The tale survives the teller, in a way that Lawrence—despite his rejection of both Victor and his Monster—would have to approve.

16. In a letter written to Elizabeth Barrett on 11 September 1845, Browning expressed his disappointment in finding that "'Mary dear' with the brown eyes, and Godwin's daughter and Shelley's wife" had become a "commonplace" travel writer who "surely was something better once upon a time" (*The Letters of Robert and Elizabeth Barrett: 1845–1846* [New York, 1898], I:196). Robert and Elizabeth (who as early as 1831 feared that "Mrs. Shelley's genius" had "exhaled" with *Frankenstein*) unquestionably saw their elopement—as did the Shelleyan George Henry Lewes and George Eliot—as a reenactment of Percy's and Mary's flight. More important, however, is the recurrent interest in animation and resuscitation found in Browning's poetry; an essay on his indebtedness to *Frankenstein* would have been a valuable contribution to this volume and should be undertaken.

Wherever we attempt to find an image of human aspiration in a technological and scientific world, wherever we attempt to find an image for the failure of that aspiration, the metaphor of Frankenstein comes immediately to hand. Ursula's quest in *The Rainbow* is in fact also a quest for perfection, although one in which mind and body are to be reconciled. But in her narrative the image for achievement cannot be Frankenstein. Ursula's dream vision, unlike Mary Shelley's, unlike Victor's, is a vision of the resurrection and the life, not of death. And it comes from Revelations, not science or radical idealism. *Frankenstein* is the perfect myth of the secular, carrying within it all the ambivalences of the life we lead here, of civilization and its discontents, of the mind and the body, of the self and society. It is, indeed, the myth of realism. To find another myth, the "new germination," the "earth's new architecture" which Ursula prophetically sees, we must look elsewhere, if we can.

II

Frankenstein as Mystery Play

JUDITH WILT

I T IS AN ARTFUL DODGE of Mary Shelley's to have moved the English
Gothic out of the God-haunted Mediterranean into the Swiss
republic. Eventually, the Gothic setting will move boldly to Dr.
Jekyll's London and Mina Harker's Whitby (before departing again
with Wells for outer space). In the early nineteenth century, however, Switzerland, with just a quick foray into Scotland, is as close
as the Gothic can be allowed to come. With the change of scene,
one set of apparent accidentals also seems to have been discarded,
the Walpole-Radcliffe machinery of Church and Sin, Angel and
Devil. In 1810, Percy Shelley still delights in the old trappings: even
when Zastrozzi, with "a smile of contemptuous atheism," proclaims
his belief in "the non-existence of a Deity," [1] he does so in the traditional setting. By 1816, however, Shelley has written *Queen Mab*
and contemplates Jupiter's overthrow in *Prometheus Unbound*. Writing her Gothic tale in the same new day, Mary Shelley decides not
to talk about God (Adam's "Maker" appears merely in the epigraph
from *Paradise Lost* on her novel's title page). God seems dead in the
Gothic, and priestcraft even eliminated as an enemy.

Still, for an atheist, the palimpsest of Bible stories contrived for
Frankenstein is suspiciously thick. Satan, Cain and Judas, Abraham,
Adam and Christ, and the thousand names of the unnameable
God, jostle in the figures of Victor Frankenstein and his creature
like ghosts in a haunted house. Literally, their name is Legion.
Shelley's protagonists wear themselves out trying to manage the
spiritual archetypes laid over them by the great Christian poets—
wear themselves and each other down to emaciation. If each is his

1. P. B. Shelley, *Zastrozzi: A Romance*, chap. 17; Eustace Chesser, *Shelley
and Zastrozzi* (London, 1965), p. 156.

own haunted body, they are also each other's Gadarene swine, fleeing with the poisoned identities exorcised out into them. Of course, this kind of vocabulary comes from reading *Paradise Lost* "as a true history," from believing that you face not a stitchery of bone and flesh but "a thing such as even Dante could not have conceived."[2] The absence of God is celebrated in the presence of metaphor. For Mary Shelley, it would seem, a poetic-Christian-literary baggage is only useful to describe the otherwise inexplicable excesses of the human soul.

Still, Shelley's book derives its special force not from eccentricity but from an eerie familiarity with an astonishing variety of contexts. And one of these contexts is exactly the God-haunted English Gothic tradition. *Frankenstein* is of a piece with Matthew Lewis's *The Monk* (1796) and James Hogg's *The Private Memoirs and Confessions of a Justified Sinner* (1824), in a tradition that is painfully acting out under the nose of the Enlightenment a long line of expunged doctrines—Justification, Creation, Damnation—and unspeakable sacraments—Holy Orders, Confession, Communion. A tradition, unmistakably, from Horace Walpole's *The Castle of Otranto* (1765) to Bram Stoker's *Dracula* (1897), the Mystery Play of the Romantic mind. We thought the Gothicists were hiding something in all that incense and chapelgloom, mitres, crosses, hosts and hoods, wimples and prayers. And they hid it, Watson, where it is hardest to find, in the most obvious place: on the surface.

I

Classic English Gothic took shape in the 1750s and '60s, after a hundred years of Enlightened Anglican revision of the Puritan Counter-Reformation, after a hundred years of safe but dull parliamentary and party rule had almost wiped out the memory of Divine Right tyrants, Anglican and Puritan. Not for another sixty years or so, until Scott's and Hogg's mad Covenanters, would the specifically English roots of the Gothic fascination with tyrannical religious establishments and distended God-men become clear. And not until Bram Stoker had to bring a Belgian scientist-saint with a satchelful of Sacred Wafer to counter the evil Transylvanian

2. Mary Shelley, *Frankenstein*, ed. M. W. Joseph (New York, 1971), p. 58. All subsequent references given in the text are to this Oxford edition.

Power that was making bloodpies out of healthily unsuperstitious Anglicans did the shamed yearning for the Great Old Faith, pre-emptive, terrible and beautiful, get openly acknowledged. Transposed in its first phase to Mediterranean Catholicism and the drama there of formation, reformation, and counterreformation, the Gothic fascination took hold. Coyly posing as antiquarian editor of a dusty text found in an old North Catholic family's library, Walpole speculates that *The Castle of Otranto* might have been a tool of the Counter-Reformation, "to confirm the populace in their ancient errors and superstitions." It was the Religious Question again; it was even the Theological Question.

It was even, I want to argue, the Trinitarian Question, the deep-structured subject of the English Gothic Mystery, the attempt to explore and explain the flight of a parental mind out of itself into what Frankenstein's Creature will gropingly call "the series" of its being.[3] As both Frankenstein and his Creature will discover, this flight involves a double peril. If the flight is successful, each member in the series is diminished; if the flight is not successful, neither movement nor growth is possible. The struggle of Frankenstein and his Creature, the Father and the Son, is in this context power-fully arresting and inconclusive. Nightmare waits on both sides: diminishment leads finally to non-being, yet the failure to extend brings the horrors of paralysis and inward diminution.

The efforts of theologians to imagine the mind of God as extending without diminishing are thus highly instructive. In a world made corruptly various by the variousness of the old gods, "the fathers" of the early Christian centuries wrestled for the pure will in one preemptive Being, while allowing force, nature, and "person" to two others, the Son and the Holy Ghost. "Special place" was allowed for another holy being, a subordinate but crafty spirit,[4] as

3. The "warm controversy between the theologians respecting the nature of God and his mode of acting and manifesting himself" occupies much of the book that inspires Frankenstein's Creature with such "strange feelings," M. Volney's *The Ruins, Or, A Survey of the Revolutions of Empires.* In chapter 21, on problems of "religious contradiction," Volney makes a re-mark that also would have interested the father-begotten creature: "after permitting the human species to damn themselves for four or five thousand years, this God of compassion ordered his well-beloved son engendered without a mother." These quotations are taken from the 1857 London edition of *The Ruins,* pp. 121, 102.
4. "A subordinate but crafty spirit" is M. G. Lewis's description of the

she would have to have been, the Virgin Mother. In its reach for the nature of God, the Trinitarian intuition has a great deal of nobility, even ecstasy about it. Separatenesses which exist for the sharp joy of choosing communion again at every second in a seamless intense serenity—these are God in the old Christian language, or perhaps, as theologian Mary Daly has recently proposed in *Beyond God the Father*, this is what is involved in the verb "to God." The dynamic of this intuition is not so much a dying to live, but the less abstract though more mysterious paradox of *kenosis*, the emptying out to be filled up. The Father pours himself out into the Son, the Son, knowing himself separate, makes the astonishing choice to curve that stream of Being back toward the progenitor; that choice separates as person, as Holy Ghost, and reflects through all matter that same curve outward with perfect confidence that the final destination is inward. Thus the emptier is always filled, the spring never runs dry. There is no heat-death threatened in this universe; even the exchanges of energy take place without loss for they are not really exchanges, body to body, but numinous participations in a world without end.

We remember that ideal. But we remember too that woman was excluded from the formal orthodox formulations of the ideal to a subordinate and crafty place, where she becomes demonic. And we remember that a great battle was fought over the first thousand Christian years to establish that orthodox unbearable balance for God and a Church both One and Catholic. The Holy Ghost is not to be separated but "proceeds" from the Father and the Son, filioque; the Son is not to be separated, not even in his human dimension, but in every aspect and moment is with and from and to the Father and the Holy Ghost, "begotten, not made," not the maker. All angles of the Godhead are "consubstantial," as the formula had it —the formula imposed upon a divided Council at Nicaea by the Godfather of the Church, Constantine. God is a communion, man is a community; if anyone dwell too long, fascinated on the moment of separation, let that one be, in the word of the ultimate curse, anathema, that is, separated.

---

demonic Mathilda in *The Monk*. Mathilda first reaches the doomed Monk's heart through her resemblance to a picture of the Virgin Mary that Ambrosio worships in his bedroom. P. B. Shelley's Matilda in *Zastrozzi* seems derived from Lewis's figure, while Mary Shelley's heroine in *Mathilda* is conceived as a Dantean figure, as Peter Scott points out on p. 185, below.

In a universe shaped by the curve of God out into a consubstantial Personhood everything that moves moves together: in the words of the theologian Teilhard de Chardin taken up in a modern Gothic work by Flannery O'Connor, everything that rises must converge. In such a universe, dread has the shape of an unmoving point, or a point whose movement affirms a straight line. In such a universe, freedom is a long curve, slavery an obsessed straight line against all the energies of Being. Dreadful, but fascinating: against the whole outward upward inward sweep, to travel straight to the edge of the curve and leap off, to find Damnation. A contemporary poet, trying to account for his interest in the Gothic, pounces on this insight: "But Ambrosio is the point: the point is to conduct a remarkable man utterly to damnation. It is surprising after all, how long it takes—how difficult it is—to be certain of damnation." [5] This is John Berryman on Lewis's *The Monk,* ten years before the poet killed and resurrected himself in *The Dream Songs* ("Noises from underground made gibber some / others collected & dug Henry up"), and twenty-two years before he leapt off the edge into the Mississippi ("insomnia-plagued, with a shovel / digging like mad, Lazarus with a plan / to get his own back, a plan, a stratagem / no newsman will unravel").

The Gothic treats of the Separated One, his search to be sure of Damnation. And it might be argued that the central tradition of the English novel, F. R. Leavis's Great Tradition of moral seriousness, was begotten from it by heretics who want to allow the Separated One his or her mission in the outward curve, allow it, and then, if possible, rescue the missionary. For as Gothic fiction shows unmistakably, and Trinitarian theology implies, the most intense moral life is always lived at the edge of separation or the edge of recommunion. The terrors of the Separated One are always more moving and more instructive than the terrors of the outraged community; and the *progress,* as Berryman called it, of the self-separated one, the Gothic hero-villain, is even more significant, in terms of human awareness, than the progress, or rather the standfastness, of the one separated by circumstance, the Gothic "victim," the orphan, the bastard, above all, the woman. Separated he may be (usually it is he), but still, in the affirmation Conrad's Marlow makes, he is "one of us," though he confirms his separation by

5. John Berryman, Introduction to *The Monk* (New York, 1952), p. 13.

walking "away from the living woman [usually it is a woman] towards some shadowy ideal of conduct," as Lord Jim does in the last paragraph of Conrad's novel.

As Victor Frankenstein does. The ideal and its shadow are familiar mysteries in *Frankenstein*, and familiar too is the place of celebration. As the Gothic has its classic plots, so it has its characteristic space, the haunted castle, as Eino Railo calls it, "the centre of suspense," the "hidden chamber where the terrifying element is housed."[6] In eighteenth-century Gothic novels it is the mystically tenanted chapel with its activating priest; in the nineteenth century it is the laboratory. Victor Frankenstein raises his hands over the mortal scraps on his table and calls down into them the ideal. There is in the ordinary celebration of this mystery always a space between the altar and the chapel; the priest is both dangerously separated from the community and together with it.

But it makes *all* the difference in the circling story of Victor Frankenstein that there is no community present at his Mass, not even an altar boy.[7] The priest is separated but together, son and brother to the congregation that calls him father, child to the Power he calls upon, brother to the Person who emerges in the mortal scraps from and with and to the Father. Without the presence of the community somewhere behind, this dynamic is lost, and a terrible simple doomful Transference occurs in the would-be priest. Choose to play God and the Deity points out that the position is already occupied.

He who separates himself as completely as Victor Frankenstein did from the curve of the community, from the marrying-begetting, giving over of life to the new generation, dying in his turn— he is by that wish a murderer and in the Gothic he gets, horribly, what he wishes for. It is an economical universe: if he wants immortality, all the life in the world, he is doomed to take it away from others. It is one thing to take it away from his mother; in the natural order he may do that, if his son may take it away from him in turn. But Victor, utterly fixed in outrage and guilt when he looks upon the death of his mother, expects to keep death at bay by reversing her example, by withholding life from his child, who would take it away.

6. Eino Railo, *The Haunted Castle* (New York, 1927), p. 171.

7. The "Igor" of cinematic fame is thus an invention absolutely counter to Mary Shelley's theme: Victor Frankenstein's creation is a solitary act.

It is a mistake to be too far misled by Victor's apparently unselfish wish to become "the father of a new race of beings." Like Walpole's Manfred, who calls in sly desperation for "more sons" when the family sin strikes his son dead, he is not so spontaneously generous with life as he seems. Look instead to these fathers' attitudes towards their daughters, objects of horror and lust to them, custodians of life barred from the fathers' control by the oldest of patriarchal taboos. Manfred does not want his daughter, and finally kills her; Frankenstein looks at his daughter/creature lying unanimated on the table, recognizes that she, unpredictable and uncontrollable, will take both the son/creature and the new race out of his power, and destroys her. With Ann Radcliffe's famous monk Schedoni, it was his brother and his brother's wife and almost his daughter; with Lewis's Ambrosio, it was his mother and sister, living their share of the familial life and by accident or design, by agent or by hand, killed and emptied of it so that the preempting father may live, may forsake his real nature as son/brother, may avoid his real Trinitarian choice to curve his life-share back to the Father.

Victor Frankenstein is a compendium of all these Gothic dooms and Mysteries. From childhood he knew himself "the idol" of an aged father and a young mother whose special tenderness to him sprang from "the deep consciousness of what they owed towards the being to which they had given life" (p. 34). When he was five he was "given" an adopted sister, Elizabeth Lavenza: "my mother had said playfully, 'it was a pretty present for my Victor.' . . . I, with childish seriousness, interpreted her words literally" (pp. 35–36). In school he was "indifferent to my schoolfellows in general," but he selected one friend, Henry Clerval, whose interest in "the moral relations of things," politics, culture, social adventure, complemented Victor's own lack of interest in these things and left him free to pursue that "curiosity about the secrets of heaven and earth" which is among the "earliest sensations" he can remember. Perhaps his deepest, and indeed most sensual memory, is the outrage he felt at the death of his mother. Death, "that most irreparable evil," seems to his questing mind the key to the significant secret of life: "to examine the causes of life we must first have recourse to death" (p. 51). Anatomy is a "not sufficient" resource; the boy spends "days and nights in vaults and charnel-houses" (p. 52). In the grisly study of worm and waste, of rot and decay, he is checked by no natural or supernatural repugnance, having had a thoroughly republican pragmatic education: "my father had taken the greatest precautions that my mind should be impressed with no supernatural horrors" (p. 51). To be free of supernatural or philosophical speculation is to regard death simply as a disease, and life as a cure, a material quantity waiting to be isolated.

Neither is he checked in his charnel house excursions by that fellow-feeling with human and natural life by which Radcliffe and the Romantic poets dramatize the harmonic universal curve: "my eyes were insensible to the charms of nature. And the same feelings which made me neglect the scenes around me caused me also to forget those friends . . . whom I had not seen for so long a time" (p. 55). Cut off, self-separated, he "lost all soul or sensation but for one pursuit" whose goal, the benevolent and disinterested creation of life, seems from the start linked with a sinister dilation of himself: "A new species would bless me as its creator and source. . . . No father could claim the gratitude of his child so completely as I should deserve theirs" (p. 54). Even the wish to so increase his consequence constitutes a profound separation, and "I shunned my fellow creatures as if I had been guilty of a crime" (p. 56).

When on that "dreary night of November" the conception is birthed, the bread and wine transubstantiated, love turns without warning to hatred, as it is wont to do in the Gothic: "I had desired it with an ardour that far exceeded moderation, but now that I had finished, the beauty of the dream vanished, and breathless horror and disgust filled my heart." He rejects and abandons his desire, his dilation of himself already criminally eight feet high. And the creation and rejection together bring on the novel's most significant dream. He is embracing his affianced Elizabeth—she is a corpse, the corpse is his dead mother—"and I saw the grave worms crawling in the folds of the flannel" (p. 58).

A Freudian might see in the whole progress of Frankenstein simply a wish to join his loved mother in the tomb; but the Gothic, as we have seen, adds an extra dimension, a profound resentment of the sources of one's being, especially the female sources, stemming from the desire to be one's own source and one's own goal, to stand fixed and to hold-in life. Thinking he has sought life in the embrace of death, Victor has in fact been seeking death in the embrace of life, seeking death to kill it like a virus. And his creature/son, his hold on immortality, his dilated self, deliberately made (not begotten) too gigantic to be overturned in the going-out of time and matter, has this same nightmare in his makeup. Insofar as he is Frankenstein's avatar, the creature proceeds with dreamlike thoroughness to cut off in fact all those whom Frankenstein cut off from his affections while he fed his obsession—his brother, his friends Justine and Clerval, eventually indirectly his father, and of course, preeminently, his "more than sister," his almost-wife, Elizabeth.

Insofar as he is his own being, first Adam, then Satan and then Cain, the creature reenacts the whole hopeless cycle. He cannot stand the state of separation. He *knows* he is the son, that his marrying and murdering-or-begetting impulse is a compensation mechanism for his real need to curve his being back to the father. But Frankenstein's fears and the creature's own deep resentments make full recommunion impossible. Since his memory constantly torments him with Frankenstein's rejection and with Frankenstein's ultimate responsibility for his being, and since he looks like what he is, the Separated One, perversely joined together, he can deceive no one, make no compromise or accommodation.

Nor can Frankenstein. Like Prospero, he finally acknowledges this thing of darkness his, even acknowledges this thing of darkness him: "my own vampire, my own spirit let loose from the grave and forced to destroy all that was dear to me" (p. 77). But he cannot bring himself to actualize woman on any level: "Alas! to me the idea of the immediate union with my Elizabeth was one of horror and dismay. . . . Could I enter into a festival with this deadly weight yet hanging around my neck?" he mourns, ambiguously clutching his albatross (pp. 151–52). The drama is inexorably, as it has always been in the Gothic, between himself and himself, since he wants to keep himself fixed and immortal, yield no atom of his being back to death. This drama, which went under the name of hypocrisy in eighteenth-century Gothic, enters the nineteenth century as schizophrenia, the actual detachment of multipersonalities. In nineteenth-century Gothic the fragment of self that escapes and must be reabsorbed is not recognized as child, as it was in Walpole and Radcliffe, but as brother, as it is in Hogg's *The Memoirs and Confessions of a Justified Sinner* and Stevenson's *Dr. Jekyll and Mr. Hyde* (1886). Mary Shelley's book, as it dramatizes both a kind of hypocrisy and a kind of schizophrenia in Victor's consciousness, both a father-child and a brother-self relationship in the two center figures, stands right at the tipping point in Gothic presentation of this dilemma.

Consciously, both beings know they are in a battle for the one available quantum of existence, "bound by ties only dissolvable by the annihilation of one of us." It is above all Frankenstein who seeks to annihilate the creature, to take back his life. His indestructible self, even in the accomplishment of pursuits and torments upon his creator that double his own agony, keeps Frankenstein alive at all costs out of a powerful sense that he cannot sustain existence alone, that alone, despite his size, he is not quite real, cannot stand his ground. Locked together in a race to the North Pole, the one steady state on the compass, the two pass and sight and lose each other in a fury of malice and thwarted love. The father has looked upon himself and that look has begotten a son; the son has looked upon the father and that look which was, as both recognize, naturally holy and creative, is now an unholy ghost of utter destruction, decreation, the last term in the series of Mary Shelley's atheistic trinity. That Unholy Ghost is the real pursuer of both beings into the ice. Frankenstein dies, hounded. Looking at the corpse, the son in this trinity keens, in the Miltonic biblical cadence that marks all their exchanges: "in his murder my crimes are consummated; the miserable series of my being is wound to its close" (p. 219). "My work is nearly complete," he repeats to Frankenstein's friend, the explorer Walton: "neither yours nor any man's death is needed to consummate the series of my being and accomplish that which must be done, but it requires my own. Do not think that I shall be slow to perform this sacrifice" (p. 222).

This has a familiar holy ring, but we should remember that *Paradise Lost* impressed the creature (and, one presumes, both Shelleys) not as a heroic sacrifice story but as the story of a God "warring with his creatures." And indeed the reader of Milton's epic learns about two trinities. One is Holy, with an arguably Arian twist to its picture of a gaudily subservient, not very separated or choice-agonized Son, and a Spirit that "came forth spontaneous" to create the world at the moment when the Father most shone in the Son. Another is Unholy, remarkably imaged in Book II as Satan, Sin, and Death. In this trinity, the just rebelling Satan looked upon himself, and that look, that self-perception, half narcissistic love, half candid disgust, burst from the Father as a Daughter, Sin, not

Son. The two curved back toward each other again in stark narcissism, and that mutuality emerged as Death: Death, repeating the narcissism that is always half love half hate ("though more, it seems / inflam'd with lust than rage"), revisited the Daughter and produced the fearful hell hounds who also endlessly repeat the enraged Lust. This trinity's dramatic climax comes when Death and Satan meet at the gates of hell, Father and Unholy Ghost ready to slay one another until the mediating Word, Sin, convinces each to turn his hate and hunger outward, upon creation. At the end of the encounter, fighting has turned to fawning, and Death, the final inevitable term in the series of Satan's being, the Unholy Ghost, spirit of Decreation, emerges through the great Gate to breathe upon the new earth his invitation to return to eldest Night and Chaos, where all movement is either purposeless strife or blind purposeless rigidity.

No wonder Victor Frankenstein shrinks at the last moment from the animation of his Daughter, the next term in what has now turned into an Unholy series of his being. No wonder that the creature, looking upon that destroying Father, shifts permanently to that Unholy series, turned in a moment from Christ to Sin. He binds Frankenstein permanently to himself as Sin did Satan, by the murder of his wife, the closing off of any positive or normal terms of his being, and by the constant saving of his life, supplying him with food during his progress to the final frozen rest. The two Persons, first and second terms of the trinity, alternately holy and unholy on that long progress, lock regards, lock wills, seek to materialize a third Person. Will it be the Holy or the Unholy Ghost?

Something in the serenity and even nobility of the ending of the novel seems to promise the former, the creative spirit, brooding over northern waters and keeping alive in the explorer Walton and his men somehow *both* prudence and aspiration. Perhaps. But the content of the wish, the Word's word at the end, seems unequivocally Decreation, the invoking of the reign of Night and Chaos. On his self-made funeral pyre the creature expects "light, feeling and sense will pass away. . . . my ashes will be swept into the sea by the winds. . . . the very remembrance of us both will speedily vanish" (p. 222).

Decreation, the pulling apart, laying asleep, washing away of body, soul, and consciousness, is a Gothic Anti-Mystery vividly dramatized in novel after novel, one that rules more strongly than the Creation mystery, the Awakening moment. The exquisite, the unbearable Awakeness that characterizes the citizens of the Gothic world, that makes them see and hear the Ghosts that we do not, gives way in the central citizen, the Gothic hero-villain, to a recognition, willing or unwilling, of Decreation, the falling asleep. This intense susceptibility is Ann Radcliffe's special province of character; pursuer and pursued share it. The sentimental hero is distinguished by it and the Gothic hero-villain by his profound attempt to deny it. Sensation bombards consciousness unmercifully in her novels in a universe with strong resemblances to Lawrence's. The hero-villain's consciousness grapples with its own moods and in a fury of bitterness pronounces the human condition intolerable, human nature evil and changeable, morally laughable. For him "hardihood" is the only possible value, a good word of Radcliffe's to express that standing fast in the rain of contradictory emotions, the wish to be the immovable object among the irresistible forces which follow the universal curve, change the mind and change the matter. In the eyes of his victims, and this by the crafty convention of the Gothic is usually the initial stance of the reader, the hero-villain seems to be the irresistible force, the master of plot, sweeping obstacles out of his way in the dash for power. Yet the twist inward that all good Gothic fiction makes, inward from the terrors or the threatened victim or community to the terrors of the monster, always shows us from his standpoint a universe sweeping him away, sucking at his ground, his identity, his meaningfulness, his "consequence." And the dilation of his power, the solidifying of his consequence, the building of himself eight feet tall, is a struggle to hold ground, to stay in place in a cosmos which moves. The brilliant transfixing eye of the Gothic hero-villain is only secondarily a search and destroy apparatus; essentially it is attempting to pin the world in place. The simple lesson of the Gothic, then, is a lesson for the Gothic hero, with whose terrors we are always brought to identify. The lesson is that eat power, eat people, extend your desires as you may, you cannot grow big enough to avoid being rolled away around the curve. One's only hope in such a universe is clearly to move from ultimate faith in (preemption of) the Creation Mystery, to ultimate ground in the Resurrection mystery, a move which the Gothic hero-villain resists with a wonderful tragic stubbornness dramatized most memorably, and most subtly, in Maturin's *Melmoth the Wanderer* (1820).

Radcliffe's murdering Confessor Monk Schedoni makes a good try at standing still; like Iago, he attempts not to change when his fortune changes and he carries some of his secrets and some of his motivations with him, so that even when he is rolled away, a rather disturbing blank is left. For the lesson made literal, dark and chilling, we can look to the end of another monk, Lewis's Ambrosio. This man too has an intimation of greatness and an even more powerful sensation of instability and shrinkage: he also has—handy Gothic machine—an androgynous demon to taunt him with nursing unacted desires. In rage, in lust, in hate, he must flesh out each desire as its baby shape is revealed to him, and finally, ripe to bursting with hypocrisy, matricide, incest, rape and blasphemy, and huge with despair, he falls, "rolled from precipice to precipice," is broken down by rocks and picked apart by birds, dissolved by sun and air, his substance eaten by insects and washed into the sand and the sea "on the seventh day" of his Decreation.

Something like that is envisioned by Frankenstein's creature, an entry into Night and Chaos, extinction without rage, though Resurrection lurks around the edges of his consciousness: "my spirit will sleep in peace, or if it thinks, it will not surely think thus" (p. 223).

II

Frankenstein is a deeply complex and somewhat ambiguous mélange of analogies that play more or less heavily at different moments. It will not do to regard Victor Frankenstein simply as mad scientist,[8] for he also has crucial existences as cloistered monk, as flawed God, as anti-husband. Readers of Romantic poetry who come to look more closely at the author of this remarkable story are now recognizing in Frankenstein a variation on the Shelleyan doomed seeker, an Alastor who refuses all comfort in the community, vile stuporous mass that it is, to seek his vision of ideal beauty with such passion that the actual loving figure of the Indian maiden beside him becomes the illusion, and the abstract illusion the reality. Or like the poet of "Epipsychidion," a man who seeks as a lover not an autonomous human being but his imagined double self, that "soul fled out of my soul" which he dreams of taking

8. As Brian Aldiss does both in his history of science fiction, *Billion Year Spree* (New York, 1973), and in *Frankenstein Unbound* (New York, 1973).

43

apart from the world into a tower on an island, where he and his recovered soul will melt back together again in a creation (love) that sounds much more like a decreation, first of the other being, then of the single soul:

> In one another's substance finding food . . .
>
> . . . .
>
> One hope within two wills, one will beneath
> Two overshadowing minds, one life, one death,
> One Heaven, one Hell, one immortality,
> And one Annihilation.
>
> [Lines 580, 584–87]

These are Shelleyan decreation poems, written in the same span that saw the great creation, or rather Resurrection Mystery, of *Prometheus Unbound*. *Frankenstein* was written in 1816 and partakes of the same ecstatic despair before the old aesthetic paradox—the poet sets out to create an image of beauty and instead looses into the world, soul out of my soul, an image of death. The poet masters himself in the arduous making of the poem, but the poem, once free, is masterless. And vulnerable. Frightened critics may turn on the artwork and attempt to kill it, or spurn it as (let us say) "a loose baggy monster." Or the poem may turn harsh and tear human nature. And in the general emotional conflagration, poet and artifact may lock together in a miserable destroying bond that leaves no room for the living woman, who is the daughter of William Godwin and Mary Wollstonecraft after all, and hence no anxious bourgeoise, but who would still quite like to be a wife.

If Frankenstein as creator is of changing import, alternately Shelleyan resurrector and Blakean Nobodaddy, even more so is the creature. Machine and poem, son and brother, alter ego to Frankenstein, not as black is to white but as mirror is to man, or as imagination is to the whole being, the creature matches Frankenstein in his progress in a straight line across the curve to the edge of Damnation. Both beings, in their stature, their capacity to think and feel more intensely than the community, in the profound sense of original grace and gift that attends them and the equally profound intuition they both have of secret and original sin and burden, are the Gothic hero-villain as Walpole's Manfred described himself, the Man of Sorrows. Yet behind that phrase in the Western Christian heritage stands another Person, of whom the Gothic hero is not a blasphemy but an appropriation. He too is a Son pursued and killed by the Father. Yet, as in the case of Manfred, it is not so much the Son who must be annihilated but the sin which the Son harbors. In the Christian vision of this second Adam the Father's Son remakes himself out of the sins of men, constructs a new being, as Frankenstein did, from the limbs and organs of criminals and vagrants. The creature, both apart from and together with his Father, recognizes his dependence and struggles against it, knowing that his father's will curves toward his death. At the end the creature decides to fulfill that will. He sets off to construct his funeral pyre partly to end his personal torment and to leave a world made cold by the absence of his creator, but also to fulfill the last wish of Frankenstein, that the creature, whose relationship to the human community if not to Frankenstein himself is now unambiguous hatred, remove that threat to the community:

Thou didst seek my extinction, that I might not cause greater wretchedness. I shall . . . consume to ashes this miserable frame, that its remains may afford no light to any curious and unhallowed wretch who would create such another as I have been. [P. 223]

Thus at the end the creature leaves unsolved in himself the two important paradoxes of the novel. The community of feeling beings is so linked that when he causes wretchedness, to Frankenstein whom he knows or even to Justine whom he does not know, he experiences wretchedness. And when they cause him misery no exertion of will or reason, not even the anticipation of his own remorse, can keep him from returning misery to them—he is "the slave of an impulse which I detested yet could not disobey" (p. 220). Yet both creature and creator, if they cannot disobey the impulse that irresistibly feeds their life, be it poisoned or nourishing, into the community, can also not resist the contrary impulse, to go apart, to seek truths where community is not, to do their greatest endeavors where men are not. This is Frankenstein at the beginning, holding his little community of family and friends in stasis, at a distance, while he pursues his object. And so he is at the end. He has in his pursuit/flight with the creature in the Arctic been succored by the explorer Walton, who also has as his object the conquest of the farthest material secrets, tracing a straight line up the round earth. Like his creature after him, Frankenstein tells his tale as a warning to all who would travel too far out of the will and the touch of community; and looks forward to his death as the exemplary seal on that warning. Yet when the men of Walton's ship vote to turn back from the dangerous ice and gales, Frankenstein harangues them to continue, to "believe these vast mountains of ice are mole-hills which will vanish before the resolutions of men" (p. 213). The impulse to move out of community into the void, to make molehills out of mountains and vice versa, is alive in Frankenstein to the very end. Embodying that impulse the creature sets off into the north wastes in the novel's last sentence—not wearily or reluctantly, he "springs" from the ship. He intends, he says, to go to extinction, or at least to sleep. Yet the novel does not show his extinction; that spirit is clearly still alive, part Holy part Unholy Ghost. And succeeding generations of the community, responding unerringly to Mary Shelley's real message, have brought him back, play by film by novel, to seek love, to be repulsed, to kill and be killed and remain unkillable.

He comes back to seek love, reaching out of the Decreation Mystery, the embrace of the living dead, beautiful and terrible staple of the Gothic, the annihilating love which is the sin against the Holy Ghost. Lawrence understood—Lawrence whom Leavis elevated higher than Joyce in the Great Tradition both as a thinker and as a literary technician because "he can truly say that what he writes must be written from the depths of his religious experience." [9] That same experience gives him language to penetrate the Gothic Tradition, to describe in his classic study of Edgar Allan Poe the sin of Poe's lovers and of all Gothic annihilating lovers, Victor Frankenstein and his creature included:

Moreover, they are 'love' stories. . . . Love is the mysterious vital attraction which draws things together, closer, closer together. . . . [*The House of Usher*] is lurid and melodramatic, but it is true. It is a ghastly psychological truth of what happens in the last stages of this beloved love, which cannot be separate, cannot be isolate, cannot listen in isolation to the isolate Holy Ghost. For it is the Holy Ghost we must live by. The next era is the era of the Holy Ghost. And the Holy Ghost speaks individually inside each individual; always, forever a ghost. There is no manifestation to the general

9. F. R. Leavis, *The Great Tradition* (New York, 1969), p. 125.

world. . . . The Ushers, brother and sister, betrayed the Holy Ghost in themselves. . . . They would love, they would merge, they would be as one thing. So they dragged each other down to death. For the Holy Ghost says you must *not* be as one thing with another being. Each must abide by itself, and correspond only within certain limits.[10]

To abide apart, yet correspond. Separate but consubstantial. Classic Gothic, the orthodox sublime, believes in correspondence, believes in love, strives against limits. It is one of the major "spines" of Romance and yet it is one of the most deeply conservative of the Romance genres, punishing first the community that declines to strive and then the striving being who preempts that function. Classic Gothic creates the Romance world of two opposite absolutes, but the special flavor of the Gothic, as Lawrence notes, is to show not the inevitability and stamina of duality, as Romance often does, but the vulnerability of it. *Pace* Lévi-Strauss, the bi-structured world is radically unstable, it seeks collapse into oneness, or else seeks to generate a third term to marshall itself into unity, not oneness. That is why in the Christian Mystery the Trinity needs the Holy Ghost, that unseen triangulation point that makes "person" possible. That is what Lawrence means by the Holy Ghost, a third dimension with no manifestation to the general world that provides space to dwell in for beings who otherwise were simply points on a line infinitely collapsing. The Gothic describes the failure of its significant people to generate that triangulation point, listen to the Holy Ghost. Romance may show the duality, the opposite absolutes, still holding apart in tension, but Gothic Romance usually shows the merge-back-together.

Frankenstein shows all these actions. At the ultimate edge of miserable hostile merging the creature seeks to generate a third term in the duality, a woman with whom he can triangulate sufficient mental space to deal with Frankenstein. And Frankenstein tries to do this himself with Elizabeth. Then, jealous and doomed, each destroys the other's triangulation point, the other's Holy Ghost. Instinctively Mary Shelley seeks this same thing in her artistic structure, creating the explorer Walton to raise and then to

10. D. H. Lawrence, *Studies in Classic American Literature* (New York, 1954), p. 79. For a different connection between this work and *Frankenstein*, see George Levine's discussion on pp. 28–29, above.

frustrate expectations of greater mental space within the novel. But though she can give Walton pertinence and even some complexity, she cannot give him weight enough to make that third dimension; so the novel tightens and tautens back into its destined shape, the Gothic Romance, the duality snapping back into merge and annihilation, "borne away by the waves and lost in darkness and distance." The Trinity was never achieved. The Mystery was Poe's Mystery, Decreation.

III

Fire and Ice in *Frankenstein*

ANDREW GRIFFIN

As HEAT AND COLD are among our most primitive bodily sensations, so fire and ice form a part of the primitive language of the mind. In *The Psychoanalysis of Fire* Gaston Bachelard even suggests that thought itself arose in reveries before the fire, taking as its first object fire itself, "the first phenomenon."[1] Fire has served man for centuries (doubtless for many millennia) not just to warm his house and cook his food but to explain his world as well, and in particular those aspects of his world that live and change. To the prescientific and poetic mind that Bachelard analyzes, fire *is* life and change, "the ultra-living element," and as such has been confidently located in the sky, deep in the earth, in everything that moves, grows, alters its shape, reproduces itself. Fire is thus "one of the principles of universal explanation," both good and bad. "It shines in Paradise. It burns in Hell."[2] But nowhere is it more confidently located, or more necessary to thought and discourse, than in the very seat of life, the inner world of human feeling. For all the intimate sensations we experience directly and daily—intestinal, libidinal, but most of all emotional—there seems to exist no language but metaphor and no metaphor so apt as this of vital fire or fiery life, glowing or smoldering, flaring up or blazing out, as we love and hate.

Ice has yet to find its phenomenologist. The Eskimo language may have more than forty words for ice, but to most of us ice seems, in contrast to fire, essentially fixed and dead. It is precisely in contrast to fire, however—in its essential fixity and uniformity— that ice finds its imaginative meaning. For unlike water (which,

1. Gaston Bachelard, *The Psychoanalysis of Fire* (Boston, 1964), p. 7.
2. *Ibid.*, p. 7.

49

though it puts fire out, rather resembles fire in its fluidity and formlessness and is, like fire, often used to represent the "life" of the feelings) ice opposes or negates fire, cooling what is hot, solidifying what is fluid, arresting motion, silencing sound. Ice opposes and suppresses life and change; it is repression and death. In the inner world of the emotions, it blights and kills what was warm and blooming, seals up and freezes over even the most volcanic passions. Its killing numbness may, of course, be welcome, bringing relief from all feeling except (in Keats's phrase about the solaces of December) "the feel of not to feel it."

To the Victorian imagination, anxious for clear alternatives in a confusing world, the polarities of fire and ice often proved irresistible. When *Jane Eyre* opens by placing its small heroine between warm red and cold white realms, we understand at once that her problem will be to avoid *both* the blaze of strong feeling *and* the frozen stillness of no feeling at all. She will seek instead a moderate and human warmth, a controlled burning, symbolized throughout the novel (and the period) by that most Victorian of symbols, the domestic hearth.

To the Romantic imagination, however, there is little comfort and less interest in hard edges and hard choices—and little to be said for the hearth. In the Romantic universe extremes meet, contraries are reconciled and even fused. *Frankenstein* begins with Walton's dream of a tropical paradise at the North Pole, and his Romantic vision in turn introduces Frankenstein's dream of the vital fire or "spark" interpenetrating and animating matter otherwise cold and dead. Both visions recall Coleridge's enthusiasm for the reconciliation of elements opposed or different *in kind*, whether in nature or in art: external with internal, intellectual with emotional, conscious with unconscious, matter with spirit, "the FREE LIFE and the confining FORM," not to mention fire and ice.[3]

But Mary Shelley, though intellectually a Romantic, seems almost a Victorian at heart. Her novel never questions the reality and the power of Romantic reconciliations—Frankenstein's quest is

3. These and other polarities recur, of course, throughout Coleridge's thought, which seems (like the imagination itself) to "dissolve, diffuse, dissipate," and especially to distinguish mainly in order "to recreate" its objects in their original unity. For "the FREE LIFE and the confining FORM," see "On the Principles of Genial Criticism," Essay Third, the discussion of Raphael's Galatea.

successful, nor are we sure that Walton's would have failed. But it does expose the disregard for simple human needs that seems inseparably a part of all Romantic exploration. Frankenstein's Prometheanism is more and more clearly revealed as obsessive and inhuman, the cause of much suffering and many deaths. More profoundly, *Frankenstein* betrays the conviction that a knowledge of the principles of life gives us no cause to rejoice: that the elements mixed in man make for disharmony, monstrosity, and tragedy. Frankenstein's creation is a monster, after all, sublime only in his Dantean ugliness. The Monster's narrative reveals a conservative distrust of Romantic extremes, a Victorian longing for security, society, and self-command, symbolized (as in *Jane Eyre*) by the domestic hearth. Only when he loses all hope of companionship does he run, as it were, to extremes: first to fire; next, in bitterness of heart, to cold and ice; finally, in a condition of almost philosophical despair, to a "Romantic" synthesis of both in his dramatic suicide-by-fire at the North Pole.

On this cruel and significant irony the novel closes. The Monster's last act realizes Walton's visionary goal, but in such a way as to parody and protest against the contradictions in existence. With mixed feelings, Walton sails for home, away from the world of Romantic poetry, toward the native regions of the Victorian novel, a temperate zone where one can tell hot from cold and where, for better or for worse, human relations flourish.

I

This is not to say that the Victorian universe is necessarily a simpler or a tamer place than the Romantic, or that it offers less scope for daring and significant action. Jane Eyre is, in her own way and her own world, as adventurous and as imaginative as Walton or Frankenstein, and as ready as they to commit herself to the unknown. Coldly dismissed from the Reed family fireside in her story's opening chapter, Jane takes refuge in an imagined cold deeper than this cruel rejection, a dim vision of "death-white realms" derived from Bewick's *History of British Birds*, especially those pages

which treat of the haunts of sea-fowl; of "the solitary rocks and promontories" by them only inhabited; of the coast of Norway, studded with isles from its southern extremity, the Lindeness, or Naze, to the North Cape. . . . Nor could I pass unnoticed the suggestion of the bleak shores of Lapland, Siberia, Spitzbergen, Nova Zembla, Iceland, Greenland, with "the vast sweep of the Arctic Zone, and those forlorn regions of dreary space,—that reservoir of frost and snow, where firm fields of ice, the accumulation of centuries of winters, glazed in Alpine heights above heights, surround the pole, and concentre the multiplied rigors of extreme cold."[4]

Here is an epic roll-call of the coldest and loneliest places on earth, in all their frigid glamor. But here is also, still more powerfully, both a concentration and a vast expansion of the idea of the Far North, the idea of ice itself. Bewick's vision of the ice-cap extends and perfects itself in every dimension, including that of time: accumulated through "centuries of winters," thickly overspreading "the vast sweep of the Arctic Zone," deepening into a "reservoir of frost," soaring into "Alpine heights above heights," the whole massively "concentred" on the axis of the pole.

This is not the language of geography but of romance and fantasy. To Jane, sadly enough, the Arctic Zone *is* a romance, "as interesting as the tales Bessie sometimes narrated on winter evenings" beside the nursery-hearth, "passages of love and adventure."

With Bewick on my knee, I was then happy; happy at least in my way. I feared nothing but interruption. . . . [P. 5]

It is disturbing to find in a child of ten what Wallace Stevens calls "a mind of winter," more at home in "forlorn regions of dreary space" than in Gateshead. In the beginning Jane is both pathetic and perverse; her tastes are morbid, her fantasies suicidal. But she is not allowed to linger long in the indulgence of neurotic pleasures. Reaction must follow, a reaction away from ice and toward fire. The interruption Jane has dreaded arrives in the person of Master John Reed, whose petty tyrannies strike an unexpected spark from the passive little girl; she rebels, strikes back, and is imprisoned, "an infantile Guy Fawkes" (p. 24). Soon afterwards she turns her newfound heat of feeling on John Reed's frigid mother, vanquishing her too.

The short-term results of her rebellion are mixed; victory over

4. Charlotte Brontë, *Jane Eyre* (New York, 1950), p. 4. All further references to this work appear in the text.

Mrs. Reed in particular brings a "fierce pleasure" but, on its heels, a black desolation.

> A ridge of lighted heath, alive, glancing, devouring, would have been a meet emblem of my mind when I accused and menaced Mrs. Reed: the same ridge, black and blasted after the flames are dead, would have represented as meetly my subsequent condition. . . . [P. 37]

In the long term, however, the results are positive: Jane's explosion brings about her release from Gateshead. And before she leaves, she makes some progress toward controlling (not repressing) her fire, exploring her emotions and turning them to some use. On the day of her fateful interview with Brocklehurst, she goes to the window and gazes out on the wintry landscape. It is mid-January and the countryside lies "still and petrified under the influence of a hard frost." But Jane no longer seeks the anesthesia of cold.

> I fell to breathing on the frost-flowers with which the window was fretted, and thus clearing a space in the glass through which I might look out on the grounds. . . .
> From this window were visible the porter's lodge and the carriage road, and just as I had dissolved so much of the silver-white foliage veiling the panes, as left room to look out, I saw the gates thrown open and a carriage roll through. [Pp. 28–29]

This delicate melting of the frost-flowers is a human use of human warmth, opening a loophole on the world. It also seems to bring on, as if by sympathetic magic, a dissolving of more meaningful barriers, as the gates of Gateshead open to admit the carriage bearing Jane's future. Before she goes downstairs to meet Brocklehurst, Jane opens the window on which she has been breathing to share her breakfast with "a hungry little robin"—aligning herself with all warm-blooded creatures who would come in out of the cold.

The Gateshead chapters show Jane moving unsteadily but with increasing control toward the proper use of fire—simultaneously, and significantly, abandoning not only her ice-fantasies but also fantasy itself. She does remain in danger from both extremes throughout her later career, being (in her own view) a creature of extremes, now frozen in "absolute submission," now "bursting . . . with volcanic vehemence" (p. 436). Thornfield exposes her to the mingled dangers and attractions of fire: Rochester's sexual heat

("He rose and came towards me, and I saw his face all kindled, and his full falcon-eye flashing" [p. 295]) and Bertha Mason's pyromania. Moor House holds for Jane the cold magnetism of her handsome cousin St. John Rivers, with his marble profile, gem-like eye, and icy kiss. To Rochester and to Bertha, Jane opposes all the cold that is in her nature, skillfully cooling the ardor of the former and throwing cold water on the bedroom fire set by the latter. And to St. John Rivers' ice Jane opposes, of course, her warm feelings, never to be wholly numbed again: "I am cold," says St. John, "no fervour infects me," to which Jane stoutly replies, "Whereas I am hot, and fire dissolves ice" (p. 417). Throughout the novel Jane steers a wavering course between extremes, the domestic hearth her lodestar as well as her goal: a hearth of her own, for warmth and for cooking, symbolic too of safe or socially approved (married) sexuality.

Frankenstein begins much as *Jane Eyre* does, with a drive (literal, in this case) into the polar regions. Walton's narrative, framing the novel, is entirely Arctic; Victor's and the Monster's stories are set much of the time amid the peaks and glaciers of Frankenstein's native Switzerland, sometimes in the almost equally desolate landscape of northern Scotland, and—finally—in the Arctic again, where the lines of all three narratives converge. "The land of mist and snow," as Walton calls it, consciously quoting Coleridge, is thus before our eyes from the beginning and, intermittently but with powerful effect, until the end. For Walton, it is the object of an enthusiastic quest; for Victor, sometimes an end in itself and always, in some form, the background of his "unhallowed" work. Only for the Monster are the mountains and glaciers an unmixed evil, a place of exile.

But for Walton, unlike young Jane Eyre, the pure idea of ice and snow holds no attractions; he dreams instead of an impossible conjunction of hot and cold, a paradise at the heart of the polar snows. It is on this Romantic vision, not on the cold fact of the ice-floes proper, that the novel really opens. "I try in vain to be persuaded," he writes his sister, "that the pole is the seat of frost and desolation":

it ever presents itself to my imagination as the region of beauty and delight. There, Margaret, the sun is forever visible, its broad disc just skirting the horizon and diffusing a perpetual splendour. There—for with your leave, sister, I will put some trust in preceding navigators—there frost and snow are banished; and, sailing over a calm sea, we may be wafted to a land surpassing in wonders and in beauty every region hitherto discovered on the habitable globe.[5]

Walton clearly realizes the surface improbability of his conviction. He writes self-consciously ("for with your leave, my sister") and even somewhat self-critically of his expedition: "there is a love for the marvellous, a belief in the marvellous, intertwined in all my projects, which hurries me out of the common pathways of men . . ." (p. 231). He is fully conscious of his own ambivalence, sometimes carried forward by boyish enthusiasm, sometimes checked by serious misgivings:

It is impossible to communicate to you a conception of the trembling sensation, half pleasurable and half fearful, with which I am preparing to depart. . . . There is something at work in my soul which I do not understand. [Pp. 15, 231]

But the same contradictions that trouble his mind have captured his imagination and lead him on; he is Romantic, where Jane is Victorian. She feels the tug of either extreme, in opposite directions; he *knows* that contraries combine somehow, somewhere, and so he travels north in search of the warm seas and relaxed living of the south.

Like much else in his journeying, this miraculous synthesis is Coleridgean. For Coleridge, both the poetic imagination and the Divine Hand reveal themselves "in the balance or reconciliation of opposite or discordant qualities."[6] It is not the least of Kubla Khan's achievements to have united fire and ice in his pleasure dome ("It was a miracle of rare device, / A sunny pleasure dome with caves of ice"—one hemisphere reflecting the other, frozen cave inverting and mirroring sunny dome). "Frost at Midnight" ends with a related vision of antitheses reconciled: summer blends with winter in the speaker's loving prophecy, "tufts of snow" and

5. Mary Wollstonecraft Shelley, *Frankenstein*, ed. James Rieger (New York, 1974), pp. 9–10. All further references to this work appear in the text.

6. Samuel Taylor Coleridge, *Biographia Literaria*, ed. J. Shawcross, (Oxford, 1907), II:12.

the "sun-thaw" simultaneously affirmed in one harmonious vision of the living year.

But the interfusion of elemental contraries is Shelleyan too. For Percy Bysshe Shelley, life is love and both are fire, "the fire for which all thirst":

> that *sustaining* love
> Which through the web of being blindly wove
> By man and beast and earth and air and sea,
> *Burns bright or dim.*

[*Adonais*, stanza 54; my italics]

In *Prometheus Unbound* it is the all-forgiving love of the fire-bringing Titan through which all things are renewed, "love, which is as fire" (III.iii.151) and which survives eons of Jupiter's implacable hatred, symbolized here by the freezing cold of the Caucasian alp to which Prometheus is chained. Prometheus' alp resembles Walton's polar paradise, only without the bliss. His vital fire exists in (tormented) opposition to the enveloping and invading ice:

> The crawling glaciers pierce me with the spears
> Of their moon-freezing crystals, the bright chains
> Eat with their burning cold into my bones.

[I.i.31–33]

Meanwhile, though Jupiter showers down his curses "like snow on herbless peaks," mankind still keeps the faith and "burns toward heaven with fierce reproach" an "unextinguished fire" of detestation for tyranny (III.i.5–12).[7] When at last the "retributive hour" arrives and Jupiter falls, Prometheus' vital heat dissolves his icy chains and kindles everything with love, first penetrating Panthea "like vaporous fire," then irradiating Asia, reaching as far as the frozen moon "with warmth of flame."

7. Jupiter's hatred is always ice and snow, but he does not always hate. When he loves, he too is fiery. At the conception of Demogorgon, Thetis cries out,

> Insufferable might!
> God! Spare me! I sustain not the quick flames,
> The penetrating presence . . . .

Even his love, however, serves less to quicken and comfort life than to oppress and destroy it. Thetis feels herself dissolving "into a dew," the echo of Hamlet's soliloquy strongly suggesting death; and Demogorgon, of course, will be death to Jupiter.

But Shelley is not always this Blakean. He is at least as likely to represent the conjunction of contraries as conflict-free, harmonious—not melted and transformed by fire but filled with a marvelous light. Even in *Prometheus Unbound* we find visions of all the elements drawing together in harmony and interpenetrated by an effulgent light.[8] "Mont Blanc" displays both kinds of conjunction, the violent and the peaceful, and seems to affirm both at once. Here, however, it is not Love but, more mysteriously and ominously, "Power" that animates and pervades all things, even the mountain world of ice and death:

> Power in likeness of the Arve comes down
> From the ice-gulfs that gird his secret throne,
> Bursting through these dark mountains like the flame
> Of lightning through the tempest.
>
> [Lines 16–19]

It is astonishing how much raw energy this image of the torrent manages to harness. Born in the glaciers, taking the form of rushing water, Shelley's Protean "Power" bursts into our ken as fire and light together: light at its most magnificent and deadly, the lightning bolt, but veiled or muffled by its contrary, the cold and vaporous cloud—which, however, the lightning heats and illuminates from within. The image is a favorite of Shelley's, doubtless because it brilliantly expresses the dynamic union of opposites which is life itself: life *is* fire wrapped in a cloud. But the combination need not be so explosive; "Mont Blanc" ends with the same image tamed and full of unearthly peace. The lightning is no longer a flame, no longer thunderous:

> Its home
> The voiceless lightning in these solitudes
> Keeps innocently, and like vapour broods
> Over the snow.
>
> [Lines 136–39]

The fire of heaven here becomes its own cloud ("like vapour") and "broods" with dovelike innocence—even, perhaps, creatively, as

8. In Asia's hymn to Earth, for example, mountains, sky, and ocean seem to press eagerly into each other's natural regions, while at the same time light plays over and links all the elements into one whole, glancing

the divine Spirit broods in *Paradise Lost*—over its own opposite, the snow.

Shelley may sometimes have believed that universal peace would follow opposition and conflict, and light supersede fire, as the world turned toward the millennium. But it seems more likely that his attitude toward the elements of which we are compounded was, like his young wife's, as mixed as the compound itself. When Shelley dwelt on revolutionary change, he thought of fire and high wind. When he dreamt of the millennium his mind turned toward the light: Milton's holy Light, almost a fifth element—unburning fire and impalpable air, the essence or abstraction of radiant energy. When Shelley imagined eternity he saw, as we know, simply a "white radiance."

II

That radiance behind or within all things calls to mind the "sudden light" that breaks in on Victor Frankenstein at the climax of his own attempt to unriddle nature and master the elemental opposition between death and life. Frankenstein is attracted to Mont Blanc by the same "Power" that Percy Shelley intuits there, alive and at work in what would seem to other eyes only "a scene terrifically desolate," a world of ruin and death. Jane Eyre's mighty "idea" of the ice-world is *natura naturata*; she welcomes the utter solitude and frozen stillness of a world without force or motion. But Frankenstein's and Shelley's Alps are *natura naturans*, "this glorious presence-chamber of imperial nature," as Frankenstein puts it, whose every sublime feature declares the immanence of a tremendous energy, "brawling . . . cracking . . . silent working," "accumulated . . . rent and torn" (p. 249). Where Jane seeks from her imagined Arctic a blessed numbness, Victor, like Shelley (and like Walton), feels a rising excitement, a return of feeling as he draws nearer nature's throne. To him, the cold peaks are "mighty

from the "icy spires," irradiating the drops of ocean spray so that they "dazzle" the eye and "spangle" the wind (*Prometheus Unbound*, II.iii.28–32). In "Lines Written Among the Euganean Hills," a meditative and anti-apocalyptic poem, it is the changing light of a whole Italian day that, again, draws all things into a unity (including the poem) by "interpenetrating" them all.

friends," and they house friends still more strange, "wandering spirits" to whom he calls out at the height of his mountain ecstasy (p. 93).

Frankenstein's science is only this sort of geographical investigation in another language, a language not of regions, journeys, and spirits, but of substances, elements, and essences. Whether in the landscape or the laboratory, both he and Walton seek to penetrate ground that seems unredeemably dead, searching for a core of vital warmth unseen before. Frankenstein's genius seems indeed essentially penetrative. It is not enough that his "mighty friends" the Alps console and attend him, he must "penetrate their misty veil and seek them in their cloudy retreats"—going without a guide, of course (p. 249). Even as a boy, in his alchemical period, what stirs him is what is hidden. "The world was to me a secret which I desired to divine," he tells us. "The hidden laws of nature" were his passion, and only those:

and whether it was the outward substance of things or the inner spirit of nature and the mysterious soul of man that occupied me, still my inquiries were directed to the metaphysical, or in its highest sense, the physical secrets of the world. [Pp. 236–37]

Victor's language is often vigorously if unconsciously phallic ("here were men who had penetrated deeper and knew more" [p. 238]); the object of his quest is sometimes clearly female ("He had partially unveiled the face of Nature, but her immortal lineaments were still a wonder and a mystery" [p. 238]). To many imaginations, therefore, if not certainly to his own, Victor's goal will present itself as a womb, the warm source and seat of being, which Victor—adolescent from first to last—desires rather to know than to possess. So it was, at least, for the alchemists, with their "seminal fire" and "seeds of fire" burning deep within matter, "in the belly" of a substance, "active at the center of each thing."[9] According to Bachelard, "This need to *penetrate*, to go to the *interior* of things, to the *interior* of beings," always arises from and sets out to confirm an "intuition of inner heat" on the part of the investigator.[10] "The equation of fire and life," he says, "forms the basis of the system of

9. Bachelard, *Psychoanalysis of Fire*, pp. 41, 47, 75.
10. *Ibid.*, p. 40.

Paracelsus."[11] Over this system and others Frankenstein "warmed" his young imagination and fed his "fervent longing to penetrate the secrets of nature," of maternal nature (p. 238).

To satisfy that longing is, however, dangerous. For not only is fire itself both life-giving and death-dealing, but the compounded fire-in-ice which is a living being is unpredictable and unstable. In a storm at his home near Belrive, Victor, age fifteen, sees an oak tree struck by lightning and destroyed. "Struck," however, is not the word:

As I stood at the door, on a sudden I beheld a stream of fire issue from an old and beautiful oak, which stood about twenty yards from our house; and so soon as the dazzling light vanished, the oak had disappeared, and nothing remained but a blasted stump. When we visited it the next morning, we found the tree shattered in a singular manner. It was not splintered by the shock, but entirely reduced to thin ribbands of wood. I never beheld anything so utterly destroyed. [P. 35]

Fortunately "a man of great research in natural philosophy" (in the novel's first edition, Victor's father) is at hand to explain the phenomenon, turning Victor's thoughts away from alchemy and towards natural science proper. What Victor actually sees and obviously feels, however, has little to do with "the laws of galvanism and electricity": a stream of fire *issues from* the oak, its exit shredding the tree. This spectacle confirms Frankenstein's intuition but greatly complicates his ambition; his vision, henceforward, is as ambiguous as Walton's. There has been a revelation of life in a "dazzling light," but there has also been, inseparably, the catastrophic ruin of the "old and beautiful oak," on which Victor dwells with a fascinated horror that would not be out of place in the vaults and charnels of his subsequent research ("blasted stump . . . shattered . . . splintered . . . entirely reduced . . . so utterly destroyed").[12] If this were animal instead of vegetable matter—if it

---

11. *Ibid.*, p. 73.

12. Later in the novel a lightning bolt again brings Victor Frankenstein this mixed elation and dread, revealing in terms much more personal than before the paradoxical oneness of life-giving and death-dealing in nature. After little William's death, Victor walks alone at night near the scene of the murder and witnesses an electrical storm over the Alps. The sublime display "elevated my spirits," he tells us, and helps to relieve his grief; but a sudden flash shows him the Monster whom he has not seen since the

were, for example, the remains of little Stevie in Conrad's *The Secret Agent*—we would be sickened. And Victor is sickened even in the midst of his profound excitement, abandoning for a time this whole line of inquiry, with its terrible contradictions, for the bloodless certainties of mathematics. When he returns to the problem of life it is, as he now warns his reader, to a personal destruction as sure and thorough-going as that of the old oak tree: "my utter and terrible destruction" (p. 239).

The movies make of Victor's laboratory a brilliant pyrotechnical display, full of light and energy. In the novel, however, it is a dark cell, a "workshop of filthy creation." All is cold horror: "unhallowed damps," "lifeless clay," "dissecting-room and slaughterhouse" (pp. 49–50). Like her husband, Mary Shelley means to emphasize that the path to the "deep mysteries" of the universal Mother lies through charnels and coffins ("Alastor," lines 18–29). Just as the cold must deepen as Walton draws nearer and nearer to his warm goal, so the corruption of death deepens around Frankenstein as he approaches the secret of life. When he reaches it at last, the "sudden light" that blazes forth "from the midst of this darkness" is something more than intellectual illumination. "Brilliant and wondrous," it bursts from its hiding place, flooding the chamber (pp. 47, 50). When Victor stoops at last over his giant creation, the fundamental metaphor clearly asserts itself: "I collected the instruments of life around me, that I might infuse a spark of being into the lifeless thing that lay at my feet" (p. 52). In a novel subtitled "The Modern Prometheus," that is clear enough.

What kind of Prometheus is Frankenstein, however? The myth itself, in its different versions, presents the Titan in two primary roles or aspects, one usually emphasized to the exclusion of the other: first, the bold thief of heaven's fire; second, the fire-giver, shaper and benefactor of mankind, in some versions (*Prometheus Unbound* included) the father of all the arts. Frankenstein is brilliantly successful as the thief of fire and, if not exactly happy in this pursuit, at least excited and ardent. But as the fire-giver he is a disaster and increasingly miserable. As chapter IV begins (with the

night of his creation, "hideous" and (as Victor instantly intuits) murderous as well. As in the case of the oak tree, a flash of lightning shows us life and death, creation and destruction, inextricably linked, inspiring in the viewer both excitement and despair.

words Mary Shelley first wrote) Frankenstein has achieved the dream of the fire-theft and is about to enter into the responsibilities of the fire-gift; he infuses the vital element into the cold form at his feet, which begins to stir fitfully. But "at this catastrophe," as Frankenstein puts it, all the horror that has been slowly accumulating through the preceding pages is precipitated, and we see not only what Frankenstein thinks of the creature he has made but also what Mary Shelley thinks of the whole romantic enterprise, and even of life:

Oh! No mortal could support the horror of that countenance. A mummy again endued with animation could not be so hideous as that wretch. I had gazed on him while unfinished; he was ugly then; but when those muscles and joints were rendered capable of motion, it became a thing such as even Dante could not have conceived. [P. 53]

Here, at the novel's imaginative center, the many issues it confronts are twisted tightly together. From Frankenstein's horrified rejection of his creature both the moral and the psychological dimensions of the tale unfold. From this point forward Frankenstein will be in flight from that to which he is inextricably linked, at once his child and *Doppelgänger*.

But what inspires this "breathless horror and disgust" in the first place, except the long-sought union of contrary elements, the compound of fire and clay? Victor's self-analysis, as far as it goes, lays heavy emphasis on the creature's physical ugliness, the distance between "the beauty of the dream" and gross reality. He feels no *horror*, however, until the spark enters the dead flesh and the mysterious combination is achieved, "muscles and joints . . . rendered capable of motion"—"the filthy mass that moved and talked" (pp. 53, 145). It is the contradiction at the root of Frankenstein's endeavor—and, for that matter, at the root of all creation—that produces the disgust. Frankenstein's nightmare on the fatal evening points in the same direction. Its cast of characters irresistibly suggests Oedipal anxieties, already implicit in Frankenstein's ambivalence regarding Mother Nature's secrets; but (as Judith Wilt rightly says in the preceding essay) the dream need not be reduced to these anxieties alone. The action of the dream (Elizabeth dissolving into a corpse within his arms) shows us, as does the Monster, a fearful fusion of opposites: bride and mother, wedding and funeral, present and past, and of course life and death. Frankenstein wakes from his dream feeling horror for the second time that night, only to find the dead-alive thing he has made peering through his bed-curtains; and for the second time that night he flies from it.

This dream, and the revulsion from the Monster that precedes and generates it, seem to me evidence of a disgust on Mary Shelley's part with something deeper than Romantic metaphors and habits of mind: a disgust with organic life or biological being itself (which, indeed, Romantic unities aspired to imitate and, by imitation, honor). Nature's workshop is as filthy as Victor's; not the Monster only but each of us is a filthy mass that moves and talks. In the "Author's Introduction" to *Frankenstein*, written a dozen years after the novel, Mary Shelley associates with her story's origins several ghost stories read in the same summer; and each of them exhibits the same intimate blending of the vital and the fatal, procreation and destruction. There was the *History of the Inconstant Lover* "who, when he thought to clasp the bride to whom he had pledged his vows, found himself in the arms of the pale ghost of her whom he had deserted." And there was "the tale of the sinful founder of his race,"

whose miserable doom it was to bestow the kiss of death on all the younger sons of his fated house, just when they reached the age of promise. . . . Eternal sorrow sat upon his face as he bent down and kissed the forehead of the boys.

These "blooming youths, cradled in healthy sleep," Mary Shelley writes, "from that hour withered like flowers snapped upon the stalk" (p. 224). Both stories show several parallels with Mary Shelley's own; but their central motif is the same as that of Frankenstein's nightmare, the fatal embrace or kiss of death overtaking and transforming "blooming youth." Here, again, is destruction *in* procreation, and "Eternal Sorrow" at the root of being. Death is the bride, the "founder of his race" is death. These equations are terrible, and so is the punishment for having glimpsed them. The last of the stories is Polidori's "terrible idea about a skull-headed lady [death-in-life again] who was so punished for peeping through a keyhole—what to see I forget: something very shocking and wrong of course" (p. 225).

Penalties of some sort we might have expected, for all these stories (*Frankenstein* most of all) point toward, if they do not actual-

ly represent, what Freud calls the primal scene: a forbidden looking at the processes by which new life is produced, the "filthy"
foundations of human being, made more than usually fearful and
forbidding in Mary Shelley's case by the circumstances surrounding her own birth. In Frankenstein's case (and in horror stories
generally), it is clear that the taboo violated has as much to do with
seeing as with *doing*, perhaps more. The "Author's Introduction"
speaks of the pale student as having looked into "the cradle of life"
only to see a "hideous corpse." In the novel it is not, strictly speaking, what Frankenstein has *done* that makes him shudder but rather
what he has *seen*: "I saw the dull yellow eye of the creature open."
He responds, not by destroying his creation, but by running away:
not, that is, by *un*doing it but by getting it out of his sight. "Unable
to endure the aspect of the being I had created, I rushed out of the
room" (p. 53).

Looking and *not looking* play at least as great a part in the novel's
inception, too, which Mary Shelley describes as a waking nightmare, an involuntary seeing:

My imagination, unbidden, possessed and guided me, gifting the
successive images that arose in my mind with a vividness far beyond
the usual bounds of reverie. *I saw—with shut eyes, but acute mental
vision—I saw* the pale student of unhallowed arts kneeling beside
the thing he had put together. *I saw* the hideous phantasm of a
man stretched out, and then, on the working of some powerful
engine, show signs of life and stir with an uneasy, half-vital motion.
Frightful must it be. . . . He would rush away. . . . He sleeps; but he
is awakened; *he opens his eyes; behold,* the horrid thing stands at his
bedside, opening his curtains and *looking on him with yellow, watery,
but speculative eyes.*
I opened mine in terror. [Pp. 227–28; my italics]

Ellen Moers discusses the "birth-myth" underlying the whole novel.
But Mary Shelley's original vision, recreated and all but relived
here, with its kneeling and lying figures, "uneasy" movements, and
"powerful engine" applied to the recumbent form, seems more
erotic than maternal. The seed of fire, after all, is being planted,
and Mary Shelley—however innocently or involuntarily—is present as a voyeur. Victor Frankenstein himself does not see more
vividly nor feel more terror of his monster than Mary Shelley in
the grip of her overwhelming fantasy; her immediate response,

like Victor's, is to deny it, to clear it away from before her eyes. Like Victor, she fails:

The idea so possessed my mind that a thrill of fear ran through me, and I wished to exchange the ghastly image of my fancy for the realities around. I see them still: the very room, the dark parquet, the closed shutters with the moonlight struggling through, and the sense I had that the glassy lake and white high Alps were beyond. I could not so easily get rid of my hideous phantom; still it haunted me. [P. 228]

The novel is her attempt either finally to exorcise or somehow to integrate the relentless "idea."

III

Either from Mary Shelley's or from Frankenstein's perspective, Walton looks naive and superficial. His enthusiasm is misplaced. The appropriate response to the kind of union he seeks is horror and revulsion. *Frankenstein* suggests that the mystery of being should be left strictly alone or, if glimpsed, covered again at once. It may suggest, further, that creation and procreation themselves, even by the usual means, might better be left alone.

But it is the great strength of this novel that, for all its deep-rooted horror of the nature of creation, it does not simply turn away from the condition of creatures (as do many of Shelley's poems) toward death and eternity—not, at least, without a struggle. If all of Mary Shelley's disgust and desperation is concentrated in Victor Frankenstein's story, all her compassion for our mixed nature and middle state is expressed in the Monster's. And all her hope as well—for with the Monster's opening words the novel makes a new beginning and turns upwards toward hope and possibility. "Poor, helpless, miserable wretch" that he is, the Monster is still a new life; his narrative brings to this novel a kind of second chance for human nature, of a kind especially attractive to eighteenth-century minds. Without social and familial ties, free of the handicaps as well as the supports of human culture, he will receive his education from Nature and Reason alone. For better or worse, what he essentially *is* from birth will have liberty to grow and act.

The Monster's self-education begins along Lockean lines; his story in general is that of dawning consciousness, first acquaintance with the world. But by far the most important discovery of his mental infancy is that of fire, a discovery he at once improves through experiment. "Overcome with delight at the warmth" of a fire abandoned by wandering beggars, he naïvely thrusts his hand into it; made cautious by experience, he explores the nature of fire, learning that fire subsists on wood, dries wet things, may be banked and so preserved through the night and fanned into life again in the morning. In addition to such basic science he learns things of immediate practical benefit, observing (in language as stiffly scientific as anything in Victor's narrative) "that the fire gave light as well as heat, and that the discovery of this element was useful to me in my food" (pp. 99–100). It is through fire, then, that the Monster first learns to exercise his considerable powers of observation and inference and, as we now say, to manipulate his environment.

In a novel dominated by the fatal results of Victor Frankenstein's esoteric science, this emphasis on his creature's natural bent toward applied science should not be passed over lightly. It is not "the hidden laws of nature" that interest the Monster but her more apparent operations, the mechanics of nature and its human uses. To him the world is not "a secret" to be divined or penetrated, but a place in which to live as comfortably as possible, pursuing pleasure, avoiding pain. As if by instinct he follows the angel Raphael's advice to a too-curious Adam: "Solicit not thy thoughts with matters hid. . . . Think only what concerns thee and thy being" (*Paradise Lost*, VII.167–74). What concerns the Monster is, before anything else, bodily health and well-being, food and warmth; fire comes to him as a godsend. One thinks of the young Jane Eyre and her clear appreciation of the need to stay alive ("I must keep in good health, and not die" [p. 31]), reaffirmed by the mature woman at the climax of her crisis with Rochester ("*I* care for myself" [p. 344]).

But fire is much more than the Monster's first tool. For it is through fire that he feels the first stirrings of sympathy and solicitude for something outside himself. His self-portrait before the fire in the forest at night is charming: he sits still, rapt, "watching the operation of the fire"; on a sudden inspiration he busies himself to gather more wet sticks and lay them near the blaze; when he must sleep, "in the greatest fear lest my fire should be extinguished," he first puts it to bed ("I covered it carefully with dry wood and leaves, and placed wet branches upon it; and then, spreading my cloak, I lay on the ground, and sank into sleep" [p. 99]). Waking the next morning, "My first care was to visit the fire." When at last he has to leave the clearing where he found the fire, it is with deep personal regret: "In this emigration I exceedingly lamented the loss of the fire." It is the first of many such emigrations, many laments for personal loss. The fire has become almost his friend and seems almost to reciprocate his care; he tends it, it comforts him.

Fire also forges the first links uniting the Monster to the De Lacey family, in whose lean-to he next comes to rest. The daily example and select library of his unsuspecting hosts teach the Monster first to understand and finally to claim the kinship he spontaneously feels for beings superficially so unlike himself. This sympathy begins, however, in the Monster's recognition that these "lovely creatures" are fire-users like himself. His first sight of the Swiss cottage interior discloses an old man seated "near a small fire." Soon a young man enters carrying "a load of wood"; a girl gathers roots and plants and, putting them in water, takes them also to the fire. The Monster understands these amenities from his own rough experience and seems pleased to recognize, amid the swimming confusion of so much that is new, the familiar business of preparing food (pp. 103–4). Of the first four words he learns, two have to do with fire (*fire, wood*) and two with food (*milk, bread*).

In short, the De Laceys introduce the Monster to a further use of fire: fire in its social dimension, housekeeping as in part a social ritual. What could be more natural, or more pathetic, than that he should try to repay his unknowing hosts by taking on himself the chore of gathering wood, or "firing"—secretly delighting in their wonder at the great piles of fuel he brings to their door and, through this gift, joining them in spirit each night around the fireplace? When at last, risking everything, the Monster dares to enter the cottage in hopes of gaining open and permanent relationship with other beings, he asks only (with as much meaning as feeling) "to remain a few minutes before the fire" (p. 129). He refuses food: "It is warmth and rest that I need." When Felix returns and drives him away, it is literally out into the cold he must go. From this moment he is doomed to the glaciers and ice-floes that symbolize (in *Frankenstein* as in *Jane Eyre*) the absence of all fellowship and warm feeling.

Looking back, the Monster asks himself why he did not then and there embrace the ultimate cold of death (as Jane does when similarly rejected, at least in fantasy), "extinguish the spark of existence" (p. 132) and "subside into dead matter" (p. 228). But the balance tips instead toward rage and revenge and, with these violent feelings, toward fire in a new form. He fans the "spark" within into a blaze that consumes house and hovel and all—his past, present, and future—in one great conflagration.

This act opens yet a third phase in the Monster's exploration of fire, his discovery of its antisocial dimension. Through the destructive power of fire he consciously allies himself, in bitterness of heart, with the fallen angels of whom he has read in the De Laceys' copy of *Paradise Lost*, perverting the life-giving and life-sustaining element into an instrument of torture and destruction. Like Satan, the Monster henceforth bears a hell within him (p. 132) and makes evil his good (p. 218).

The passage that describes his carefully orchestrated burning of the beloved cottage is, however, as two-edged and ambiguous as fire itself.

As the night advanced, a fierce wind arose from the woods and quickly dispersed the clouds that had loitered in the heavens; the blast tore along like a mighty avalanche and produced a kind of insanity in my spirits that burst the bounds of reason and reflection. I lighted the dry branch of a tree and danced with fury around the devoted cottage, my eyes still fixed on the western horizon, the edge of which the moon nearly touched. A part of its orb was at length hid, and I waved my brand; it sank, and with a loud scream I fired the straw, and heath, and bushes, which I had collected. The wind fanned the fire, and the cottage was quickly enveloped by the flames, which clung to it and licked it with their forked and destroying tongues. [P. 135]

Howling in frenzy and dancing around the "devoted" hut, the Monster seems possessed by some universal spirit of destruction or plastic Shelleyan "Power"; he acts in concert with the rising wind and setting moon, so that the whole cosmos seems to conspire in his revenge. It was the moon, "a radiant form" (p. 98), that first taught him what pleasure was; it is fitting that he should take its setting as the cue for his dedication to pain. The symbolic burning in itself, however, is an act tragically mixed, in which the Monster seems almost to be loving to death what remains of the De Laceys. In heaping up the "combustibles" with which to fire their hut, he makes, of course, one last grand offering in his year-long series of love-gifts of fuel. And even as the flames consume the house they seem to embrace it: they "clung to it and licked it with their forked and destroying tongues," a masterpiece of ambivalence, in which satanic longing merges seamlessly into satanic enmity toward mankind.

But the Monster is more than satanic. As he waves the burning branch or "brand" overhead, he is Adam and the avenging angel rolled into one, his own "dreadful face" and his own "fiery arms" barring the way back into his brief Eden.

> They looking back, all the Eastern side beheld
> Of Paradise, so late their happy seat,
> Waved over by that flaming brand, the gate
> With dreadful faces thronged and fiery arms.
>
> [XII.641–44]

With conscious irony he asks himself two sentences later, "And now, with the world before me, whither should I bend my steps?" The Monster knows, of course, that the world contains for him neither Providence as guide nor any place of rest at all.

> It was late in autumn when I quitted the district.... Nature decayed around me, and the sun became heatless; rain and snow poured around me; mighty rivers were frozen; the surface of the earth was hard, and chill, and bare, and I found no shelter. [P. 136]

From this point it is but a step (though many chapters intervene) to the last act in the Monster's tragedy, his suicide by fire at the North Pole. "I shall quit your vessel on the ice raft which brought me hither," he informs Walton,

> and shall seek the northernmost extremity of the globe; I shall collect my funeral pile and consume to ashes this miserable frame, that its remains may afford no light to any curious and unhallowed wretch who would create such another as I have been. [Pp. 210–11]

But to end his sufferings and to frustrate Frankenstein's science, the Monster need not go to the North Pole nor arrange his death by fire. His extraordinary plan is, for all its extreme privacy, dramatic in the extreme and highly symbolic, as much a statement as an act. It is, first, a bitter parody of both Walton's and Frankenstein's dream of the fire in ice, underscoring the sorrow and fatality in that dream. At the end of his life the Monster affirms, or bitterly concedes, the truth in the Romantic vision of being; but his suicide implies that to recognize the truth is to loathe being, as his maker has come to do, and to choose not to be. In his last act, then, he declares (as the hero of any tragedy must somehow declare at the end) his conscious recognition and grim acceptance of the conflict in nature that has brought him to this pass.

But there is more to be said about his suicide, and in fact the Monster says it:

"But soon," he cried with sad and solemn enthusiasm, "I shall die, and what I now feel be no longer felt. Soon these burning miseries will be extinct. I shall ascend my funeral pile triumphantly and exult in the agony of the torturing flames. The light of that con-flagration will fade away; my ashes will be swept into the sea by winds. My spirit will sleep in peace, or if it thinks, it will not surely think thus. Farewell." [P. 221]

Like so much else in the imagery of fire, the fantasy of one's own funeral pyre combines contradictory attractions. On the one hand, it offers complete destruction and nonentity, seen here in the Monster's anticipatory vision of the fading light of the flames, the wind-blown ashes, the spirit's sleep. On the other hand, it offers (as in the legend of the phoenix) a promise of regenerated or renewed life—faintly suggested here in the Monster's last clause—or, failing that, at least one final intense experience of what it is to be alive. As the Monster stands by the ship's cabin-window, soon to be "lost in darkness and distance," the note of triumph and enthusiasm in his voice belies the expressed wish for death and oblivion. He exults in the blaze he will make ("the light of that conflagration") and even in the "agony" he will feel. That agony and that light, indeed, will only make outward and visible the "burning miseries" he now feels inwardly and which are, in fact, his life: soon to be "extinct," but not before the pyre goes out.

As Bachelard elegantly observes, speaking of paradox in pyre-imagery generally:

When the fire devours itself, when the power turns against itself, it seems as if the whole being is made complete at the instant of its final ruin and that the intensity of the destruction is the supreme proof, the clearest proof, of its existence.[13]

13. Bachelard, *Psychoanalysis of Fire*, p. 78.

We know well the Monster's desperate need, always frustrated in life, for acceptance from others, even for simple acknowledgment of the fact of his existence. The spectacular character of death by fire, then, has a special appeal for him. Even while it ends his misery the funeral pyre will affirm and liberate to view a spirit systematically denied and abused while confined in clay. The Monster's total destruction, like the memorable shredding of Frankenstein's oak tree, will disclose in one great pulse of blazing light and heat the fire of intense inner being.

IV

Such an end would be unthinkable for the heroes and heroines of Victorian fiction, and not only because (until Hardy) they tend to survive their novels' conclusions. Death by fire is generally reserved for those characters whose lives have been given over to some fiery excess; moderation would have saved them all. Thus Krook, in *Bleak House*, dies by the spontaneous combustion of the fire-water he has consumed immoderately in life; Miss Havisham, in *Great Expectations*, perishes in the flames of feeling so long and so successfully repressed that, when unexpectedly rekindled in old age, they cannot be controlled. In *Jane Eyre*, to return to our starting point, Bertha Mason dies as she has lived, by the fire of passion, taking Thornfield down with her and, very nearly, Rochester too.

These and many others like them are the monsters of Victorian fiction: monsters of excess, grotesque exaggerations of natural human appetites or faculties that have become unnaturally isolated and grossly overdeveloped. Bertha Mason is both "monster" and "goblin," her "pigmy intellect" long since overwhelmed by her "giant propensities" (pp. 332–33); in her red eyes, empurpled skin, and bloated features Jane sees the image of "the foul German spectre—the Vampyre" (p. 307). Bertha indeed resembles Dracula, a true vampire and hard-core monster, in her monomaniacal intensity and superhuman strength, not to mention her habit of nocturnal prowling and her taste for blood. But it is Mr. Hyde, at the end of the century, who best epitomizes Victorian monstrosity. Where Frankenstein, a Romantic scientist, labors to unite contrary elements and to make a man, Dr. Jekyll labors to dissociate them and to *un*make man, to separate and liberate from each other the "polar twins" he finds perpetually at war within human nature. The result is Edward Hyde, a being artificially simple, one-half of human nature masquerading as a whole, a walking appetite.

As such, of course, Dr. Jekyll's monster could not be more different from Frankenstein's, whose nature is only our own writ large and whose self-consciousness and sadness are our own, too. The monsters of Victorian fiction are not sad but, on the contrary, diabolically gleeful, inhumanly confident; they do not recoil from their reflections in horror, as does Frankenstein's Monster (and as Jane Eyre does too, in lesser degree), but study them eagerly; they can never be the heroes, much less the narrators, of novels. Frankenstein's Monster is horrible—to himself, to his maker, and to us—because he shows us what we are. The monsters of Victorian fiction, on the contrary, show us what to avoid, what we must on no account allow ourselves to become: as Jane, seeing Bertha's blood-swollen features under her own bridal veil, in her own bedroom mirror, must take warning and take control of the "animal" side of herself that is, in fact, like Bertha. The Monster can at best accept despair with dignity, and die. But Jane survives, not in tortured contradiction but in balance between opposite extremes, having learned to adjust her figurative temperature much as Alice learns to adjust her size in Wonderland: first a nibble of this, then a nibble of that, until one is no longer a monster ("'Serpent!' screamed the pigeon," at Alice's long neck) but only a human being ("'I—I'm a little girl,' said Alice, rather doubtfully") fit for the business of life.

The denouement of Jane's story helps to reveal the depth of tragedy in the Monster's and brings into relief Mary Shelley's dark view of human existence. As Jane approaches Ferndean where Rochester sits, blind and alone, one cannot help but remember the Monster's half-eager, half-terrified approach to the "devoted" cottage where M. De Lacey sits, also blind, also alone. For Jane as for the Monster, all hope of future happiness depends upon her reception. Like the Monster, Jane delays her revelation, first studying her man from a distance ("To examine him, myself unseen, and alas! to him invisible" [p. 470]) and then, after she enters, withholding her identity until Rochester (like De Lacey) has to cry out "Who is this?"

But Jane, of course, can count on a welcome from her blind consort and, almost as certainly, on a life of happiness at his side. Her delay is half calculating, half playful, a return to the old teasing—

72

not like the Monster's agony of hesitation while he summons all his strength to face "the moment of decision" (p. 129). As Jane sees at once, the fires of life and passionate feeling, having flared up much too high, have now sunk correspondingly low: "'Can there be life here?' I asked" (p. 470). Rochester's retreat is dank, decayed, and desolate; he is scarred and darkened, his lips "sealed," his "brow of rock"; and as we might have predicted, "a neglected handful of fire burnt low in the grate" (p. 472). But Jane knows what to do:

Now, let me leave you an instant, to make a better fire, and have the hearth swept up. Can you tell when there is a good fire? [P. 476]

Despite appearances, he can indeed; for as he says himself (beginning to warm to Jane again), is he not a kind of Vulcan, "a real blacksmith," used to fire and careless of a singe or two? As Jane puts it in a related metaphor,

His countenance reminded one of a lamp quenched, waiting to be relit. . . . I had wakened the glow: his features beamed. [P. 479]

And now, at long last, so do Jane's. After her near-death from cold and his from fire, both find in the end what Jane calls—with deep physical satisfaction, but with a strong moral meaning as well —"a good fire," crackling away merrily within its proper bounds, like the warmth of the "good" marriage they now make. Each warms and illuminates the other:

There was no harassing restraint, no repressing of glee and vivacity with him; for with him I was at perfect ease, because I knew I suited him: all I said or did seemed either to console or revive him. Delightful consciousness! It brought to life and light my whole nature: in his presence I thoroughly lived; and he lived in mine. Blind as he was, smiles played over his face, joy dawned on his forehead: his lineaments softened and warmed. [P. 476]

So naturally and completely do the metaphors of heat and light express the emotional and social realities described in this passage that *hearth* and *marriage*, *light* and *joy*, *heat* and *feeling*, almost become one. Extremes of freezing cold and scorching fire are forgotten. United, Jane and Rochester will dwell in (they appear to radiate) a human warmth, a glowing or flickering light. Nothing could be farther from the Monster's last lonely beaconing across the polar ice, for none to see.

PART
TWO

BIOGRAPHICAL
SOUNDINGS:

*Of Mothers
and Daughters*

IV

Female Gothic

ELLEN MOERS

A baby at birth is usually disappointing-looking to a
parent who hasn't seen one before. His skin is coated
with wax, which, if left on, will be absorbed slowly and
will lessen the chance of rashes. His skin underneath
is apt to be very red. His face tends to be puffy and
lumpy, and there may be black-and-blue marks. . . .
The head is misshapen . . . low in the forehead, elongated at the back, and quite lopsided. Occasionally
there may be, in addition, a hematoma, a localized
hemorrhage under the scalp that sticks out as a distinct bump and takes weeks to go away. A couple of
days after birth there may be a touch of jaundice,
which is visible for about a week. . . . The baby's body
is covered all over with fuzzy hair. . . . For a couple of
weeks afterward there is apt to be a dry scaling of the
skin, which is also shed. Some babies have black hair
on the scalp at first, which may come far down on the
forehead. . . .
— Dr. Spock: *Baby and Child Care*

W HAT I MEAN by Female Gothic is easily defined: the work that
women writers have done in the literary mode that, since the
eighteenth century, we have called the Gothic. But what I mean—
or anyone else means—by "the Gothic" is not so easily stated except
that it has to do with fear. In Gothic writings fantasy predominates
over reality, the strange over the commonplace, and the supernatural over the natural, with one definite auctorial intent: to scare.
Not, that is, to reach down into the depths of the soul and purge it
with pity and terror (as we say tragedy does), but to get to the body
itself, its glands, muscles, epidermis, and circulatory system, quickly
arousing and quickly allaying the physiological reactions to fear.
Certainly the earliest tributes to the power of Gothic writers

tended to emphasize the physiological. Jane Austen has Henry Tilney, in *Northanger Abbey*, say that he could not put down Mrs. Radcliffe's *Mysteries of Udolpho*: "I remember finishing it in two days—my hair standing on end the whole time." According to Hazlitt, Ann Radcliffe had mastered "the art of freezing the blood": "harrowing up the soul with imaginary horrors, and making the flesh creep and the nerves thrill." And Mary Shelley said she intended *Frankenstein* to be the kind of ghost story that would "curdle the blood, and quicken the beatings of the heart." Why such claims? Presumably because readers enjoyed these sensations. For example, in a work the Shelleys knew well, Joanna Baillie's verse play on the theme of addiction to artificial fear, the heroine prevails upon a handmaiden, against the best advice, to tell a horror story:

> Tell it, I pray thee.
> And let me cow'ring stand, and be my touch
> The valley's ice: there is a pleasure in it.
> Yea, when the cold blood shoots through every vein;
> When every pore upon my shrunken skin
> A knotted knoll becomes, and to mine ears
> Strange inward sounds awake, and to mine eyes
> Rush stranger tears, there is a joy in fear.
>
> [*Orra: A Tragedy* (1812)]

At the time when literary Gothic was born, religious fears were on the wane, giving way to that vague paranoia of the modern spirit for which Gothic mechanisms seem to have provided welcome therapy. Walter Scott compared reading Mrs. Radcliffe to taking drugs, dangerous when habitual "but of most blessed power in those moments of pain and of languor, when the whole head is sore, and the whole heart sick. If those who rail indiscriminately at this species of composition, were to consider the quantity of actual pleasure which it produces, and the much greater proportion of real sorrow and distress which it alleviates, their philanthropy ought to moderate their critical pride, or religious intolerance." A grateful public rewarded Mrs. Radcliffe by making her the most popular and best-paid English novelist of the eighteenth century. Her preeminence among the "Terrorists," as they were called, was hardly challenged in her own day, and modern readers of *Udolpho* and *The Italian* continue to hail her as mistress of the pure Gothic form.

As early as the 1790s, Ann Radcliffe firmly set the Gothic in one of the ways it would go ever after: a novel in which the central figure is a young woman who is simultaneously persecuted victim and courageous heroine. But what are we to make of the next major turning of the Gothic tradition that a woman brought about, a generation later? Mary Shelley's *Frankenstein*, in 1818, made the Gothic novel over into what today we call science fiction. *Frankenstein* brought a new sophistication to literary terror, and it did so without a heroine, without even an important female victim. Paradoxically, however, no other Gothic work by a woman writer, perhaps no literary work of any kind by a woman, better repays examination in the light of the sex of its author. For *Frankenstein* is a birth myth, and one that was lodged in the novelist's imagination, I am convinced, by the fact that she was herself a mother.

Much in Mary Shelley's life was remarkable. She was the daughter of a brilliant mother (Mary Wollstonecraft) and father (William Godwin). She was the mistress and then wife of the poet Shelley. She read widely in five languages, including Latin and Greek. She had easy access to the writings and conversation of some of the most original minds of her age. But nothing so sets her apart from the generality of writers of her own time, and before, and for long afterward, than her early and chaotic experience, at the very time she became an author, with motherhood. Pregnant at sixteen, and almost constantly pregnant throughout the following five years; yet not a secure mother, for she lost most of her babies soon after they were born; and not a lawful mother, for she was not married—not at least when, at the age of eighteen, Mary Godwin began to write *Frankenstein*. So are monsters born.

What in fact has the experience of giving birth to do with women's literature? In the eighteenth and nineteenth centuries relatively few important women writers bore children; most of them, in England and America, were spinsters and virgins. With the coming of Naturalism late in the century, and the lifting of the Victorian taboo against writing about physical sexuality (including pregnancy and labor), the subject of birth was first brought to literature in realistic form by the male novelists, from Tolstoy and Zola to William Carlos Williams. Tolstoy was the father of thirteen babies born at home; Williams, as well as a poet and a Naturalist, was a small-town doctor with hundreds of deliveries to his professional credit, and thus well equipped to write the remarkable account of a birth that opens *The White Mule*. For knowledge of the sort that makes half a dozen pages of obstetrical detail, they had the advantage over woman writers until relatively recent times.[1]

Mary Shelley was a unique case, in literature as in life. She brought birth to fiction not as realism but as Gothic fantasy, and thus contributed to Romanticism a myth of genuine originality: the mad scientist who locks himself in his laboratory and secretly, guiltily, works at creating human life, only to find that he has made a monster.

It was on a dreary night of November, that I beheld the accomplishment of my toils. With an anxiety that almost amounted to agony, I collected the instruments of life around me, that I might infuse a spark of being into the lifeless thing that lay at my feet. . . . The rain pattered dismally against the panes, and my candle was nearly burnt out, when, by the glimmer of the half-extinguished light, I saw the dull yellow eye of the creature open; it breathed hard, and a convulsive motion agitated its limbs. . . . His yellow skin scarcely covered the work of muscles and arteries beneath; his hair was of a lustrous black, and flowing . . . but these luxuriances only formed a more horrid contrast with his watery eyes, that seemed almost of the same color as the dun white sockets in which they were set, his shrivelled complexion and straight black lips.

1. Two very popular women novelists (and Nobel laureates), Pearl Buck and Sigrid Undset, were probably responsible for establishing pregnancy, labor, and breast feeding as themes belonging to twentieth-century women's literature. The miscarriage is a powerful new theme in the hands of Jean Rhys and Sylvia Plath, and the unwed mother's labor inspires a spirited obstetrical chapter ("Don't Have a Baby Till You Read This") in the memoir of the young poet Nikki Giovanni, who has a fine sense of the incongruity of the experience. "'A BABY? BUT I DON'T KNOW ANYTHING ABOUT HAVING A BABY! I'VE NEVER HAD A BABY BEFORE.' And I started crying and crying and crying. What if I messed up? You were probably counting on me to do the right thing and what did I know? I was an intellectual. I thought things through. I didn't know shit about action."

But Colette's note of skepticism is most worth recalling, because she was the first to pick and choose for literature among all the ramifications of female sexuality. In *La Maison de Claudine* she tells of fainting away in horror when, as a young girl, she first came upon a gruesome birth scene in Zola. "Oh, it's not such a terrible thing, the birth of a child," she has her mother comment. ". . . The proof that all women forget it is that it's never anybody but men—and what business was it of his, that Zola?—who make stories about it."

That is very good horror, but what follows is more horrid still: Frankenstein, the scientist, runs away and abandons the newborn Monster, who is and remains nameless. Here, I think, is where Mary Shelley's book is most interesting, most powerful, and most feminine: in the motif of revulsion against newborn life, and the drama of guilt, dread, and flight surrounding birth and its consequences. Most of the novel, roughly two of its three volumes, can be said to deal with the retribution visited upon Monster and creator for deficient infant care. *Frankenstein* seems to be distinctly a *woman's* mythmaking on the subject of birth precisely because its emphasis is not upon what precedes birth, not upon birth itself, but upon what follows birth: the trauma of the afterbirth.

Fear and guilt, depression and anxiety are commonplace reactions to the birth of a baby, and well within the normal range of experience. But more deeply rooted in our cultural mythology, and certainly in our literature, are the happy maternal reactions: the ecstasy, the sense of fulfillment, and the rush of nourishing love which sweep over the new mother when she first holds her baby in her arms. Thackeray's treatment of the birth of a baby in *Vanity Fair* is the classic of this genre: gentle Amelia is pregnant when her adored young husband dies on the field of Waterloo, a tragedy which drives the young woman into a state of comatose grief until the blessed moment when her baby is born. "Heaven had sent her consolation," writes Thackeray. "A day came—of almost terrified delight and wonder—when the poor widowed girl pressed a child upon her breast . . . a little boy, as beautiful as a cherub. . . . Love, and hope, and prayer woke again in her bosom. . . . She was safe."

Thackeray was here recording a reality, as well as expressing a sentiment. But he himself was under no illusion that happiness was the only possible maternal reaction to giving birth, for his own wife had become depressed and hostile after their first baby was born, and suicidal after the last; at the time of *Vanity Fair*, Thackeray had already had to place her in a sanitarium, and he was raising their two little girls himself. So, in *Vanity Fair*, he gives us not only Amelia as a mother, but also Becky Sharp. Becky's cold disdain toward her infant son, her hostility and selfishness as a mother, are perhaps a legacy of Thackeray's experience; they are among the finest things in the novel.

From what we know about the strange young woman who wrote

Frankenstein, Mary Shelley was in this respect nothing like Becky Sharp. She rejoiced at becoming a mother and loved and cherished her babies as long as they lived. But her journal, which has set the tone of most of the discussion of the genesis of *Frankenstein*, is a chilly and laconic document in which the overwhelming emphasis is not on her maternity but on the extraordinary reading program she put herself through at Shelley's side. Mary Shelley is said—and rightly—to have absorbed into *Frankenstein* the ideas about education, society, and morality held by her father and her mother. She is shown to have been influenced directly by Shelley's genius, and by her reading of Coleridge and Wordsworth and the Gothic novelists. She learned from Sir Humphry Davy's book on chemistry and Erasmus Darwin on biology. In Switzerland, the summer she began *Frankenstein*, she sat by while Shelley, Byron, and Polidori discussed the new sciences of mesmerism, electricity, and galvanism, which promised to unlock the riddle of life, and planned to write ghost stories.

Mary Shelley herself was the first to point to her fortuitous immersion in the literary and scientific revolutions of her day as the source of *Frankenstein*. Her extreme youth, as well as her sex, have contributed to the generally held opinion that she was not so much an author in her own right as a transparent medium through which passed the ideas of those around her. "All Mrs. Shelley did," writes Mario Praz, "was to provide a passive reflection of some of the wild fantasies which were living in the air about her."

Passive reflections, however, do not produce original works of literature, and *Frankenstein*, if not a great novel, was unquestionably an original one. The major Romantic and minor Gothic tradition to which it *should* have belonged was to the literature of the overreacher: the superman who breaks through normal human limitations to defy the rules of society and infringe upon the realm of God. In the Faust story, hypertrophy of the individual will is symbolized by a pact with the devil. Byron's and Balzac's heroes; the rampaging monks of Mat Lewis and E. T. A. Hoffmann; the Wandering Jew and Melmoth the wanderer; the chained and unchained Prometheus: all are overreachers, all are punished by their own excesses—by a surfeit of sensation, of experience, of knowledge and, most typically, by the doom of eternal life.

But Mary Shelley's overreacher is different. Frankenstein's exploration of the forbidden boundaries of human science does not cause the prolongation and extension of his own life, but the creation of a new one. He defies mortality not by living forever, but by giving birth. That this original twist to an old myth should have been the work of a young woman who was also a young mother seems to me, after all, not a very surprising answer to the question that, according to Mary Shelley herself, was asked from the start: "How I, then a young girl, came to think of, and to dilate upon, so very hideous an idea?"

Birth is a hideous thing in *Frankenstein*, even before there is a monster. For Frankenstein's procedure, once he has determined to create new life, is to frequent the vaults and charnel houses and study the human corpse in all its loathsome stages of decay and decomposition. "To examine the causes of life," he says, "we must first have recourse to death." His purpose is to "bestow animation upon lifeless matter," so that he might "in the process of time renew life where death had apparently devoted the body to corruption." Frankenstein collects bones and other human parts from the slaughterhouse and the dissecting room, and through long months of feverish and guilty activity sticks them together in a frame of gigantic size in what he calls "my workshop of filthy creation."

It is in her journal and her letters that Mary Shelley reveals the workshop of her own creation, where she pieced together the materials for a new species of Romantic mythology. They record a horror story of maternity of the kind that literary biography does not provide again until Sylvia Plath.

As far as I can figure out, she was pregnant, barely pregnant but aware of the fact, when at the age of sixteen she ran off with Shelley in July 1814. Also pregnant at the same time was Shelley's legal wife Harriet, who gave birth in November "to a son and possible heir," as Mary noted in her journal. In February 1815 Mary gave birth to a daughter, illegitimate, premature, and sickly. There is nothing in the journal about domestic help or a nurse in attendance. Mary notes that she breast-fed the baby; that Fanny, her half-sister, came to call; that Claire Clairmont, her stepsister, who had run off with Mary, kept Shelley amused. Bonaparte invaded France, the journal tells us, and Mary took up her incessant reading program: this time, Mme. de Staël's *Corinne*. The baby died in March. "Find my baby dead," Mary wrote. "A miserable day."

In April 1815 she was pregnant again, about eight weeks after the birth of her first child. In January 1816 she gave birth to a son:

more breast-feeding, more reading. In March, Claire Clairmont sought out Lord Byron and managed to get herself pregnant by him within a couple of weeks. This pregnancy would be a subject of embarrassment and strain to Mary and Shelley, and it immediately changed their lives, for Byron left England in April, and Claire, Shelley, Mary, and her infant pursued him to Switzerland in May. There is nothing yet in Mary's journal about a servant, but a good deal about mule travel in the mountains. In June they all settled near Byron on the shores of Lake Geneva.

In June 1816, also, Mary began *Frankenstein*. And during the year of its writing, the following events ran their swift and sinister course: in October Fanny Imlay, Mary's half sister, committed suicide after discovering that she was not Godwin's daughter but Mary Wollstonecraft's daughter by her American lover. (The suicide was not only a tragedy but an embarrassment to all. Godwin refused even to claim Fanny's body, which was thrown nameless into a pauper's grave.) In early December Mary was pregnant again, as she seems to have sensed almost the day it happened. (See her letter to Shelley of December 5, in which she also announced completion of Chapter 4 of her novel.) In mid-December Harriet Shelley drowned herself in the Serpentine; she was pregnant by someone other than Shelley. In late December Mary married Shelley. In January 1817 Mary wrote Byron that Claire had borne him a daughter. In May she finished *Frankenstein*, published the following year.

Death and birth were thus as hideously intermixed in the life of Mary Shelley as in Frankenstein's "workshop of filthy creation." Who can read without shuddering, and without remembering her myth of the birth of a nameless monster, Mary's journal entry of March 19, 1815, which records the trauma of her loss, when she was seventeen, of her first baby, the little girl who did not live long enough to be given a name. "Dream that my little baby came to life again," Mary wrote; "that it had only been cold, and that we rubbed it before the fire, and it lived. Awake and find no baby. I think about the little thing all day. Not in good spirits." ("*I thought, that if I could bestow animation upon lifeless matter, I might in process of time renew life where death had apparently devoted the body to corruption.*")

So little use has been made of this material by writers about *Frankenstein* that it may be worth emphasizing how important, because how unusual, was Mary Shelley's experience as a young woman writer. Though the death of one of their babies played a decisive role in the literary careers of both Harriet Beecher Stowe and Elizabeth Cleghorn Gaskell, two of the rare Victorian women writers who were also mothers, both were about twice Mary Shelley's age when their babies died; and both were respectably settled middle-class women, wives of ministers. The harum-scarum circumstances surrounding her maternity have no parallel until our time, which in its naïve celebrations upon family life (and in much else, except genius) resembles the Shelley era. The young women novelists and poets of today who are finding in the trauma of inexperienced and unassisted motherhood a mine of troubled fantasy and black humor are on the lookout for Gothic predecessors, if the revival of *The Yellow Wallpaper*—Charlotte Perkins Gilman's macabre post-partum fantasy—is any indication. The newborn returns again to literature as monster.

> At six months he grew big as six years
> . . . One day he swallowed
> Her whole right breast . . .
> . . . both died,
> She inside him, curled like an embryo.
> [Cynthia Macdonald: "The Insatiable Baby"]

Behind them all stands the original fantasy and the exceptional case of Mary Shelley. She hurtled into teenage motherhood without any of the financial or social or familial supports that made bearing and rearing children a relaxed experience for the normal middle-class woman of her day (as Jane Austen, for example, described her). She was an unwed mother, responsible for breaking up a marriage of a young woman just as much a mother as she. The father whom she adored broke furiously with her when she eloped; and Mary Wollstonecraft, the mother whose memory she revered, and whose books she was rereading throughout her teen-age years, had died in childbirth—died giving birth to Mary herself.

Surely no outside influence need be sought to explain Mary Shelley's fantasy of the newborn as at once monstrous agent of destruction and piteous victim of parental abandonment. "I, the miserable and the abandoned," cries the Monster at the end of *Frankenstein*, "I am an abortion to be spurned at, and kicked, and trampled on. . . . I have murdered the lovely and the helpless. . . .

I have devoted my creator to misery; I have pursued him even to that irremediable ruin."

In the century and a half since its publication, *Frankenstein* has spawned innumerable interpretations among the critics, and among the novelists, playwrights, and filmmakers who have felt its influence. The idea, though not the name, of the robot originated with Mary Shelley's novel, and her title character became a byword for the dangers of scientific knowledge. But the work has also been read as an existential fable; as a commentary on the cleavage between reason and feeling, in both philosophical thought and educational theory; as a parable of the excesses of idealism and genius; as a dramatization of the divided self; as an attack on the stultifying force of social convention, including race prejudice, for Stephen Crane's *The Monster* must surely be counted among the most powerful descendants of *Frankenstein*.

The versatility of Mary Shelley's myth is due to the brilliance of her mind and the range of her learning, as well as to the influence of the circle in which she moved as a young writer. But *Frankenstein* was most original in its dramatization of dangerous oppositions through the struggle of a creator with monstrous creation. The sources of this Gothic conception, which still has power to "curdle the blood, and quicken the beatings of the heart," were surely the anxieties of a woman who, as daughter, mistress, and mother, was a bearer of death.

Robert Kiely's suggestive study of *The Romantic Novel in England* includes one of the rare serious discussions of *Frankenstein* as a woman's work. For Professor Kiely does more than interpret; he also responds, as one must in reading *Frankenstein*, to what he calls the "mundane side to this fantastic tale":

In making her hero the creator of a monster, she does not necessarily mock idealistic ambition, but in making that monster a poor grotesque patchwork, a physical mess of seams and wrinkles, she introduces a consideration of the material universe which challenges and undermines the purity of idealism. In short, the sheer concreteness of the ugly thing which Frankenstein has created often makes his ambitions and his character—however sympathetically described—seem ridiculous and even insane. The arguments on behalf of idealism and unworldly genius are seriously presented, but the controlling perspective is that of an earthbound woman. [P. 161]

The "mundane side" to *Frankenstein* is one of its most fertile and original aspects. Mary Shelley comes honestly to grips with the dilemma of a newly created human being, a giant adult male in shape, who must swiftly recapitulate, and without the assistance of his terrified parent, the infantile and adolescent stages of human development. She even faces squarely the Monster's sexual needs, for the denouement of the story hangs on his demand that Frankenstein create a female monster partner, and Frankenstein's refusal to do so.

But more than mundane is Mary Shelley's concern with the emotion surrounding the parent-child relationship. Here her intention to underline the birth myth in *Frankenstein* becomes most evident, quite apart from biographical evidence about its author. She provides an unusual thickening of the background of the tale with familial fact and fantasy, from the very opening of the story in the letters a brother addresses to his sister of whom he is excessively fond, because they are both orphans. There is Frankenstein's relationship to his doting parents, and his semi-incestuous love for an abandoned, orphan girl brought up as his sister. There is the first of the Monster's murder victims, Frankenstein's infant brother (precisely drawn, even to his name, after Mary Shelley's baby); and the innocent young girl wrongly executed for the infant's murder, who is also a victim of what Mary Shelley calls that "strange perversity," a mother's hatred. (Justine accepts guilt with docility: "'I almost began to think that I was the monster that my confessor said I was. . . .'") The material in *Frankenstein* about the abnormal, or monstrous, manifestations of the child-parent tie justifies, as much as does its famous monster, Mary Shelley's reference to the novel as "my hideous progeny."

What Mary Shelley actually did in *Frankenstein* was to transform the standard Romantic matter of incest, infanticide, and patricide into a phantasmagoria of the nursery. Nothing quite like it was done in English literature until that Victorian novel by a woman which we also place uneasily in the Gothic tradition: *Wuthering Heights*.

V

Thoughts on
the Aggression of Daughters

U.C. KNOEPFLMACHER

Parental affection, indeed, in many minds, is but a
pretext to tyrannize where it can be done with impun-
ity.

> —Mary Wollstonecraft, *A Vindication of
> the Rights of Woman* (1792)

I will keep a good look out—William is all alive—and
my appearance no longer doubtful—you, I daresay,
will perceive the difference. What a fine thing it is to
be a man!

> —Mary Wollstonecraft to William Godwin,
> 10 June 1797

There never can be perfect equality between father
and child . . . the ordinary resource is for him to pro-
claim his wishes and commands in a way sometimes
sententious and authoritative and occasionally to utter his censures with seriousness and emphasis. . . .
I am not, therefore, a perfect judge of Mary's character. . . . [She] shows great need to be roused.

> —William Godwin to William Baxter,
> 8 June 1812

I learned from your papers that you were my father,
my creator; and to whom could I apply with more
fitness than to him who had given me life?

> —Mary Wollstonecraft Godwin Shelley,
> *Frankenstein* (1818)

O N THE FIRST PAGE of *Frankenstein*, beneath the title and subtitle,
appears a three-line quotation from *Paradise Lost*, X.743–45:
"Did I request thee, Maker, from my clay / To mould me Man, did
I solicit thee / From darkness to promote me?" The following page

contains an inscription that seems far more tame and submissive: "To WILLIAM GODWIN / Author of Political Justice, Caleb Williams, &c. / These Volumes / Are respectfully inscribed / By / The Author."

The bitterness of Milton's Adam is intensified in *Frankenstein* by the companionless Monster: "I remembered Adam's supplication to his Creator; but where was mine? he had abandoned me, and, in the bitterness of my heart, I cursed him."[1] Though recognizing "Satan as the fitter emblem of my condition," the Monster also seems to remember Adam's fit of rebellion in Book Ten of *Paradise Lost* when it sarcastically reproaches its own indifferent maker: "Oh truly, I am grateful to thee my Creator for the gift of life, which was but pain" (p. 115). In the speech from which Mary Shelley takes her novel's epigraph, Adam revolts againt that same Spirit of Creation earlier described "brooding on the vast Abyss" and making "it pregnant" (I.20–22). When Adam considers that he can only increase and multiply his own progeny's "curses," Eve invites him to abjure creation, to remain the first and last Man. In Mary Shelley's revenge story, the Adamic Monster who has turned into a Satan forces its neglectful father-creator to experience its own desolation; in Milton's paternal universe, however, the rebellious child Adam must be forced to accept his own role as parent, even if parenthood does convert him into a death-bringer, the father of Cain and Abel. Adam's revolt is short-lived. To deny God's design would be tantamount to submission to a far more terrifying "Universe of death" and to a banishment into the Satanic abode of "many a frozen Alp"—so like the ice-scapes into which the Monster lures its creator—a region where "all life dies, death lives, and Nature breeds / Perverse, all monstrous, all prodigious things / Abominable, inutterable, and worse, / Than Fables yet have feign'd, or fear conceiv'd, / *Gorgons* or *Hydras*, and *Chimeras* dire" (II.622, 624–28).

If the three lines quoted on the title page of *Frankenstein* thus evoke a locus for the "anger and hatred" that so irreconcilably separate the Monster from its father and creator, the novel's dedication seems to stem from quite opposite an intention. The "Au-

1. *Frankenstein; or, The Modern Prometheus*, ed. James Rieger (Indianapolis and New York, 1974), chap. 7, p. 127. All future references in the text are to this edition of the 1818 version of the novel.

thor," who so "respectfully" aligns herself with that other "Author" she will not publicly address as her father, assumes a stance that is as dutiful and self-effacing as that adopted by the exemplary Elizabeth Lavenza, the orphan whom Alphonse Frankenstein cherishes as "his more than daughter, whom he doated on with all the affection a man feels, who, in the decline of life, having few affections, clings more earnestly to those that remain" (pp. 195–96). In her 1831 introduction to the revised version of *Frankenstein*, Mary Shelley speaks of herself "as the daughter of two persons of distinguished literary celebrity." Her 1818 dedication, however, pays tribute only to the father who had been her mentor in the decline of his life; it ignores the famous mother whose conflicts with a tyrannical father had helped shape her first published work, a pamphlet entitled *Thoughts on the Education of Daughters*. Had Mary Shelley forgotten the rebellious mother who had written that "respect for parents is, generally speaking, a much more debasing principle" than marriage and who had insisted that the "father who is blindly obeyed is obeyed from sheer weakness, or from motives that degrade the human character"?[2]

Before I attempt to answer that question, let me point out that the quotation from *Paradise Lost* and the dedication to Godwin have a connection that is so obvious that it can easily be missed. In each passage, a father is addressed by the offspring he has "moulded." And, what is more important, in each passage the father addressed is that offspring's only parent. Like Adam, and like the Monster who calls himself "an abortion to be spurned at" (Walton's last letter, p. 219), Mary Shelley never knew a mother's nurture.

Frankenstein is a novel of omnipresent fathers and absent mothers. It is no coincidence that after killing the child who boasts of his powerful "papa," the Monster should stop to gaze at "the portrait of a most lovely woman" and be momentarily calmed by her maternal beauty, only to remember angrily and ruefully that "I was for ever deprived of the delights that such beautiful creatures could bestow" (p. 139). Nor is it a coincidence, I think, that the Monster's previous "rage of anger," the "kind of insanity in my spirits" that

2. Mary Wollstonecraft, "Duty to Parents," *A Vindication of the Rights of Woman, with Strictures on Political and Moral Subjects* (New York, 1833), chap. 11, p. 167.

leads him to burn down the De Lacey cottage and to seek "redress," is the direct result of his realization that he will never be accepted as a member of the family of "the old man"—the blind father whose hand he had seized in his unsuccessful plea for affection and kinship (pp. 134–35, 136).

Frankenstein resurrects and rearranges an adolescent's conflicting emotions about her relation both to the dead mother she idealized and mourned and to the living, "sententious and authoritative" father-philosopher she admired and deeply resented for his imperfect attempts at "moulding" Mary Wollstonecraft's two daughters. Fanny "Godwin" emulated the mother who had twice attempted to commit suicide. Her hardier half-sister attempted to master guilt and hostility in the "voyage of discovery" begun by Walton the mariner. As she tries to explain in her 1831 introduction—written after she had completed *Valperga, The Last Man, Perkin Warbeck*, and nearly a dozen short stories—*Frankenstein* is unique among her productions. It differs from her other works because in it she refused to "exchange the ghastly image of my fancy for the realities around" (p. 228). The adolescent mother and wife could confront "frightful" fantasies—destructive and aggressive thoughts—which the matured professional writer still entertained, yet carefully defused and disguised in most of her subsequent fictions.

I

Critics have inevitably ventured into biographical speculations in their attempts to come to terms with *Frankenstein*. In the preceding essay in this collection, Ellen Moers demonstrates the significance for this novel of the death of Mary Shelley's first (unnamed) "female child" in 1815, of the birth of the son she named after her father in 1816, and of the death by suicide, later in that same year and when *Frankenstein* was well under way, of Mary's half-sister Fanny, whom Godwin had described in 1812 as possessing "a quiet, modest, unshowy disposition," quite the reverse of his own daughter's "singularly bold, somewhat imperious" manner.[3] Like Professor Moers, I tend to read *Frankenstein* as a "phantas-

3. Quoted in C. Kegan Paul, *William Godwin: His Friends and Contemporaries* (London, 1876), II:214; the letter was written to an "unknown correspondent" who had inquired about Godwin's theories of education.

magoria of the nursery," a fantasy designed to relieve deep personal anxieties over birth and death and identity. Yet I prefer to stress the importance of an earlier nursery—of the nurture denied to Mary herself when her mother died of a retained placenta eleven days after her birth and of the highly inadequate substitute for a nursery which she found in her remarried father's household.

Since in my reading of *Frankenstein* William Godwin may appear almost a villain, it ought to be acknowledged that he was genuinely solicitous about the care and welfare of Mary Wollstonecraft's two daughters. (Indeed, his very solicitude contributed to Mary Shelley's conflicting emotions of allegiance and resentment; had he been more like her maternal grandfather, Edward John Wollstonecraft, a drunkard and a bully, Mary might have found it easier to emulate her mother's rebellious detachment.) Godwin himself had been "brought up in great tenderness" as a child. Just as, in a passage added to elaborate on Victor Frankenstein's happy youth, Victor describes "the ardent affection that attached me to my excellent parents" (p. 31), so did Godwin gratefully remember his own parents. He claimed that his mother had "exercised a mysterious protection over me" and yet, significantly, he never could bring himself to forgive her for sending him away from home while an infant "to be nourished by a hireling."[4] This personal understanding of the need for mothering must have been decisive in Godwin's stubborn quest for a second wife to act as surrogate mother for the two orphans in his care. Still, as every biographer has pointed out, Mrs. Clairmont was hardly a Mary Wollstonecraft. Vulgar, mundane, preoccupied with the welfare of her own two children, she failed to establish a good relationship with her two stepdaughters. Rather than compensating Mary for her deprivation, as Godwin had intended, she actually helped activate in Mary a lifelong desire to compensate her father for the loss of his exquisite first wife and their short-lived marital happiness. The situation was hardly improved when, in 1803, before Mary's sixth birthday, the new Mrs. Godwin presented her husband with the son he had actually expected in 1797 when he and the pregnant Mary Wollstonecraft, strangely overconfident of the sex of the child she was carrying,

4. *Ibid.*, I:7; see also Ford K. Brown, *The Life of William Godwin* (London and Toronto, 1926), p. 3.

had repeatedly promised themselves a "little William" in their letters.[5]

Professor Moers hints that the Monster's wanton destruction of little William in the novel is an expression of a young mother's anxieties over the precarious health of her own baby William. The speculation is not entirely new. Back in 1928, Richard Church also thought he detected a "miserable delight in self-torture" and a prophetic "anticipation of disaster" in Mary Shelley's decision to depict the fictional murder of "that fair child" who bears the name of her actual son:

At the time that she was writing this book, the baby William was in the tenderest and most intimate stage of dependent infancy. The mite five months of age was passionately tended—but not very knowledgeably or hygienically—by both his parents. It is almost inconceivable that Mary could allow herself to introduce a baby boy in her book; deliberately call him William; describe him in terms identical with those in which she portrays her own child in one of her letters [in which she alludes to the real boy's identical blue eyes in similar rhapsodic terms]—and then let Frankenstein's monster waylay this innocent in a woodland dell and murder him by strangling.[6]

Church's clue is valid, as we shall see; but his surmise remains as incomplete as Muriel Spark's added suggestion that the murder of the boy who bears the name of "the child Mary loved more than any" is symptomatic of a split between feeling and intellect that led her "automatically" to identify the threatened child with her own threatened emotions.[7]

Church, Spark, and Moers are undoubtedly correct in linking the Monster's first murder to Mary Shelley's fears for her second child. Yet these fears, which proved so sadly justified when William died in 1819, also stemmed from deeper and more primal associations. For, in addition to her own son, there were two other "little Williams" who played a crucial role in the fantasy life of Mary Shel-

5. See *Godwin and Mary: Letters of William Godwin and Mary Wollstonecraft*, ed. Ralph M. Wardle (Lawrence, Kansas, 1966), pp. 80, 82, 88, 92, 102; the passage used as the second epigraph to this essay ("William is alive") occurs on p. 94.

6. Richard Church, *Mary Shelley* (London, 1928), pp. 54–55.

7. Muriel Spark, *Child of Light: A Reassessment of Mary Wollstonecraft Shelley* (Southend-on-Sea, Essex, 1951), p. 138.

ley's formative years. The first of these was none other than Mary herself, the little William expected in 1797 who turned into a little girl responsible for her mother's death and father's grief. The second was the half-brother born to Mary's stepmother, William Godwin the Younger, whose arrival she must have regarded as a threat to her relationship with a father to whom she so desperately wanted to make amends.

Even after the birth of this rival man-child, Mary eagerly tried to repair her father's loss both of the philosopher-wife he had worshipped and the philosopher-son he had hoped for from his first union. In the same 1812 letter in which Godwin contrasts Mary's imperiousness to Fanny's passivity, he notes approvingly that, unlike her half-sister, his daughter had shown herself true to her parental stock by responding to his teachings: "Her desire for knowledge is great, and her perseverance in anything she undertakes almost invincible." It seems fairly obvious that this extreme eagerness to learn was related to Mary's even greater eagerness to please the father for whom she had, as she later would put it, from very early on entertained an "excessive and romantic passion." Still, her deep thirst for knowledge and her active identification with his own learning, so like the impulse that binds the Monster and Walton to the more deeply studied and "philosophical" Victor, seems to jar both with Mary's lifelong insistence on her ignorance, timidity, and "horror of pushing" and with Percy Shelley's self-justificatory, yet believable, description in "Epipsychidion" of an unresponsive and indifferent wife. Indeed, visitors who came to the Godwin home detected no real distinction between Mary and the torpid and unambitious Fanny; Coleridge, for instance, found "the cadaverous silence of Godwin's children quite catacombish."[8]

This discrepancy is crucial to *Frankenstein* and to Mary Shelley's self-divisions into aggressive and passive components, a raging Monster and a "yielding" Elizabeth. But the discrepancy itself is easy enough to reconcile. In 1838, two years after Godwin's death, Mary Shelley was finally able to voice her disappointment in the exacting father-tutor she had tried to please:

My Father, from age and domestic circumstances, could not *"me faire valoir."* My total friendlessness, my horror of pushing, and

8. Quoted in Edna Nixon, *Mary Wollstonecraft: Her Life and Times* (London, 1971), p. 248.

94

inability to put myself forward unless *led, cherished, and supported*—all this has sunk me in a state of loneliness no other human being ever before, I believe, endured—except Robinson Crusoe.[9]

It is clear from this account that Mary could, when "led, cherished, and supported," be the active and responsive, even "somewhat imperious," child described by Godwin in his 1812 letter; but like "Lucy," who lost her mother as an infant and whose case history is described in Erna Furman's *A Child's Parent Dies: Studies in Childhood Bereavement*, she could also resort to the defence of withdrawal and passivity whenever thwarted in this acute need for support.[10]

Mary Shelley's identification with the total isolation of Robinson Crusoe is significant. By 1838 she might have allowed another fictional analogue to characterize her sense of desertion. Yet the qualifying use of the adjective "human" prevents an identification with the Monster: the motherless creature who clings to the blind De Lacey to plead for affection and support is pointedly distinguished by its "un-human" features. What is more, the Monster is aggressive. As a male, albeit a male who wishes a female complement to subdue its "evil passions," it can find an outlet for hatred not permissible for nineteenth-century daughters. Fearful of releasing hostilities which—without a maternal model—she regarded (or wanted to regard) as exclusively male attributes, Mary Shelley could resort only to passivity as a safer mode of resistance. Again like "Lucy," Mary experienced a depressive crisis at the age of fifteen in the same year in which her father had hailed her "invincible" drive for knowledge. Noting that his "bold" daughter had suddenly become so listless that she showed "a great need to be roused," Godwin sent the teenager to the Baxters in Scotland, where she observed a happy family nucleus for the first time in her life. Recalled from Scotland by her father two years later (is it sheer coincidence that Victor Frankenstein should destroy the female monster in the Hebrides?), she soon became reacquainted with Shelley, the anti-authoritarian son of Sir Timothy. It was during their honeymoon at Marsluys that Shelley, perhaps to help her weather the bitterness of her father's disapproval, encouraged

9. *Mary Shelley's Journal*, ed. Frederick L. Jones (Norman, Oklahoma, 1947), p. 205; the entry occurs on 21 October 1838.

10. *A Child's Parent Dies: Studies in Childhood Bereavement* (New Haven and London, 1974), p. 176; see also pp. 194–95.

Mary to write her first piece of fiction. The title of that story, now lost, was "Hate."[11]

Yet, unlike Shelley the iconoclast, she was not cast for the role of rebel. Even her elopement could not be construed as an act of open defiance. The poet, after all, had presented himself as her father's eager disciple, as one who would—and could—put into practice the principles of the "inestimable book on 'Political Justice.'" It is not too fanciful therefore to suppose that the young girl who pledged her love to Shelley over her mother's grave at St. Pancras Churchyard hoped to revive or resurrect the short-lived union between her own parents. Shelley had been betrayed, Mary was willing to believe, into a marriage with one inferior and unsympathetic to his genius. Had she not seen her father debased by just such a union with her stepmother? She would nobly rescue Shelley from her father's fate, and, in the process, repair the damage done by her own birth. Through her, the "little William" her parents had expected could be born again, and, by giving it the nurture she had herself lacked as a child, she would be able to assume her dead mother's identity and role. Yet the child once again was a female, and again the bond between mother and daughter was short-lived; after recording her successful nursing of the baby for three consecutive days, Mary Shelley laconically wrote: "Find my baby dead. Send for Hogg. Talk. A miserable day. In the evening read 'Fall of the Jesuits.' Hogg sleeps here."[12] The unemotional, seemingly indifferent tone of this and subsequent entries (the next one ends: "Not in good spirits. Hogg goes at 11. A fuss. To bed at 3") is broken when she records her dream, on 19 March 1815, "that my little baby came to life again; that it only had been cold, and that we rubbed it before the fire, and it lived."[13]

As Professor Moers observes, this dream is linked to the fantasy of animation that underlies *Frankenstein*; yet it could hardly have been Mary Shelley's first wishful "dream" of making the dead come alive. Before, a child had wished to restore a mother; now, a mother wished to restore a child. The restoration again became a possibility after the birth of a male "babe" in January of 1816.[14] By nam-

11. For a fuller account of Mary's early life with Percy see Peter Dale Scott's discussion on pp. 178–183, below.

12. *Journal*, p. 39; 6 March 1815.

13. *Ibid.*, p. 41; 19 March 1815.

14. Mary Shelley's journal for May 1815–July 1816 is lost; since it

ing her first male child after her father, Mary could signify the reparation she had so long intended. The offering was as deferential as the dedication of her first literary offspring to the "Author" of *Political Justice*, of *Caleb Williams*, and of herself. But, like that dedication, it was also double-edged.

II

By 1816, the surrogate life with Shelley had already been sorely tested. No "little William" could breach the sense of loneliness and desertion she once more intensely experienced. Not only her father, but also her father's substitute, had been found wanting.[15] The integration that she, like the Monster, had yearned to find through a mate who might take the place of a rejecting father seemed impossible. Although she clung tenaciously to her second child, the rebelliousness and self-pity she had previously stifled began to surface. Like the Malthusian Adam of Book Ten who resents his own birth and decides to resist his Father by not procreating, she resented her role as perpetuator of a male line.

The 1831 introduction makes much of the "hideous" thoughts that went into the making of *Frankenstein*. As if to deny that these thoughts germinated within her, Mary Shelley overemphasizes her passivity, the defense to which she had previously resorted to her father's (and to Shelley's) chagrin. She insists that she had no control over her revenge story: "My imagination, unbidden, possessed and guided me." If this tactic recalls Coleridge's own distancings from an "unhallowed" and possibly demonic imagination, it also strongly resembles both Victor Frankenstein's trancelike activities and the Monster's repeated claim that its vengeful crimes are solely attributable to the neglect of, and contempt for, all its eager efforts to please.

At least in the early stages of its growth and education in the

---

would have contained entries about the first six months of her "little William's" life, it is possible that she herself destroyed it after the boy's death in 1819.

15. Why had Mary Shelley called for Hogg immediately after the death of her first child? In her letter to Shelley of 27 July 1815 she pleads that he "attend to" and "comply with" her feeling that they "ought not to be absent any longer": "We have been now a long time separeted [*sic*]" (*The Letters of Mary Shelley*, ed. Frederick L. Jones [Norman, Oklahoma, 1944], I:16–17).

ways of "man" (Mary Shelley deliberately seems to eschew the words "humanity" or "mankind") the Monster is a most willing student. Not only does it quickly master the lessons intended for Safie (whose name means "wisdom"), but it is eager to please the De Laceys by anonymously performing the most menial tasks. Like a child who reveres grownups, it looks upon the family "as superior beings, who would be the arbiters of my future destiny." The Monster fantasizes "that it might be in my power to restore happiness to these deserving people," particularly to "the venerable blind father" whose losses have been greater than his children's (p. 103). De Lacey first wins the Monster's "reverence" by the soul-stirring music of his violin. Significantly, the ugly Monster and the beautiful Agatha respond identically to the "sweet mournful air." Indeed, when the Monster later kneels at De Lacey's feet, it hopes to win the same recognition earlier accorded to De Lacey's kneeling daughter:

He played a sweet mournful air, which I perceived drew tears from the eyes of his amiable companion, of which the old man took no notice, until she sobbed audibly; he then pronounced a few sounds and the fair creature, leaving her work, knelt at his feet. He raised her, and smiled with such kindness and affection, that I felt sensations of a peculiar and overpowering nature. . . . I withdrew from the window, unable to bear these emotions [Pp. 103–4]

Frankenstein clearly draws on Mary Shelley's recollection of her vain attempts to win "notice" and approval as her father's pupil. (Indeed, after her elopement she remained most interested in the "conduct" of the second "little William" being "moulded" in her father's house.[16]) In her 1831 introduction she depicts herself as

16. *Journal*, p. 15; 16 September 1814. As a male child, the younger William Godwin was permitted to go away to school: from 1811 to 1814 he went to the Charterhouse, from 1814 to 1818 to a school in Greenwich run by the younger Dr. Burney. Described as "wayward and restless" as a youth, he became a successful journalist and wrote a novel called *Transfusion*. He died of cholera at the age of twenty-nine, leaving a wife but no children (Mary's Percy Florence thus was William Godwin's only grandchild). In 1818, Godwin described his son as "the only person with whom I have been any way concerned in the course of education, who is distinguished from all others by the circumstance of always returning a just answer to the questions I proposed to him"; this habit of mind apparently seemed more important to Godwin than the boy's "very affectionate dispo-

"a devout but nearly silent listener" to Byron's and Shelley's discourses on "the principle of life." She deliberately belittles both her "tiresome unlucky ghost story" and her ideas, which, she says, required "communication with [Percy's] far more cultivated mind." But the belittlement can hardly conceal her ready appropriation of the subject discussed by the two poets and "poor Polidori." Their conversation about the piece of flesh that twitched "with voluntary motion" may well have evoked, in her mind, the piece of flesh that caused her mother's death. But it was clearly their speculation that perhaps a "corpse would be re-animated" that attracted and repelled her so powerfully.

Mary could not acknowledge to her 1831 English readers that the topic which the three men had so casually touched upon was integral to a private fantasy she had by 1816 long cherished and recently despaired of—the fantasy of restitution that would reconcile the apparently antagonistic aims of resurrecting a mother and regaining a father's undivided love. In the 1831 introduction it is Shelley, and not his wife, who soon starts a story "founded on the experiences of his early life." Although Mary Shelley dwells on her own early life in Scotland (an "eyry of freedom" in which she was "not confined to my own identity"), she ostensibly dwells on this past only to suggest her subsequent acquisition of a greater sense of "reality." The wife of a husband "anxious that I should prove myself worthy of my parentage" thus wants above all to stress her maturation. She has outgrown "the indulging of waking dreams" and must apologize for the "so very hideous" production of a "young girl." Nonetheless, it is noteworthy that the introduction should depict her Scottish fantasy life as wholly "pleasant" and thus in no way connected to the "ghastly image" that overwhelmed her in 1816 when forbidden and ugly material had, like the Monster itself, come to life.

That "hideous progeny," Mary Shelley insists in 1831, is her very own. Though she acknowledges Shelley's "incitement," she stresses her originality with unaccustomed forcefulness: "I certainly did not owe the suggestion of one incident, nor scarcely of one *train of feel-*

---

sition" (Paul, *William Godwin*, II:258). After his son's death, Godwin published the novel he had left behind and added, in Paul's words, a "gravely self-restrained Memoir" (II:321).

ing, to my husband" (p. 229; italics added). Indeed, there is a faint note of resentment at the two "illustrious poets" who, "annoyed by the platitude of prose, speedily relinquished their uncongenial task" (p. 225). The seed they have so carelessly implanted in Mary (and "poor Polidori") becomes a burden that is hers alone. It is she who has to give birth to a "hideous progeny," because she can better understand the pains of abandonment. Like the Monster, the author has been deserted. And, if we are to trust her account, she began her story neither with Walton's frame or Victor's account of his idyllic youth, but with the scene of desertion in chapter 4, with a father who rejects the stretched-out hand ("seemingly to detain me, but I escaped") of the "miserable monster whom I had created" (p. 53). Victor's repulsion of "the demoniacal corpse I had so miserably given life" will unleash antagonistic emotions that Mary Shelley had resisted and would stoutly continue to resist.

Yet the Monster does not become truly demoniacal until it murders little William and thereby causes the death of the guiltless Justine. As it explains to its creator, "I was benevolent and good; misery made me a fiend." Unlike the "fallen angel" he professes to have become, the Monster insists that evil need not be its good: "Make me happy, and I shall again be virtuous" (p. 95). The words recall another male demonist created by a female imagination, Emily Brontë's Heathcliff, who asks Nelly to "make me good." Yet Mary Shelley was far less willing than her Victorian successors to acknowledge her attraction to the anarchic and the destructive. Her violent figures are inevitably males; she could not have depicted a Jane Eyre who bloodies a boy's nose or a Maggie Tulliver who mutilates her dolls. And, whereas Emily Brontë quickly passes over the particulars of Heathcliff's early deprivation, Mary Shelley lingers over the Monster's painful degradation before she will depict it as an enraged murderer and fiend.

By the time the Monster does strangle little William our sympathies have so fully shifted from Frankenstein to the Monster that the action almost seems justifiable. Like little William, the Monster has been an innocent more sinned against than sinning. Though no "darling of a pigmy size," it is a genuine Wordsworthian child who has been able to "wander at liberty" and to derive intense "pleasure" in the natural world. It is as delighted by "the bright moon" and "the little winged animals" (p. 98) as any Romantic child of a feminine Nature.[17] But unlike Wordsworth's asocial children, this grown-up child desires socialization, human contact. On observing the De Laceys, who are exiled from society and yet remain self-sufficient as a family unit, the Monster discovers that its "heart yearned to be known and loved by these amiable creatures" (p. 127). It is from them that it—like the Mary Shelley who observed the Baxter family—learns the rudiments of kinship:

The youth and his companion had each of them several names, but the old man had only one, which was *father*. The girl was called *sister*, or *Agatha*; and the youth *Felix*, *brother*, or *son*. I cannot describe the delight I felt when I learned the ideas appropriated to each of these sounds, and was able to pronounce them. I distinguished several other words, without being able as yet to understand or apply them; such as *good*, *dearest*, *unhappy*. [Pp. 107–8]

The absence of a "mother" in this paragraph (which ends on the word "unhappy"!) is conspicuous. Less apparent, I think, is the strange fact that Agatha is called "sister" but never "daughter," even though "brother" Felix, who will tear away the old man with the single name of "father," is accorded the name of "son."

It is its own exclusion from such a system of relations that later leads the Monster to maintain that both the killing of little William and the execution of the innocent Justine have been a warranted retaliation, the outcome of "the lessons of Felix, and the sanguinary laws of man" (p. 140). Felix had removed his father from the Monster's reach after mistaking its Agatha-like feelings for the contrary emotions of hatred and violence. That the creature should still so vividly remember this potential brother's action after the deaths of William and Justine seems rather poignant. For, in its way, the murder of William was a delayed fratricidal act.

After it has burned the De Lacey cottage the Monster manages to reassert its softer nature. On entering "a deep wood," it blesses the sun and "dared to be happy." But its "hatred" for its "unfeeling, heartless creator" is soon reactivated when it is accidentally cast in a life-giving role like that of its own deserting father. Just as

17. Juliet Mitchell points out that in the conditions established by "patriarchal human history," the growing girl learns "that her subjugation to the law of the father entails her becoming the representative of 'nature'" ("A Woman's Place," *Psychoanalysis and Feminism* [New York, 1974], p. 405).

Victor had animated the corpse from which he created the Monster, so the Monster tries "to restore animation" to a young girl it has rescued from drowning. But again a gesture of kinship is rewarded with a wound—a literal injury this time—from the "ball" shot by "the man" who, like Felix, misreads an expression of the benevolent side of the Monster's divided personality as an act of aggression. Unlike a Mary Shelley who desperately clung to her Agatha- or Elizabeth-self, the Monster now yields to its destructive impulses and vows "eternal hatred and vengeance."

Yet the Monster wavers still one more time when it sees, not an adult male rival, but a "beautiful child, who came running into the recess I had chosen with all the sportiveness of infancy" (p. 138). The vague syntax almost seems designed to confuse us momentarily—does "the sportiveness of infancy" refer to little William or to the Monster? Assuming "this little creature" to be as "yet unprejudiced," the larger creature is "seized" by the idea to "seize him, and educate him as my companion and friend." The child, however, displays Victor's own adult horror: "monster! ugly wretch! you wish to eat me, and tear me to pieces—You are an ogre—Let me go, or I will tell my papa" (p. 139). Significantly, the scene both reverses and matches the earlier encounter with Felix: whereas the threatened little boy invokes his father to protect him, Felix tried to protect his own father from the Monster's threat. In both cases, however, this threat is only imaginary: just as the Monster has revoked its vows of "eternal hatred" on seeing the harmless child, it had earlier "refrained" from strangling Felix. But when little William utters the name of his father, the oath of revenge is remembered. Assuming that "M. Frankenstein" and his own creator are one and the same, the Monster has found its "first victim": "Frankenstein! you belong then to my enemy" (p. 139). The murder is a delayed act of revenge, not only against a father but also against a father's rival son, like Felix a brother-figure. A huge and alienated Cain kills an Abel who can be sure of his father's support and secure in that father's identity.

If, as Church was the first to suggest, the fictional little William were no more than an analogue for Mary Shelley's real-life "baby boy," then the sympathetic, almost exculpating, attention devoted to all the psychic wounds inflicted on the Monster before it commits the murder would be distracting and illogical, as well as inartistic. The Monster's first choice of "victim" derives its fitness as much from the unattainability of a father as from fraternal slights. Little William possesses the birthright the Monster longs for. Only a course of aggression can obtain for the Monster the parental recognition it desires. And that course will prove irreversible—despite the Monster's pleas for a restraining female counterpart. It will also prove self-destructive.

III

Frankenstein is a fiction designed to resist that potential self-destruction. The destruction of little William can obviously be related to Mary Shelley's own muted hostility toward her younger half-brother: unlike herself, the younger William Godwin possessed a mother and, as a male, had received his father's identity and approbation. Simultaneously, however, the Monster's murder of the little boy must also be recognized as a self-mutilation which the novel as a whole tries to resist and conquer. Just as Mary Shelley must have feared that the possible death of her own little William might damage her identity, so does the death of the fictional boy mark the irreparable loss of the "benevolent" or feminine component of the Monster's personality, making it indistinguishable from Victor Frankenstein, similarly alienated from his feminine self—a self represented both by his dead mother and by the wife who dies on his wedding night.

I have said that *Frankenstein* is a novel of fathers and absent mothers, and it is time to examine this statement more closely. The book's central relationship is obviously that between father and child. After his mother's death, the secluded Frankenstein pursues feminine Nature "to her hiding places" to appropriate for himself the maternal role and the blessings of a new "species" created without a mother's agency: "No father could claim the gratitude of his child so completely as I should deserve theirs" (p. 49). After the destruction of its female complement ("a creature of another sex, but as hideous as myself"), the Monster becomes father to the man and relentlessly imposes on its creator the same conditions of dependency and insecurity that it was made to suffer.[18] Once able to

18. Frankenstein describes himself as "passive" in the arrangements of his return to Geneva immediately after he has agreed to the Monster's dictates; when, "trembling with passion, [he tears] to pieces the thing on which I was engaged," the Monster soon forces him into passivity again

identify with Agatha, the daughter, and to respond so powerfully to the "benign divinity" of little William's and Victor's mother, the Monster culminates its revenge by depriving Victor of Elizabeth. This contest between males divorced from female nurturance is framed by a series of forbidding fathers—the father whose "dying injunction" forbade Walton to embark on a sea-faring life; Henry Clerval's father, who insists that his son be a merchant rather than a poet; the "inexorable" Russian father who tries to force his daughter into a union she abhors; the treacherous Turkish father who uses Safie to obtain his freedom yet issues the "tyrannical mandate" that she betray Felix.

There are kinder fathers in the novel, to be sure, but their kindness is tainted: as Kate Ellis shows on pp. 129–130 below, the "proud and unbending disposition" of Beaufort leads him to seek an exile that results in his loyal daughter's total degradation; the "Italian gentleman" who is Elizabeth's father in the 1818 version (in 1831 she is the daughter of an imprisoned patriot and a German lady who "had died on giving her birth") decides, on remarrying, that it would be preferable to have her educated by her uncle and aunt rather than have her "brought up by a step-mother"—a decision that, in reversing William Godwin's own choice, may be construed as an act of kindness, but nonetheless involves an abdication of parental responsibility. De Lacey and Alphonse Frankenstein are impaired by an impotence and lack of discrimination that Mary must often have regretted in a father who "from age and domestic circumstances could not '*me faire valoir*.'" De Lacey can welcome Safie as a daughter but cannot respond to the Monster's need for affection; Alphonse Frankenstein values Elizabeth as a replica of Caroline Beaufort yet cannot believe in the innocence of Justine Moritz. A rationalist, like Godwin, the elder Frankenstein rather cruelly chastens his son's youthful imagination; his disparagement of Cornelius Agrippa actually may have produced, according to Victor, "the fatal impulse that led to my ruin" (p. 33). The 1818 version of the novel is even harsher on the old man whose heart is finally broken by Elizabeth's death. In a contradiction which Mary Shelley emended in her 1831 revisions, Alphonse is also blamed for leading his son to science when he conducts a Franklin-like

(pp. 145, 164). By the time the two reach Walton's ship, the presumed aggressor, Victor, is clearly the victim of the Monster he thinks he is pursuing.

experiment and draws some electrical "fluid" down from the clouds (p. 35). The Monster's confusion of Alphonse with Victor, when he encounters William, thus seems quite warranted. When, after Clerval's murder, the calm but "severe" magistrate, Mr. Kirwin, informs Victor that a "friend" has come to visit him, the prisoner believes that the visitor is the Monster: "I know not by what chain of thought the idea presented itself that the murderer had come to mock me at my misery." Surprised, Mr. Kirwin rejoins: "I should have thought, young man, that the presence of your father would have been welcome, instead of inspiring such violent repugnance" (p. 177). To the reader, however, the "chain of thought" seems quite intelligible: Alphonse, Victor, and the Monster have all become manifestations of the same truncated male psyche.

Frankenstein questions the patriarchal system (see Kate Ellis on this, pp. 135–136), yet the novel is more than an indictment of fathers as potential monster-makers. If in his parental neglectfulness Victor resembles William Godwin (as well as Percy Shelley), his obsessive "desire for knowledge" and "perseverance" are the very same qualities displayed by the younger Mary Shelley when she wanted to signify her oneness with her father. The novel's attack on a male's usurpation of the role of mother therefore goes beyond a daughter's accusation of a father who could not "me faire valoir." It is also an expression of Mary Shelley's deep fears about an imbalance within herself—the imbalance of a personality that had developed one-sidedly, without a feminine or maternal model. Karen Horney points out that a "girl may turn away altogether from the female role and take refuge in a fictitious masculinity" in order to assuage "disappointments in the father" or "guilt feelings towards the mother."[19] It seems obvious that the young woman who addresses the readers of Frankenstein (including the "Author" to whom the book is dedicated) through three male speakers acquired such an attitude in her own childhood. Yet Frankenstein represents a desperate attempt to recover "the female role." Despite its use of male masks and its emphasis on male aggression, the

19. "Inhibited Femininity," Feminine Psychology (New York, 1967), p. 79; see also, in the same volume, "The Flight from Womanhood": "the desire to be a man is generally admitted comparatively willingly and . . . once it is accepted, it is clung to tenaciously, the reason being the desire to avoid the realization of libidinal wishes and fantasies in connection with the father" (p. 66).

novel tries to exorcise a sadistic masculinity and to regain the female component of the novelist's threatened psyche.

Just as the novel oscillates in its sympathies between Victor and the increasingly demonic monster, so does it oscillate in the sexual characterization of these two antagonists. At first, though nurtured by loving women, Frankenstein is phallic and aggressive, capable of torturing "the living animal to animate the lifeless clay" (p. 49). Conversely, the Monster—purposely not called a "he" in this discussion—initially displays feminine qualities. It identifies with both Agatha and Safie and is respectful of that same Wordsworthian and feminine Nature whose "recesses" its creator is so eager to "penetrate" (p. 42).[20] These sexual associations, however, shift with the Monster's first act of aggression, the "mischief" that leads it to plant the portrait of maternal "divine benignity" into one "of the folds of [Justine's] dress" (p. 140). The Monster now assumes Victor's phallic aggression; and Victor becomes as tremulous and "timid as a love-sick girl" (p. 51).

Victor's desire to marry Elizabeth is presented as a pathetic and hopeless attempt to reenter the broken circle of affection over which his dead mother had presided. Conversely, the Monster's similar yearning for a female companion is treated as highly dangerous. Victor's marriage to Elizabeth evokes the image of a debilitated patient in need of a nurse (an image corroborated in James Whale's film *The Bride of Frankenstein*, which implies that the newly wed "Henry" Frankenstein is far too frail to consummate his marriage to the voluptuous Elizabeth). The Monster's desire for a mate, however, raises the specter of "a race of devils" to be "propagated on the earth" (p. 163). Even an unconsummated union holds dangers: Victor fears that the female monster might "turn with disgust from [the Monster] to the superior beauty of man" or that the Monster's own aggression (so far limited to the murder of William and the death of Justine) might be exacerbated upon his beholding his own "deformity" in "female form" (p. 163).

But above all Victor fears the possibility of a female creature not only more aggressive than the novel's remarkably passive female characters, but also capable of surpassing the sadistic and "un-

20. The contrast between the two figures, in fact, resembles that between "Man of Science" and poet developed by Wordsworth in his 1800 "Preface": the scientist "seeks truth" in "solitude," while the creative poet carries "everywhere with him relationship and love."

paralleled barbarity" of the killer of little William: "she might become ten thousand times more malignant than her mate, and delight, *for its own sake*, in murder and wretchedness" (p. 163; italics added). The implications are clear. Victor seems to acknowledge that the Monster's aggression has been partly justified, but a female who might delight in sadism "for its own sake" is a horror he cannot contemplate. Mary Shelley may well intend to have her readers see the speciousness in Victor's rationalizations—his decision is made when he "had not sufficient light" for his "employment." Still, Victor's terror seems also to be Mary Shelley's. The specter of female sadism is resisted by the novelist who fears her own aroused anger and desire for revenge. Victor rejects the Monster when he destroys the half-formed shape of its female companion; Mary Shelley, too, distances herself from the demonic figure at the casement, whose "ghastly grin" proclaims the retaliations that will follow: the deaths of Clerval, Alphonse Frankenstein, and Elizabeth. Only after the death of Victor will the Monster turn its aggression on itself. In a parody of the self-sacrificing Son, the feminine principle of compassion in *Paradise Lost* who balances the exacting justice of God the Father, the Monster will immolate itself to save humanity from its own violence.

The only surviving male speaker of the novel, Walton, possesses what the Monster lacks and Frankenstein denies, an internalized female complementary principle. Walton begins his account through self-justificatory letters to a female ego-ideal, his sister Margaret Saville (the British pronunciation of her name sounds like "civil"). The memory of this civilizing and restraining woman, a mother with "lovely children," helps him resist Frankenstein's destructive (and self-destructive) course. Frankenstein and the Monster are the joint murderers of little William, Justine, Clerval, Alphonse Frankenstein, and Elizabeth; Walton, however, refuses to bring death to his crew. In a skillful addition to the 1831 version, Mary Shelley has Walton remind his sister that a "youth passed in solitude" was offset by "my best years spent under your gentle and feminine tutelage."

Mary Shelley, who likened her own "state of loneliness" to that of Robinson Crusoe, lacked the "feminine tutelage" that rescues Walton. Bereft of a maternal model that could teach her how to acknowledge and channel her own aggression, fearful of the unleashed aggression that consumes both Victor and the Monster, she turned to passivity as a stabilizing force. In her story "The Sisters of Albano" (published in *Keepsake* for 1829), the young nun Maria sacrifices herself for her more passionate sister Anina (who then becomes herself a nun). In *Frankenstein* the falsely accused Justine Moritz meets her degradation and death with "an air of cheerfulness"—in total contrast to the Monster's rage at the injustices it is forced to suffer (p. 84). In "The Sisters," Anina, "her only wish to find repose in the grave," delays this death-wish (so like both Fanny Imlay's and that of Richardson's Clarissa) until the death of her own "miserable father," whose loss she tries to repair through constant "filial attentions";[21] in *Frankenstein*, Justine can die peacefully since she, "the favourite of her father" until the day of his death, has no such amends to make (p. 60).

This equation of femininity with a passivity that borders on the ultimate passivity of death is, in *Frankenstein* and in Mary Shelley's own life, associated with a dead mother. Caroline Beaufort Frankenstein, who nurses her dying father "with the greatest tenderness" and is the perfect daughter-wife to Alphonse Frankenstein, is a model accepted by Justine and by Elizabeth yet rejected (or forgotten) by the Monster and by Victor. Caroline is found by the elder Frankenstein near her father's coffin; on her own deathbed, she enjoins the "yielding" Elizabeth to take her place as mother and "supply my place to your younger cousins" (p. 38). It is significant that both she and Elizabeth are invoked in Victor's dream just after he has seen "the dull yellow eyes of the creature" to which he has given life. Presumably one of Victor's objects in finding "a passage to life" is to restore his mother and "renew life where death had apparently devoted the body to corruption" (p. 49); but his dream only underscores his rejection of the maternal or female model.

In the dream, Victor embraces Elizabeth, about whom he had said that she and he "were strangers to any disunion and dispute" (p. 30); when Elizabeth turns into the "corpse of my dead mother" (p. 53) the startled dreamer awakes and beholds "the miserable monster whom I had created." The conjunction of dream and reality, both equally frightening to Victor, forces us to link the four personages, the two females and the two males. The relation between Caroline and Elizabeth is one of fusion: although Elizabeth,

21. *Tales and Stories by Mary Wollstonecraft Shelley*, ed. Richard Garnett (London, 1891), p. 19.

like Mary Shelley, is the accidental agent of the mother's death, the "amiable woman"[22] harbors no resentment and insists that Elizabeth take her place. The relation between Victor and the two female corpses and the relation between Victor and the Monster are both based on "disunion"; his reaction is identical in each case: he recoils from the association.

But what is the relation between the two female corpses and the Monster? Like the Elizabeth of the 1831 version, the Monster is an orphan; like the young woman whose single remonstrance in the entire novel is her regret "that she had not the same opportunities of enlarging her experience, and cultivating her understanding" (p. 151) as her male friends, the Monster is denied a formal education. It is customary by now to discuss Frankenstein and the Monster as the feuding halves of a single personality. Yet the beautiful and passive Elizabeth and the repulsive, aggressive Monster who will be her murderer are also doubles—doubles who are in conflict only because of Victor's rejection of the femininity that was so essential to the happiness of his "domestic circle" and to the balance of his own psyche.[23]

Victor's dream, then, can be read as an intrapsychic conflict that has its roots in Mary Shelley's deprivation of a maternal model. Though Frankenstein is the dreamer, it is Caroline, Elizabeth, and Monster who dramatize this conflict. The Elizabeth whose mother died on giving her birth in the 1831 version and whose father deserted her in the 1818 version can find a feminine model in Caroline, and inherit her place. The motherless Monster deserted by its father finds this model in the picture of Caroline, only to be triggered by it into a course of revenge that ends with Elizabeth's death. Victor's dream thus contains an ominous warning. Though male, ugly, and deformed, the Monster is a potential Elizabeth (indeed, what if Frankenstein had created a little Galatea instead of

22. Mary Shelley seems to have had difficulties choosing the right adjective to describe the mother who is infected by Elizabeth; "amiable" was originally "admirable," but in the 1831 edition the novelist had apparently become less hesitant about identifying Caroline with her own mother: "this amiable woman" now becomes "this best of women."

23. In a way, it is Mel Brooks, in his script for the comic *Young Frankenstein*, who has been the most acute reader of the novel when he reunites the Monster, not with Victor, but with Elizabeth; Brooks also recognizes the novel's fluid interchanges when he has young Frahnkensteeeeen become endowed with the Monster's brain.

a heroic male of Brobdingnagian proportions?). Yet Victor fails to recover the feminine ideal of nurture represented by Caroline, that sentimentalization of a forgiving Mary Wollstonecraft. By rejecting his child as a Monster, he will also be responsible for the death of Elizabeth, that less monstrous, yet also unduly passive, component of Mary Shelley's personality.

Death remains the only reconciler in *Frankenstein*, as the dream of Elizabeth's corpse and the reality of the corpse turned Monster foreshadow. For not only Victor and the Monster, but also the Monster and Elizabeth fuse through death into a single personality. Like Keats and Percy Shelley, but for rather different reasons, Mary Shelley was half in love with easeful death. The demise of Caroline so early in the novel suggests that Mary Shelley could endorse this escape from a world of fathers, brothers, husbands, and male justices and identify it with the repose found by her own mother.[24] There is strong empathy, too, with the grief the Monster feels as it hangs "over the coffin" of its dead parent, a scene that parallels Caroline Beaufort's own grief by her father's coffin. The Monster's lament ("Oh, Frankenstein! generous and self-devoted being! what does it avail that I now ask thee to pardon me?") may seem out of character, as Walton rather self-righteously points out, but Walton of course fails to understand that the Monster has also recovered that softer, feminine side that enabled it before to identify with Agatha and Safie. Indeed, as we shall see in the next section, the very phrasing of the Monster's tribute to Victor resembles the speeches of penitent daughters in *Mathilda* and "The Mourner."

The conclusion of *Frankenstein* exorcises aggression. With the death of Victor, the Monster turns its hatred against itself. "You hate me" it tells Walton, "but your abhorrence cannot equal that with which I regard myself" (p. 219). These words echo the expression of Mary Shelley's own revulsion, in her 1831 introduction, over the "hideous" embodiment of anger she had allowed herself to create. The Monster now sees justice in destroying its own "miserable frame"; its sadism has turned into self-pity: "I, the miserable

---

24. It may not be necessary to remind the reader that in both males and females the longing for death is associated with the longing for a reunion with the mother; in women, however, this death-wish seems to be free of the fears which lead men to paint a destructive *femme fatale* who brings death rather than life into the world.

and the abandoned, am an abortion, to be spurned at, and kicked, and trampled on." Sadism becomes masochism, the outlet for self-inflicted anger: "Polluted by crimes, and torn by the bitterest remorse, where can I find rest but in death?" (p. 220). Rest rather than restitution. The Monster must welcome the death so eagerly embraced by many of Mary Shelley's female penitents, figures often far more guiltless than it has been.

One such figure is that other victim of "injustice," the ironically named Justine Moritz. Mary Shelley asks us to regard the revengeful Monster and the passive Justine who is falsely accused of the murder of little William as exact opposites. Yet are they? If the child's murder can be construed as a fratricidal act on the part of the Monster, why are we told shortly before the murder that Madame Moritz has accused poor Justine of "having caused the deaths of her brothers and sisters"? (p. 61). The accusation is as false as the later indictment: it comes from one who—like Mrs. Clairmont in the Godwin household—clearly prefers the other children to this Cinderella and "neglected daughter." But why is the detail inserted? We must trust the novel rather than the novelist, and the suggestion that Justine may harbor thoughts as aggressive as the Monster's is corroborated by her willingness to confess to the murder. "Threatened and menaced" by her father confessor, charged "with the blackest ingratitude" for killing the child of the woman who had adopted her, Justine tells Elizabeth that she "almost began to think that I was *the monster* that he said I was" (p. 82). And so she dies for the Monster's crime. She is an innocent—and yet so is the Monster. She is its associate: her passive death becomes almost as much a retaliation against injustice as its murderous passion. She can also cause pain: her self-deprecating speeches are as agonizing to Victor as the Monster's later accusations. And Elizabeth, by identifying with Justine's death-wish ("I wish," cried she, "that I were to die with you; I cannot live in this world of misery" [p. 84]), also manages, ever so sweetly, to sharpen Victor's guilt and pain over William's death. Passivity, used correctly, as Mary Shelley knew but could not admit, can be as powerful a weapon as rage.

IV

Novels, as we all know, are relations based on relations: narratives based on the interconnection of characters as well as on the links between these characters and their creator. In a famous illustration in *Vanity Fair*, Thackeray drew his own mournful and timid face peering out behind the removed mask of laughing jester; in a celebrated passage in *Middlemarch*, George Eliot, who had privately claimed that Casaubon was based on no other "original" but herself, rejected the notion that Dorothea's mummified husband ought to be regarded as a heartless monster: "some ancient Greek," the narrator volunteers, must have "observed that behind the big mask and the speaking-trumpet, there must always be our poor little eyes peeping as usual and our timorous lips more or less under anxious control."[25] In *Frankenstein*, too, the lifting of a monstrous mask produces a startling unveiling: beneath the contorted visage of Frankenstein's creature lurks a timorous yet determined female face.

The unveiling should not really surprise us. For *relatio*, as Percy Bysshe Shelley seemed to remember in his distinction between poetry and logic, once simply meant evocation: the recalling or bringing back of forgotten or dormant associations that the conscious will must then rearrange and recombine. The fluidity of relations in *Frankenstein*, which converts each character into another's double and makes a male Monster not only a counterpart of Victor and Walton but also of little William, Agatha, Safie, Caroline, Justine, and Elizabeth, stems from common denominators that can be traced back, as I have tried to show, to Mary Shelley's childhood and to her threatened identity as an adult daughter, wife, and mother. Yet this fluidity of relations, which makes *Frankenstein* so powerful as an exploration of the very act of kinship and relation, is absent in the novelist's later fictions, even though these later works are equally obsessed with the same intrapsychic conflicts. The later Mary Shelley, who suffered severe new shocks through the deaths of her own William, her daughter Clara, and Shelley himself, seemed no longer capable of the imaginative strength that had enabled her to relate her own adolescent deprivations to the Monster's development and education. Whereas only a matured George Eliot, could, after much experimentation, have produced *Middlemarch*, maturity for Mary Shelley involved a loss of the powers she had been able to tap in her first novel. Her gradual acceptance of her father's deficiencies, her Amelia Sedley-like cult of the

25. *Middlemarch*, ed. Gordon S. Haight (Cambridge, Mass., 1956), p. 297.

dead Shelley, and her devotion to little Percy Florence, permitted her to domesticate the daemon within and to advocate, in fiction as in life, the renunciatory virtues of an Elizabeth-Justine.

To be sure, there was one more important imaginative outburst and it came, not unexpectedly, after William died in Rome in June 1819. Mary had been able to bear the deaths of her first female child in 1815 and of the year-old Clara in 1818, but the loss of the little boy overwhelmed her as powerfully as the death of the fictional little William had unsettled Frankenstein. Life (or death) threatened to imitate art as the grieving mother indulged the same deathwish to which Justine had yielded. Writing to Amelia Curran three weeks after the burial, Mary Shelley asked to hear about the child's tomb, "near which I shall lie one day & care not—for my own sake —how soon—I shall never recover that blow—I feel it more now than at Rome—the thought never leaves me for a single moment— Everything has lost its interest to me."[26] But again, life and creativity came to the rescue: she had been pregnant since March, and Percy Florence was born in November 1819; angered by a new affront from her father and increasingly alienated from Shelley, she was "roused" once more into writing a fiction that might master these turbulent emotions, the novella *Mathilda*, on which she worked feverishly in August and September.

Shelley had written to Godwin to ask him to "soothe" Mary "on account of her terrible state of mind." Instead, the philosopher (who could not remember his grandson's age) wrote to berate Shelley and to ask for more money to help him fight a litigation. A second letter to Mary proved equally insensitive; instead of consolation for the loss of the boy she had named after Godwin, Mary found herself threatened once more with the withdrawal of her father's love: "Remember too," wrote Godwin, "though at first your nearest connections may pity you in this state, yet that when they see you fixed in selfishness and ill humor, . . . they will finally cease to love you, and scarcely learn to endure you."[27] That this bullying accusation of selfishness was taken seriously by Mary Shelley is evident in *Mathilda*, her most autobiographical piece of fiction, the writing of which must have been almost as therapeutic as the birth, after its completion, of her new male child.

Unlike *Frankenstein*, with its three male narrators, *Mathilda* is told

26. 29 June 1819, *Letters*, I:74.
27. Quoted in Spark, *Child of Light*, p. 62.

by a twenty-two-year-old woman (Mary Shelley's own age in 1819). And unlike Walton who successfully repels the death that consumes Victor and the Monster, this narrator is engulfed by death: in one version of the manuscript, she is a penitent soul in limbo who addresses herself to a female listener who (unlike Walton's sister) is also dead, possibly after committing suicide on suffering a "misfortune" in Rome that reduced her "to misery and despair."[28] Elizabeth Nitchie, the critic most extensively concerned with *Mathilda*, has stressed the biographical implications of the novella's second half in which the lonely Mathilda meets a deprived young poet called Woodville and tries to cajole him into a suicide pact (in the days before their elopement, it had been Shelley who suggested to Mary that they both commit suicide). Nitchie is undoubtedly correct when she reads this second half as a self-castigation on Mary's part for her estrangement from Shelley: "*Mathilda* expresses a sense of estrangement from, even of physical repulsion toward, one whom she had deeply loved, a realization of her own selfish, petulant, and unreasoning absorption in her grief."[29] But in the first half of the narrative Mathilda's guilt and grief are traced to their source in her relationship to her father.

Like Mary Shelley, Mathilda is the daughter of a beautiful, intelligent, and adored woman who dies a few days after Mathilda's birth; like Godwin, her father is crushed by his loss. Although, unlike Godwin, he does not remarry, he leaves his child in the care of a stern and unsympathetic foster mother and (like De Lacey) becomes an exile. Again like Mary Shelley—who in the 1831 preface to *Frankenstein* speaks of living "in the country as a girl" and of passing a "considerable time in Scotland"—Mathilda grows up in the Scottish countryside. Her sole "pleasures," like the Monster's, "arise from the contemplation of nature alone; I had no companion."[30] At this point Mary Shelley begins to invert the fictional parallels: whereas she was recalled from Scotland by her father, Mathilda's father visits her in Scotland when she is sixteen; whereas

28. *Mathilda*, ed. Elizabeth Nitchie (Chapel Hill, 1959), p. 90. The Bodleian notebook simplifies the implausibility of a dead narrator by having Mathilda write out her story just before her death. The fullest account of the bibliographical and biographical history of the manuscript is to be found in the third appendix of Elizabeth Nitchie's *Mary Shelley: Author of "Frankenstein"* (New Brunswick, N.J., 1953), pp. 211–17.

29. Nitchie, *Mary Shelley*, p. 212.

30. *Mathilda*, p. 10.

Mary found herself as neglected as before by Godwin after her return, Mathilda's father tries to compensate for his earlier desertion by lavishing attentions on his daughter; and, lastly, while Mary gave up her "excessive and romantic" attachment to Godwin when she eloped with Shelley, Mathilda discovers, to her horror, that her father's love for her is incestuous. After she repels him, he leaves her a letter in which he acknowledges that he had hoped to find in her a substitute for his beloved dead wife. She dreams that she pursues him to a high rock, and her dream (like Frankenstein's) is prophetic: she finds her father's corpse in a cottage on a cliff. Guilt-stricken, she withdraws from society until she meets Woodville, himself a guilty mourner.

This melodramatic fable obviously displays in a different fashion the passive and aggressive impulses I have examined in *Frankenstein*. Mathilda's passive withdrawal clearly stems from parricidal wishes which the narrative conveys and yet never fully dares to acknowledge. Just as the Monster protests that it has not willed its crimes, so is Mathilda absolved from wishing her father's death— an event she dutifully tries to prevent. Why, then, should she feel such inordinate guilt over the death of the incestuous lecher who can love her only after she has become a fully developed woman? Though far less artistic than *Frankenstein*, the story must be read as a pendant to the novel, as still another self-exploration and confrontation with acknowledged hatred and wishful self-destruction; moreover, by dispensing with the protective masks of male protagonists, the story places Mary Shelley's marital difficulties at her father's doorstep.

How could Mary Shelley have had the temerity to send the manuscript of *Mathilda* to Godwin? She asked Maria Gisborne to take the manuscript to London, show it to her father, and obtain his advice about publishing it. When Maria demanded its return, Godwin held on; he told her that he did "not approve of the father's letter" in the story and that he found the entire subject "disgusting and detestable."[31] Had Mary Shelley finally succeeded in unsettling the revered "Author" of *Political Justice*? Was he finally forced to recognize what was so much more elliptically presented through Victor's rejection of the disgusting and detestable Monster? Godwin made sure that *Mathilda* would never be published.

---

31. Quoted in Nitchie, *Mary Shelley*, p. 214n.

But when his daughter sent him *Valperga* to help him defray new debts and expenses, he gladly saw this new novel to press. Begun in 1820, yet not published until February of 1823, well after Shelley's death, *Valperga* had again anticipated an actual disaster, as Mary recognized: "it seems to me that in what I have written hitherto I have done nothing but prophecy [sic] what has [? arrived] to. Mathilda foretells even many small circumstances most truly—and the whole of it is a monument of what now is."[32]

What "now" was in 1823, however, was the death of Shelley and not the death of the father, who calmly wrote his daughter early that year that he had "taken great liberties with [*Valperga*], and I am afraid your *amour propre* will be proportionately shocked."[33] He need not have worried. The wife who had deferred to Percy's "far more cultivated mind" while composing *Frankenstein* did not resent her father's editorial tampering with *Valperga*. Yet the old conflicts could not be exorcised, and they would continue to surface in her fictions—particularly in her short stories.

In "Transformation" (1831), perhaps her best short story, a monster—this time a deformed Satanic dwarf—must be killed before an "imperious, haughty, tameless" young man, who has shown sadistic traits and whose thirst for revenge against his beloved's father leads him to exchange bodies with the monster, can win his Elizabeth-like bride: by mutilating himself on his enemy's huge sword while feebly plunging in his tiny dagger, Guido the rebel can regain his manly shape, marry the kind Juliet, and be henceforth known as "Guido il Cortese." If "Transformation" is a fantasy in which the aggression and monsterhood induced by two fathers—Guido's "generous and noble, but capricious and tyrannical" father and Juliet's "cold-hearted, cold-blooded father"—can be overcome, "The Mortal Immortal" (1834) reverses the emphasis. In this story, which George Eliot must have read before writing her own horror tale "The Lifted Veil" (1859), the alchemist's apprentice Winzy (another ironic name suggestive of the Pyrrhic victories of "Victor" and "Lavenza") becomes responsible for the death of Cornelius Agrippa (the youthful Frankenstein's own mentor) when he drinks the elixir of life the old master had prepared

32. Mary Shelley to Maria Gisborne, 2–6 May 1823, *Letters*, I:224; by a coincidence, a stern portrait of Godwin faces the pages from which this passage is taken.
33. February 1823, quoted in Paul, *William Godwin*, II:277.

for himself; he thus not only becomes a parricide of sorts who is forced to see his "revered master" expire before his eyes, but also a passive victim of his own longevity as he watches the gradual deterioration of his beloved Bertha into a "mincing, simpering, jealous old" hag. Nursing her until her death "as a mother might a child," Winzy, like the Monster, seeks some place where he might end his life-in-death.[34]

It is the tale called "The Mourner" (1830), however, which most pronouncedly allegorizes the self-division first manifested in *Frankenstein*. The story's narrative interest is itself split between a grief-stricken Mathilda-figure called Ellen (her real name turns out to be Clarice) and the Guido-like narrator Neville, a young man whose impetuosity is checked by Ellen much in the way that Walton is restrained by the feminine fosterage of his sister. Neville's rebellious feelings toward education and parental authority are carefully contrasted to Ellen-Clarice's feelings about her own dead father and tutor. At Eton Neville has only met "a capricious, unrelenting, cruel bondage, far beyond the measured despotism of Jamaica" (p. 87); his outrage and sense of "impotence" reach their apex when he is abused by a tutor. He rebels and, like the Monster, gives in to a "desire of vengeance." After the departure of the De Laceys, the Monster is "unable to injure any thing human" and turns its "fury towards inanimate objects" (*Frankenstein*, p. 134); Neville too wants to leave a "substantial proof of my resentment," and, like Proust's Marcel who destroys the hat of Charlus, he tears his tutor's belongings to pieces, "stamped on them, crushed them with more than childish strength," finally dashing a "time-piece, on which my tyrant infinitely prided himself" (*Stories and Tales*, p. 88). Neville flees to Ellen's cottage, sure that his violent outburst has forever alienated him from his father, but she persuades him that he will be forgiven.

Ellen-Clarice may be able to reclaim Horace Neville from exile and monsterhood, but she cannot overcome her own self-loathing as a female monster; her alienation can be conquered only through a withdrawal into death. Like so many of Mary Shelley's fictional orphans, Ellen-Clarice is the daughter of a widower who, after the "deadly blight" of his wife's death, leaves his surviving "infant

---

34. *Tales and Stories*, p. 161; future references to stories in this collection will be given in the text.

daughter" to be reared by others (p. 96). He returns when Clarice is ten and devotes himself to her education. Their relationship, totally unlike that between Mathilda and her returning father, is ideal and she quickly becomes "proficient under his tutoring": "They rode—walked—read together. When a father is all that a father may be, the sentiments of filial piety, entire dependence, and perfect confidence being united, the love of the daughter is one of the deepest and strongest, as it is the purest passion of which our natures are capable" (p. 96). This wishful harmony between parent and child is disrupted by an incident that links Clarice's passivity to Neville's aggression much as Justine–Elizabeth are linked to the Monster. During a raging storm, Clarice's father deposits her in a lifeboat in which there is room for but one more passenger. He dies, fighting the waves and battling "with the death that at last became the *victor*" (p. 100) and leaves Clarice haunted by the idea of "self-destruction." Neville's attempts to dispel her "intense melancholy" ("what do I not owe to you? I am your boy, your pupil") are fruitless. Unable to bear her guilt, sure that no young man would ever want "to wed the parri—," she wills her death (p. 106), joins her "father in the abode of spirits" (p. 105), and leaves Neville to tell her story to his own bride.

Mary Shelley's deep ambivalence about William Godwin informs most of her works of fiction. While thesis-novels such as *The Last Man* (1826) show the impress of her father's philosophical tutorship by incorporating some of his ideas on institutions and government, *Frankenstein* and tales like those discussed above reveal the impact of a very different legacy.[35] The philosopher who had so strongly inveighed against "coercion" of any sort, who had written that all "individuals" ought to be left "to the progress of their own

35. A study of the ways in which *Frankenstein* and some of the other novels enlist, yet also subvert, Godwinian ideology is beyond the scope of this essay. Such an investigation, however, I am convinced, would yield fruitful results. It would show, for instance, that the Monster I have called a Wordsworthian child of Nature is also a Godwinian child whose freedom from social institutions paradoxically proves as injurious as Justine's degradation at the hands of the legal system, which Godwin pronounced to be "an institution of the most pernicious tendency" (*An Enquiry Concerning Political Justice and Its Influence on General Virtue and Happiness*, edited and abridged by Raymond A. Preston [New York, 1926], II:210). It would also show that in her rebellious moods Mary Shelley sided with the idea of Godwin's former disciple, T. R. Malthus, against her father, who, by 1818, was preparing his reply to the *Essay on Population*.

minds,"[36] clearly failed to apply his precepts during the early development of his daughter. His effect on her was as inhibiting as that which James Mill, another rationalist prescriber of felicity, was to have on the emotional life of his son.

When Godwin died in April 1836 at the age of eighty, Mary Shelley was at work on her last piece of fiction, *Falkner* (1837), a novel about remorse and redemption. The fact that she wrote no more novels or stories in the fifteen years after his death can be attributed to a variety of reasons, among them, no doubt, her greater financial independence. Still, the fact remains intriguing. Intriguing, too, is her decision to postpone the edition of Godwin's manuscripts and the composition of his biography. Like George Eliot's Casaubon, Godwin had left her a message adjuring her not to allow his papers "to be consigned to oblivion." Yet, very much like the Dorothea Brooke who no longer could think that the "really delightful marriage must be that where your husband was a sort of father, and could teach you even Hebrew, if you wished it,"[37] Mary Shelley now stoutly resisted the hold of the dead hand. She had once wanted "little William" to be recognized by her father. Now she could adduce her maternal solicitude for another boy as a foil to "the sense of duty towards my father," whose "passion for posthumous fame," so like Victor Frankenstein's eagerness to receive the blessings of future generations, she no longer professed to share: "With regard to my Father's life," she wrote Trelawny, "I certainly could not answer it to my conscience to give it up—I shall therefore do it—but I must wait. This year I have to fight my poor Percy's battle—to try to get him sent to College without further dilapidation of his ruined prospects."[38] To see Percy Florence reinstated in the graces of Sir Timothy Shelley, that other forbidding father, had become more important than to make amends for guilty thoughts and feelings. Aggressive at last in a sanctioned way, she had become a militant mother rather than a daughter penitent for not being a son. Godwin had squelched the publication of *Mathilda* in 1820; when Mary Shelley died in 1851, the promised biography consisted of only a few manuscript pages, largely about Godwin's relation to Mary Wollstonecraft.

"Little William" had been revenged at last.

36. *An Enquiry Concerning Political Justice*, II:27.
37. *Middlemarch*, p. 8.
38. To Edward John Trelawny, 27 January 1837, *Letters*, II:119.

PART
THREE

CONTEXTS:

Society and Self

VI

Monsters in the Garden:
Mary Shelley and the Bourgeois Family

KATE ELLIS

> Nature has wisely attached affections to duties, to
> sweeten toil, and to give that vigour to the exertions
> of reason which only the heart can give. But, the af-
> fection which is put on merely because it is the appro-
> priate insignia of a certain character, when its duties
> are not fulfilled, is one of the empty compliments
> which vice and folly are obliged to pay to virtue and
> the real nature of things.
> —Mary Wollstonecraft, *A Vindication*
> *of the Rights of Woman*

THE 1818 PREFACE to *Frankenstein* tells us that the author's "chief
concern" in writing the novel had been limited to "avoiding
the enervating effects of the novels of the present day and to the
exhibition of the amiableness of domestic affection, and the excellence of universal virtue." Perhaps Percy Shelley's statement was
simply one of those ritual declarations of moral intent that we find
in prefaces written before the novel became a respectable genre.
But if Shelley meant to be descriptive, he was certainly reading
Frankenstein selectively. It is true that each of the novel's three in-
terconnected narratives is told by a man to whom domestic affection is not merely amiable but positively sacred. Yet each narrator
also has been denied the experience he reveres so highly, and cannot, because of this denial, transmit it to a future generation.

The three narratives are thematically linked through the joint
predicament of those who have and those who have not the highly
desirable experience of domestic affection. The recurrence of this
theme suggests that Mary Shelley was at least as much concerned
with the limitations of that affection as she was with demonstrating
its amiableness. She is explicit, moreover, about the source of these

limitations. It is not domestic affection but the context in which it manifests itself that brings death into the world of her novel. And that context is what we have come to describe as the bourgeois family.

In her analysis of domestic affection Mary Shelley carefully sifts the degree to which members of the various families in the novel accede to the separation of male and female spheres of activity characteristic of the bourgeois family. Historically, this separation of spheres had an economic base as factory production replaced cottage industry and as wealth increasingly represented by capital eroded old ties of economic interdependency, not only between landlords and tenants but also between husbands and wives.[1] Female wage laborers were rarely paid even subsistence wages; middle-class wives, on the other hand, welcomed their separation from paid work, now done exclusively by their husbands, as a sign of bourgeois status. Pursuits once restricted to the aristocracy were thus opened to a much larger class of women. Accordingly, considerable attention was paid, by many a writer, to the "nature" of the female sex, the education best suited to its cultivation, and the duties arising from its new relationship to the masculine world of production. An important contributor to this debate was Mary Wollstonecraft, who saw domestic affection undermined by an exaggerated separation between female charm and social usefulness. The success with which she transmitted this view can be seen in both the narrative method and the content of her daughter's first novel.

The structure of *Frankenstein*, with its three concentric narratives, imposes upon the linear unfolding of the plot the very sort of order that Mary Shelley is commenting on in the novel as a whole: one that separates "outer" and "inner," the masculine sphere of discovery and the feminine sphere of domesticity. Moreover, the sequence in which the reader encounters the three narrators gives the plot line a circular as well as a linear shape. It begins and ends with Walton, writing to his English sister from the outer periphery of the civilized world, the boundary between the known and the unknown. From there we move inward to the circle of civilization, to the rural outskirts of Geneva, birthplace of the Protestant ethic,

1. See Alice Clark, *Working Life of Women in the Seventeenth Century* (London, 1968), p. 12 and *passim*.

the spirit of capitalism. Then, in the physical center of the novel, accessible only if one traverses many snowy mountains, we come upon the limited Paradise Regained of the De Lacey family. Here males and females learn together, role distinctions are minimal, and domestic bliss is eventually recovered, largely through the initiative of Safie, a young woman who comes from a world outside the sphere of Western Protestantism. Yet we are not allowed to end with this fiction of the isolated triumph of domestic virtues. Elizabeth Bennett can remove herself to Pemberley away from her family's pride and prejudice; but we follow the dispossessed Monster back into the outer world, witness his destruction of the remnants of Victor's harmonious family circle, and finally behold Walton's defeated attempt to discover in the land of ice and snow a Paradise beyond the domestic and the familiar.

The circularity of *Frankenstein* underscores Mary Shelley's critique of the insufficiency of a family structure in which the relation between the sexes is as uneven as the relationship between parents and children. The two "outside" narrators, Walton and Frankenstein, are both benevolent men whose exile from the domestic hearth drives them deeper and deeper into isolation. Neither, however, can see that his deprivation might have been avoided through a better understanding of the limits of the institution into which he was born. Even the De Lacey family, where these limits are meaningfully transcended, is basically innocent of what Mary Wollstonecraft, in the title of chapter 9 of her *Vindication of the Rights of Woman*, had called "the pernicious effects which arise from the unnatural distinctions established in society." The "rational fellowship"[2] of this family nucleus has been enforced by necessity. De Lacey's blindness, combined with the primitive conditions in which his family must create a refuge from the world's injustice, simply makes rigid roles impractical, if not impossible to maintain. Safie has asserted her independence from her Turkish father in the belief that she will be able, in a Christian country, "to aspire to higher powers of intellect, and an independence of spirit, forbidden to the female followers of Mahomet."[3] She has no idea, in

2. Mary Wollstonecraft, *A Vindication of the Rights of Woman*, ed. Carol H. Poston (New York, 1975), p. 150.
3. Mary Shelley, *Frankenstein, or The Modern Prometheus*, ed. M. K. Joseph (New York, 1971), p. 124; future references to this edition will be given in the text.

other words, that what she has done would be unthinkable to Elizabeth Lavenza and her virtuous nineteenth-century middle-class counterparts. She and Felix learn from Volney's *Ruins of Empires* "of the division of property, of immense wealth and squalid poverty; of rank, descent, and noble blood" (p. 120). But they do not read *A Vindication of the Rights of Woman*, where Mary Wollstonecraft connects the "pernicious effects" of these divisions with the tyranny of husbands over wives and parents over children in the middle-class home.[4]

This leaves only the Monster to articulate the experience of being denied the domestic affections of a child, sibling, husband, and parent. In his campaign of revenge, the Monster goes to the root of his father's character deformation, when he wipes out those who played a part, however unwitting, in fostering, justifying, or replicating it. If we view his violent acts as components of a horror story, the novel can be read either as a warning against uncontrolled technology and the ambition that brings it into being, or as a fantasy of the return of the repressed, a drama of man at war with alienated parts of himself, variously identified.[5] But an additional meaning emerges if we also take the violence in the novel to constitute a language of protest, the effect of which is to expose the "wrongs" done to women and children, friends and fiancés, in the name of domestic affection. It is a language none of the characters can fully decode because they lack the perspective on bourgeois domesticity that Mary Shelley had learned, principally from her mother's writings, and which she assumed, perhaps naively, in her readers.

I

To grasp the subversiveness of Shelley's critique of the family we need to look more closely at her depiction of the various domestic groupings in the novel. Each of the families in the outer two narratives illustrates a differently flawed model of socialization, ranging from the "feminine fosterage" of Walton's sister and the "silken cord" employed by Victor's parents, to the wrongheaded class pride of Caroline Beaufort's father and the overt tyranny of Mme. Moritz. None of these arrangements provides the younger genera-

4. *A Vindication*, chaps. 9–11, pp. 140–57.
5. See George Levine on pp. 15–16, above.

tion with adequate defences against powerful forces in the outside world, forces that can neither be controlled nor escaped through the exercise of domestic affection.

Mary Shelley makes clear that Robert Walton's career has been nourished and shaped by conflicting cultural artifacts. From his uncle's travel books he learned that his culture confers its highest praise on those who endure great personal hardships to bring "inestimable benefits" to all mankind. This knowledge, he tells us, "increased the regret which I had felt, as a child, on learning that my father's dying injunction had forbidden my uncle to allow me to embark on a seafaring life." The fact that he was told this before he began to read suggests that his contact with his father, if any, had taken place very early in his life. There is no mention of a mother, only of the sister whose influence upon him he so persistently acknowledges:

A youth passed in solitude, my best years spent under your gentle and feminine fosterage, has so refined the groundwork of my character that I cannot overcome an intense distaste for the usual brutality exercised on board ship. [P. 20]

Walton's brief account of his "best years" parallels in two particulars the more lengthily elaborated early life of Victor. The parental injunction (which he transmits without any explanation) has the same effect on him that Alphonse Frankenstein's cursory dismissal of the work of Paracelsus and Cornelius Agrippa has on the youthful Victor. The other similarity is between the brother-sister relationship he values so highly and the ersatz sibling bond between Victor and Elizabeth. Lacking a Clerval among his friends, the orphaned Walton regards his sister as his better, because more refined, self. He is markedly uncomfortable in the presence of men who have not been similarly "fostered" by women like his sister. His lieutenant's "endowments," he notes, are "unsoftened by cultivation." In telling his sister the "anecdote" of the sailor's generosity in bestowing his "prize-money" on a rival suitor of the "young Russian lady" who spurned him, Walton suggests that such disinterestedness is nonetheless tainted: "'What a noble fellow!' you will exclaim. He is so; but then he has passed all his life on board a vessel, and has scarcely an idea beyond the ship and the crew."

Walton's stance prevents him from acknowledging that his lieutenant possesses a natural generosity that is instinctive (not unlike that of the Monster). The sailor, he notes, had amassed sufficient wealth to buy himself the hand of the woman he loved. But on discovering that her heart belonged to another, he relinquished his entire fortune to an impoverished rival—thus enabling the lovers to conform to the prevailing social definition of marriage as an economic transaction. The realization that domestic affection may be simply a commodity to be purchased on the marketplace has apparently left the lieutenant highly disenchanted.

Walton, too, possesses sufficient wealth to have made him the target of some real-life Mr. Harlowes and Mrs. Bennetts. "My life might have been passed in ease and luxury," he tells his sister, "but I preferred glory to every enticement that wealth placed in my path" (p. 17). His quest for glory alienates him from the crew whose physical work is necessary to the success of his venture. Although, unlike nineteenth-century factory owners, Walton does not plan to enrich himself at the expense of his seafaring "hands," he is as baffled by their lack of commitment to his "glorious expedition" as factory owners were by their workers' unwillingness to subordinate their needs to the higher cause of industrial expansion. Determined to find for himself and all mankind a substitute for the domestic affections, Walton nonetheless cannot exorcise the effects of his sister's "gentle and feminine fosterage." The drastic separation of home and workplace enforced on the Arctic explorer cannot be maintained. Walton must behold the "untimely extinction" of the "glorious spirit" that had driven him into the land of ice: "My tears flow; my mind is over-shadowed by a cloud of disappointment. But I journey towards England, and may there find consolation."

In Walton we see a benevolent man made incapable of happiness by the very forces that make him an exemplary, self-denying bourgeois male. Since Victor is caught in the same double bind, it is not surprising that similar forces shape his early life, especially those that separate domestic life from work. The Frankensteins have been, Victor recounts, counsellors and syndics for many generations, distinguished members of the bourgeoisie of Calvinist Geneva, and respected servants of the state as public office holders. Victor's father "had passed his younger days perpetually occupied by the affairs of his country . . . nor was it till the decline of life that he became the husband and father of a family." Although eager to bestow "on the state sons who might carry his virtues and his name down to posterity," Alphonse Frankenstein retired from public life entirely in order to pursue this self-perpetuation. The very first paragraph of Victor's narrative thus presents the same dichotomy between public service and domestic affection already exemplified in an extreme form by Walton's career—a dichotomy, moreover, which will widen for Victor himself as his narrative progresses.

After describing his father's retreat from public life, Victor supplies a second example of such a removal, though not into felicity. Beaufort, Alphonse Frankenstein's friend, was a merchant who, "from a flourishing state, fell, through numerous mischances, into poverty" (p. 31). Fortunately for him, his motherless daughter follows him into exile, where she descends voluntarily into the working class to support them so that her father may be spared a humiliation his male pride could not have endured. Caroline Beaufort's self-sacrifice says a good deal about her conception of domestic affection. De Lacey in the Monster's narrative is blind, and thus actually disabled from sharing the burden of maintaining the family economy. But we are told nothing from which to conclude that Beaufort was unable to work. In the face of misfortune he is passive, a characteristic of other males in the novel, and condones, by that passivity, the exploitation of his daughter.

It is in this nobly submissive attitude that Victor's father finds his future bride, weeping by the coffin of her dead father. This, it would seem, was her finest hour, the shadow of her future idealization and just the kind of scene sentimental nineteenth-century painters loved. Victor's father rescues her from the painful fate of working-class womanhood, bringing her back, after a two-year courtship, by the only route that women can return, that is, through marriage. Yet Beaufort's response to economic reversal, and the success of one friend in finding him, act as a comment on the relationship between class and friendship that one exceptional act does not negate. All of Beaufort's other friends have apparently conformed to the usual pattern of bourgeois behavior when one of their number drops over the economic edge. Given the economic turbulence that marked capitalist development in the later eighteenth and early nineteenth centuries, the experience of being "ruined" was even more common in life than in novels. Yet in the fiction of the same period it is rare to find the victims of that upheaval sustained by friendship made in better days. Class solidarity was not large enough, it would seem, to encompass misfortune.

Of course Beaufort's personality has not helped the situation. He was, says Victor, "of a proud and unbending disposition, and could not bear to live in poverty and oblivion in the same country where he had formerly been distinguished for his rank and magnificence" (p. 31). Still, his self-removal into oblivion, which his fellow merchants would have imposed had he remained where he was, implies that he is not unique but rather disposed to view a loss of money in much the same way the others do, that is to say, as a fall from grace. Like Robert Walton, Beaufort has internalized an ideology which, though painful to him and his daughter, advances the interests of his class as a whole by purging it of its failures. Domestic affection may be heavily taxed, but it is the one source of self-esteem left to him once he and his neighbors have collaborated in his emotional "ruin."

At the center of this ideology is the belief that material prosperity and social recognition are conferred on superior merit, and thus the lines that divide the bourgeoisie from the rest of humanity reflect worth, not birth. Nevertheless, this view, while often expressed in the public sphere without shame,[6] was difficult to reconcile with other Christian teachings. One popular fictional device that obfuscates this ideological contradiction is that of the "noble peasant" and his various fairy tale counterparts, male and female. Caroline Beaufort's devotion to her father is the glass slipper that gives her entrée to her new role as child bride. For her, this role involves revisitations to the fallen world of poverty from which she had been so fortuitously rescued. Her son explains:

This, to my mother, was more than a duty; it was a necessity, a passion—remembering what she had suffered and how she had been relieved—for her to act in turn the guardian angel to the afflicted. [P. 34]

Like her husband, Caroline rejects the harsher side of an ideology that views poverty as a problem to be solved only through hard work on the part of those afflicted. Motherless herself, she attempts to alleviate social injustice by becoming a "good mother" to those for whom no Prince Charming is likely to appear. Yet when she

6. See, in this connection, Sidney and Beatrice Webb, *English Poor Law History* (Hamden, Conn., 1963); Ivy Pinchbeck and Margaret Hewett, *Children in English Society* (London, 1969), vol. I; J. J. Tobias, *Urban Crime in Victorian England* (New York, 1972).

finds one who clearly does not belong where fate has placed her, Caroline's response is to single out this exception and give her more than periodic bounty. In fact, she gives Elizabeth everything she had: a bourgeois father, a mother who dies young, a Prince Charming, and a view of the female role as one of constant, self-sacrificing devotion to others.[7] What is more, she remains dependent, as Elizabeth will be, on male energy and male provision. When Victor tells us that "My father directed our studies, and my mother partook of our enjoyments," he unwittingly suggests much about Caroline's reduced sphere of action.

To say that domestic affection, extended into the public sphere, is an inadequate remedy for the ills of an industrial society would be to fly in the face of an idea that gained immense popularity in the Victorian era, both in England and in the United States. But to say that Elizabeth's early death, like her adopted mother's, was a logical outgrowth of the female ideal she sought to embody, is a radical statement indeed. Mary Shelley may well have thought she was going too far in this direction when she revised her account of Caroline's death from the following:

Elizabeth had caught the scarlet fever; but her illness was not severe, and she quickly recovered. During her confinement, many arguments had been urged to persuade my mother to refrain from attending upon her. She had, at first, yielded to our entreaties; but when she heard that her favorite was recovering, she could no longer debar herself from her society, and entered her chamber long before the danger of infection was past. On the third day my mother sickened. . . .[8]

In 1831 Mary revised this ironic passage. It is precisely because Elizabeth "was in the greatest danger" that Caroline now

7. In his discussion, U. C. Knoepflmacher draws numerous parallels between Mary Shelley and her characters. The links between Mary and both Caroline Beaufort and Elizabeth Lavenza are reenforced in other ways: Mary's mother also died young, leaving her orphaned daughter with a father who "passed his younger days perpetually occupied in the affairs of his country; a variety of circumstances had prevented his marrying early, nor was it until the decline of life that he became a husband and father of a family." If both Caroline and Elizabeth are retrieved by Alphonse Frankenstein, a Prince Charming also rescued Mary (or so she at first thought) from the family with which she could not be happily accommodated.

8. *Frankenstein, or The Modern Prometheus*, ed. James Rieger (New York, 1974), p. 37.

had, at first, yielded to our entreaties; but when she heard that the life of her favorite was menaced, she could no longer control her anxiety. She attended her sick-bed—her watchful attentions triumphed over the malignity of the distemper—Elizabeth was saved but the consequence of this imprudence were fatal to her preserver. On the third day my mother sickened. . . . [Pp. 42–43]

In the revision Caroline's death is tragic, but not gratuitous. Her motherly touch would seem to have been crucial, whereas in the first version it kills her without benefiting anyone else.

The revised Caroline becomes a heroine in death, but her daughter's self-effacing behavior throughout the novel is singularly ineffectual in actual crisis situations. Her most dramatic public act is her attempt to save Justine, yet all she seems able to do is to display her own goodness, her willingness to trust the accused, to have given her the miniature of her mother, had Justine but asked for it. Yet feminine sweetness does not win court cases. It may captivate male hearts, and even elicit "a murmur of approbation" from those in the courtroom. But making a convincing argument before a male judge and jury requires skills that Elizabeth hardly possesses.

Elizabeth seems unaware of her ineffectuality. She hopes that Victor "perhaps will find some means to justify my poor guiltless Justine." Still, like Alphonse Frankenstein, who believes in Justine's guilt, Elizabeth is uninterested in pursuing the truth: that the "evidence" that convicts Justine has been planted. The description of Justine's apprehension makes this oversight seem truly incredible. Ernest, Victor's younger brother, tells the story:

He related that, the morning on which the murder of poor William had been discovered, Justine had been taken ill, and confined to her bed for several days. During this interval, one of the servants, happening to examine the apparel she had worn the night of the murder, had discovered in her pocket the picture of my mother, which had been judged to be the temptation of the murderer. The servant instantly showed it to one of the others, who, without saying a word to any of the family, went to a magistrate; and, upon their deposition, Justine was apprehended. [P. 79]

This act on the part of two servants is certainly one that might reasonably arouse suspicion on the part of their employers, but the Frankensteins appear to view their inability to suspect anyone as one of their greatest virtues. Furthermore, for a murderer to keep such a damning piece of evidence on her person is at least questionable, yet none of the bereaved family even thinks of raising the issue in Justine's defence. Instead, believing in the power of domestic affection unaided by deductive reasoning, they follow the lead of the elder Frankenstein, who urges his family to "rely on the justice of our laws, and the activity with which I shall prevent the slightest show of partiality."

Elizabeth's passivity, however, goes beyond a suspension of the need to find little William's true murderer. On hearing of the boy's death, she immediately blames herself for having given him the miniature to wear. And if this is her response, when no finger is pointing at her, how much less able to defend herself is Justine, whose very confusion is interpreted as a sign of her guilt. Both Justine and Elizabeth have learned well the lessons of submissiveness and devotion to others that Caroline Beaufort epitomized for them. Their model behavior similarly lowers their resistance to the forces that kill them.

Of the education Justine received in the Frankenstein household we know only that it was "superior to that which [her mistress] intended at first," and that Justine thought this second mother of hers to be "the model of all excellence, and endeavoured to imitate her phraseology and manners" (p. 65). We know a lot more about Elizabeth's education, particularly from the second edition of the novel, where Mary Shelley expanded two sentences that appear in her husband's handwriting in the original manuscript. In the original,

I delighted [says Victor] in investigating the facts relative to the actual world; she busied herself in following the aerial creations of the poets. The world was to me a secret, which I desired to discover; to her it was a vacancy, which she sought to people with imaginations of her own.[9]

Here we see the crucial difference in the respective educations of the two figures: Victor translates his interest in science into a career aspiration, while Elizabeth translates her interest into a substitute for experience, a way of filling a void created by her lack of contact with the outside world.

In her 1831 revision, Shelley lays even greater stress on the domestic harmony that formed the context of the early education of Elizabeth, Victor, and their friend Clerval. She develops the divi-

9. *Ibid.*, p. 30.

sion of the realm of masculine knowledge between Victor and Clerval, connecting (in Clerval's case especially) their studies and their future aspirations:

It was the secrets of heaven and earth that I desired to learn; and whether it was the outward substance of things, or the inner spirit of nature and the mysterious soul of man that occupied me, still my enquiries were directed toward the metaphysical, or, in its highest sense, the physical secrets of the world.

Meanwhile, Clerval occupied himself, so to speak, with the moral relations of things. The busy stage of life, the virtues of heroes, and the actions of men, were his theme, and his hope and his dream was to become one of those whose names are recorded in story, as the gallant and adventurous benefactors of our species. [P. 37]

Elizabeth's literary studies, on the other hand, have been dropped rather than developed. She is now shown to spend her entire time shining "like a shrine-dedicated lamp in our peaceful home." To whom, one may ask, is this shrine dedicated? Both editions remark that Elizabeth and Victor "were strangers to any species of disunion or dispute." But in the first they learn Latin and English together so that they "might read the writings in those languages," while in the second her participation in the studies of the other two is quite different:

She was the living spirit of love to soften and attract: I might have become sullen in my study, rough through the ardour of my nature, but that she was there to subdue me to a semblance of her own gentleness. And Clerval—could aught ill entrench on the noble spirit of Clerval?—yet he might not have been so perfectly humane, so thoughtful in his generosity—so full of kindness and tenderness amidst his passion for adventurous exploit, had not she unfolded to him the real loveliness of beneficence, and made the doing good the end and aim of his soaring ambition. [P. 38]

What Mary Shelley spells out, in these additions, is Elizabeth's role in maintaining the atmosphere of continual sunshine in which Victor claims he spent *his* best years.

One might argue that Elizabeth was not harmed by having her mind filled with these exclusive demands, that she was in fact happy with the "trifling occupations" that took up all her time after Victor and Clerval left their common schoolroom, occupations whose reward was "seeing nothing but happy, kind faces around me" (p. 64). Or one might say that she was being excessively modest, that keeping others happy generally and softening the "some-times violent" temper and "vehement passions" (p. 37) of two male students in particular, is no trifling occupation. Thomas Gisborne, whose extensive treatment of *The Duties of the Female Sex* was first published in 1797, was one of the many debaters on the nature of women who held this latter view. He posited three general categories of female duties, "each of which," he insisted, "is of extreme and never-ceasing concern to the welfare of mankind." The second of these sets of duties entails "forming and improving the general manners, dispositions, and conduct of the other sex, by society and example." Female excellence, he observed, was best displayed in "the sphere of domestic life," where it manifests itself

in sprightliness and vivacity, in quickness of perception, fertility of invention, in powers adapted to unbend the brow of the learned, to refresh the over-laboured faculties of the wise, and to diffuse throughout the family circle the enlivening and endearing smile of cheerfulness.[10]

But Mary Wollstonecraft, debating from the other side, had very different views on the kind of education Elizabeth receives in the second version of *Frankenstein*. For her "the only way to make [women] properly attentive to their domestic duties" was to "open" political and moral subjects to them. "An active mind," she asserts, "embraces the whole circle of its duties and finds time enough for all."[11] Victor praises his adopted sibling for her charms and graces, for which "everyone loved" her. But her education has no content, and she does not live long enough for Victor to test Wollstone-craft's assertion that "unless the understanding be cultivated, su-perficial and monotonous is every grace." What is not evident to Victor is certainly evident to the reader, however. Elizabeth is not a real force in the novel: she is too superficial and monotonous.

II

The division into roles that takes place in the Frankenstein schoolroom corresponds roughly to the divisions described in Plato's *Republic*. There the citizens learn in earliest childhood a

10. Thomas Gisborne, *An Enquiry into the Duties of the Female Sex* (London, 1798), pp. 20–21.
11. *A Vindication*, p. 169.

"myth of the metals" which divides them into groups according to whether intellect, courage, or neither predominates in their makeup. The purpose of the indoctrination is to eliminate friction in the kingdom. But in *Frankenstein* the division has the opposite effect: Victor, divided from his courageous, moral self as well as from his ability to subdue his own vehement passions, sets in motion a chain of events that will destroy those parts of a potentially whole human psyche that he has already partly lost through his conflict-free upbringing.

There is in Victor much that could not find expression without disrupting the tranquility of his happy home. On leaving that home he indulges at first "in the most melancholy reflections." But, he continues,

as I proceeded my spirits and hopes rose. I ardently desired the acquisition of knowledge. I had often, when at home, thought it hard to remain during my youth cooped up in one place, and had longed to enter the world, and take my station among other human beings. [P. 45]

Unfortunately for him, these other human beings turn out all to be male, their sisters and daughters being busied with "trifling occupations" within the safety of the domestic circle. Only males, in the world of the novel's second narrator, are seen acting upon their longings to acquire knowledge, to leave a home that coops them up, and to take their places in the world.

Thus Victor discovers a flaw in the wall that keeps his hearth untouched by evil from the outside: you cannot take its protective magic with you when you leave. For Elizabeth's power "to soften and attract" does him little good if he must leave it behind when he goes "to take [his] station among other human beings." He may be devoted to preserving her innocence, grounded in passivity, and revere her for her self-denying dedication to the happiness of others. But since these qualities cut her off from any active engagement in his life, and thus deprive him of a real companion, her supposed perfection only intensifies his isolation. Unable to detect any flaws in his mother's and Elizabeth's unreproaching dependency, he creates in the Monster a dependent child who does reproach him for his neglect. Furthermore, by making this child ugly he can justify his neglect by appealing to a prejudice shared by all the characters in the novel: resentment toward (and cruelty to) an ugly helpless creature is perfectly appropriate human behavior. Indignation is aroused in the novel only by cruelty to beautiful children like Elizabeth and William. Thus Victor can vent on his Monster all the negative emotion that would otherwise have no socially acceptable object and remain unaware of the transference he has made from his child bride to his "child."

From Victor's remarks about spending his youth "cooped up in one place," we may surmise that his feelings of resentment, for which the Monster becomes an uncontrollable "objective correlative," had their first stirrings while the would-be scientist-hero was still blissfully lodged in the womb of domesticity. But resentment in Paradise, for Victor no less than for Satan himself, leads to an expulsion that intensifies the resentment. Outside the home, there is nothing to prevent that feeling from growing until it reaches literally murderous proportions. Had Victor not been so furtive about his desire to astound the world, he might have allowed himself time to make a creature his own size, one who mirrored the whole of him, not just the part of himself he cannot bring home. But to do that he would have had to be a whole person outside the home and a whole person within it.

Repeatedly throughout the novel Shelley gives us examples of the ways in which the insulated bourgeois family creates and perpetuates divided selves in the name of domestic affection by walling that affection in and keeping "disunion and dispute" out. We have noticed already that those whose role is to embody domestic affection cannot go out into the world. "Insiders" cannot leave, or do so at their peril. At the same time Shelley dramatizes, through the experiences of Victor's creature, that "outsiders" cannot enter; they are condemned to perpetual exile and deprivation, forbidden even from trying to create a domestic circle of their own. This point is emphasized by the fate of Justine, who succeeds in imitating to perfection the similarly rescued Caroline Beaufort, but who is abandoned at the first suggestion of rebellion. By having Justine abandoned first by her own jealous mother, Shelley is making her most devastating indictment of bourgeois socialization: another family cannot, as Milton put it, "rectify the wrongs of our first parents."

The Frankenstein family fails Justine because its response to her at a time of crisis was passivity. Yet here the distinction between "outsiders" and "insiders" breaks down: the Frankensteins respond to one another, when crises come, in the same way, adjuring one another to repress their anger and grief for the sake of maintaining tranquility.

Their repressed emotions, especially anger, are acted out by others. We can see this in the behavior of the jurors at Justine's trial: they are ruled by the spirit of vengeance that the family members themselves refuse to admit into their consciousness. Of course the Monster is the example *par excellence* of this process of projection, and his victims come from within the family circle as well as outside it. Their only crime is that they participated (voluntarily) in the process of self-division that left Victor incapable of being a loving father, passive in the face of crises, and content to let other people complete him.

The one murder that does not seem to fit into this scheme is that of "little William." What we know of him comes only from Elizabeth, who notes his beauty and his precocious interest in domestic affection in its traditional form:

When he smiles, two little dimples appear on each cheek, which are rose with health. He has already had one or two little *wives*, but Louisa Biron is his favorite, a pretty little girl of five years of age. [P. 66]

Ernest Frankenstein is drawn to a life of adventure and a career in the foreign service, though he does not have, Elizabeth reports, Victor's powers of application. Thus William, preparing to be just like his "papa," is the one on whom Victor can indirectly visit, through the agency of the Monster, a resentment against a childhood spent in domestic role-playing.

The hothouse atmosphere in which Victor and later William play with their "pretty little" child brides stands in contrast to the mutually supportive, matter-of-fact life of Felix and Agatha De Lacey. Nor is this the only point on which the De Laceys contrast with the other families in the novel. They are the only family that perpetuates itself into the next generation, largely bcause no one in it is striving for the kind of personal immortality that propels Victor and Walton out of their respective domestic Edens. De Lacey *père*, like Beaufort and Frankenstein the elder, was once a prosperous member of the bourgeoisie. He was exiled and stripped of his fortune and place in the social order because his son, motivated by benevolence, impulsively aided in the escape of a Turk who was a victim of French racism and political injustice. But his idealistic impulse precipitates events in "the world" that are beyond his control, events that bring down ruin on his whole family.

The De Laceys exhibit a great deal less rigidity, however, when coping with misfortune than either of the two Genevese families who are called upon to deal with ruin or bereavement. Not that they are entirely happy. Although the father encourages "his children, as sometimes I found that he called them, to cast off their melancholy" (p. 112), his blindness prevents him from seeing that there is often not enough food for himself and them too. But if the land nurtures them meagerly even with the help of the Monster, it is at least a resource for meeting real needs. The relationship of the De Laceys to nature significantly differs from that of Victor, for whom nature can only provide occasions for the repeated display of a histrionic sensibility.

Furthermore, the social exile of the De Laceys is involuntary; they did not choose it, nor do they blame Felix and exile him as a punishment for the fate they must all share. Victor's family is incapable of such action. Returning home after his first encounter with the Monster as a speaking creature, he notes:

My haggard and wild appearance awoke intense alarm; but I answered no question, scarcely did I speak. I felt as if I were placed under a ban—as if I had no right to claim their sympathies—as if never more might I enjoy companionship with them. [P. 149]

One might almost think this was the Monster speaking of his relationship with the De Lacey family. Victor's refusal, or inability, to be an accepting father to his creature, and to give him a companion who would share his sorrows as well as his joys, is a repetition of his own father's refusal to accept or give to him. His exile, as he portrays it in this passage and elsewhere, is largely self-imposed. He "answered no question," but questions were asked. Nevertheless, everything we have seen about the Frankenstein family's mode of dealing with the disturbing reality outside their circle indicates that Victor is right to keep quiet, that his revelations might provoke a response even more damaging than alarm: they might pretend he had never spoken.[12]

12. Examples of this mode of paternal interaction, and of the schizophrenia it elicits, may be found in R. D. Laing and A. Esterson, *Sanity, Madness, and the Family* (Middlesex, England, 1970).

III

The deficiencies of Victor's family, dramatized in his inability to bring the Monster home (openly, that is), to deal with evil in the outside world, or to own the repressed impulses that others are acting out for him, stem ultimately from the concept of domestic affection on which the continuing tranquility of the family depends. The root of this evil lies in the separation of male and female spheres for purposes of maintaining the purity of the family and the sanctity of the home. The effect of domestic affection on both Victor and Walton is "an invincible repugnance to new countenances" that leads them toward the solitary pursuit of glory, which paradoxically disqualifies them for domestic affection. Once touched by the outside world, they cannot reenter the domestic circle without destroying its purity. Victor's rejection of the Monster also makes it impossible for him to embrace Elizabeth without destroying the purity that is her major attraction in his eyes.

Scholarly interest in the bourgeois family, the target of Mary Shelley's critique of domestic affection, has received a good deal of impetus in the last ten years from the feminist movement's attempts to name and trace the origins of what Betty Friedan has called "the problem that has no name."[13] Shelley seems to suggest that, if the family is to be a viable institution for the transmission of domestic affection from one generation to the next, it must redefine that precious commodity in such a way that it can extend to "outsiders" and become hardy enough to survive in the world outside the home. It is not surprising that a woman should be making this point. Eradicating the artificial gulf between the work of the world and the work of the home is of greater concern to women than men since they experience in almost every aspect of their lives the resultant "unnatural distinctions established in society" against which Mary Wollstonecraft protested almost two hundred years ago. If we can imagine a novel in which a woman scientist creates a monster who returns to destroy her family, the relevance to wom-

13. Betty Friedan, *The Feminine Mystique* (New York, 1965). For an overview of recent scholarship on the family, see Christopher Lasch, "The Family and History," *New York Review of Books*, November 13, 1975, pp. 33–38. For a feminist view of this material see Barbara J. Harris, "Recent Work on the History of the Family: A Review Article," in *Feminist Studies*, vol. 3, nos. 3–4 (spring–summer 1976): 159–72.

en of the problem that Mary Shelley has imagined becomes more immediately apparent.

The one character who clearly exemplifies such a redefined notion of domestic affection is Safie, the daughter of a Christian Arab woman who, "born in freedom, spurned the bondage to which she was now reduced" upon her marriage to the Turk. Safie's father had rescued his wife from slavery, just as Victor's father had rescued Caroline Beaufort from poverty. But instead of translating her gratitude into lifelong subservience and sporadic charity, this woman taught her daughter "to aspire to higher powers of intellect, and an independence of spirit forbidden to the female followers of Mahomet" (p. 124). Safie's lucid perception of the rightness of her mother's views was doubtless only confirmed by her father's selfish duplicity in encouraging her union with Felix when it served his purposes while at the same time he "loathed the idea that his daughter should be united to a Christian."

Although Safie is, like Mary Shelley, motherless when she must put her early training to the test, she applies her mother's teachings in a way that is intended to contrast, I believe, with the behavior of the passive Elizabeth, equally influenced by her adopted mother's teachings and example. Safie discovers that her mind is

sickened at the prospect of again returning to Asia, and being immured within the walls of a harem, allowed only to occupy herself with infantile amusements, ill suited to the temper of her soul, now accustomed to grand ideas and the noble emulation of virtue. [P. 124]

In consequence, she not only refuses to wait for the possibility that her lover will miraculously find her, but actively seeks Felix out, traveling through Europe with only an attendant for protection. Had Elizabeth been encouraged "to aspire to higher powers of intellect, and an independence of spirit," she might have followed Victor to Ingolstadt and perhaps even have insisted that he provide the Monster a companion for his wanderings. As it is, Victor cannot conceive of involving Elizabeth in his work on any level; both are petrified in fatally polarized worlds.

In her essay, Ellen Moers observes that *Frankenstein* "is a birth myth, and one that was lodged in the novelist's imagination . . . by the fact that she was herself a mother" (p. 79). But women are daughters before they are mothers, and daughters of fathers as well as mothers, as U. C. Knoepflmacher points out. The kind of family that Shelley is describing shapes us still: its most distinctive feature is that of the dominant yet absent father, working outside the home to support a dependent (or underpaid), subservient wife and children, all roles circularly functioning to reinforce his dominance. *Frankenstein* is indeed a birth myth, but one in which the parent who "brought death into the world, and all our woe" is not a woman but a man who has pushed the masculine prerogative past the limits of nature, creating life not through the female body but in a laboratory.

Victor's father seems to be the exception that proves the rule. He is an absent father for Victor not because he leaves home every day but because he does not. He is so uninvolved in matters that do not pertain directly to the domestic tranquility that he does not act to guide Victor's interest in science—an interest he shared with his son in the first version of the novel but not the second. Likewise, Victor is alienated from his "child" not by his work but by his desire to flee to the shelter of domesticity, which gives a further twist to the already novel image of a man giving birth and then escaping his parental responsibility. The price paid for the schisms that are encouraged behind the pleasant façade of "domestic affection" may be higher than even Mary Shelley could imagine.

The modern world can create worse monsters.

VII

Mary Shelley's Monster: Politics and Psyche in *Frankenstein*

LEE STERRENBURG

> ... out of the tomb of the murdered monarchy in France has arisen a vast, tremendous, unformed spectre, in a far more terrific guise than any which ever yet have overpowered the imagination, and subdued the fortitude of man. Going straight forward to its end, unappalled by peril, unchecked by remorse, despising all common maxims and all common means, that hideous phantom overpowered those who could not believe it was possible she could at all exist.
> —Edmund Burke, *Letters on a Regicide Peace* (1796)[1]

Mary Shelley was the daughter of two of England's foremost intellectual radicals, Mary Wollstonecraft and William Godwin. For a number of reasons—not all of which can be considered here—she rejected her utopian and radical heritage and opted for a more conservative and pessimistic view of the world. Her mother's early death, her quarrels with William Godwin, her marital difficulties with Percy Shelley, her own political instincts, her extensive readings on the French Revolution, along with the fact that she came to intellectual maturity during the decline of Napoleon and the Metternichian Restoration that followed, all contributed to her growing detachment from radicalism. Her gravitation toward conservatism was more overt and explicit later in her career. But it is

---

1. Edmund Burke, *Letters on the Proposals for Peace with the Regicide Directory of France, Letter I* (1796), in *The Works and Correspondence of the Right Honorable Edmund Burke*, new edition (London, 1852), V:256.

already apparent in her first novel, *Frankenstein*, which was written in 1816–17, just after the beginning of the Restoration.

In *Frankenstein*, Mary Shelley's critique of her father's utopianism occurs mainly on the level of metaphor and narrative form. In her attempts to move beyond the utopian politics of William Godwin, Mary Shelley appropriated several literary conventions from the conservative opposition. My essay concentrates on three of these antecedent traditions. In the first section I begin with what might be described as the anti-Godwinian debate in a narrow and specific sense, along with some of Godwin's own literary responses to his conservative critics; I suggest that the character and utopian aspirations of Victor Frankenstein echo parts of this debate. In the second section I expand my focus to include writings on the Revolution in France; I suggest how Mary Shelley's Monster echoes demonic imagery in the revolutionary tradition, including the resurrected monsters and specters of Edmund Burke. In my conclusion, I briefly relate the confessional narrative structure of *Frankenstein* to earlier conservative confessional modes, in which repentant ex-radicals renounce their reforming ways. As I shall try to demonstrate, *Frankenstein* goes beyond both the radical and conservative traditions it appropriates. Though relying on images drawn from these traditions, Mary Shelley writes a novel that is, in many ways, a subversion of all ideology.

Viewed in its historical context, *Frankenstein* poses a question about the relationship of literature and political ideology. As the art historian T. J. Clark suggests, works of art may draw upon surrounding ideological structures, without being reducible to them. Clark argues that

the encounter with history and its specific determinants is made by the artist himself. The social history of art sets out to discover the general nature of the structures he encounters willy-nilly; but it also wants to locate the specific conditions of one such meeting. ... The work of art may have an ideology (in other words, those ideas, images, and values which are generally accepted, dominant) as its material, but it *works* that material; it gives it a new form and at certain times that new form is in itself a subversion of ideology.[2]

2. T. J. Clark, *Image of the People: Gustave Courbet and the Second French Republic 1848–1851* (Greenwich, Conn., 1975), p. 13.

Frankenstein may well serve as a case in point. Mary Shelley draws upon political images and values that were already current. She echoes such standard anti-Jacobin motifs as grave-robbing, reviving the dead, and monsters who destroy their own creators. Conservatives had often used these images to warn of the dangers of reform. They pictured the radical regeneration of man in demonic terms, as the unleashing of parricidal monsters and specters from the grave. In appropriating these images for her novel, however, Mary Shelley gives them a "new form" which partially subverts their original political import.

The "new form" of her novel is more subjective, complex, and problematic than earlier monster fictions in the political tradition. Mary Shelley translates politics into psychology. She uses revolutionary symbolism, but she is writing in a postrevolutionary era when collective political movements no longer appear viable. Consequently, she internalizes political debates. Her characters reenact earlier political polemics on the level of personal psychology. In the 1790s, writers like Edmund Burke had warned of a collective, parricidal monster—the revolutionary regime in France—that was haunting all of Europe; in the aftermath of the revolution, Mary Shelley scales this symbolism down to domestic size. Her novel reenacts the monster icon, but it does so from the perspective of isolated and subjective narrators who are locked in parricidal struggles of their own.

Structurally, *Frankenstein* introduces a major innovation in the demonic confessional story that had been used by George Walker, Hannah More, and by William Godwin himself. Like later works such as James Hogg's *Private Memoirs and Confessions of a Justified Sinner* (1824) and Thomas Carlyle's *Sartor Resartus* (which was originally begun just after the July Days Revolution of 1830), we are presented with the confessions of isolated protagonists who are, at least symbolically, reenacting heroic and messianic quests from a previous revolutionary age. Political themes are translated into private and psychological terms. The messianic struggles of the hero are presented subjectively, in an autobiographical confession we cannot fully trust, and surrounded by equally subjective editors, interlocutors, and interpreters, whose presence further complicates our hope of finding a simple ideological meaning. The identity of the demonic forces is no longer clear. The specter haunting

Europe is no longer the monster Jacobin. The messianic impulse remains, but its political content has been called into question.

I

If we want to understand why Godwinian reforms produce monsters in *Frankenstein*, we can begin by noting the pervasiveness of analogous symbolism in the period before Mary Shelley wrote her novel. The symbolic association between Godwin and monsters was forged in the years 1796–1802, when the conservative reaction against him reached its peak.[3] During those years demonism and the grotesque were frequently used to deflate Godwin's theories about the utopian regeneration of humanity. Conservatives depicted Godwin and his writings as a nascent monster that had to be stamped out, lest England go the way of revolutionary France.[4] The demonic style of these attacks against radical philosophers was established in part by Edmund Burke, who wrote in 1796 of "metaphysical" social theorists:

... a more dreadful calamity cannot arise out of hell to scourge mankind. Nothing can be conceived more hard than the heart of a thoroughbred metaphysician. It comes nearer to the cold malignity of a wicked spirit than to the frailty and passion of a man. It is like that of the principle of evil himself, incorporeal, pure, unmixed, dephlegmated, defecated evil.[5]

William Godwin served as a chief example of this evil reforming type. Burke called Godwin's opinions "pure defecated atheism . . . the brood of that putrid carcase the French Revolution."[6] Horace Walpole called Godwin "one of the greatest monsters exhibited by history."[7] The *Anti-Jacobin Review*, which championed the attack

3. On the rise and duration of the reaction against Godwin see B. Sprague Allen, "The Reaction Against William Godwin," *Modern Philology* IV, no. 5 (September 1918): 57–75; Ford K. Brown, *The Life of William Godwin* (London, 1926), pp. 151ff.
4. The use of anti-Jacobin imagery against domestic liberals is discussed in Gerald Newman, "Anti-French Propaganda and British Liberal Nationalism in the Early Nineteenth Century: Suggestions Toward a General Interpretation," *Victorian Studies* XVII, no. 4 (June 1975): 385–418.
5. Edmund Burke, *Letter to a Noble Lord* (1796), *Works*, V:241.
6. Cited by Brown, *Godwin*, p. 155.
7. *Ibid.*

upon William Godwin and Mary Wollstonecraft, denounced the couple's disciples in 1800 as "the spawn of the monster."[8] The previous year, the *anti-Jacobin* published a print and an accompanying poem entitled "The Nightmare," a take-off on Fuseli's famous painting.[9] The print shows the opposition Whig leader Charles James Fox asleep on his bed, while a grinning French Jacobin monster, resurrected from the dead, replete with revolutionary cap and grinning skeletal face, rides the horse of death across the sleeper's chest. And the cause of Fox's nightmare is not hard to find. At the foot of the bed lies a copy of his nighttime reading, William Godwin's *Political Justice*. Long before Mary Shelley wrote her novel, Godwin's utopian theories were symbolically reviving the dead. Looking back at the reactionary 1790s, Thomas de Quincey later declared, somewhat anachronistically, that "most people felt of Mr. Godwin with the same alienation and horror as of a ghoul, or a bloodless vampyre, or the monster created by Frankenstein."[10]

In fiction, too, monster imagery is evoked to depict Godwin and Wollstonecraft as the begetters of anarchy and destruction. In George Walker's conservative propaganda novel *The Vagabond* (1798), a "new philosopher" named Stupeo lectures an English crowd on the utopian principles of Godwin and Wollstonecraft, only to have them riot and turn against the lecturer, who cries out helplessly: "What shall be done? . . . This enraged beast, this many-headed monster will devour us."[11] This is a standard conservative trope. Utopian reformers breed monsters who threaten to destroy them. Throughout the novel, Stupeo remains a steadfast disciple of Godwin and continues trying to apply his master's theories. His doom comes at the hand of metaphorical monsters of a different sort. After being run out of England by Church and King mobs, Stupeo, accompanied by Frederick Fenton and Dr. Alogos, two of the novel's other Godwinian radicals, goes off to the wilds of Kentucky to found a new utopian community. Just as the wishes of Frankenstein's Monster are aborted when the destruction of his mate takes with it his plan to "go to the vast wilds of South America," so does Stupeo's desire to resettle the new world go up in

8. *The Anti-Jacobin Review* V (1800): 427.
9. *The Anti-Jacobin Reviw* III (1799): 98–99.
10. *Tait's Magazine* (March 1837), reprinted in *The Collected Works of Thomas de Quincey*, ed. David Masson (Edinburgh, 1890), III:25.
11. George Walker, *The Vagabond*, 4th ed. (Boston, 1800), p. 150.

flames. In symbolic punishment for his misdeeds, he is burned alive at the stake by marauding Indians, savage "monsters" who are supposedly more delighted with their wanton killing than "the fair daughters of France, who danced the Carmagnole round the guillotine."[12] The "great philosopher, metaphysician and politician" Stupeo and his utopian plans are thereby "reduced . . . to the idea of a few cinders."[13] The meaning is perfectly apparent. Utopian theories beget savage mobs, who rage out of control like the revolutionaries in France.

Frankenstein might well be described as a descendant of the anti-Godwinian novel of the 1790s. Although Mary Shelley dedicated her novel to William Godwin, her dedication, as U. C. Knoepflmacher suggests elsewhere in this anthology, was secretly invidious. If her novel surreptitiously criticizes Godwin in personal and autobiographical terms, it also mounts a critique of Godwin's philosophical ideas—especially his schemes for regenerating the human race. As some critics have pointed out, Victor is a latter-day Godwinian. Victor's attempts to regenerate human life echo both Godwin and the conservative critique of Godwin's ideas. It is as if Mary Shelley has appropriated the standard conservative portrayal of Godwinianism, and then added her own private and domestic perspective to it.

Godwin entertained millennial expectations in *An Enquiry Concerning the Principles of Political Justice* (1793), where he exulted in nothing less than the coming of a new human race. This race, to emerge once overpopulation had been scientifically brought under control, was to be produced by social engineering, not sexual intercourse. Godwin's scheme summarily dispenses with sexual reproduction, mothers, and children. In his famous chapter on population, Godwin envisions a future form of humanity. He writes:

The men . . . who exist when the earth shall refuse itself to a more extended population, will cease to propagate, for they will no longer have any motive, either of error or duty, to induce them. In addition to this they will perhaps be immortal. The whole will be a race of men, and not of children. Generation will not succeed generation, nor will truth have in a certain degree to recommence her career at the end of every thirty years. There will be no

12. *Ibid.*, p. 224.
13. *Ibid.*

war, no crimes, no administration of justice as it is called, and no government.[14]

Viewed in the revolutionary context of the 1790s, these utopian speculations on human immortality may have seemed plausible, at least to their author. Many people at the time were talking about the regeneration of society and humanity. Godwin simply took the matter more literally than most. But his abstract, overly philosophical, and thoroughly male-oriented vision of the coming utopia is hardly something his daughter could have been expected to embrace.

Godwin's utopia is public, political, and messianic. It foresees the salvation of the human species as a correlative of the coming state of anarchism. Restraining institutions will be dissolved and oppression will come to an end. Humanity will be reborn socially and physically. Mary Shelley parodies these heroic hopes in the quest of Victor Frankenstein. But she also shifts the emphasis from politics to psychology. Godwin's disinterested utopianism is parodied through Victor Frankenstein's self-centered creation of a new Adam of "gigantic stature." In Godwin's paternalistic utopia, children were eliminated entirely. Victor does seem to want offspring, but only as a glorification of himself. He anticipates:

A new species would bless me as its creator and source; many happy and excellent natures would owe their being to me. No father could claim the gratitude of his child so completely as I should deserve their's.[15]

Victor foresees a utopia that reflects his own subjective desires. What was previously a form of social millenarianism has been reduced or narrowed to the status of a psychic obsession.

To a large extent, the sections of the novel narrated by Victor Frankenstein concern themselves with his subjective hopes and fears, his millenarian expectations and his demonic sufferings, and his emotional inability to cope with the Monster he has unleashed. In representing Victor's psychology, Mary Shelley deliberately draws on the features of earlier political literature. Conservative

14. William Godwin, *An Enquiry Concerning the Principles of Political Justice*, the essay on "Property," ed. H. S. Salt (London, 1890), pp. 126–27.
15. Mary Shelley, *Frankenstein* (the 1818 text), ed. James Rieger (Indianapolis, 1974), p. 49. All subsequent references are to this edition.

writers had parodied Godwin's bloodless, "incorporeal" theories by rendering them into something demonic, grotesque, and ghoulish. Where Godwin foresaw the triumph of mind over matter, and the banishment of death and disease from the human frame, his conservative opponents saw something promiscuous, perverted, and unnatural. They denounced Godwin's theories as a virtual invitation to grave-robbing and trafficking with the dead.

When Victor Frankenstein exhumes and revives the dead he is thus enacting a role that was standard fare for previous fictions. In George Walker's *The Vagabond* the young Frederick Fenton joins forces with a radical anatomist who is experimenting on the dead in order to prove that humans have no souls. The anatomist soon convinces Fenton that death is meaningless and that "all things in nature [are] merely modifications of the same matter, there being no difference between a putrid carcase and a bank of violets, except in the perception of our ideas."[16] When Fenton willingly digs up cadavers for the anatomist's experiments, his ghoulish task is presented as the ultimate expression of his radical philosophy. Fenton tells us:

My practice of plundering church-yards at the most solemn hours, under danger of detection, and what was worse, under fear of infection from diseases nearly advanced to putrescence before the interment; to break open a coffin, and to carry in my arms a naked body, whose scent was sufficient to ferment a plague, was an undertaking that required all the resolution of philosophy, and fitted me for the event of any revolution or combustion of nature.[17]

Victor Frankenstein claims an analogous indifference toward death and the grave. He tells us "a church-yard was to me merely the receptacle of bodies deprived of life, which, from being the seat of beauty and strength, had become food for the worm" (p. 47). Victor's career as a bodysnatcher sounds a great deal like Frederick's. But there are also subtle and important differences. Victor is more isolated and withdrawn. He works in secret, totally alone. He is no longer working in the name of "philosophy." His description lacks the codewords which would identify him as part of a movement trying to effect revolutions or combustions, either in

16. Walker, *The Vagabond*, pp. 141–42.
17. *Ibid.*, p. 142.

nature or politics. Rhetorically, he emphasizes the subjective "I" who eagerly pursues success even to the grave. Victor recounts:

I collected bones from charnel houses; and disturbed, with profane fingers, the tremendous secrets of the human frame. In a solitary chamber, or rather cell, at the top of the house, and separated from all other apartments by a gallery and staircase, I kept my workshop of filthy creation; my eyeballs were starting from their sockets in attending to the details of my employment. The dissecting room and the slaughter-house furnished many of my materials; and often did my human nature turn with loathing from my occupation, whilst, still urged on by an eagerness which perpetually increased, I brought my work near to conclusion. [P. 50]

These two scenes suggest a major stylistic difference between *Frankenstein* and conservative writings of the 1790s. Walker's melodramatic style in *The Vagabond* assumes a rigid schism between inner and outer. Evil comes from without. It is like an alien, invading force that threatens to take over the mind. Originally, Fenton was not a radical philosopher. It was only after he met his evil mentor, the Godwinian disciple Stupeo, that philosophy invaded and took possession of his mind. That erstwhile external influence is now in control, and it leads him into contact with further dangers and horrors from without. Fenton's mind is now armed with the "resolution of philosophy." He may have other thoughts and emotions, but we do not see them. Psychically, he has been flattened out into a sterotype, the ideologically blinded radical philosopher. When Fenton robs graves, he is moving inexorably from one external influence (radical philosophy) to its natural sequel (graveyard horrors and monsters). Radical philosophy and demonism both come from without, at least in conservative writings. The former leads straight to the latter. As soon as Fenton becomes infected by philosophy, he is further assailed by threats of detection and punishment, by plagues and diseases, and by the grim realities of the naked, rotting carcasses he carries in his arms. As mentioned earlier, Fenton and Stupeo also find themselves surrounded and assailed from without by "monsters" in the form of riotous mobs and wild Indians. For Walker, evil influences—such as radical philosophy and armed uprising—are always alien forces arising from without, perhaps from France, or, more metaphorically, from hell itself. Characters like Fenton and Stupeo serve as warnings of what happens when these alien forces take over. We are led straight to the nether realm of demonism, anarchy, and destruction.

Victor Frankenstein enacts a similar graveyard melodrama. But he does so in more psychological terms. He is not simply the victim of invasions from without. The innate benevolence of his "human nature" is at war with a counter tendency, his perpetually increasing "eagerness" to revive the dead. His fanatical desires (which are symbolized by his staring eyes and incessant nighttime labors) do battle with his natural "loathing" of the horrors around him. The fanaticism wins. But a battle has taken place within. And that battle renders Victor into a more complex character than Frederick Fenton, who is merely an ideological conduit for Godwinism.

Stylistically, then, the rigid schisms and dualisms of Walker's world have been shifted within. Disturbing and demonic forces are no longer simply portrayed as invasions from without. The world is still dualistic. But the contending poles of the dualism are now contained within the parameters of a single psyche. Victor Frankenstein goes through the motions of a 1790s melodrama. He robs graves, revives the dead, and spawns a monster who rises parricidally against him. But the vector of external forces assumed by writers of the 1790s is largely dissipated. There is no longer a Jacobin Revolution at hand, so robbing graves ceases to be a revolutionary act. It is a private act, carried out in isolation. The psychology is also private. Victor responds not primarily to outer influences, but rather to obscure drives within. These drives prompt him to reenact—in private terms—an anti-utopian melodrama from the age of the French Revolution.

II

The stylistic distance between *Frankenstein* and the 1790s is even more graphically illustrated when we turn to writings dealing directly with the Revolution in France. If the characterization of Victor Frankenstein owes much to Godwin's utopian writings and to the body of literature that grew up in response to him, Frankenstein's Monster, in contrast, rises from the body of writings on the French Revolution. Mary Shelley's reading was by no means confined to the philosophical tradition of her father. As Gerald McNiece has shown, Mary and Percy Shelley were ardent students of the literature and polemics written about the French Revolution, the Reign of Terror, and the meteoric career of Napoleon.[18] During their trip to the continent in 1816, the year she began writing *Frankenstein*, Mary and Percy toured various revolutionary landmarks, noted the spot where the King and Queen had appeared before the Paris insurrectionaries, and even tried to find the chambers where the demonstrators had allegedly burst in upon and captured the royal pair. In their attempts to understand the Revolution and how it had issued forth into Napoleonic despotism, Mary and Percy systematically studied the works of the radicals, including Thomas Paine, Mary Wollstonecraft, and William Godwin. But they also read widely in the works of the conservatives and anti-Jacobins, including Edmund Burke, Abbé Barruel, John Adolphus, and the anonymous *French Revolutionary Plutarch*. In all these latter works appear metaphors that depict the revolutionary crowd as demons and monsters. These monsters are the precursors of Mary Shelley's creature in *Frankenstein*, although she again internalizes the metaphor and adapts it to new ends.

According to the conservative myth of the French Revolution, that event was the result of sinister external influences. In fact, the "revolution" itself is often rhetorically rendered as an external influence that has invaded and altered the human mind, thereby giving rise to unprecedented evils and monstrous horrors. The stylistic focus on externals is by no means confined to the psychology of single fictional characters, like Frederick Fenton. It also serves to depict the collective psychology of revolutionary France. Like Fenton, the French revolutionaries are depicted as the victims of a twofold attack from without. First they are invaded and infected by "revolution" or radical philosophy. Then they set about rebelling, robbing graves, tampering with the dead, and calling forth deadly monsters. The resurrected dead constitute a second attack from without, which descends upon those who succumbed to revolution in the first place. This etiology of political demonism informs Edmund Burke's passage on grave-robbing in his *Letter to a Noble Lord* (1796). Burke haughtily warns:

Before this of France, the annals of all time have not furnished an instance of a *complete* revolution. That revolution seems to have ex-

18. See especially Gerald McNiece's chapter "The Literature of Revolution," *Shelley and the Revolutionary Idea* (Cambridge, Mass., 1969), pp. 10–41.

tended even to the constitution of the mind of man. . . . They [the French Revolutionaries] have so determined hatred to all privileged orders, that they deny even to the departed the sad immunities of the grave. . . . they unplumb the dead for bullets to assassinate the living. If all revolutionists were not proof against all caution, I should recommend it to their consideration, that no persons were ever known to history, either sacred or profane, to vex the sepulchure, and, by their sorceries, to call up the prophetic dead, with any other event, than the prediction of their own disastrous fate.[19]

Burke echoes the standard conservative melodrama of invading externals. He himself views the Revolution from the outside and without sympathy. It is a drama happening to foreigners, who are the pawns of alien, external forces. The social revolution has "extended" itself into the minds of the French, thus revolutionizing their mental economy as well. They have been turned into a new and unprecedented race of grave-robbers. But Burke caustically warns these revolutionaries that their demonic nemesis is near at hand. The prophetic dead will awaken, and turn upon the sorcerers of the revolutionary tribunal.

Burke also develops an externalized, Gothic melodrama in his *Reflections on the Revolution in France* (1790). He denounces armed insurrection as a pernicious monster, set free by experimenters and reformers. He pointedly warns that military democracy is "a species of political monster, which has always ended by devouring those who have produced it."[20] For Burke, even resurrected monsters and the prophetic dead are animated by external forces, "radical and intrinsic" evil.[21] He uses a Gothic symbolism of transmigrating spirits to suggest the new, unexpected shapes rebellion can assume once it begins its rampages. As history moves forward, he suggests, the spirit of evil invades new bodies and works in new ways. Now, during the French Revolution,

vice assumes a new body. The spirit transmigrates; and, far from losing its principle of life by the change of its appearance, it is renovated in its new organs with the fresh vigour of a juvenile activity.

19. Burke, *Letter to a Noble Lord*, *Works*, V:216.
20. Edmund Burke, *Reflections on the Revolution in France*, ed. Conor Cruise O'Brien (Harmondsworth, England, 1968), p. 333.
21. Burke, *Reflections*, p. 339.

It walks abroad; it continues its ravages; whilst you are gibbeting the carcass, or demolishing the tomb.[22]

Burke's personifications are effective. It is difficult to sympathize with a revolution that springs forth from the tomb and stalks abroad like some evil monster, specter, or phantom haunting its hapless victims.

It would perhaps be relevant at this point to suggest the social and historiographical import of these demonic personifications. Conservatives often divide their political melodramas along class or factional lines. The *philosophes*, or sometimes the moderates and reformers from the early phases of the Revolution, play the role of the sorcerer who calls up the prophetic dead. The monster they call into being personifies the extreme factions of the Revolution, such as the radical bourgeois Jacobins and their sansculotte allies, who turn upon and destroy the moderates. This symbolic division of labor preserves the theory of external causes: philosophical ideas of reform are seen to filter from the wealthy and educated classes above down to the level of the revolutionary masses, who translate them into violence and anarchy. Sometimes, the appearance of the monster or specter also serves as a temporal designation, marking a turning point in the course of the Revolution. This is the case in the passage from Burke's *Letters on a Regicide Peace* I cited at the beginning of my essay. A "spectre" or "hideous phantom" springs forth from the tomb of the "murdered monarchy," thus signifying the increasingly demonic nature of the Revolution after 1793. Such symbolic watersheds are common. As J. M. Roberts points out, after 1793 "battle-lines were much more clearly drawn and on the anti-revolutionary side the general swing to reaction led to greater readiness to accept extreme statements about the origins of the Revolution."[23]

In its most extreme form, the melodrama of external influences emerges as a full blown theory, which holds the French Revolution to be the result of a vast, organized international conspiracy. This theory emerges most overtly, perhaps, in Abbé Barruel's lurid *Memoirs Illustrating the History of Jacobinism* (1797), which, according to Thomas Jefferson Hogg, was a favorite work of Percy Shelley's

22. Burke, *Reflections*, p. 248.
23. J. M. Roberts, *The Mythology of the Secret Societies* (London, 1972), p. 180.

during his days at Oxford. Hogg says that Shelley read all four volumes of Barruel again and again, and that he was particularly taken with the conspiratorial account of the Illuminati. We know that Mary and Percy both studied Barruel during their continental tour of 1814, and that Percy read parts of the *Memoirs* to her out loud at that time.[24] Barruel sets out to expose the secret conspiracies he sees lurking behind the French Revolution. He uncovers a vast, proliferating cabal, which originates with the Illuminati in Ingolstadt, and descends downward through the Freemasons, the *philosophes*, the Jacobins, and finally reaches the revolutionary crowds in the streets. He depicts the Jacobins and the revolutionary crowds as a monster incarnate. This monster is an offspring of the Illuminati, whose reforming philosophies have brought it into being. At the end of his third volume, Barruel looks forward to his fourth with an ominous warning to the reader:

Meanwhile, before Satan shall exultingly enjoy this triumphant spectacle [of complete anarchy] which the Illuminizing Code is preparing, let us examine how . . . it engendered that disastrous monster called Jacobin, raging uncontrolled, and almost unopposed, in these days of horror and devastation.[25]

The international conspiracy theory here takes the form of a sexual or parenting metaphor. The secret code of the Illuminati has "engendered" a "monster called Jacobin," who now rages out of control across Europe. Barruel makes extensive use of the parent-child metaphor. He writes: "the French Revolution has been a true child of its parent Sect; its crimes have been its filial duty; those black deeds and atrocious acts the natural consequences of the principles and systems that gave it birth."[26] The symbolic projection of external causes and external agents could hardly be more extreme. Without the parent philosophical sect, there would be no childlike monster arising to terrorize Europe. Without the secret conspiracy of the Illuminati at Ingolstadt, there purportedly would

24. Thomas Jefferson Hogg, *The Life of Percy Bysshe Shelley*, ed. Humbert Wolfe (London, 1933), I:367. See also W. E. Peck, "Shelley and Abbé Barruel," *PMLA* XXXVI (1921): 347–53; McNiece, *Shelley and the Revolutionary Idea*, pp. 22–24; and Peter Dale Scott's essay, pp. 176–77, below.

25. Abbé Barruel, *Memoirs Illustrating the History of Jacobinism*, trans. Robert Clifford (London, 1798), III:414.

26. Barruel, *Memoirs*, I:viii.

have been no French Revolution, either. For Barruel reforming philosophies lead directly and inevitably to the production of rebellious monsters.

There is reason to assume that Mary Shelley had Barruel in mind when she composed *Frankenstein*. Victor Frankenstein of course does not produce a real Jacobin monster. But he does create his Monster in the same city, Ingolstadt, which Barruel cites as the purported secret source of the French Revolution—and as the place in which the "monster called Jacobin" was originally conceived. Victor, in effect, is producing the second famous literary monster to issue forth from the secret inner sanctum of that city. This second coming differs significantly from the first. Even though the demonic personification remains intact and though the story is nominally set in the 1790s, the French Revolution has simply disappeared. Mary Shelley retains the monster metaphor, but purges it of virtually all reference to collective movements. Her monster metaphor explains the coming of a domestic tragedy. Political revolution has been replaced by a parricidal rebellion within the family. And, as Kate Ellis suggests above, that family is essentially bourgeois.

The form of Mary Shelley's novel further serves to depoliticize the monster tradition. Instead of watching the birth and career of the monster from without, as we do in Burke and Barruel, we watch it from within, from the personal viewpoint of the participating parties. This shift within opens up subjective perspectives left untapped in the political milieu of the 1790s. Mary Shelley's new formal subjectivity does more than efface and replace politics. It also subverts the clear, definable melodrama of external ideological causes that informed writings of the 1790s. The world is now much more problematic. Monsters are still abroad, but we are no longer quite sure why. In order to find out, we have to piece together and compare the various subjective explanations offered by Victor, by the Monster, and even by the frame narrator, Robert Walton. But these narratives are patently at odds with one another, especially when it comes to explaining causes. Mary Shelley's worldview is less political than Godwin's or Burke's; it is also far more labyrinthine and involuted when it comes to telling us why things fall apart.

For writers of the 1790s, the world could be improved, saved, or destroyed by manipulating external and environmental influences. William Godwin thought that humans might become immortal, once the pressures of overpopulation were brought under control. Edmund Burke was Godwin's political enemy and a bitter opponent of Enlightenment philosophies. But he too used social and environmental explanations, at least when it came to dealing with the threat of revolution. Godwin wanted to eliminate misery, and he thought this could be done by eradicating excess population. By the end of his career, when Burke actively wanted to eliminate the international revolutionary menace, he thought (or hoped) this could be done by locating and eradicating revolutionaries at home and abroad. Both writers were thus the heirs of Enlightenment thinking, at least rhetorically, in the sense that they held forth the practical hope of isolating and doing away with a social cause of suffering.

To put the matter in moral terms, both Godwin and Burke presumed to know where evil resided. For Godwin, it was in social institutions that maintained arbitrary inequality, oppression, and want. For Burke, evil resided in those philosophers and rebels who wanted to strip away the protection of social hierarchies and institutions. Both these world-views contain an element of melodrama. They are also typical expressions of the polarized thinking which emerged, during the revolutionary 1790s, as a political extension of the Enlightenment world-view. The cultural historian J. M. Roberts comments on the style of this "new political universe" as follows:

Its essence was a view of politics whose roots lay in the Enlightenment itself and sometimes proclaimed by the revolutionaries; it rested on the assumption of one great and general antithesis, Good versus Evil, Right versus Wrong. Practically, it was expressed in the rapid crystallisation of the day-to-day politics of the Revolution into a straight two-sided confrontation and the appearance of a Left-versus-Right Convention. This confrontation was soon expanded to become an ideological antithesis which could find room for any piece of historical data which people wished to fit into it. . . . The idea of the struggle between the Revolution and the ancien régime, reason and religion, rich and poor, talent and birth (or whatever translation was given to the idea from time to time), helped to create behavior exemplifying its own reality.[27]

27. Roberts, *Secret Societies*, pp. 203–4.

Viewed in its wider cultural context, Mary Shelley's shift from politics to psyche in *Frankenstein* should be seen, not merely as a reaction against the utopianism of Godwin, nor against the conservatism of Burke, but rather as a reaction against this entire world-view of the revolutionary age. Mary Shelley does not escape from the schisms of that polarized world. Hers is still a world of good versus evil, rich versus poor, men versus monsters. But she does set about internalizing those dualisms. Instead of depicting the vast political dramas of the revolutionary age, she narrows the focus to a few isolated characters, who are often too subjectively rendered to conform neatly to the old political labels. In *Frankenstein*, the very act of perceiving and defining a monster has become problematic.

The confessional structure of *Frankenstein* pulls our attention away from the world of politics. We shift our attention from the social object to the perceiving subject. The novel often deals with the problems of the subjective viewer, who is projecting upon others a private vision of demonic persecution. Mary Shelley pays a good deal of attention to how characters misperceive or half invent the social forces aligned against them. For example, she goes to great lengths to portray Victor's subjective fantasies of the Monster he has created. Subjective images of the fiend intrude upon Victor's nighttime dreams; they also appear during his waking hours as a kind of spectral hallucination. The first such imaginary visitation takes place the morning after Victor has revived his creature from the dead. Henry Clerval notices that Victor appears upset and asks him what is wrong. Victor responds in a paroxysm of fear:

"Do not ask me," cried I, putting my hands before my eyes, for I thought I saw the dreaded spectre glide into the room; "*he* can tell. —Oh save me! save me!" I imagined that the monster seized me; I struggled furiously, and fell down in a fit. [P. 56]

Victor becomes feverish in the days that follow. He continues to be haunted by fears of the Monster's return. He recalls "the form of the Monster on whom I had bestowed existence was ever before my eyes, and I raved incessantly concerning him" (p. 57). Victor sometimes accounts for these subjective fears as a form of mental possession or derangement. Thus he recalls the period just after he agreed to make a mate for the Monster: "Can you wonder," he narrates, that sometimes a kind of insanity possessed me, or that I saw continually about me a multitude of filthy animals inflicting on me incessant torture, that often extorted screams and bitter groans? [P. 145]

Imaginary attacks also take place in Victor's dreams. Just after his release from the Irish prison he sleeps fitfully through one night and then,

towards morning I was possessed by a kind of nightmare; I felt the fiend's grasp in my neck, and could not free myself from it; groans and cries rung in my ears. [P. 181]

Repeatedly, Victor experiences subjective persecutions of the most intimate and personal kind. The imaginary Monster fastens upon his throat, or seems to be torturing or killing him. Although Victor plays the familiar role of the reformer who produces a monster, his narrative often reduces itself to extremely subjective renditions of the creature's revenge.

Mary Shelley internalizes the dualisms of utopian expectation and demonic reversal which partisan writers like Robert Walker had portrayed from without. Victor's account is complicated by the fact that he often perceives the creature as an imago of his own blasted hopes. Victor continually talks in terms of dualistic reversals. Within the space of a single disjunctive sentence, he can pass from utopian hope to demonic suffering and catastrophic failure. Victor recalls the moment the creature opened his eyes for the first time: "now that I had finished, the beauty of the dream vanished, and breathless horror and disgust filled my heart" (pp. 52–53). Victor's dualistic sentences chart emotional convulsions that take place within his own psyche. *He* is the focal point of his own narrative. *His* utopian expectations have been blasted by failure. And his responses to the Monster are often a function of that disappointment. Thus the frequently self-reflexive nature of his syntax: "dreams that had been my food and pleasant rest for so long a space, were now become a hell to me; and the change was so rapid, the overthrow so complete" (p. 54). Hells and demons are, for Victor, the symbolic reversals of his extravagant hopes and desires.

When Victor finally meets and speaks with his Monster, we are implicitly witnessing a clash of rival world-views. Victor speaks in his typically subjective and self-reflexive manner. The Monster retains much more of the Enlightenment political style. He talks analytically about the social influences that have shaped his life. The Monster speaks like a *philosophe*, while Victor rages in Romantic agony. The first time Victor ever speaks with his creature, he breaks out in a fit of wild imprecations, and the Monster replies:

"I expected this reception, . . . All men hate the wretched; how then must I be hated, who am miserable beyond all living things." [P. 94]

There is considerable irony in this stylistic reversal. The novel assigns to Victor the conventional role of the experimenting *philosophe*-scientist; but he raves like a mad demon. Conversely, the novel assigns to the creature the role of the mad, Jacobin demon, risen from the grave to spread havoc abroad. But he talks like a *philosophe*, indicting the social system for the suffering it causes individuals. Mary Shelley does not always escape from the stereotypes of the revolutionary age, but she does conflate and mix them in new and subversive combinations.

The confrontation of world-views continues. Oblivious of his own cruel neglect, Victor remains fixated on the crimes and innate evils of his adversary and continues to rave in a dire, apocalyptic style ("Abhorred monster! fiend that thou art! the tortures of hell are too mild a vengeance for thy crimes"). Yet the Monster's rhetorical style tells us that his identity as a rebel was learned, not innate. In direct contradiction to the Burkean tradition of the monster as evil incarnate, the creature tells Frankenstein: "I was benevolent and good; misery made me a fiend" (p. 95). This disjunctive rhetoric itself reenacts a passage from benevolence to rebellion. In part, the Monster has been converted to his demonic identity, and does not deserve Victor's reactionary labeling, which assumes that he is the principle of evil incarnate. And Victor's rejection is all the more ironic because the utopia projected by the monster is highly paternalistic: he wants to be cared for by Victor, whom he calls his "natural lord and king" (p. 95).

The Monster proves a very philosophical rebel. He explains his actions in traditional republican terms. He claims he has been driven to rebellion by the failures of the ruling orders. His superiors and protectors have shirked their responsibilities toward him, impelling him to insurrection. He says of the De Laceys: "My protectors had departed, and broken the only link that held me to the world. For the first time feelings of revenge and hatred filled my bosom, and I did not strive to controul them" (p. 134). This rebellion against irresponsible superiors soon turns against Victor, who has rejected the creature from the moment of its awakening. The Monster's rebellion is parricidal; he rises against his own creator. He defiantly tells Victor: "I will revenge my injuries: if I cannot inspire love, I will cause fear; and chiefly towards you my archenemy, because my creator, I do swear inextinguishable hatred" (p. 141). This imprecation echoes a motif in the political literature of the 1790s. Especially for republican historiographers, parricidal monsters serve as emblems of the consequences of misrule. For republicans, monsters rebel not because they are infected by the evils of radical philosophy, but because they have been oppressed and misused by the regnant order. In the language of *Frankenstein*, social misery turns them into fiends.

Mary Shelley's readiest source for this stereotype of a republican monster would have been her mother's study, *An Historical and Moral View of the Origin and Progress of the French Revolution* (1794). Mary Wollstonecraft grants one concession to the Burkean conservatives. She admits that rebels are monsters. But she resolutely insists that these monsters are social products. They are not the living dead, nor are they specters arisen from the tomb of the murdered monarchy. Rather, they are the products of oppression, misrule, and despotism under the *ancien régime*. The lower orders are driven to rebellion. They have been "depraved by the inveterate despotism of ages,"[28] and they eventually turn against their oppressors in parricidal fashion.

Mary Wollstonecraft uses this imagery to depict the female rebels of Paris in the opening days of the Revolution. The Paris women, exacerbated to the point of frenzy, execute Old Foulon and Berthier, two hated agents of the old regime, stick their severed heads on pikes, and parade them triumphantly through the streets. The old regime receives its due. In mock surprise, Mary Wollstonecraft exclaims of these female rebels:

28. Mary Wollstonecraft, *An Historical and Moral View of the Origin and Progress of the French Revolution* (1795; reprint of 2d ed., Delmar, N.Y., 1975), p. 252.

Strange that a people . . . should have bred up such monsters! Still we ought to recollect, that the sex, called the tender, commit the most flagrant acts of barbarity when irritated.[29]

Wollstonecraft is not an overt partisan of these French female insurrectionaries. She analogizes their acts to the bloody crimes of Lady Macbeth, and she conjectures that we may never be able to "erase the memory of those foul deeds, which, like the stains of the deepest dye . . . can never be rubbed out."[30] But she does account for these foul deeds in social and historical terms. Oppression, she argues, always tends to breed parricidal monsters. Continuing her analogy to Lady Macbeth, she finds parricide inevitable under certain circumstances: "Since . . . we cannot 'out the damned spot,' it becomes necessary to observe, that, whilst despotism and superstition exist, the convulsions, which the regeneration of man occasions, will always bring forward the vices they have engendered, to devour their parents."[31]

The critics who see Mary Shelley's Monster as a furtively female character have a historical precedent on their side. The most extravagant and demonic pictures of mass insurrectionary violence in both Wollstonecraft and Burke concern female rebels. Wollstonecraft depicts the sansculotte women of July 1789 as devouring, cannibal-like monsters destroying their own parents. Burke depicts the women who marched on Versailles to bring back the King and Queen on October 6, 1789, in the following terms:

. . . the royal captives who followed in the train were slowly moved along, amidst the horrid yells, and shrilling screams, and frantic dances, and infamous contumelies, and all the unutterable abominations of the furies of hell, in the abused shape of the vilest of women.[32]

Mary Shelley knew these passages well. She had available to her models of monsters, specters, and furies who actually were female. These female monsters are a collective force; they have behind them the weight and resonance of actual historical events, includ-

29. Wollstonecraft, *French Revolution*, p. 258.
30. *Ibid.*
31. *Ibid.*, p. 259.
32. Burke, *Reflections*, p. 165.

ing the march on Versailles. But Mary Shelley turns her Monster into a lone male, rebelling on his own. She thereby denies herself many of the sexual and political implications already inherent in the image of the female, parricidal monster.

She settles instead for a rebellion within and against the bourgeois family. The Monster kills off Victor's friends and kin, promises to be with him on his wedding night, and murders his new wife. If nothing else, his rebellion effectively brings about the demise of one socially prominent family with a long history of public service. Victor comes from a long line of officials and syndics. His father gives him a university education, so he might better perpetuate the family fame and tradition. Victor also inherits a "competent fortune" (p. 149) that enables him to carry on his scientific researches without having to work for a living. Victor is in a position to further the social responsibilities historically associated with his family, but he does not do so. The Monster ensures the end of this "distinguished" line (p. 27) by killing little William and finally leading Victor to his death.

The Monster accompanies these specific acts of rebellion with a verbal indictment of social oppression in general. His experiences have turned him into an articulate social critic. Rejected by his creator, the Monster has to eke out a miserable existence on the lower fringes of rural society. He gleans food from shepherds, peasants, and wandering beggars (pp. 99–101). The De Laceys, with whom he identifies for a while, are reduced to the level of poor cottagers, who support themselves by gardening a rented plot and sending their son out as a hired farm laborer. From the De Laceys' plight and their family discussions, he extrapolates what sounds like a radical critique of oppression and inequality: "I heard of the division of property, of immense wealth and squalid poverty; of rank, descent, and noble blood" (p. 115). Both his prose style and his message portray a world of social schisms and polarities. He speaks in the manner of revolutionary-era radicals:

"I learned that the possessions most esteemed by your fellow-creatures were, high and unsullied descent united with riches. A man might be respected with only one of these acquisitions; but without either he was considered, except in very rare occasions, as a vagabond and a slave, doomed to waste his powers for the profit of the chosen few." [P. 115]

The creature utters an explicit verbal critique of the chosen few who live on the toil of others and care not at all for the plight of the multitudes. And as he very well knows, this economic critique of society in general bears directly on his own plight:

"And what was I? Of my creation and creator I was absolutely ignorant; but I knew I possessed no money, no friends, no kind of property. I was besides, endowed with a figure hideously deformed and loathsome; I was not even of the same nature as man. . . . When I looked around, I saw and heard of none like me. Was I then a monster, a blot upon the earth, from which all men fled, and whom all men disowned?" [Pp. 115–16]

This existential protest harkens back to the revolutionary age of the 1790s, yet also stands at a considerable distance from it. Had Mary Shelley's Monster "looked around" in the 1790s, he might have found many other defiant literary monsters, ready to do battle against the *ancien régime*. But there are no other monsters in the post-Napoleonic era to join his cause, and he is destined to remain alone.

Still, Mary Shelley's Monster would have been unique and isolated even in the 1790s. He is a hybrid, a cross between two traditions that produces a unique third. From the Burkean tradition of horrific, evil, and revolutionary monsters, he seems to have derived the grotesque features that physically mark him and set him apart; he has risen from the tomb like a revolutionary monster, and the mark of death is still upon him. All men flee from such ugliness and apparent evil, as the Monster knows only too well. From the republican tradition of social monsters, he seems to have derived his acerbic, verbal critique of poverty and injustice, which serves as his stated rationale for insurrection. As he tells us with pointed eloquence, monsters are driven to rebellion by suffering and oppression. People flee from this monster, and they try to kill him as well. The Monster in *Frankenstein* thus suffers the consequences of two symbolic traditions.

But Mary Shelley does more than conflate two traditions. She molds them into a unique third. She moves inside the mind of the Monster and asks what it is like to be labeled, defined, and even physically distorted by a political stereotype. The Monster in *Frankenstein* is the victim of Burkean circumstances: he is resurrected from the grave. He is also the victim of circumstances a republican might single out: he is oppressed and misused by the social orders above him. Mary Shelley is able to represent the consequences of these influences subjectively, through the eyes of a victim who is also a rebel. This is a new perspective. It is something her Enlightenment forerunners could not see, preoccupied as they were with charting, explaining, and debating the external influences that enkindle revolution.

III

If, as I have tried to show, *Frankenstein* draws on, yet greatly complicates, the revolutionary and antirevolutionary political metaphors of the 1790s, the novel itself furnished a political metaphor for the later nineteenth century. Written at a time of "severe distress," when Regency England was facing "the most widespread, persistent, and dangerous disturbances, short of actual revolution and civil war, that England has known in modern times,"[33] *Frankenstein* was evoked during subsequent periods of crisis. The image of the "Frankenstein monster" surfaced during the revolutionary scares and reform agitation of the early 1830s, the climax of Chartism in 1848–49, the enfranchisement of the working classes in the late 1860s, and the Irish troubles of the 1880s.

Commenting in 1830 on the atheistic and revolutionary tenor of the times, the radical Tory *Fraser's Magazine* remembered Mary Shelley's Monster:

A state without religion is like a human body without a soul, or rather like an unnatural body of the species of the Frankenstein monster, without a pure and vivifying principle; for the limbs are of different natures, and form a horrible heterogeneous compound, full of corruption and exciting our disgust.[34]

Similarly forgetting the sympathy that Mary Shelley had managed to create for the Monster's plight, other writers and cartoonists preferred to dwell on the dangers of animating social monsters through hopes of political reform. The metaphor used by Burke and Mary Wollstonecraft had found a new palpable shape. Parry's

33. Frank Darvall, *Popular Disturbances and Public Order in Regency England* (London, 1934), p. 306.
34. *Fraser's Magazine*, November 1830, p. 481.

1. *Reform BILL's First Step Amongst his Political Frankensteins.* This 1833 lithograph by the portraitist and engraver James Parry depicts the Satanic giant "Bill" (no little William!) emerging from "Laboratory 1832," eclipsing worthier causes such as the abolition of slavery and free trade, and thumbing his nose at his legislative creators.

illustration, "Reform Bill's First Step Among His Political Frankensteins" (1833), depicts a devilish creature—the sovereignty of the masses—overwhelming the privileged classes who had reluctantly brought him into being (see illustration 1).[35] Elizabeth Gaskell's allusions to the Frankenstein monster in *Mary Barton* are only slightly more sympathetic: likening the "actions of the uneducated" to "those of Frankenstein, that monster of many human qualities,

35. Michael W. Jones, *The Cartoon History of Britain* (New York, 1971), p. 62.

ungifted with a soul, a knowledge of the difference of good and evil," the novelist fears the masses who "rise up to life."[36]

A similar return to the stereotypes that had preceded *Franken-stein* is evident in two later cartoons by John Tenniel. "The Brummagem Frankenstein" (1866) depicts a timid reformer, John Bright, tiptoeing past a recumbent monster who clearly stands for the huge working class demonstrations at Birmingham (see illustration 2).[37] And in the lurid "The Irish Frankenstein," which appeared shortly after the Phoenix Park murders of 1882, the Irish terrorist yoked with Parnell is a barbaric, ape-like beast—who resembles Stevenson's Mr. Hyde as much as Shelley's creature (see illustration 3).[38] In all of these instances, reforming or seditious ideas transform the new classes into political monsters. And in each case, the metaphor is derived from a novel written by the daughter of two radical writers.

Mary Shelley herself, of course, eventually rejected the radicalism that had been her birthright. In October of 1838 she recorded in her *Journal*: "since I had lost Shelley I have no wish to ally myself to the Radicals—they are full of repulsion to me—violent without any sense of Justice—selfish in the extreme—talking without knowledge—rude, envious, and insolent—I wish to have nothing to do with them."[39] In 1818, however, the writer who dedicated *Frankenstein* to her father and let herself be guided by her husband, was far more ambivalent towards her radical heritage. An anti-revolutionary confessional such as Hannah More's *The Death of Mr. Fantom, The Great Reformist*, published in 1817, some months before *Frankenstein*, would have been unthinkable to her. Hannah More revived one of her old characters from the 1790s, the demonic reformer Fanton, who now is made to renounce radicalism and to warn others of the monstrosities of rioting and sedition. Like Frederick Fenton in Walker's *The Vagabond*, More's Fanton is merely a vehicle for a sustained antirevolutionary and anti-utopian critique.

36. Elizabeth Gaskell, *Mary Barton*, ed. Myron F. Brightfield (New York, 1958), p. 162.

37. *Punch*, September 8, 1866, p. 103.

38. *Punch*, May 20, 1882, p. 235; see also Matt Morgan's "The Irish Frankenstein," *The Tomahawk*, December 18, 1869, reproduced in Thomas Milton Kemnitz, "Matt Morgan of *Tomahawk* and English Cartooning, 1867–1870," *Victorian Studies* XIX, no. 1 (September 1975): 31.

39. *Mary Shelley's Journal*, ed. Frederick L. Jones (Norman, Okla., 1947), p. 481.

2. *The Brummagem Frankenstein* (1866).
The *Punch* cartoon by Sir John Tenniel
(1820–1914) mocks the reformer John
Bright (1811–1889). Bright stutters,
"I have no fe-fe fear of Ma-Manhood
Suffrage," but is made more than uneasy
by the Brobdingnagian monster who
watches his steps.

3. *The Irish Frankenstein* (1882). Tenniel's
sarcastic inscription, purportedly an
"Extract from the Works of C. S. P-rn-ll,
M. P." (Charles Stewart Parnell, the Irish
nationalist leader), exploits the master-
slave inversion of Mary Shelley's novel:
"The hateful and blood-stained Monster
. . . yet was it not my Master to the very
extent that it was my Creature? . . . Had I
not breathed about my own spirit?"

If *Frankenstein*, too, contains a political critique, it does so by availing itself of a far more subtle confessional form. The dilemma of the Godwinian philosopher is seen from within. Godwin's own self-doubts, dramatized in his confessional romance *St. Leon* (1799), are revived in Victor and his creature. Like St. Leon, an alchemist who discovers an elixir of life that gives him immortality, Frankenstein is led to admit that his powers for melioration have resulted in anarchy and chaos. Each character bemoans the "fatal legacy" of his redemptive powers; each bemoans the deaths of others caused by his own neglect and malfeasance. St. Leon admits: "I possessed the secret of immortal life; but I looked upon myself as a monster that did not deserve to exist." When Frankenstein animates the "lifeless thing that lay at my feet" (p. 52), he must likewise confront self-loathing: "but now that I had finished, the beauty of the dream vanished, and breathless horror and disgust filled my heart" (pp. 52–53).

In *Frankenstein* Mary Shelley relies on political symbols to depict a psychological struggle. She could therefore animate what, in the political writings from which she drew her symbolism, had hardened into stereotype and rhetoric. Victor Frankenstein is more than a Godwinian theorist; the rebellious Monster, the offspring of utopian ideas, is more than the vindictive and "hideous phantom" envisioned by Burke. The earlier stereotypes are nonetheless encrusted in the novel. Like the monsters depicted in conservative writings, the nameless creature arises from the grave and perishes in flames. He acts out the apocalyptic paradigm when he destroys his formerly benevolent creator and consigns himself to a fiery holocaust. Mary Shelley can imagine a positive side to radical hopes for reform, yet she also sees their degeneration into carnage and disaster. Unlike the polemicists who assailed her father and the French Revolution, however, she can go beyond ideology, from the world at large to the quarrel within.

VIII

Vital Artifice: Mary, Percy, and the Psychopolitical Integrity of *Frankenstein*

PETER DALE SCOTT

T HE EXTRAORDINARY SCOPE of Mary Shelley's *Frankenstein* is attested to by the diversified labors of its critics. The Monster whom U. C. Knoepflmacher sees as an aggressive projection of Mary's childhood resentments emerges in Lee Sterrenburg's essay as an implicit critique of her father's political ideas. I shall argue that the book's greatness is precisely this fusion of the personal and the political, the private and the ideological. Yet I also hope to show that the conflicting feelings of resentment and love that Mary originally felt toward her father could only be articulated after transference to another insensitive but idealistic Utopian, her father's disciple, Percy Bysshe Shelley.

Percy helped Mary escape into the freedom of a premature adulthood. But his role as liberator was defective; Mary was soon forced to recognize old forces of sexually imbalanced oppression working through him. Thus I shall argue that the excessively ideological and masculine figure of Victor Frankenstein is modeled primarily, though not exclusively, on Percy Shelley, and that the motherless generation of the Monster symbolizes something at once political and intensely personal—the corrigible errors of her own experimental life with him. Her responses to both were not hostile but profoundly and creatively ambivalent, and ultimately open-minded.

Percy's Promethean vision of shaping new persons in new sexual relationships both inspired and disrupted the lives of the women around him. His powerful but erratic energy, marred by abstractness and eccentricity, affected Mary's life more deeply than his

own. It is no accident that Percy's early philosophical poems—
Queen Mab, Alastor, or *The Revolt of Islam*—should strike us as less
realized productions than the novel subtitled *The Modern Prometheus.* Percy was still distracted by ideas, many of them gathered
from outlandish and ponderous books. Mary's novel, though en-
riched by some of these ideas, crystallized around a shaping gift
from her own unconscious—her horrific but cathartic dream. Her
ambivalent reactions to that early flamboyantly experimental life
with Percy were jolted into dreams and then art by the traumatic
death of her first child.

Frankenstein does not merely confront, in the form of the Monster, the threat of dehumanizing alienation which attended the
Shelleys' vision of a revolutionary scientific spirit. Mary goes further: the rejected Monster whom she faced in herself, her husband,
and the age they lived in, is seen as "susceptible of love" (p. 217).
More soberly than Rousseau, Godwin, or Percy, her novel still reasserts, in the face of tragedy, the transcendent human potential
for change.

I

Two recent books[1] have made clear that Percy Shelley's perverse
virtues had their part in inspiring the obsessive character of Victor
Frankenstein, as well as that of his rejected *Doppelgänger.* It would
be wrong, in documenting this fact, to distinguish too sharply
between the personal reminiscences in *Frankenstein* of Percy, and
the philosophical or political echoes of his ideas. For better or
for worse, Percy tried to live his ideas, and to make others live
them too: there was artifice in his own projected life-style. This
followed from what in his preface to *Prometheus Unbound* he called
his own "passion for reforming the world," and what Mary later,
with less enthusiasm, would call his "abstract imagination."[2] Of
their first year of hectic convivial experiment together in a *ménage à
trois* Mary later noted: "it was acting a novel, being an incarnate
romance."[3]

1. Christopher Small, *Ariel Like a Harpy: Shelley, Mary and Frankenstein*
(London, 1972); Richard Holmes, *Shelley: The Pursuit* (London, 1974).
2. Percy Bysshe Shelley, *Poetical Works* (Boston, 1975), pp. 164, 161.
3. Claire Clairmont, *Journals,* ed. Marion Stocking (Cambridge, Mass.,
1968), p. 21.

In writing out her ambivalence towards Percy's libertarian scientism, Mary had to reconcile that part of herself that thought and felt like Percy with her own protofeminist resentment of him. In its drama of hyperintellectual men and overly passive women, her novel explores the paradox that the two modern intellects most admired by the professed sexual egalitarian Percy—Milton and Rousseau—are precisely the two who are criticized at length in *The Rights of Woman* for their subordination of women.[4] (In Safie, *Frankenstein* proffers an androgynously balanced corrective to Rousseau's docile, domestic, and affectionate Sophie, a figure reproved by Mary Wollstonecraft.) On an ideological level, then, one might say that "The Modern Prometheus" is a pendant to *Emile* and *La Nouvelle Héloise*. As Kate Ellis suggests in her contribution to this volume, Victor's abandonment of Elizabeth for a male-oriented course of study "weaken[s] . . . his domestic affections"[5] and thus underscores the tragic consequences of an imperfect sexual balance in self and society.

All this is not, of course, to ignore the great mythic innovation of the frightful but sympathetic man-made Monster. On the political level, the Monster, as Lee Sterrenburg points out, acts as an emblem of the revolutionary ideas which radicals like Mary Wollstonecraft viewed as an "experiment in political science."[6] Wollstonecraft repeatedly alluded to the "monsters" brought forth by that convulsion, even though her purpose was always to prove that, despite "acts of ferocious folly . . . the people are essentially good" and had only been "rendered ferocious by misery" (I: 71). Her daughter's

4. Mary Wollstonecraft, *A Vindication of the Rights of Woman*, ed. Helen Poston (New York, 1975), pp. 20 ff.

5. Mary Wollstonecraft Shelley, *Frankenstein; Or, The Modern Prometheus* (the 1818 text), ed. James Rieger (Indianapolis and New York, 1974), cited in the text by page number: "the little Elizabeth . . . shewed signs even then of a *gentle and affectionate* disposition . . . and a desire to bind as closely the ties of domestic love. . . . She was *docile* and good-tempered . . ." (p. 51). Cf. Wollstonecraft: "Gentleness, docility, and a spaniel-like affection are, on this ground, consistently recommended as the cardinal virtues of the sex" (*A Vindication of the Rights of Woman,*" p. 34).

6. Mary Wollstonecraft, *An Historical and Moral View of the Origin and Progress of the French Revolution; and the Effect It Has Produced in Europe* (London, 1795), I:13. While Wollstonecraft is writing here about the "practical success" of the American Revolution's effort to establish a government "on the basis of reason and equality," the French Revolution is in this respect comparable.

Monster echoes these beliefs; "misery made me a fiend," he insists (p. 95).[7] On a more personal level, then, the Monster's rebellious outbursts stem from resentments very similar to those nurtured by Percy and Mary, both of whom were obsessed with, and rejected by, their fathers.

Percy's most recent biographer, Richard Holmes, has noted how the poet, in his review of Mary's book, implicitly accepted the identification of the Monster's "malevolence and selfishness" with his own waywardness as Sir Timothy's rejected son:

In this the direct moral of the book consists. . . . Treat a person ill and he will become wicked. . . . It is thus that too often in society, those who are best qualified to be its benefactors and its ornaments, are branded by some accident with scorn, and changed by solitude of heart into a scourge and curse.[8]

Characteristically, Percy does not write as if he had been the initiating agent of rejection, only as the victim.

Yet Percy is first of all Victor. "Victor" was the pseudonym Percy chose on publishing his first volume of childhood poems—along with the productions of his sister Elizabeth, whose namesake in the novel is Victor Frankenstein's cousin and playmate "or rather his sister" (p. 79).[9] The victimized and isolated Monster, on the other hand, can be taken to represent Mary as well as Percy. He also symbolizes the artifice of their innovative and problematic life to-

7. Years later, when Mary would no longer admit any ambivalence about her dead husband, and when "Frankenstein's monster" had entered the vocabulary of political reaction, Mary reverted to a more simple and classical notion of *hubris*. She wrote in her 1831 Preface to *Frankenstein* that "supremely frightful would be the effect of any human endeavour to mock the stupendous mechanism of the Creator" (p. 228). Victor is made to see his tragedy more fatalistically: "Chance—or rather the evil influence, the Angel of Destruction, which asserted omnipotent sway over me from the moment I turned my reluctant steps from my father's door" (p. 240). But the slow genesis of the Monster's hatred, in the 1818 edition, is a matter not of tragic predestination but of missed opportunity, unsustained purpose, and love denied.

8. Percy Bysshe Shelley, "On *Frankenstein*," in *The Complete Works of Percy Bysshe Shelley*, ed. Roger Ingpen and Walter E. Peck (New York, 1965), hereafter cited in text as *Works*, VI:264.

9. Percy is said once to have fainted on reading the lines comparing the Ancient Mariner (quoted in *Frankenstein* at p. 54) to one who "Doth walk in fear and dread / Because he knows a frightful fiend / Doth close behind him tread" (Small, pp. 101, 158).

gether, a vital artifice that offered hopes of a new age while it had also become guiltily associated in Mary's mind with the death of their premature first child. Victor Frankenstein's irresoluteness, which leads him first to promise and then to deny a spouse to his creation, is a key to the tragedy, and is likewise attributable to an ideologue's insufficient awareness of human nature. Mary Shelley depicted this blend of fitful irresolution and abstract rhetoric with compassionate intensity, for they were qualities she had come to know in her own husband.

The Victor Frankenstein who is cured by experiments with lightning of his eccentric love for Cornelius Agrippa, Albertus Magnus, and Paracelsus (p. 35) is clearly modeled on the pale atheist at Oxford, the young Percy who (according to his friend T. J. Hogg) purchased "treatises on magic and witchcraft, as well as those modern ones detailing the miracles of electricity and galvanism." [10] Victor, like Percy, is dominated by his first love for his "playmate" Elizabeth; yet he leaves her to travel because, like Dante's Ulysses, he "ardently desired the acquisition of knowledge" (p. 40).

Ingolstadt, on the other hand, alludes not to Percy's life but to his ideas, for it is the place where in May 1776 the secret revolutionary conspiracy of the Illuminati had been founded by Dr. Adam Weishaupt. This Masonic brotherhood, according to the compendious four-volume history of Jacobinism by the French émigré Abbé Augustin Barruel, was dedicated to the destruction of private property, religion, and "superstitious" social forms such as marriage (*Shelley: The Pursuit*, p. 52). The Abbé Barruel expected that the mere exposure of this litany of antinomian ideas would shock foreigners, and particularly the Anglo-Saxons, into outraged reaction; indeed, his *Memoirs* still have some currency among the American radical right. But as is well known they had the opposite effect on the young Oxonian Percy Bysshe Shelley, who found them a convenient index of the very ideas on marriage and society, the personal and the political, that he would later weave into *Queen Mab*.

On reading Barruel in 1810 Shelley's immediate response was characteristically impulsive and improvident: a defiant show of atheism that led indirectly to his being sent down from Oxford. In his first letter to Leigh Hunt, then a stranger, Shelley proposed an

10. Thomas Jefferson Hogg, *The Life of Percy Bysshe Shelley* (London, 1858), I:58; quoted by Holmes, p. 24.

association, analogous to Illuminism, which might work for "rational liberty" rather than "the visionary schemes of a completely-equalized community" (*Shelley: The Pursuit*, p. 52).

In 1812, Shelley dabbled briefly in this utopian fantasy, to the alarm of his new mentor William Godwin. Writing in 1810 to his one close friend, Hogg, Shelley revealed passions more violently reminiscent of the Monster's vows:

Oh! I burn with impatience for the moment of Xtianity's dissolution, it has injured me; I swear on the altar of perjured love [here Percy refers to his rejection by his cousin Harriet Grove, but his resentment against his father and whole family situation is unmistakable] to revenge myself on the hated cause of the effect which *even now* I can scarcely help deploring.—Indeed I think it is to the benefit of society to destroy the opinions which can annihilate the dearest of its ties. . . . Adieu—Ecrasez l'infame ecrasez l'impie.[11]

The closing words are of course Voltaire's, but as a call to action they were (at least in the imagination of Barruel and his young readers Shelley and Hogg) the watchword of the Illuminati. It is unlikely that Mary Shelley ever saw this letter, but she had seen and heard only too much of her husband's bursts of rage and revenge in the name of love. Indeed her Monster's oaths of vengeance ("I vowed eternal hatred and vengeance to all mankind" [p. 138]) seem far less rhetorical than some of her husband's parricidal gesturings in real life:

Yet here I swear, and as I break my oath may Infinity Eternity blast me, here I swear that never will I forgive Christianity! . . . Oh how I wish I *were* the Antichrist, that it were *mine* to crush the Demon, to hurl him to his native Hell never to rise again. . . .[12]

This self-absorption in one's sense of grievance, even more visible in Victor Frankenstein than in his Monster, is akin also to the "selfish" grief for which Mary castigated herself in her autobiographical novel *Mathilda*. Her reactions to Percy's self-absorption

11. Percy Bysshe Shelley, *Letters*, ed. Frederick L. Jones (Oxford, 1964), I:27.

12. Shelley, *Letters*, I:35. Mary must undoubtedly have heard outbursts from Percy like that in a letter of March 6, 1816, to her father William Godwin: "Do not talk of *forgiveness* again to me, for my blood boils in my veins, and my gall rises against all that bears the human form, when I think of what I, their benefactor and ardent lover, have endured of enmity and contempt from you and from all mankind" (*Letters*, I:459).

must soon have been extremely ambivalent. The intensity of their early relationship seems to have owed much to their shared sense of alienation and rejection ("I detest Mrs. G[odwin]," Mary wrote in October 1814, and the thought can hardly have been a new one) from family dramas in which there were also strong incestuous side-currents. (Percy wrote in verse to Mary at this time that she offered him an awakening from a life of cursing and "the soul's mute rage," while he tried to interest his wife Harriet in Mary's "sufferings, & the tyranny which is exercised on her.")

But from the first, as in the notorious suicide proposal, it seems to have been Percy who indulged his fantasies, Mary who restrained them. The elopement itself, during which Percy revived his dormant Promethean visions, probably does not deserve to be described as "in every way a disaster" (p. xiv); but undeniably it also suffered, as their marriage would later, from Percy's geographical and sexual restlessness. In particular Jane ("Claire") Clairmont (the daughter and reminder of the detested Mrs. G.) was a source of tension from the beginning, encouraging both Percy to experiment and Mary to withdraw toward the more domestic aspect of her divided make-up—a nostalgia that we know in her from her early dependence on the Baxter family in Scotland, and also from the eulogy of family tranquillity in *Frankenstein*.

The polarities in the novel between civil injustice at home and disastrous private experiments abroad reflect the tensions of that first year together, as do the Monster's homelessness and his sensitivity in his inadequate hovel to the passage of the seasons. Even Walton's abandonment of his "great purpose" of finding some paradisal Ultima Thule beyond the Arctic ice—a recurring fantasy of Percy's early epics (*Poetical Works*, pp. 19, 59, 618)—reflects the Shelleys' absurd moment of truth in the wintry rains of Lake Lucerne: only three days after arriving at their intended destination, they abandoned it, and decided not to head on over the frozen Alps to Italy but to return home.

Most laughable to think [wrote Claire] of our going to England the second day after we entered a new house for six months—All because the stove don't suit.[13]

The flippant tone of this entry suggests that the stove would not have been Claire's problem—let alone Percy's.

13. Claire Clairmont, *Journals*, p. 31; Holmes, p. 247; cf. *Works*, VI:104.

At this stage Mary was still more creature than creator; she was still the young woman who wrote in her copy of *Queen Mab* that the book was "sacred" to her, and that she loved the author "beyond all power of expression" (*Shelley: The Pursuit*, p. 232). Though the abstract, indeed the escapist, aspects of Percy's communitarian philanthropy were beginning to shrivel up her own, she was still willing not only to study Percy's ideas but to help put them into practice. The journals of Mary and Claire record that, for the four days preceding the abrupt decision to return home, the three of them had been reading Percy's cherished copy of Barruel. Frustrated in his earlier efforts at political organization in Ireland, Shelley's interests were shifting toward more intimate, erotic notions of fellowship for a select radical vanguard—the intimacy of the early idylls with his sister Elizabeth at Field House now recreated as part of a plan for human enlightenment.

Barruel's account of the Illuminist and incestuous infanticide Weishaupt ("like the sinister owl . . . which glides in the shadow of the night, this baleful Sophist will be remembered in history only as the Demon"[14]) offers many reasons why his University of Ingolstadt should be presented in *Frankenstein* as the antithesis to Victor's domestic happiness with his playmate Elizabeth in Geneva. The Illuminati wished to deny family love and to replace it with universal love (III:129)—just as Victor forgets his family while eagerly pursuing the "undertaking" that might endear him to an entire "new species." There was even a proposal to create two orders of Illuminist women—one of bluestockings, the other of *femmes volages* "to satisfy those Brothers with a penchant for pleasure" (III:29)—though Weishaupt rejected this proposal and restricted the higher secrets of his order (as Mary in her novel restricted Ingolstadt) to men alone.

Percy at least may have been interested in the rejected proposal —not only in his poetry but also in his own small community of women. In the chilling rain and mist at Brunnen, while encouraging Claire to study further in Barruel, Percy began with Mary's help to compose *The Assassins*, a romance about an isolated fellowship whose unwavering goal is to cause "at whatever expense, the greatest and most unmixed delight."

14. M. l'Abbé Barruel, *Mémoires pour servir à l'histoire du Jacobinisme* (Hamburg, 1803), III:2.

By the rapidity of their fervid imaginations . . . a new and sacred fire was kindled in their hearts. . . . They were already disembodied spirits; they were already the inhabitants of paradise. [*Works*, VI:160]

From his source-book Percy had read that the assassins inaugurated their mission of political terror and murder with one day of total sexual license, a fantasy which can be read into the rites of Liberty with which Cythna, in *The Revolt of Islam*, inaugurated her liberation of the city (*Shelley: The Pursuit*, p. 397). There is an echo of this paradisal fixation in the initial portrait of Walton, who is twice described (in an echo of Dante's Ulysses) as "ardent" in his desire for knowledge. Just as Percy in *Queen Mab* imagined a future "sweet" Arctic "of purest spirits" (vi.40), so Walton seeks an imaginary Ultima Thule where "snow and frost are banished" (p. 10)—a "region of beauty and delight" where "the sun is for ever visible" (p. 9). As Walton first writes to *his* "dear sister," "I feel my heart glow with an enthusiasm which elevates me to heaven" (pp. 9–10). Walton's renunciation of this fantasy can be seen as a judgment on the youthful Percy, one which, albeit more ambivalently, Percy had already made in his Preface to *Alastor*: "The Poet's self-centered seclusion was avenged by the furies of an irresistible passion pursuing him to speedy ruin" (*Poetical Works*, p. 33).

It is not clear what Mary thought in 1814 about the Assassins' mountain paradise of "love, friendship and philanthropy" (*Works*, VI:57).[15] But in her journal of the return journey down the Rhine the tone is clearly one not of philanthropy but of an emerging and possibly displaced anger toward her fellow-passengers; three years later she would admit this in a rhetoric far less egalitarian than her husband's:

Nothing could be more horribly disgusting than the lower order of smoking, drinking Germans . . . ; they swaggered and talked . . . and, what was hideous to English eyes, kissed one another. [*Works*, VI:109).[16]

15. What appears in Mary's journal as collaboration ("We arrange our apartment and write") was revealed by Mary in 1817 to have been more one-sided ("I wrote to his dictation"): Mary Shelley, *Journal*, ed. Frederick L. Jones (Norman, Okla.: University of Oklahoma Press, 1947), p. 11; Mary Shelley, *History of a Six Weeks' Tour* (London, 1817), in *Works*, VI:104.

16. Mary Shelley, *Journal*, p. 12: "We . . . surveyed at our ease the horrid and slimy faces of our companions in voyage . . . to which we might

As the three waited to cross the Channel, Percy returned to *The Assassins* without Mary's help. The stepsisters, who by now had Percy and each other very much on their minds, began their own stories. Claire's, about a misunderstood nonconformist, was called "Idiot"; all we know of Mary's is its intriguing title, "Hate."

The next seven months of exacerbated tensions and experimentation in the beleaguered Shelley household saw the crisis that engendered *Frankenstein*. As Ellen Moers shows, these tensions climaxed with Mary's guilt and nightmares after the death of her first baby ("Dream that my little baby came to life again, and that we rubbed it before the fire, and it lived"),[17] which so clearly anticipate her waking dream one year later of a "hideous phantasm" which she saw "show signs of life" (p. 228).

It was a time of separation. Mary, pregnant and increasingly bedridden, saw less and less of Percy, who, now hounded by avenging bailiffs for his unpaid debts, at one point could only visit his home on the legal holiday of Sunday. One thinks of the moment when Victor, now the slave of his creature, becomes engaged to Elizabeth and immediately, like Ulysses–Walton, departs on a two-year voyage for "knowledge and discoveries" (p. 149).

But Percy exploited this separation as a chance to test in real life his abstract political dreams of an expanded erotic community. He spent more and more time with Claire, whose journal of October 7, 1814, records the gradual build-up of undischarged energy:

Mary goes to Bed—Shelley & myself sit over the fire—we talk of making an Association of philosophical people [Percy's journal entry reads "subterraneous community of women"]. . . . at one the conversation turned upon those unaccountable & mysterious feelings about supernatural things that we are sometime subject to.

On October 18 she wrote (a partially deleted entry):

Mary goes to bed—Talk with Shelley over the fire till two—Hogg —his letter—friendship—Dante—Tasso & various other subjects.

Mary's own journal records, with perhaps exaggerated detachment, the extent to which Shelley and Claire were exciting each other with tales of supernatural terror. On at least one occasion

have addressed the Boatman's speech to Pope—"'Twere easier for God to make entirely new men than attempt to purify such monsters as these.'"

17. Mary Shelley, *Journal*, p. 41.

when Claire could not sleep for "thinking of ghosts," Percy counseled her to read his *Zastrozzi*, *Queen Mab*—and the Abbé Barruel (*Shelley: The Pursuit*, p. 261).

Soon Mary was developing some degree of erotic intimacy with Percy's old friend T. J. Hogg (whom he had first urged to fall in love with his sister Elizabeth and later involved with his first wife Harriet). Hogg had just published his novel, *Prince Alexy Haimatoff*, in a review of which Percy had expressed shock at the male chauvinism of the prince's tutor:

We cannot regard his commendation to his pupil to indulge in promiscuous concubinage without horror and detestation. . . . No man can rise pure from the poisonous embraces of a prostitute. . . . Whatever the advantages of simple and pure affections, these ties, these benefits are of equal obligation to either sex. [*Works*, VI:178–79]

Percy's abhorrence of prostitutes, at least, was sincere. From one he had probably once contracted a venereal disease, a clue not only to the sexual ambivalence and grey hair of *Alastor*, the *Revolt*, and *Epipsychidion*, but very possibly to complications now arising between Percy and his pregnant wife.[18] At any rate, Percy went on to praise Hogg's "new and unparalleled powers," adding, suggestively, "we think the interesting subject of sexual relations requires for its successful development the application of a mind thus organized and endowed" (*Works*, VI:181–82).

This review was written in the same week that Hogg returned to Percy's company. Soon afterwards, as "dear, dearest Alexy," he was becoming Mary's spiritual lover, and the recipient of letters that spoke ambiguously of an even more intimate future bliss:

that also will come in time & then we shall be happier, I do think, than the angels who sing for ever and ever, the lovers of Jane's [Claire's] world of perfection. [*Shelley: The Pursuit*, p. 278]

One senses that Mary may have valued Hogg, as in the next year she would value Byron, as a friend of Percy's who might bring him a little down to earth. Yet it is clear from her letters as from her

18. Thornton Hunt, "Shelley—by One Who Knew Him," *Shelley and Keats as They Struck Their Contemporaries*, ed. Edmund Blunden (London, 1925), pp. 30–31; quoted in K. N. Cameron, *The Young Shelley: Genesis of a Radical* (New York, 1950), p. 125.

journal that, as a woman (not to mention a pregnant woman) she was increasingly unhappy to be schooled in the manners of this intellectual and philanthropic *ménage à quatre*.

By April 1815 this build-up of tension led to a brief storm. Claire (now described in Mary's no longer discreet journal as "the lady" or "his friend") was sent away to Devonshire; Hogg (whom Mary would soon dislike) also disappeared, despite a written offer from Shelley at one point "to give you your share of our common treasure of which you have been cheated for several days" (*Shelley: The Pursuit*, p. 282). To three of Shelley's biographers this letter suggests strongly that Hogg's intimacy "had reached a sexual stage and that Mary, at least briefly, had been shared" (*Shelley: The Pursuit*, p. 282). Rieger, mindful that "the Shelleyan ménage derived its belief in erotic pluralism from Plato and Dante," believes that the fellowship "was physically monogamous at all times" (p. xv). Cameron notes judiciously that the air was heavy with discretion as well as flirtation.[19] The whole situation in early 1815 was perhaps almost as ambiguous to the four principals as it is to us, who can only wonder about those excisions from both women's journals.

Whatever the realities, they were more than Mary could cope with; the experiment in a new sexual politics was so far not a success. It was in the midst of these tensions that Mary's first baby girl was born two months prematurely, lived for twelve days, and then —after yet another of the Shelleys' restless moves—died one night at Mary's side. On the day of this appalling discovery Mary summoned Hogg ("you are so calm a creature and Shelley is afraid of a fever from the milk") and then "in the evening read *Fall of the Jesuits*" (*Shelley: The Pursuit*, p. 281). The title has never been identified; but once again the recipe for calming female nerves may have been Barruel.[20]

In this period it would hardly have been surprising if Mary had simply resented Percy as an ideological Prometheus with herself as his victim. Yet when their second daughter Clara died in 1818, a victim of Shelley's impetuous decision to rejoin his family with Byron in Venice, Mary clearly internalized the guilt. The second

19. Kenneth Neill Cameron, *Shelley: The Golden Years* (Cambridge, Mass., 1974), p. 26.

20. One chapter of the English translation has the subtitle "The Extinction of the Jesuits."

death was followed by a second and much less disguised novel, *Mathilda*, written in 1819, in which Percy appears as better than Prometheus and herself as a monster. Both descriptions are relevant:

Woodville [Percy]:
He was glorious from his youth. Every one loved him; no shadow of envy or hate cast even from the meanest mind ever fell upon him. He was, as one the peculiar delight of the Gods, railed and fenced in by his own divinity, so that nought but love and admiration could approach him. . . . It is one of the blessings of a moderate fortune, that by preventing the possessor from bestowing pecuniary favors it prevents him also from diving into the arcana of human weakness or malice—To bestow on your fellow men is a Godlike attribute—So indeed it is and as such not one fit for mortality;—the giver like Adam and Prometheus, must pay the penalty of rising above his nature by being the martyr to his own excellence. Woodville was free from all these evils; and if slight examples did come across him he did not notice them but passed on in his course as an angel with winged feet might glide along the earth unimpeded by all those little obstacles over which we of earthly origin stumble.

Mathilda [Mary]:
I believed myself to be polluted by [my father's] unnatural love I had inspired, and that I was a creature cursed and set apart by nature. I thought that like another Cain, I had a mark set on my forehead to shew mankind that there was a barrier between me and they [sic]. . . . Why when fate drove me to be come this outcast from human feeling; this monster with whom none might mingle in converse and love; why had she not from that fatal and most accursed moment, shrouded me in thick mists and placed real darkness between me and my fellows so that I might never more be seen?[21]

This polarization of the pair into angel and monster, neither of them human, reflects Mary's despondence of 1818–19, her loss of confidence in herself, and her distance from Percy, from which she, her marriage, and her art never really recovered. Both passages are psychologically complex but artistically oversimplified. We must turn to their biographies to remember that Mary resented and distrusted Percy (and Claire) for the very angelic unworldli-

21. Mary Wollstonecraft Shelley, *Mathilda*, ed. Elizabeth Nitchie (Chapel Hill, [1959]), pp. 55, 71.

ness she praised in Woodville; and that her father, who had already extracted £4,700 from his patron Percy, was writing nasty letters from London in which he encouraged Mary in her bitterness toward Percy in the hope of extorting still more money for himself. These powerful ambivalences hover near the misleading surface but are not articulated in *Mathilda*, just as Mary, at this stage, did not dare admit them to herself. The one artistic insight is when Mathilda (so named from Dante's *Purgatorio*, where she is the more humble terrestrial precursor of the celestial Beatrice) blames her monster-like alienation from human "converse and love" on nothing else than her own belief in her guilt—indeed, on her own self-condemnation for the guilt of others.[22]

Frankenstein brilliantly articulates the same ambivalences of guilt and anger that *Mathilda* suppresses. Written when Percy and Mary were still close, it does not simply contrast their personalities but also fuses them: there are aspects of Mary in the overly masculine Victor, as well as of both Mary and Percy in the suffering daemon. This was possible because, as Grylls has written, "in essentials Mary and [Percy] Shelley were at one."[23]

The creative richness of *Frankenstein* reflects Mary's relatively high spirits in 1816–17, when even her dreams could now recognize and confront (as in the dream of the revivified monster) rather than merely compensate for (as in the dream of the revivified baby) the horrors in her own subconscious and past. Mary was even more courageous in her ability to accept the monster-dream as a creative challenge, and hence to dive (as she later shrewdly wrote that Woodville–Percy could not) "into the arcana of human weakness or malice."[24] In this period her life was no longer a mere artifice

22. Compare the speech of Cythna which so angered John Taylor Coleridge in the *Quarterly Review*: "Reproach not thine own soul, but know thyself, / Nor hate another's crime, nor loathe thine own" (*Revolt of Islam*, VIII.22).

23. R. Glynn Grylls, *Mary Shelley: A Biography* (London, 1938), p. xvi. Small agrees (*Ariel Like a Harpy*, p. 12).

24. Mary later wrote in her journal for February 25, 1822, about this capacity for honest introspection: "let me, in my fellow creature, love that which is ... and, above all, let me fearlessly descend into the remotest caverns of my mind, carry the torch of self-knowledge into its deepest recesses: but too happy if I dislodge any evil spirit" (Mary Shelley, *Journal*, pp. 169–70). Mary may have had in mind Cythna's self-description in *The Revolt of Islam*, VII.31: "My mind became the book through which I

dominated by Percy's whims; she moved in the company of other men (Byron and Polidori) whose suspicions of Percy's utopianism reinforced her own.

Percy of course was not incapable of self-confrontation, but he was clearly less willing to go so far in pursuing it:

> Thine own soul still is true to thee,
> But changed to a foul fiend through misery.
>
> This fiend, whose ghastly presence ever
> Beside thee like thy shadow hangs,
> Dream not to chase;—the mad endeavor
> Would scourge thee to severer pangs.
> Be as thou art. Thy settled fate,
> Dark as it is, all change would aggravate.
>
> [*Poetical Works*, p. 351]

This interesting poem, published just before Mary wrote *Frankenstein*, casts light not only on the absence of psychological realism and self-knowledge in his early poetry, but on his failure to validate poetically the vision of change on which in life he set such store. What Mary had learnt from her dreams Percy continued to read about in books.[25]

II

One could compare at length the two major works produced by the Shelleys in 1817: *Frankenstein* and *The Revolt of Islam*. Seemingly disparate, each work deals with the complementary themes of despair and revenge, now denounced by Percy as the forces in history that obstruct the triumph of justice and love (*Poetical Works*, p. 85, cf. pp. 81, 163). Each work, based on earlier models of Gothic

grew / Wise in all human wisdom, and its cave, / Which like a mine I rifled through and through, / To me the keeping of its secrets gave—" (to be contrasted with Percy's own pedantic "knowledge from forbidden mines of lore," *To Mary* — —, v). Both cave images derive from St. Augustine's *Confessions*, bk. X, chap. 17.

25. For an independent corroboration of Shelley's inability to recreate his own dreamwork poetically, cf. Alethea Hayter, *Opium and the Romantic Imagination* (Berkeley and Los Angeles, 1968), pp. 77–78: "Shelley's visionary powers, extraordinary as they were, do not seem to have included the experience of remembered imaginative dreams in normal sleep."

revenge tales, narrates a story of vengeful carnage contrasted with love, climaxing with the death of the protagonists but not ending there.

In each work the heroine is an orphan who falls in love with her childhood friend; in the *Revolt* this orphan (like Mary, to whose "young wisdom" the poem is dedicated with Percy's most intimate and self-revealing praise) then gives birth to a child that is soon taken away, leaving the mother with swollen breasts (*Revolt of Islam*, VII.22–24).[26] In each work the hero (like Percy) is schooled by a gentle tutor, who teaches "doctrines of human power," and accompanied by a male friend, for whom the models are Dr. Lind (Percy's tutor at Eton) and T. J. Hogg. Each work is cast on a global scale, and even introduced by a narrator who tells of his own voyage through "mountains of ice" (*Revolt of Islam*, I.47; *Frankenstein*, pp. 204, 211) toward a paradise beyond the polar seas.

Each work, on a more philosophical level, attributes the madness of its protagonists to the brutality of the world. (Special condemnations are reserved for judicial institutions, which at this time were so harassing the family arrangements of the Shelleys.) Each work sees the human condition as one of alienation brought about by a satanic dialectic in which "ill has become their good" (*Revolt of Islam*, IV.26; cf. *Frankenstein*, p. 218). Nevertheless, each work, incorporating the historical perspectives of Volney's *Ruins*, is structured so as to suggest that human nature, at bottom benevolent and meliorable as Rousseau described it, may in the end transcend this historical alienation.[27]

Above all, each work, when studied closely, makes the free and equal reunion of the sexes and their attributes the key to liberation and order in both self and society. In Laon's words

> Well with this world art thou unreconciled;
> Never will peace and human nature meet
> Till free and equal man and woman greet
> Domestic peace. . . .
>
> [*Revolt of Islam*, II.37]

26. Mary Godwin to T. J. Hogg, March 6, 1815, in *Shelley and His Circle 1773–1822*, ed. K. N. Cameron (New York, 1961), III:453.

27. Volney's *Ruines*, "the book from which Felix instructed Safie," is summarized in *Frankenstein* at pp. 114–15; cf. K. N. Cameron, "A Major Source of *The Revolt of Islam*," *PMLA*, LVI (1941): 175–206; *Shelley: The Golden Years*, pp. 315–26.

Each work views its present in the light of William Godwin's eighteenth-century commonplace that in our culture the male sex "is accustomed more to the exercise of its reasoning powers" and that women, "in proportion as they receive a less intellectual education, are more unreservedly under the empire of feeling" (cf. also Ellis, above, p. 135). Though Percy's handling of sexuality in the *Revolt* would justify an entire essay, what emerges is almost an equality by reversal. Reiman somewhat oversimplifies when he writes that "Cythna, the feminine member, embodies the power of knowledge and reason, whereas Laon embodies forgiving love."[28] But he correctly underlines the symbolic importance of their androgynous reunion, which anticipates that of Prometheus and Asia in *Prometheus Unbound*.

Thus we see in the *Revolt* an ironic sexual reversal of the polarity in *Frankenstein*: Percy's Laon is as fatally passive as Mary's Elizabeth, so that the personal salvation of each is in the hands of the opposite sex. Each work is made more interesting by the personal self-doubt that lurks beneath the surface of philosophical optimism (through love such sexual one-sidedness may be transcended); and more interesting also by the author's ability to identify to some degree with his character (and partner) of the opposite sex. Thus Cythna the saving heroine draws some of her good qualities, such as her introspective wisdom (*Revolt of Islam*, VII.31), from Mary, while her characteristic Shelleyan self-pity (IX.31) is Percy's own.[29] But in her philosophical role she owes not a little to Dante's Beatrice: as a "prophetess of Love" who "will fill / The world, like light" (IX.20, VIII.16), her fellowship is of "the purest and the best" hearts (IX.9), while her "smile was Paradise" (IX.36).

It may seem farfetched to compare Mary's popular and unaffected contemporary novel with the historical epic couched by Percy in awkward Spenserian stanzas. My point is to suggest the

28. Donald H. Reiman, *Percy Bysshe Shelley* (New York, 1969), p. 60. Reiman overlooks the countervailing trend in the poem by which Cythna is "the prophetess of Love" (*Revolt of Islam*, IX.20), and "Love when Wisdom fails makes Cythna wise" (IX.34).

29. For Mary, cf. supra at note 23. Holmes notes Percy's own "mood of martyrdom and self-sacrifice" while writing this poem, citing a letter of September 24, 1817, to Byron: "As to me, I can but die; I can but be torn to pieces, or devoted to infamy most undeserved . . ." (*Shelley: The Pursuit*, p. 377; *Letters*, I:557).

developing intellectual stimulation and encouragement between Mary and Percy during that productive year at Marlow in 1817. The works seem to indicate that both authors had had occasion to reconsider, without wholly rejecting, their earlier more experimental attitudes toward love and society, and that the tragedy of the lost child rested in Percy's imagination as well as Mary's. Thus it is not fanciful to suggest that each work may have been influenced to some degree by the other; and hence that the high-minded ideas of Percy's ambitious but bookish epic are, not surprisingly, found to some degree in Mary's more modest novel, the story that originated in a dream and was aimed at that wide public which Percy (in his preface and dedicatory verses) confessed he wished to reach but was not likely to.

Despite its occasional immaturities of structure and style, *Frankenstein* succeeds where the *Revolt* fails; the novel can be studied closely for its settled and insightful vision not only of the monstrous in the human psyche and society, but also of the means for amendment. From the germ of Mary's personal difficulties with those ideas and shortcomings of Percy that had so transformed her life, she expanded her holistic consciousness to a hopeful critique of civilization and its discontents. Essentially a feminist critique, *Frankenstein* locates the initial error of Victor and Walton in excessive "masculinity" and insensitivity to feeling, and ultimately leaves Walton conscious of that error's consequences. The symbolism works as well on the cultural level as on the personal, because Mary was able to expand her own personal responses to a dominating father, absent mother, and imbalanced husband into a compassionate study of an overly masculine society and its offspring. One might even say that the novel describes Victor's fall as Androgyny Lost, and that it at least offers the prospect of an Androgyny Regained.

Victor himself admits his share of "blame" (p. 51) to Walton in terms of a voyage which leads to inner psychological disequilibrium and loss, from which the whole course of civilization has suffered:

I pursued my undertaking with unremitting *ardour*. My cheek had grown pale with study. . . . A resistless, and almost frantic impulse, *urged me forward*; I seemed to have lost all soul or sensation but for this one pursuit. . . . My father . . . was justified in conceiving that I should not be altogether free from blame. . . . If the study to which you apply yourself has a tendency to *weaken your affections*, and to destroy your taste for those simple *pleasures* in which no alloy can possibly mix, then that study is certainly unlawful, that is to say, not befitting the human mind. If this rule were always observed; if no man allowed any pursuit whatsoever to interfere with the *tranquillity of his domestic affections*, Greece had not been enslaved; Caesar would have spared his country; America would have been discovered more gradually; and the empires of Mexico and Peru had not been destroyed. [Pp. 49–51; emphasis added]

Five years later Percy, in the *Defence of Poetry*, would himself criticize that pursuit of science, unrestrained by the imagination, which in turn contributed to political tyranny:

We want the creative faculty to imagine that which we know. . . . The cultivation of those sciences which have enlarged the limits of the empire of man over the external world has, for want of the poetical faculty, proportionally circumscribed those of the internal world; and man, having enslaved the elements, remains himself a slave. . . . The rich have become richer and the poor have become poorer, and the vessel of state is driven between the Scylla and Charybdis of anarchy and despotism. Such are the effects which must ever flow from an unmitigated exercise of the calculating faculty. [*Works*, VI:134, 132]

But apparently Percy did not perceive this psychic imbalance in androgynous terms, nor attribute it, like Mary, to weakened "domestic affections."[30] That imbalance is stressed in Victor's repeated and precise definition of his Percy-like restlessness:

I ardently desired the acquisition of knowledge. I had often, when at home, thought it hard to remain during my youth cooped up in one place. . . . Learn from me . . . how dangerous is the acquirement of knowledge, and how much happier that man is who believes his native town to be the world, than he who aspires to become greater than his nature will allow . . . . [Pp. 40, 48]

30. This is not the only place in this protofeminist novel where "domestic affections" may be given a more positive value than Kate Ellis indicates. The well-balanced Safie, "accustomed to grand ideas," exhibits "the simplest and tenderest affections" (pp. 119–20); her guitar performance in the cottage, at the feet of the elder De Lacey, almost anticipates the Victorian drawing room (p. 113). In like manner the Monster is made more sensitive by the "gentle and domestic manners . . . combined with lofty sentiments and feelings" that he and the De Laceys encounter in the *Sorrows of Werter* (p. 123).

The one-sidedness of male exploratory reason is dramatized by the symbolic death of Victor's mother at the moment of his departure for Ingolstadt; subsequently those whose rejections will so deprave his creature—Victor, William, the three De Laceys, Safie—will all be presented to us as motherless. Thus the tragedy is by no means as inscrutable as critics like Small suggest:

What went wrong? Within the Godwinian scheme . . . it is extremely difficult to answer. Frankenstein has suffered no deprivation, on the contrary he has been doted on, and his upbringing . . . approaches the Rousseau-Godwin ideal . . . .[31]

One answer Small overlooks, the loss of a mother, is both Mary's obsession and that of the novel, where one-sided patriarchy and intellectual domination are presented as not just Victor's condition, but Western culture's.

Victor's moral self-portrait reiterates that of the orphaned Walton at the outset of the novel, who also needs "affection enough for me to endeavour to regulate my mind" (p. 14):

I shall satiate my ardent curiosity with the sight of the world never before visited. . . . These are my enticements, and they are sufficient to conquer all fear of danger or death . . . I have read with ardour the accounts of the various voyages which have been made in the prospect of arriving at the North Pacific Ocean. . . . These volumes were my study day and night. . . . Do I not deserve to accomplish some great purpose? . . . My courage and my resolution is [sic] firm; but my hopes fluctuate, and my spirits are often depressed . . . . [Pp. 10–12]

Thus both men, as Victor seems to recognize at their first encounter, are voyagers after knowledge after the model of Dante's Ulysses, and with the same psychological imbalance:

You seek for knowledge and wisdom as I once did; and I ardently hope that the gratification of your wishes may not be a serpent to sting you, as mine has been. [P. 24]

Like the Victor who left behind his "amiable companions" in Geneva and set out on a solitary journey because he "ardently desired the acquisition of knowledge," so too Dante's Ulysses defines his obsession in terms of a willful rejection of domestic feelings and bonds:

31. Small, *Ariel Like a Harpy*, pp. 65–66.

Not fondness (*dolcezza*) for a son, nor piety (*pieta*) towards an aged father, nor the due love (*amore*) which should have made Penelope happy, could conquer in me the *ardor* (*ardore*) I had to gain experience of the world and of the vices and worth of men; and I put forth on the open deep with but one ship.   [*Inferno*, xxvi.94–101]

Dante makes Ulysses note his rejection of those very qualities (*dolcezza, pieta, amore*) which mark the more feminine grace offered by Beatrice and the *dolce stil novo*, and by responding to which Dante (unlike Ulysses) will succeed in reaching paradise. Analogously, Victor notes how he turned his back both on Elizabeth and (in the 1831 edition) on his father ("the Angel of Destruction . . . asserted omnipotent sway over me from the moment I turned my reluctant steps from my father's door" [p. 240]) and ultimately rejected the appeal of his *Doppelgänger* son.

When Mary has Victor see in his own character the defect that enslaved Greece, Rome, and America (p. 51), she is adding to the psychological insight of Dante the historical insight of Volney. The Monster himself tells us how Volney's *Ruins*

gave me an insight into the manners, governments, and religions of the different nations of the earth. I heard of the slothful Asiatics; of the stupendous genius and mental activity of the Grecians; of the wars and wonderful virtue of the early Romans—of their subsequent degeneration. . . . I heard of the discovery of the western hemisphere, and wept with Safie over the hapless fate of its original inhabitants . . . . [Pp. 114–15]

This suggests that Mary was particularly intrigued by the chapter in which Volney attributed cultural decay to political despotism, and despotism to paternal tyranny:

Paternal tyranny laid the foundation of political despotism. . . . In every savage and barbarous state, the father, the chief of the family, is a despot, and a cruel and insolent despot. The wife is his slave, the children his servants. . . . It is remarkable, that parental authority is great accordingly as the government is despotic. China, India, and Turkey are striking examples of this. . . . In opposition to this the Romans will be cited; but it remains to be proved that the Romans were men truly free; and their quick passage from their republican despotism to their abject servility under the emperors, gives room at least for considerable doubts as to that freedom . . . .[32]

32. M. [Constantin François] Volney, *The Ruins, or, A Survey of the Revolutions of Empires* (London, 1857), p. 35n.

The master-slave relationship produces in the people "a state of depression and despair, out of which arise both "gloomy and misanthropic systems of religion" (of the type abominated by Percy) and an irresolute other-worldliness in man (of the type that Mary reproved in Percy and delineated in Victor):

The states of opulent Asia become enervated. . . . To appease [the despotic gods] man offered the sacrifice of all his enjoyments. . . . he endeavoured to cherish a passion for pain, and to renounce self-love. . . . But as provident nature had endowed the heart of man with inexhaustible hope, perceiving his desires disappointed of happiness here, he pursued it elsewhere: by a sweet illusion, he formed to himself another country, an asylum, where, out of the reach of tyrants, he should regain all his rights. Hence a new disorder arose. Smitten with his imaginary world, man despised the world of nature: for chimerical hopes he neglected the reality. . . . A sacred sloth then established itself in the world. . . . Thus, agitated by their own passions, men . . . have been themselves the eternal instruments of their misfortunes.[33]

By thus fusing Dante's portrait of the sexually imbalanced psyche with Volney's portrait of a sexually imbalanced society, Mary elevates her portrait of Victor beyond personal observations of Percy into a feminist critique of her age. The Victor whose dreams were "undisturbed by reality" (p. 34), who like Percy was obsessed with the "raising of ghosts" (p. 34), who resented having to "exchange chimeras of boundless grandeur for realities of little worth" (p. 41)—this caricature of her husband was at the same time Volney's exemplar of man under patriarchal despotism. Far more than either Dante's Ulysses or Volney's slave, Mary's Victor is a study in what Fromm would later call a social character.

In depicting a hero who would solemnize his engagement to Elizabeth and in the same breath announce his departure for two years in search of knowledge, Mary elevated her personal frustrations with Percy to the level of a cultural critique. But she also shows that science need not be so alienated from affection: besides the "gruff," "repulsive," and dogmatic Krempe (shades of the Illuminist Weishaupt) there is the good scientist Waldman (modeled, like Laon's hermit, on Dr. Lind), "whose gentleness was never tinged by dogmatism" (p. 45). Victor (the bad Percy) has also his friend Clerval (the ideal Percy), whose "imagination was too vivid

33. *Ibid.*, pp. 40–42.

for the minutiae of science" (p. 64), who drew Victor away from Ingolstadt, and "in imitation of the Persian and Arabic writers . . . invented tales of wonderful fancy and passion" (p. 66). "How different from the *manly* and heroical poetry of Greece and Rome," comments Victor (again echoing Dante) on the more romantic passions of Clerval's favored "orientalists" (p. 64).

Victor is temporarily healed by Clerval's influence, which unfortunately has come too late:

Study had before secluded me from the intercourse of my fellow-creatures, and *rendered me unsocial*; but Clerval called forth the *better feelings of my heart*; he again taught me to love the aspect of nature, and the cheerful faces of children. Excellent friend! how sincerely did you love me. . . . A selfish pursuit had cramped and narrowed me, until your gentleness and affection warmed and opened my senses; I became the same happy creature who, a few years ago, loving and beloved by all, had no sorrow or care. [P. 65]

It is not the "yielding" Elizabeth but Clerval who represents both a more androgynously balanced temperament, and the counterweight to the excessively Ulyssean Victor:

He was a being formed in the very "poetry of nature." His wild and enthusiastic imagination was chastened by the sensibility of his heart. His soul overflowed with ardent affections, and his friendship was of that devoted and wondrous nature that the worldly-minded teach us to look for only in the imagination. [Pp. 153–54]

Victor rightly sees in Clerval not an opposite, but the "image of my former self" (p. 155); and Mary seems to have envisaged him as an idealized Percy, more "devoted and wondrous" in his friendship than her unpredictable husband.

Mary nicely adumbrated these differences between the two characters by their preferences for landscape: the solitary Frankenstein (whose name is translatable as "open rock") inclines to the "awful and majestic" scenery of Mont Blanc; the sociable and agreeable Clerval ("clear valley"), to the cultivated valley of the Rhine.[34] Victor says that the Montanvert glacier on Mont Blanc

filled me with a sublime ecstacy that gave wings to the soul, and allowed it to soar from the obscure world to light and joy. . . . I

34. "Clerval" also echoes the famous French monastery Claravallium or Clairvaux, a center of medieval culture. The equilibrated Clerval is thus

determined to go alone, for . . . the presence of another would destroy the solitary grandeur of the scene. [P. 92]

In contrast to this lofty escapism (revealing, in its last clause, another hint of Mary's resentments about her marriage),[35] Clerval explicitly prefers the peopled landscape of the Rhine, which Mary herself now remembered (despite those dreadful fellow-passengers) as "the loveliest paradise on earth" (*Works*, VI.109). "The mountains of Switzerland," says Clerval,

are more majestic and strange; but there is a charm in the banks of this divine river, that I never before saw equalled. Look at that castle which overhangs yon precipice; and that also on the island, almost concealed amongst the foliage of those lovely trees; and now that group of labourers coming from among their vines; and that village half-hid in the recess of the mountain. Oh, surely, the spirit that inhabits or guards this place has a soul more in harmony with man, than with those who [sic] pile the glacier, or retire to the inaccessible peaks.[36] [P. 153]

The imagery here is drawn partly from Mary's own memories, partly from Canto III of *Childe Harold's Pilgrimage* (with its "blending of . . . foliage, crag, wood, cornfield, mountain, vine, / And chiefless castles"), which Byron completed at Lake Leman in July 1816, in the company of the Shelleys. Indeed the description in the next paragraph of Clerval as a being "formed in the very poetry of nature"—Leigh Hunt's line in praise of the incestuous-adulterous Paolo Malatesta—reinforces our suspicion that there is more than a hint of Mary's oddly perceived friend Lord Byron in Clerval, and perhaps in the sister-loving, child-rejecting figure of Frankenstein himself.[37]

---

the analogue of the unaffected, down-to-earth Waldman ("Forester"), as contrasted to the overeducated and artificial Krempe ("Hatbrim").

35. Mary was allowed to accompany her husband to the Montanvert glacier, where Percy was infuriated by the presence of some English tourists; but the day before, when Percy visited the Boisson glacier, "Mary and Cla[i]re remained at home" (*Letters*, I:498).

36. Compare: "We saw . . . craggy cliffs crowned by desolate towers, and wooded islands, whose picturesque ruins peeped from behind the foliage. . . . We heard the songs of the vintagers . . . memory . . . presents this part of the Rhine to my remembrance as the loveliest paradise on earth" (*History of a Six Weeks' Tour, Works*, VI:109).

37. Mary reread Canto III with deep emotion right after finishing

More important to the structure of the novel, however, is the recapitulation in Clerval's speech of the Shelleys' life-restoring return down the Rhine to England, after that chilly moment of choice on Lake Lucerne. Clerval's speech, like Mary's own *History*, explicitly remembers that lake as a place of sexual transgression and death.

I have visited the lakes of Lucerne and Uri, where the snowy mountains descend almost perpendicularly to the water, casting black and impenetrable shades. . . . I have seen this lake agitated by a tempest . . . and the waves dash with fury the base of the mountain, where the priest and his mistress were overwhelmed by an avalanche, and where their dying voices are still said to be heard.[38] [P. 153]

Was Mary here mindful of her own illicit liaison with Percy? Certainly Clerval's speech, like her *History*, associates the voyage to England down the Rhine with a restored pastoral "harmony" and "tranquillity"—a harmony denied to those who, like Victor, or like Napoleon in the *Childe Harold* passage, "retire to the inaccessible peaks." Mary thus prepares the reader for Walton's ultimate rejection of the Arctic's "excessive" cold and "mountains of ice" in favor of "dear England."

Though identifying the excessively intellectual and grandiose as the key to cultural alienation, Mary avoids seeking the corrective in a purely domestic realm. On the contrary, women like Justine and Elizabeth, as Kate Ellis and U. C. Knoepflmacher have shown, are likewise criticized for a feminine passivity that suffers male injustice and fails to restore balance. If Victor errs towards the scientism of Krempe, Justine herself errs towards the religious possibility of her Roman Catholic mother, who accepts her sufferings, on the encouragement of her confessor, as "a judgment from heaven" (p.

Frankenstein, and was moved to recall her memories of the absent Byron in the same elegiac tones with which Victor proceeds to recall the departed Clerval (Mary Shelley, *Journal*, p. 80; cf. *Frankenstein*, pp. 153–54). For the importance to Mary of Byron and his friendship with Percy, see *Journal*, p. 184; Ernest J. Lovell, Jr., "Byron and Mary Shelley," *Keats–Shelley Journal* II (1953): 35–49.

38. Cf. *Works*, VI:103: "opposite Brunen, they tell the story of a priest and his mistress . . . an avalanche overwhelmed them, but their plaintive voices are still heard in stormy nights."

61). The dead mother of Justine compares poorly with the dead mother of Safie,

> a Christian Arab . . . who, born in freedom spurned the bondage to which she was now reduced. She instructed her daughter in the tenets of her religion, and taught her to aspire to higher powers of intellect, and an independence of spirit, forbidden to the female followers of Mahomet. [P. 119]

Safie is the ideal androgynous complement to Clerval: though "accustomed to grand ideas and a noble emulation for virtue" (p. 119), she can exhibit toward Felix "the simplest and tenderest affection" (p. 120). Clerval and Safie, the ideal Percy and Mary, are presented not as utopian pastoral fantasies of harmonious souls, but as undistorted prototypes of their analogues, Victor and Elizabeth.

III

In her critique of mere science and mere superstition, and her depiction of more androgynous alternatives to these unnatural excesses, Mary ultimately adds little to the ideas of her husband, her two parents, the Lake Poets, and Rousseau. The great originality of *Frankenstein* lies in Mary's recognition of her own dream-monster as an artifice of life that is simultaneously parodic, damned, and quintessentially human. Mary's complexly ambivalent but loving depiction of the Monster arose out of her complexly ambivalent but loving responses to the artifice of her own life with Percy, in which fears, resentments, and even self-hatred, alternated with real hopes of personal and political transcendence. Despite his imperfections, the Monster emerges as more human than his double-going creator: what has exhausted and dehumanized the father has served to ennoble the artificially prodigious son.

Mary Shelley very deliberately stresses the changed moral awareness of the two avengers, and also of Walton, in the last ten pages of her novel. That moral self-criticism which we noted in Dante's Ulysses, and in Victor's first imitation of him, is absent from Victor's final peroration to Walton's crew. This is a heightened parody of Ulysses' speech to his own crew, and a parody also of those "manly and heroical" epics of antiquity from which its rhetoric was drawn. In contrast to Ulysses' chastened reminiscence of his speech before the "mad flight," Victor now appeals directly, and without self-awareness, for the extinction of domestic affection:

"What do you mean? . . . For this was it a glorious, for this was it an honourable undertaking. You were hereafter to be hailed as the benefactors of your species; your name adored, as belonging to brave men who encountered death for honour and the benefit of mankind. And now, behold, with the first imagination of danger, or, if you will, the first mighty and terrific trial of your courage, you shrink away, and are content to be handed down as men who had not strength enough to endure cold and peril; and so, poor souls, they were chilly, and returned to their warm fire-sides. . . . Oh! be men, or be more than men. Be steady to your purposes, and firm as a rock. This ice is not made of such stuff as your hearts might be; it is mutable, cannot withstand you, if you say that it shall not. Do not return to your families with the stigma of disgrace marked on your brows. Return as heroes who have fought and conquered, and who know not what it is to turn their backs on the foe." [P. 212]

From its opening "What do you mean?" (*Quid struis?*), the speech, even more than that of Dante's Ulysses, self-consciously imitates the lofty rhetoric of Virgil's *alti versi*. In this decay into stylistic formalism, Victor has lost the moral self-awareness of his opening speeches earlier in the week; and what he has lost, Walton, who like Ulysses now admits his voyage to be a "rash" one (p. 211), has gained. But at the same time the false counselor reveals the perversity of his appeal to "be more than men" by *unconscious* irony —as when he reverses the usual lover's complaint (your heart is as hard and immutable as ice) into the complaint that theirs are not more immutable and harder.

In thus ignoring nature ("it is mutable, cannot withstand you, if you say that it shall not") and glorifying the loss of feeling, Victor epitomizes the madness he no longer recognizes, when his last three words construe Walton's voyage as a voyage of hate.[39] After

39. Another example of this unconscious self-condemnation is Victor's reversed allusion to the mark set upon Cain ("Do not return to your families with the stigma of disgrace marked on your brows"). In Genesis 4: 11–16 Cain has been cursed for his brother's murder and sent forth, "a fugitive and a vagabond . . . out from the presence of the Lord." Cain has been marked by God as a warning *against* vengeance, precisely that which Victor now insists on. Recall how when Mary's Mathilda describes herself as a "monster": "I believed . . . I was a creature cursed and set apart

the exaggerated rhetoric of a "momentary vigour" (p. 212), the speaker is next seen "sunk in languor, and almost deprived of life." Mary's critical portrait of the unspontaneous intellect owes much to Dante, yet also is an uncanny caricature of languid Percy's fitful and sometimes bookish Promethean pretensions.

The Monster, in contrast, is seen at his least menacing and most human in his final speech. Whereas on the glacier he had perversely refused to see the justice of Victor's accusations (p. 94), he now, in "wild and incoherent self-reproaches," willingly confesses his "frightful selfishness" and "remorse" (p. 217). At times his hyperbolic self-portrait of "impotent passions" and "bitter and loathing despair" anticipates that later product of the chemist's retort, Dostoevsky's underground man. But of course the Monster has acted out those crimes of spite that obsess the underground man only in fantasy; by acting out, the "insatiable passion" has ended (p. 218); and the Monster is now free to forgive Frankenstein and to ask for forgiveness in turn. "Oh, Frankenstein! generous and self-devoted being! what does it avail that I now ask thee to pardon me?" (p. 217). The modern ambiguity of the word "self-devoted" merely reinforces an irony implicit in the praise itself, reflecting Mary's ambivalence toward her husband.[40] The phrase "generous and self-devoted" is authentically Shelleyan; unconsciously or consciously, it has been lifted verbatim from one of Percy's self-gratulatory letters at this time.[41]

The impact of the two last speeches on Walton is problematic: we

by nature. I thought that like another Cain, I had a mark set on my forehead to shew mankind that there was a barrier between me and they" (*Mathilda*, p. 71, quoted in note 20). Clearly, the way for Walton's mariners to avoid such a stigma is to return home, not to pursue vengeance and isolation.

40. "Self-devoted," to mean "characterized by devotion of self," rather than to self, is cited by the OED from Addison (1713), Wordsworth (1814), and Scott (1831). Even without the modern shift in the word's connotations, the daemon's extravagant praise is surely undercut by Frankenstein's persistent failure to respond to the feelings of others.

41. Percy Shelley to Leigh Hunt, December 8, 1816, *Letters*, I:517: "I am an object of compassion to a few more benevolent than the rest, all else abhor & avoid me. With you, & perhaps some others . . . my gentleness & sincerity finds favour, because they are themselves gentle & sincere; they believe in self-devotion and generosity because they are themselves generous & self-devoted."

know only that his first impulses, to obey Victor's dying request "in destroying his enemy, were now suspended by a mixture of curiosity and compassion" (p. 217). Did Mary intend more, and were these intentions inhibited, either out of her own tactful deference to Percy, or even by Percy's own numerous editorial revisions of the manuscript's closing pages? Or did she, from her artist's sense of when to stop, intend to leave us guessing? The allusions to the *Comedia* suggest that, just as Dante the voyager was enlightened by learning of Ulysses' distemper, so may Walton have been enlightened by Victor's. This at least was Victor's own original intention:

"Listen to my tale. I believe that the strange incidents connected with it will afford a view of nature, which may enlarge your faculties and understanding." [P. 24]

Walton is moved by Victor's final speech, yet rejects its male goals of "glory and honour" (p. 213). Victor greets Walton's decision to return with an impassioned defense of his own dedication:

"You may give up your purpose; but mine is assigned to me by heaven, and I dare not. I am weak; but surely the spirits who assist my vengeance will endow me with sufficient strength." Saying this, he endeavoured to spring from the bed, but the exertion was too great for him; he fell back, and fainted. [P. 214]

Yet Victor is deluded in regarding his mission as heaven-sent. On the contrary, Walton's humiliation, his time of sorrow when his "tears flow" (p. 216), can be seen, like Dante's, as a healing crisis. The voyage, which began with his sister's "evil forebodings" (p. 9), is now reversed, to the sailors' "shout of tumultuous joy" (p. 214). Even the imagery is that of Dante's liberating contrition: "The ice cracked . . . a breeze sprung from the west, and . . . the passage . . . became perfectly free" (pp. 213–14; cf. *Purgatorio*, xxx.85–99, 142–45).

Dante is above all the poet of what we might call epic catharsis, the poet who teaches us that by speaking out our repressed anger we can recognize, and thus correct, not only our own distemper but that of our civilization. Both Shelleys seem to have responded to Dante on this high level. Their male and female visions of liberty may have differed; their contrived efforts at an artificial Dantean fellowship may have contributed at one early stage to Mary's nightmares. But the confrontation with Frankenstein's Monster does more than leave the reader, like Coleridge's wedding guest, "a sadder and a wiser man." For the Monster not only embodies our fears of the way science can artificially pervert nature in ourselves and our society, he also speaks to us knowledgeably of nature and in a human voice, as he did to Walton, to tell us we need not be afraid.

IV

It would take a more qualified historian of the Romantic period to ascertain the originality of *Frankenstein*. There appears to be no other work like it, and no such mythic creature since Shakespeare's Caliban. It would be wrong, for example, to read Mary's novel as a mere fulfillment of her dead mother's exhortations for hope amid contemporary disaster:

Sanguinary tortures, insidious poisonings, and dark assassinations, have alternately exhibited a race of monsters in human shape, the contemplation of whose ferocity chills the blood, and darkens every enlivening expectation of humanity: but we ought to observe, to reanimate the hopes of benevolence, that the perpetration of these horrid deeds has arisen from despotism in the government, which reason is teaching us to remedy.[42]

Mary Wollstonecraft anticipated those nineteenth-century writers who attributed the alienation of contemporary social character to the dehumanizing division of labor and the artificial isolation of men in large factories.[43] But her argument for sexual equality and community, like that of other revolutionary theorists, was essentially an abstract intellectual one, which relied on the repugnant dialectic of the master-slave relationship.

Frankenstein, by contrast, explores the same problems on the affective level: it depicts the tragic consequences of sexual isolation through artificial roles of "masculinity" and "femininity," and (from the experience of Mary's own unnatural childhood) focuses on one-sided parenting, in addition to schooling, as the ultimate source of these roles. Mary's proto-Freudian dialectic of fathers and sons, of motherless doubles who deny a female sexual partner

42. Wollstonecraft, *French Revolution*, I:515.
43. *Ibid.*, p. 519.

to each other, shows more awareness than Wollstonecraft or the author of *Caleb Williams* of the libidinal processes whereby psychic and social deprivations reinforce one another in history.

Like her husband Percy, Mary is more profoundly aware of sexuality, if only in the perverted form of one-sided sex roles, as a shaping energy for good or evil in political society. Percy, a visionary, wrote fitfully of love and science as abstract forces for revolutionary change. Mary, the intuitive realist, without renouncing change, studied the limitations of character in what Adrienne Rich has since called "this savagely fathered and unmothered world."[44] *Frankenstein*, with its subtle but unhostile critique of Percy's revolutionary ideology, deserves recognition as a testimony of hope for the evolution of a new consciousness: one which someday will be neither male, nor even feminist, but quintessentially human.

---

44. Adrienne Rich, "From an Old House in America," *Poems: Selected and New, 1950–1974* (New York, 1974), p. 237.

PART
FOUR

TEXTURE:

*Language
and the Grotesque*

IX

"Godlike Science/Unhallowed Arts": Language, Nature, and Monstrosity

PETER BROOKS

MARY SHELLEY'S *Frankenstein* continues to solicit and disturb us not only through its creation of a decisive image of Gothic horror, but also by the pathos of a monsterism in doomed dialectic with nature and with culture. It is above all in the question of language, both as explicit theme of the novel and as implicit model of the novel's complex organization, that the problem of the monstrous is played out. We might approach the network of issues dramatized in the novel first through Victor Frankenstein's crucial interview with his monstrous creation, the interview which leads to the Monster's telling his tale to Frankenstein, the story-within-a-story (itself a story-within-a-story-within-a-story, when we consider the role of Robert Walton as initial and ultimate narrator). Following the first murders committed by his Monster—William strangled, Justine judicially done to death through maliciously falsified evidence—Frankenstein seeks solace in the mountains above Chamonix. He penetrates into the "glorious presence-chamber of imperial Nature," climbs to Montanvert and the Mer de Glace, hoping to recapture a remembered effect of "a sublime ecstasy that gave wings to the soul, and allowed it to soar from the obscure world to light and joy."[1] His ascension takes him to a "wonderful and stupendous scene," overlooking the Mer de Glace, facing the

1. Mary Shelley, *Frankenstein, or, The Modern Prometheus*, ed. M. K. Joseph (New York, 1971), pp. 96–97. Subsequent references will be given between parentheses in the text, and are to this edition, which reprints the text of 1831. I have also consulted the valuable critical edition prepared by James Rieger (Indianapolis and New York, 1974), which gives the 1818 text (with the corrections of 1823) and notes the variants occurring in the text of 1831.

"awful majesty" of Mont Blanc; his heart once again opens to joy, and he exclaims, in the tones of the Ossianic bard, "Wandering spirits, if indeed ye wander, and do not rest in your narrow beds; allow me this faint happiness, or take me, as your companion, away from the joys of life" (p. 98). Whereupon a superhuman shape comes bounding over the ice. It is, of course, no spirit of the departed, nor any beneficent spirit of nature, but the Monster himself, who has at last tracked down his creator, and will force him into parley.

It is worth noting here that virtually every time "nature" is invoked in the novel, as moral presence presiding over human life, it appears to produce only the monstrous. Thus, earlier, as Frankenstein returns to Geneva after learning of William's death, a tremendous thunderstorm breaks out over the Lake, a "noble war" in the sky that elevates his soul so that he cries out: "William, dear angel! this is thy funeral, this thy dirge!" (p. 76). No sooner is the apostrophe uttered than Frankenstein perceives in a flash of lightning the figure of the Monster nearby and with this apparition comes the moral certainty that here is William's murderer. We will find other instances in the fate of Henry Clerval, the poet figure in the Wordsworthian mold, nourished on "the very poetry of nature," and the creation of the Monster itself. But already it may be apparent that the call upon nature the Preserver—the moral support and guardian of man—produces instead the Destroyer, the monstrous, what Frankenstein calls "my own vampire" (p. 77).

Frankenstein's initial reaction to the encounter with the Monster consists in curses and an abortive attempt to do battle with him. Still the Monster pleads for a hearing. A hearing that need not be a seeing: when Frankenstein commands, "Begone! relieve me from the sight of your detested form," the Monster responds by placing his huge hands over Frankenstein's eyes: "Thus I relieve thee, my creator . . . thus I take from thee a sight which you abhor. Still thou canst listen to me, and grant me thy compassion" (p. 101). The Monster understands that it is not visual relationship that favors him—indeed, his only favorable reception by a human being has come from a blind man—but rather the auditory, the interlocutory, the relationship of language.

For the Monster is eloquent. From his first words, he shows himself to be a supreme rhetorician of his own situation, one who controls the antitheses and oxymorons that express the pathos of his existence: "Remember, that I am thy creature; I ought to be thy Adam; but I am rather the fallen angel, whom thou drivest from joy for no misdeed. Everywhere I see bliss, from which I alone am irrevocably excluded. I was benevolent and good; misery made me a fiend. Make me happy, and I shall again be virtuous" (p. 100). When we learn of the Monster's self-education—and particularly his three master-texts: *Paradise Lost*, Plutarch's *Lives*, and *Werther*— we understand the sources of his eloquence, and of the conception of a just order of things that animates his plea to his creator. But it is of primary importance to register Mary Shelley's radical and saving decision to stage a deformed and menacing creature who, rather than using grunts and gestures, speaks and reasons with the highest elegance, logic, and persuasiveness. In the Monster's use of language the novel poses its most important questions, for it is language alone that may compensate for a deficient, monstrous nature.

I

Frankenstein is touched by the Monster's eloquence. When he looks at this "filthy mass that moved and talked," he feels horror and hatred; yet by the end of the Monster's tale he avows: "His words had a strange effect upon me. I compassionated him" (p. 147). Through the medium of language, a first relationship is created. Like Coleridge's Wedding Guest, Frankenstein is compelled to hear out the tale of this cursed being. The force of the compulsion here is no "glittering eye," but the power of language itself to link speaker and listener. In the narrative situation of the Monster facing and speaking to his creator, we have an instance of what we might call, in the terms of Jacques Lacan, the imaginary versus the symbolic order.[2] The imaginary order is that of the specular, of the mirror-stage, and is based on deception, the subject's relation to itself as other. The symbolic order is that of language, the systematic and trans-subjective order of the signifier, the cultural system into which individual subjects are inserted. In any specular

2. I adapt these terms from Lacan without giving them their full context in his thought, and without full exposition of their import. On the Lacanian concepts used in this essay, see Jacques Lacan, "Le Stade du miroir" and "L'instance de la lettre dans l'inconscient ou la raison depuis Freud," in *Ecrits* (Paris, 1966), and *Le Séminaire, Livre I* (Paris, 1975).

relationship the Monster will always be the "filthy mass;" only in the symbolic order may he realize his desire for recognition.

The Monster hence produces a tale, based, like any tale, on the "narrative contract" between narrator and narratee. Its very possibility depends on an order of cultural symbolic which implies that network of intersubjective relations from which the Monster protests he has been excluded.[3] The close of his narrative suggests the importance of language as relation. In arguing that Frankenstein create a female monster to be a companion to him, the Monster asserts that only in communication with a similar being can he "become linked to the chain of existence and events, from which I am now excluded" (p. 147). The wish for a *semblable* may itself belong to the imaginary order, as an instance of speculary narcissism and deception. The term *chain*, however, identifies meaning as residing in a systematic network of relation, in the symbolic order. It suggests Lacan's exposition of the "signifying chain" of language. Exclusion from this chain could be the very definition of monsterism. The fact of the interlocutionary relationship established by the tale-within-the tale (within-the-tale) implies the Monster's lack and his desire. Only through those linked signs whose rules he has mastered can the Monster hope to enter "the chain of existence and events," to *signify*.

Language is also the principal theme of the Monster's story of his life up to this point. His first experience with humankind has laid bare the hopelessness of speculary relationship, its necessary result in alienation and rejection: the shepherd he encounters in a hut flees shrieking from his sight. Retreating into the hovel adjoining the de Lacey cottage, he then begins his education, seeing, but himself unseen. From his hiding place, he discovers that "these people possessed a method of communicating their experience and feelings to one another by articulate sounds" (p. 112). What particularly impress him are the emotional effects wrought by these sounds, which "sometimes produced pleasure or pain, smiles or sadness, in the minds and countenances of the beholders. This was indeed a godlike science."

Mary Shelley's Monster is in many respects an Enlightenment

3. On the "narrative contract," see Roland Barthes, *S/Z* (Paris, 1970); English trans. (New York, 1974). The term "narratee" is adapted from Gérard Genette's "narrataire": see "Le Discours du récit" in *Figures III* (Paris, 1972).

natural man, or noble savage; his first ideas demonstrate the processes of Lockean sensationalism and Hartleyan associationism. His discovery of language implies Rousseau's argument, in the *Essai sur l'origine des langues*, that language springs from passion rather than need: need cannot form the necessary social context for voiced language, since its effect is to scatter men; and need can make do with the barest repertory of visual signs, gestures, imperatives. Passion, on the other hand, brings men together, and the relation of desire calls forth voice.[4] It is hence no accident that what language first reveals to the Monster is human love, and that his rhetorical plea to his creator ends with the demand for a creature whom he might love.

The Monster also discovers an important corollary to Rousseau's postulate of the emotional origin of language: the radical figurality of language, its founding statute as misnaming, transference. The sign is not consubstantial with the thing it names: "the words they uttered, not having any apparent connection with visible objects, I was unable to discover any clue by which I could unravel the mystery of their reference" (p. 112). The Monster in this manner uncovers the larger question of the arbitrariness, or immotivation, of the linguistic sign, postulated by Ferdinand de Saussure as the foundation of modern linguistics. And the consequences of this recognition will be consonant with Saussure's: the understanding that the "godlike science" of language depends, not on simple designation, on passage from the signifier to the signified, but rather on the systematic organization of signifiers. The Monster intuitively grasps that language will be of importance to him because by its very nature it implies the "chain of existence and events" within which he seeks a place, defines the interdependency of senders and receivers of messages in that chain, and provides the possibility of emotional effect independent of any designation.

The Monster unerringly discovers language to be on the side of culture rather than nature, and to imply the structures of relation at the basis of culture. The discovery is a vital one, for the side of "nature" is irreparably marked by lack, by monsterism. Against the Monster's hearing of the cottagers' language is set his discovery of his own features mirrored in a pool—a sinister parody of Eve's discovery of her fair features in the pool of Eden, on the day of her

4. See Jean-Jacques Rousseau, *Essai sur l'origine des langues* (Paris, 1970).

creation, in Book IV of *Paradise Lost*. In *Frankenstein*, the reflected image convinces the beholder "that I was in reality the monster that I am" (p. 114). This speculary *cogito*, where the Monster witnesses his outward identity as alien to his inner desire, estranged, determined by the view and judgment of the Other, clinches the importance of language as the symbolic order that must compensate for nature. The Monster understands that he must not show himself to the cottagers until he has mastered their language, "which knowledge might enable me to make them overlook the deformity of my figure" (p. 114).

The thematization of language becomes so rich at this point in the narrative that one is forced to abridge discussion. There is, first of all, a criss-crossing of languages implicit in the text: with the arrival of Safie, we have a lesson in French being offered to a Turkish Arab, in a German-speaking region, the whole rendered for the reader in English. This well-ordered Babel calls attention to the fact and problem of transmission and communication, the motive for language, and reminds us that the framing structure of the novel—Walton's letters to his sister, to which we shall return—evokes the same concerns. The Monster learns language through overhearing the instruction of Safie by Felix and Agatha; though excluded, he is learning the means by which to be included. Since the Monster needs language to compensate for a deficient nature, it is fitting that the first use to which he puts his new science is reading, the written word being for Rousseau precisely the supplementary and mediate state of language, its transmissible (hence also potentially deceitful) form, which does not demand presence for its operation. The three texts which the Monster finds and reads—Plutarch's *Lives*, Goethe's *Werther*, and *Paradise Lost*—cover the public, the private, and the cosmic realms, and three modes of love; they constitute a possible Romantic *cyclopedia universalis*. The Monster's literalist reading of *Paradise Lost* poses in acute, emblematic, and literary terms his problem: he appears to be a unique creation, like Adam "united by no link to any other being in existence," yet by his condition more resembling Satan (p. 129). The paradox of his origin and nature will be resolved by another piece of writing, Frankenstein's lab journal, which substitutes for myths of creation a literal account of the Monster's manufacture, a "disgusting" tale of an "accursed origin," by which the Monster discovers that he has indeed been created in another's image, but as a "filthy type" (p. 130). The "godlike science" has led him to learn of his origins in Victor Frankenstein's "unhallowed arts" (p. 89).

Thus far language, and especially writing, must appear to the Monster, as it did to Rousseau, ambiguous in effect, like the Promethean gift of fire, so strange in its production of "opposite effects" (p. 104). Yet it remains the necessary compensation, the only hope for linkage to humankind. The Monster will try its effects first on the blind De Lacey. And here the godlike power of the science does reveal itself, as De Lacey responds: "I am blind, and cannot judge of your countenance, but there is something in your words which persuades me that you are sincere" (p. 134). Mutual sympathy, benefaction, protection, and relation are close to being sealed through language, when Felix, Agatha, and Safie enter and throw the situation brutally back into the speculary order: Agatha faints, Safie flees, and Felix "tore me from his father, to whose knees I clung" (p. 135). The result is Fall. The Monster becomes explicitly satanic—"I, like the arch-fiend, bore a hell within me" (p. 136), sets fire to the De Laceys' abandoned cottage, and sets forth into the world in search of his creator, the *deus absconditus* who alone now can restore, through a second creation, the Monster to the chain of living sympathies. It is during this search that the Monster commits his first murder. This act implicates the question of relation through its displacement of Oedipal conflict: the Monster strangles William when the boy protests that his "papa" is M. Frankenstein; he then stands fascinated, erotically medused by the portrait of William's and Victor's mother hanging round William's neck. The result of his baffled desire is the perverse planting of the portrait on Justine Moritz, thus condemning the mother substitute ("not indeed so beautiful as her whose portrait I held; but of an agreeable aspect, and blooming in the loveliness of youth and health"), whose possession is forever denied to him (p. 143).

At its completion, the Monster's narrative implies that use of language has failed to gain him entry into the "chain of existence and events," but has rather made him fully aware of his unique and accursed origin. In his confrontation with humankind, speculary relationship and the imaginary order appear to have reasserted their dominion. Yet if language has failed to accomplish the Monster's desire, it has nonetheless provided the means for construction of a story within Frankenstein's story that will subvert the entire set of relations of which Frankenstein is part. The Monster's use of language has contextualized desire itself as a systematic chain of signifiers whose rhetorical effect cannot be denied by the narratee. The symbolic order is operational.

In the passage from the Monster's narrative back to Franken-stein's, desire reveals its functioning as metonymy, explicated by Lacan as a perpetual "sliding" of the inaccessible signified under the signifier. Desire is born from an original lack or want, in the discrepancy between need and demand, which in the relationship of Monster to creator (as in the infant-mother relationship) is es-sentially the demand for recognition. In constructing his narrative appeal, the Monster has made language the vehicle of desire, has built a construct of signifiers which figures his initial want and lack without fulfilling it, so that language itself as relation becomes the medium of his truth, which is want of relation. The metonymic sliding passes desire on to his interlocutor, charged now with cross-ing the "bar" between signifier and signified, finding access to the meaning of desire. Frankenstein is forced to accept the establish-ment of relation and the contagion of desire: "His tale, and the feelings he now expressed, proved him to be a creature of fine sensations; and did I not as his maker owe him all the portion of happiness that it was in my power to bestow?" (p. 146). This re-sponse is the basis for a contract or even covenant: the Monster will desist from acts of vengeance against mankind, while Frankenstein will undertake creation of a female monster.

The covenant is violated by the creator himself when he destroys the nearly completed form of the Monster's companion. This violent rupture may serve notice that Frankenstein has come to understand that the Monster's expressed wish is a figure for some-thing else that could endanger the whole dialectic of desire and repression. He has agreed to create the monsteress because, while he is moved by the Monster's narrative, he cannot "sympathize with him" (p. 147). This creation, then, would be a *substitute* for the Monster's inclusion within the human chain; Frankenstein may obscurely recognize that the Monster's desire for his mate may it-self be a substitute for his real, his absolute demand, which is for recognition by his creator. To create the monsteress would be to create the possibility of that demand being laid bare, and this in turn would confront Frankenstein too blindingly with the mon-strous element in his own nature, would force him to recognize what he wishes to deny. The Monster would be his *symptom* ("my own spirit let loose from the grave" [p. 77]), which in Lacanian terms is metaphor, the figure of access to repressed truth.

Whatever the value of such a speculative interpretation, Frankenstein's decision to break his promise to the Monster explicitly concerns the "chain of existence and events." It occurs to Frankenstein that the inevitable result of "those sympathies for which the daemon thirsted" will be a race of monstrous progeny that may wreak havoc on mankind (p. 165). Precisely because the special creation demanded by the Monster has as its purpose the inception of an affective chain *outside* humanity—a new family, a new society —it raises the frightening possibility of a new and uncontrollable signifying chain, one with unknown rules and grammar. Milton's Eve after the Fall considers that the divine command to reproduce now means "propagated curse." The idea of the propagation of his aberrant signifier, through unforeseeably monstrous messages, leads Frankenstein to destroy what the Monster considers his authentic desired signified, and to accept the consequences in terms of his own chain of affections—consequences that are immediately ghastly.

The Monster is now hopelessly condemned to the order of words that does not match the order of things, that has not produced the desired referent but has only brought knowledge of the unappeasable lack or difference that defines his monsterism. The godlike science itself proves deceptive: his eloquence can achieve no more than a state of permanently frustrated desire for meaning; his language is metonymic advance without a terminus. The way in which, out of his frustration, he seeks vengeance on Frankenstein exactly mirrors this situation. He does not strike directly at his creator—at the sacred name that is the signified of all signifiers—but, by displacement, by metonymy, at closely related elements in Frankenstein's own chain of existence and events: at his friend Clerval, at Elizabeth when she becomes Frankenstein's bride. Despite the Monster's words, "I will be with you on your wedding night," Frankenstein seems obtusely blind as to the threatened object. The reader understands at once that it must be Frankenstein's bride who will be sacrificed to the bride denied to the Monster.

One could pause over Frankenstein's blindness, the convergence of Eros and death on his wedding night, and the apparent fear of erotic union. "Oh! peace, peace, my love," he murmurs to Elizabeth, "this night, and all will be safe: but this night is dreadful, very dreadful" (p. 134). Elizabeth may be the interdicted because incestuous bride: she has been raised as sister to Frankenstein, and has furthermore assumed the nurturing role of Frankenstein's dead mother.[5] The necrophilic embrace which is all that Frankenstein obtains follows the logic of his creative project, which has usurped the power to make life from the dead. Fulfillment with Elizabeth would mark Frankenstein's achievement of a full signified in his life, accession to plenitude of being—which would leave no place in creation for his daemonic projection, the Monster. That projection must act out Frankenstein's sadistic impulses in destruction of the being who would bring rest, and arrest, to Frankenstein's movement of desire, must maintain the lack that led to the Monster's creation in the first place.

Frankenstein and his Monster are in fact by now engaged in an exacerbated dialectic of desire, in which each needs the other because the other represents for each the lack or gap within himself. Frankenstein sets out in pursuit of the Monster intending to destroy him, but also with a firm intuition that the Monster's death will be his own death—that in destroying the daemonic side of himself, he will also destroy the whole of self. For, like the Monster, he too bears "a Hell within me," and destruction of the representative of that hell will entail destruction of the ego, now mastered by its sadistic drives. The Monster flees from Frankenstein, yet never escapes completely, intent that Frankenstein maintain his pursuit, the only form of recognition by his creator that he can exact, his last tenuous link to the signifying chain. Hence as he flees the Monster leaves his mark and trace to guide his pursuer, messages carved in trees, even caches of food to sustain the chase. "Come on, my enemy," reads one inscription, in a nice balance of hatred and affection (p. 205). The pursuit finally leads toward the very heart of non-meaning, toward the lifeless pole, the immaculate icecap.

II

What we have said about the Monster's efforts to achieve recognition and to enter the signifying chain may pose with new force the question with which we began, the relation of the monstrous on

5. Compare Frankenstein's dream—immediately following his animation of the Monster—in which he meets Elizabeth, but finds her changing, on his embrace, into the corpse of his dead mother.

the one hand to nature, on the other to culture. The question of origins has been of utmost importance to the Monster since his first initiation into language. Like Oedipus, he has felt that his very definition depended on the discovery of his generation: "Who was I? What was I? Whence did I come?" (p. 128). His origin turns out to be not the defining plenitude of parenthood—the two who make one—but an undecidable borderline instance. He appears to have been generated at the very frontier between nature and the supernatural, from Frankenstein's studies in physics and chemistry, which are always on the verge of becoming metaphysics and alchemy. When Frankenstein discovers the principle of animation (the Promethean revelation which the text never speaks, but maintains as a central interdiction and dumbness), he must proceed through death to create a new life. "Life and death," he recalls, "appeared to me ideal bounds, which I should first break through, and pour a torrent of light into our dark world" (p. 53). Thus he works within the very "citadel of nature" (p. 38) with its first principles, but he is engaged in an overreaching quest which from its inception bears the mark of the counternatural. For his "loathesome" task he collects "with profane fingers" pieces of the dead; he becomes "insensible to the charms of nature," and the seasons pass unnoticed. The Monster comes into existence as a product of nature—his ingredients are one hundred percent natural—yet by the fact and process of his creation he is unnatural. Yet since he is a unique creation, without precedence or replication, he has no cultural context. He remains, so to speak, postnatural and precultural.

Despite the ambiguities and profanity of his creation, the Monster comes into existence potentially good, an Enlightenment savage with essentially benevolent instincts. The story of his education is a classic study of right natural instinct perverted and turned evil by the social milieu, a counterexample to such pedagogical utopias as Rousseau's *Emile*. He understands perfectly what has happened to him: "I am malicious because I am miserable," he says, (p. 145); and we must believe that the establishment of links between himself and the human community would restore his benevolence. Natural goodness is real but not sturdy; rejection and isolation easily turn us back to an original accursedness, to the satanic *non serviam*: "Evil henceforth be thou my good."

"Nature" in *Frankenstein* appears to be a fragile moral concept of ambiguous implication. It is as if the Monster, generated within the sanctum of nature, at home in its most sublime settings, might himself represent the final secret of nature, its force of forces. The novel dissents from the optimistic assumption that nature is support and comfort and source of right moral feeling—"The guide, the guardian of my heart, and soul / Of all my moral being," as Wordsworth writes in "Tintern Abbey." This dissent is suggested most forcefully through the figure of Henry Clerval, who balances Frankenstein's pursuit of science with study of the poets and is described as "a being formed in 'the very poetry of nature'" (the quotation is from Leigh Hunt). Frankenstein quotes Wordsworth in description of Clerval:

> The sounding cataract
> Haunted *him* like a passion: the tall rock,
> The mountain, and the deep and gloomy wood,
> Their colours and their forms, were then to him
> An appetite; a feeling, and a love,
> That had no need of a remoter charm,
> By thought supplied, or any interest
> Unborrow'd from the eye.

The lines from "Tintern Abbey" are usually taken to represent the poet's first, immediate, unreflective relation to nature, now lost to him but apparent in his sister Dorothy, to whom he can say that "Nature never did betray / The heart that loved her." As Peter Scott points out above, Clerval cleaves to nature with a Wordsworthian child-like love and trust; yet when he falls victim to the Monster the ensuing scenario curiously implicates nature. Frankenstein has defied the Monster by destroying the nearly complete monsteress, and has rowed out to cast the *disjecta membra* into the sea. He then loses consciousness, a storm blows up, his skiff is blown off course and finally comes to ground on the Irish coast, where he is arrested as a murderer and confronted with Clerval's corpse. Nature does not protect Clerval from its own malignant possibilities. It contains more than sounding cataracts and sublime mountains: there are also unaccommodated monsters and disseminated pieces of monstrous creation.

Nature is not one thing, and those who think it so are caught in a self-destructive blindness. This Frankenstein eventually recognizes, when he cries out to the Genevan magistrate who refuses to credit his tale of the Monster, "Man . . . how ignorant art thou in thy pride of wisdom!" (p. 201). Nature is preserver and destroyer. It possesses the awesome and ambiguous Power evoked in P. B. Shelley's "Mont Blanc," a poem written in the same summer that Mary Shelley composed *Frankenstein*, which takes us back to the scene on the Mer de Glace, where, in "the glorious presence-chamber of imperial nature," Victor evokes the spirit of the majestic mountain and instead summons forth his created daemon. The daemonic virtuality of Power in "Mont Blanc" "dwells apart." *Frankenstein* brings it into human existence, as the destructive potential of the creative drive, or Eros, of nature's creature man.

The fact of monsterism suggests that nature in *Frankenstein* has something of the radical amorality described by Sade. For Sade, nature permits everything and authorizes nothing. Since all tastes and pleasures are in nature, no perversion can outrage and no crime alter nature; if one searches for an underlying pattern or principle in nature, what one finds is destruction itself. Therefore man's destruction—torture, murder—merely does nature's work. The impassibility of nature, the regulatory principle of life which yet refuses to offer any ethical principle, is a source of anguish for Sade; and his compilation of pleasures and crimes *contra naturam* can be read as an ever-frustrated effort to make a human mark on nature, to break nature's bonds, to reach through to some transcendent principle. There are perhaps parallels to be found in Victor Frankenstein's manic quest to push nature to a frontier where it becomes meta-nature, where it releases its own principle of being. Certainly Frankenstein's assault on and in the citadel of nature produces a monsterism that both reveals and mocks the arcane principle. The overriding fact of nature in the book—dominating Mont Blanc, the Lake of Geneva, the Hebrides, and all the other sublime natural settings—is the fact and possibility of monsterism itself. It is to this, I believe, that the Monster returns in his peroration, as he says farewell to Walton and to the dead Frankenstein: "Blasted as thou wert, my agony was still superior to thine" (p. 223). He attributes his superior torture to remorse; yet surely it first of all derives from the condition of monstrosity itself. This is the supreme agony, and the properly monstrous blot upon nature: that nature should be capable of producing the monstrous. It is a nature that eludes any optimistic Romanticism, and finally most resembles Freud's "uncanny": the Monster perfectly illustrates the *Unheimliche*, a monstrous potentiality so close to us—so close to home—that we have repressed its possibility, and assigned an *un* as the mark of censorship on what is indeed too *heimisch* for comfort.[6]

The ambiguous and paradoxical nature of nature in *Frankenstein* —its seemingly equal potential as essentially good and as self-negatingly evil—cannot be resolved within the orders of the real or the imaginary, but only within the symbolic order, and only in structural terms. That is, the creations of nature will be bad or good only through the play of difference and relation, only in terms of their place in the signifying chain. This is what the Monster has understood by the time he makes his appeal to his creator for a *semblable*, what indeed he has already grasped when he intuits the possibilities of the "godlike science." In the play of sameness and difference that founds the system of our signs for things, then in grammar and syntax, we have the basis of relation and the possibility of exchange of tokens, communication. The Monster's failure—what establishes him irremediably *as* monster—is his inability, despite his eloquence, to find relation.

There finally remains as interlocutor for the Monster only Walton, who has been warned by Frankenstein that though the Monster is "eloquent and persuasive," he is not to be listened to. By the time of his confrontation with Walton that closes the book, the Monster states his recognition that his effort to enter into the signifying chain is at an end: "the miserable series of my being is wound to its close" (p. 219). This expression, "the series of my being," is used twice in the final scene. The now obsolete sense of series as "sequence," "order," suggests the meaning of "chain" in the word's etymology, and well implies the metonymic "sliding" of the Monster's effort to reach satisfaction of desire, the movement ever forward that can reach no point of arrest and no ultimate structuring relationship. It is a textual movement that can never cover over and fill in its central lack, that can reach an end only in extinction.

Yet in a larger context, the "series" does not stop with the Monster's self-immolation. The fact of monstrosity has established its own chain, with its own syntax and significance. The contamination of monsterism is a kind of accursed signifier that has come to inhabit the novel's principal actors. We must here reflect on the sig-

6. See Sigmund Freud, "The Uncanny" (*Das Unheimliche*), in Standard Edition, vol. 17.

nificance of the outer frame of the novel, which encloses Franken-stein's narrative as his encloses the Monster's. Walton's initial letters to his sister strike the very note of the Monster's narrative: Walton has "no friend . . . no one to participate my joy . . . to sustain me in dejection" (p. 19). He is reduced to committing his thoughts to paper, "a poor medium for the communication of feeling" when really "I desire the company of a man who could sympathize with me; whose eyes would reply to mine." In the uninhabited polar regions he meets his first friend in a man who has had similar visions of Promethean discovery and fame, and whose understanding of friendship—since the death of Clerval—articulates Walton's own feelings: "I agree with you . . . we are unfashioned creatures, but half made up, if one wiser, better, dearer than ourselves—such a friend ought to be—do not lend his aid to perfectionate our weak and faulty natures" (p. 28). Friendship is thus defined as specularity and as complementarity, the longing of two incomplete creatures for fullness in androgynous fusion. But this dream is no more to be realized than the Monster's hope of union. Walton loses Frankenstein to death. And he loses his dream of Promethean discovery, as his mutinous sailors vote to turn southward. His hopes are "blasted"—the term applied to Frankenstein's aspirations, and which the Monster will at the last apply to himself.

All aspirations, then, lie blasted and wasted at the end, as if the original act of overreaching, of sacrilegious creation, had tainted the world. Each tale interlocked within tale touches its listener with the taint of monsterism: Frankenstein receives it from the Monster's tale—his life, contracted to the Monster's desire, becomes torment thereafter—and Walton receives it from Frankenstein's. Walton remains, like the Ancient Mariner—or perhaps, more accurately, like the Wedding-Guest—the bearer of a tale of unnatural wisdom, the bearer of the taint of monsterism. The fate of this monsterism can perhaps best be described as textual. The ostensible recipient of Walton's letters (and hence of the interpolated manuscript of Frankenstein, itself containing the Monster's narrative) is Margaret Saville, Walton's sister. (Is there, once again, a suggestion of incest in the choice of the object of affection?) But she has no more existence in the novel than a postal address. She is inscribed as a kind of lack of being, leaving us with only a text, a narrative tissue that never wholly conceals its lack of ultimate reference and its interminable projection forward to no destination.

The absent Mrs. Saville, faceless addressee of all the textual material that constitutes *Frankenstein*, is exemplary of the situation of language and desire as they have been dramatized in the novel. If the Monster's story demonstrates that the godlike science of language is a supplement to a deficient nature, an attempt to overcome a central gap or lack of being, the inner and outer frames—Frankenstein's narrative and Walton's letters—indicate that language never can overcome the gap, that the chain established has no privileged limits, no mode of reference, but signifies purely as a chain, a system or series in which everything is mutually interrelated and interdependent but without any transcendent signified. There is no transcendent signified because the fact of monsterism is never either justified nor overcome, but is simply passed along the chain, finally to come to inhabit the reader himself who, as animator of the text, is left with the contamination of monsterism. Desire—Walton's, Frankenstein's, the Monster's—cannot overcome the monstrous but only reproduce it. Monsterism comes rather to be contextualized; the text remains as indelible record of the monstrous, emblem of language's murderous lack of transcendent reference.

In his essay on the *Unheimliche*, Freud speculates on the special capacity of literature to evoke and to control the feeling of the uncanny. Literature appears to be a kind of controlled play with the daemonic. It may belong to the logic of literature that Mary Shelley's daemon should understand that his place lies within the symbolic order of language, that the daemon should fail of arriving at meaning, and become rather the very image of a desire that can never fix or pin down meaning, but merely pass on the desire and the curse of meaning. Yet here we find the logic of desire in literature, desire of the text and for the text. The text solicits us through the promise of a transcendent signified, and leaves us, on the threshold of pleasure, to be content with the play of its signifiers.[7] At the same time, it contaminates us with a residue of meaning that cannot be explained or rationalized, but is passed on as affect, as taint.

---

7. See Roland Barthes, *Le Plaisir du texte* (Paris, 1973); English trans., *The Pleasure of the Text* (New York, 1975).

Ⅹ

Frankenstein and Comedy

PHILIP STEVICK

HERE WAS SOMETHING PLAYFUL, no doubt, about the circumstances during the wet summer in which *Frankenstein* was bargained for and conceived, but there is also no doubt that the book is as utterly serious in intent as it is utterly serious in execution. If we speak of irony in connection with *Frankenstein*, what we mean is the tendency of the novel to organize itself around some fairly predictable quirks of fate. We do not use the word irony of the verbal texture of the book, because there is no feigning, no indirection, no undercutting, no mocking of forms, no doubleness, no play. Other novels that strike us as serious, those of Hardy for example, will allow a small interlude to "relieve" the relentless seriousness of the execution, a rustic or a fool who momentarily diverts us with his incomprehension of the unfolding tragedy. There are no such episodes in *Frankenstein*, and the movement of its action is as serious as its verbal texture. Moreover, the import of the book, its significance as a cultural event and as a continuing influence in the imaginations of so many readers and other artists who have followed it, are all deeply serious, complicated, awesome to contemplate, and not at all ridiculous. Having said this once, I will find it necessary to say it again. Because it does not stay said, in the face of a fact more overwhelming than the seriousness of the book, namely its capacity to provoke laughter.

Say "Frankenstein" to anybody (well, almost anybody) and he (or she) laughs. What he (or she) laughs at, of course, are largely the burlesque associations that have come to surround the idea of the book. So many parodic possibilities have accumulated around the Monster that these are what one thinks of first. Films are made in parody of other *Frankenstein* films. Nightclub comics remind us that the Monster had a bolt in his neck and sutures on his forehead.

221

Small children who have never seen the Boris Karloff film version, asked to "do Frankenstein," will walk, arms outstretched, legs stiff, brow menacing, finally convulsed with laughter. If the laughter were merely an impertinent and irrelevant association attaching to a serious text, we could dismiss it as an unfortunate accretion distorting a classic work, of interest to the social historian and the collector of folk fads but not to the literary critic. But, whether we think so or not, our laughter is rooted in certain aspects of Mary Shelley's text. And it is the nature of that problematic comedy, existing in a wholly serious work, that I wish to define. For in defining it one discovers a clear continuity between Mary Shelley's text and a class of works, among them some of the greatest in all of prose fiction, that also generate simultaneously mythic seriousness and uncomfortable laughter. And in defining it one further finds that the comedy can only be understood by defining the experience both of *reading Frankenstein*, and books like it, and of *remembering Frankenstein*, and books like it.

One experiences the comic aspects of *Frankenstein* in different ways according to one's distance from the book. Before the fact, one tends to expect the book to be, in some respects, funny. It seems likely that such an expectation is a mid-twentieth-century phenomenon and that no reader before, say, the nineteen-thirties had any such expectation. As one actually reads the book, it seems rarely, perhaps never, funny; scarcely anyone laughs at *Frankenstein* page by page. After the fact, the book is often comic, as one remembers certain set pieces, as one tries to retell them, or as one tries to translate the action of the book into another form. The amusement one feels, in fact, is directly proportionate to one's distance from the reading. One remembers events as being amusing that, in the reading, one did not find amusing at all; and the less perfectly one remembers them, the more amusing they become.

Perhaps the best way of keeping in mind the quality I am beginning to define is to consider the peculiar contrasts that *Frankenstein* contains—of energy and torpor, movement and rest, obsessive frenzy and virtually pathological detachment. They are strange and amazing contrasts that bear directly on the reader's response. But such contrasts are not unique to *Frankenstein*. Odysseus, man of action, trickster, archetypal hero, is caught, again and again, in postures of immobility that are, at once, distressing for the reader, deeply significant, highly charged with mythic power, and, in retrospect, in some perverse and eccentric sense, amusing. Gulliver, man mountain, puller of armadas and pisser on castles, is caught, again and again, in postures of immobility that are likewise distressing to the reader, significant, mythically powerful, and, in retrospect, funny. In the twentieth century, Kafka serves up appropriate parallels and analogues from the modern imagination of the strange and haunting alternation between willing to do, doing, and being unable to do. This is a rhythm especially common to that class of works described below, a class with *Frankenstein* at its center. For if one sees *Frankenstein*, and one's responses to it, not as being atypical and *sui generis* but centrally characteristic of a very distinguished kind, then *Frankenstein* becomes both more intelligible and more aesthetically defensible.

I

The event most loaded with value in *Frankenstein*, most problematic in one's response to it, is, of course, the moment of creation. Before the fact, one thinks of mad scientists with bulging eyes, crackling and badly controlled electrical charges, the table, the covering sheet, the monster, the uncertainty, the blinking eyes, the attempt to rise. It is all rather baroque, almost alchemical, in its prescientific intricacy, its bubbling tubes, its smoking retorts. The passage, however, is very different from our imagination of it, both in detail and tone.

It was on a dreary night of November, that I beheld the accomplishment of my toils. With an anxiety that almost amounted to agony, I collected the instruments of life around me, that I might infuse a spark of being into the lifeless thing that lay at my feet. It was already one in the morning; the rain pattered dismally against the panes, and my candle was nearly burnt out, when, by the glimmer of the half-extinguished light, I saw the dull yellow eye of the creature open; it breathed hard, and a convulsive motion agitated its limbs.[1]

Nobody would be so arrogant as to say what response *is* appropriate to that passage, but it is certainly not laughter.

For one thing, Mary Shelley has no interest in scientific tech-

1. Mary Shelley, *Frankenstein, or The Modern Prometheus*, ed. M. K. Joseph (London, 1969), p. 57. Subsequent references are incorporated into the text.

nique. She diverts our attention elsewhere, to the rain, the time, the light, and the attendant emotions. We may find the techniques of biological creation amusing, but we supply those techniques; they are not in Mary Shelley's text. For another thing, at the moment of creation the monster is not actually rendered but only implied. We may find the image of the patchwork monster amusing, but again it is we who supply the image. We may also look for a participant, an assistant, someone perverse enough to share in the experiment and able to register for us his anticipation. But in the text, Frankenstein is alone (and, as Judith Wilt argues above, it is thematically crucial that he be alone).

One characteristic of the passage, however, not at all comic in the reading, is amusing as we remember and reconstruct it in reflection. Moreover, unlike those other associations which we unfairly bring to the text, it is an aspect of the action that is really in the text. Victor calls his creation a "lifeless thing," an object. His phrase carries connotations of disdain, which are, of course, not random and uncontrolled connotations but are here, as at other points in the book, Victor's consistent view of his masterpiece. Having made the creature, Victor doesn't like it very well, indeed is repelled by it, a response underlined by the "yellow eye" of the next sentence, from which the conclusion follows that Victor Frankenstein, overreacher, nineteenth-century Anglo-Germanic Faust, fallen angel, Ancient Mariner, autodidact, player at God, modern Prometheus, is not very good at his trade.

Consider the surrounding details. Rather than imparting life to a plausible corpse, Frankenstein has assembled anatomical parts so as to make a creature *eight feet tall*. No thought of the social problems of an eight foot creature crosses his mind. During the period of the experiment, he visibly disintegrates, becoming obsessive and compulsive, moved by thoughts of the creation of a new race grateful to him for its creation—yet he speaks of his work as horrible, filthy, and loathsome. As he recounts this period, he lapses into lyricism on the passing seasons (he is nearly two years at his work), interjects platitudes and facile praises of domesticity, and finally has to be reminded by his implied reader to keep to the subject. At last he imparts life and sees, apparently for the very first time, that the creature's skin does not fit its frame, that its eyes are watery and its lips are black. He leaves the room for his bedchamber, where he paces the floor, distraught and nearly delirious, while the creature rises from the table and walks away. But Frankenstein sees one last glimpse of him; the monster beckons and smiles but Frankenstein, immobilized, cannot respond. Frankenstein, in short, is a failure, not in a grand and tragic manner but in a manner closer to low comedy, bumbling, inattentive, inept, and ineffectual. Yet he does not seem so line by line, and it would take a large measure of cynicism to read those pages with sustained laughter.

In works of any period there are passages that we laugh at in which the implicit intention is comic but the execution is serious, for example, those portions of *Gulliver's Travels* in which Gulliver's comic opacity is played off against his flat and uncomprehending style. (*Gulliver's Travels*, in fact, strikingly parallels *Frankenstein* in several ways, with its seriocomic juxtapositions of size and in its contrasts of energy, motion, and potency with failure, confinement, and stasis.) In works of any period there are also passages we laugh at in which the implicit intention is serious but the execution is comic: the banter of Lear's fool. And there are, lastly, works we laugh at even though both the intention and the execution are serious, such as the poems in *The Stuffed Owl*. Mary Shelley's book has affinities with all three of these modes. But, despite affinities with other kinds of writing in which some kind of radical disjunction occurs between elements of seriousness and elements of the comic, *Frankenstein*, I would suggest, occupies a peculiar kind of subgenre, characterized by dream-like mechanisms and by much rather directly rendered psychic material, and also by a tension so unsettling as to confound our sense of how to feel about it. Understanding the place of *Frankenstein* in such a subgenre does much to explain the amazing diversity of its many reincarnations, versions differing precisely in the degree to which they ask us to take the narrative seriously. (It is not irrelevant in thinking about that subgenre to recall that the two great bodies of narrative materials which Freud used as means for describing the contours of the unconscious were dreams and jokes, that he was variously disturbed and intrigued by the fact that the two bear remarkable formal and functional similarities to each other.)

Paul Zweig describes the impotence of the characters in Walpole's *Castle of Otranto*, "their inability to make anything happen at all."

This failure, I would argue, is the principal theme of *Otranto*. All of
its human characters have a genius for ineptitude. When decisive
acts are called for, they lunge about and make a mess of things.
The children hurry enthusiastically toward disaster like rabbits into
a headlight. The fathers—Manfred, the monk Jerome, Frederick
the good knight—are bunglers. Hippolyte, the mother, is so desperately obedient that she seems to call down her husband's abuse,
and deserve it.[2]

Zweig takes very seriously the mythic power that seems to have
been set in motion by Walpole's strange and artless book. Yet as he
summarizes the characteristic action of the book, his diction becomes, almost as if against his will, quite comic: "lunge about and
make a mess of things," "like rabbits into a headlight," "bunglers,"
"desperately obedient."

Zweig's view of *Otranto* is not the conventional one; yet it seems,
both in its argument and its tone, irrefutable. And, looked at with
Zweig's eyes, *Otranto* is transformed into an analogue of *Frankenstein*. Although both books are artistically flawed, a direct response
to their quality as objects of finished art seems if not irrelevant at
least secondary. In both books a strange tension exists between
their psychic power (Walpole himself reported that *Otranto* originated in a dream and that its early composition was rather like
automatic writing) and the nature of an action so ineffectual and
bumbling as to be comic at some remove from the experience of
reading.

Nineteenth-century American fiction offers many variants of
that basic narrative situation, works often with a strained or crude
or "operatic" quality about them, carrying a heavy freight of
psychic baggage, in which the action is easily reducible to repeated
frustrations and ritual failures, the tone at all points utterly serious,
the action in its outlines perversely comic. Poe wrote such tales, as
did Hawthorne. In *The American Notebooks* Hawthorne's ideas for
his fiction read like pure prototypes of the comic impulse, waiting
to be fleshed out with solemn prose: "A person to be writing a tale,
and to find that it shapes itself against his intentions; that the characters act otherwise than he thought; that unforeseen events occur;
and a catastrophe occurs which he strives in vain to avert. It might
shadow forth his own fate—he having made himself one of the

2. *The Adventurer* (New York, 1974), pp. 174–76.

personages."[3] Melville's *Bartleby the Scrivener* is perhaps the best
known and most artistically successful example; a desperate and
depressing story of ritual nihilism, in which Melville obviously invested large amounts of his own anxieties and artistic motives,
Bartleby is, for all that, quite comic. (Try telling the story of Bartleby
aloud to anyone who does not know it.)

The supreme example, for the twentieth-century imagination, of
this narrative situation is the fiction of Kafka, in which humor lies
just beneath the surface of the flat, underplayed style and the grim
desperation of his narratives. Max Brod recalls:

When Kafka read aloud, this humor became particularly clear.
Thus, for example, we friends of his laughed quite immoderately
when he first let us hear the first chapter of *The Trial*. And he himself laughed so much that there were moments when he couldn't
read any further. Astonishing enough when you think of the fearful earnestness of this chapter. But that is how it was.[4]

The Metamorphosis, more concentrated than *The Trial*, is, as more
than one commentator has observed, at once harrowing, almost
intolerable in its psychic power, and a very funny story about a man
who, though transformed into a giant insect, still worries that he
might miss his train.

II

What I wish to put together, then, is a group of fictional works,
with *Frankenstein* at the center, in which the basic events not only
are detached from the everyday concerns of the reader but also
possess a heightened and distorted quality, especially pronounced
because of their lack of causal sufficiency and by the characters' inability to effect the consequences they strive for.[5] Such events and

3. *The American Notebooks*, ed. Claude M. Simpson, *Works, Centenary Edition* (Columbus, Ohio, 1972), VIII:16.
4. Max Brod, *Franz Kafka: A Biography* (New York, 1960), p. 178.
5. I have assembled works that are not exactly novels and stories, not
exactly romances, not exactly dream allegories. The fact, in itself, that such
works do not fit established genres has something to do with their power.
Jonathan Culler asks, "Why are our most crucial and tantalizing experiences of literature located at the interstices of genres, in this region of
non-genre literature?" and then speculates on the reasons why ("Towards a
Theory of Non-Genre Literature," in *Surfiction: Fiction Now and Tomorrow*,
ed. Raymond Federman [Chicago, 1975], pp. 255–62).

such works remind us of the events of our own dream life, our dreams, in retrospect, often seeming to us both portentous and nonsensical, terrifying and silly. More particularly, the unity that connects these literary forms can be found in the last stage of Freud's (and others') description of the dream process, namely that waking stage known as "secondary elaboration," in which the recollection of the dream, which, as it was dreamed, was necessarily illogical, causally discontinuous, absurd, and fragmentary, is arranged, made sequential, and fleshed out with a kind of narrative logic that makes the telling of it tolerable to the waking, conscious mind.

The classic description of the process of secondary elaboration occurs in Freud, who quotes Havelock Ellis with amusement and approval: "'As a matter of fact, we might even imagine the sleeping consciousness as saying to itself: "Here comes our master, Waking Consciousness, who attaches such mighty importance to reason and logic and so forth. Quick! gather things up, put them in order—any order will do—before he enters to take possession."'"[6] The writing of most prose fiction, of course, is analogous not to the telling of dreams but to the telling of remembered events from one's conscious past. The much smaller body of prose fiction (and a significant body of narrative and lyric poetry) that is analogous to the telling of dreams carries with it both the compulsiveness and the indeterminacy of the relating of dreams in experience; the Ancient Mariner is model both for the compulsiveness of the teller and the oddity of the rhetoric, for whom is it that one tells one's dreams to? And what is the appropriate tone?

Literature created out of dream images can either leave the dream images with much of the absurdity intact or transform them into "made," "told," fully "elaborated" works, still with some aspects of the dream work exposed, such as its detachment from empirical reality and its unabashed symbolism, but with the illogic and absurdity neutralized. In prose fiction, dream allegories of the past such as *Pilgrim's Progress* or visionary fantasies of the future like H. G. Wells's *The Time Machine* are examples of entirely different aesthetic motives, united only by the common effort to superimpose a maximum of conscious control on a body of dream-like

6. *The Basic Writings of Sigmund Freud*, Modern Library edition (New York, 1938), p. 464.

images. We could isolate individual passages in either Bunyan's book or Wells's as legitimately dream-like, but neither work *reads* at all like a dream being told. At the other extreme, Rabelais is full of passages that read rather like unmediated dream scenes, told with a minimum exercise of the elaborative mechanisms; and in modern literature the "Nighttown" episode in *Ulysses* is the best known and most sustained example of a passage that allows the primal dream material to stand, in all of its irrational power.

At some midpoint between these extremes are those forms I am attempting to describe, in which the secondary elaboration is incomplete, part of the conscious mediation left undone, some of the illogic left unrationalized, some of the absurdity left intact, as if the author, as dreamer, wished to leave the strangeness of the dream largely unchanged by deliberately withholding some of the art. The result is a story that risks seeming ridiculous for the sake of preserving a measure of the psychic authority of the dream work that gave the initial impetus to the creation of the work.

Most of Poe's stories obviously had their origins in dream work or in images comparable to and derivative of dreams. But their syntax is conventional, the order of events is intelligible, sufficient gestures are made toward the explanation of motive, the criteria for inclusion of images and events are implicitly clear, and Poe's desired effect can be inferred from the finished story—which is to say that the fragmentary silliness and the arbitrary illogic of the primal materials with which Poe begins are written out in the interests of a unified art story. "The Pit and the Pendulum" is a bad dream, but the reading of it conveys not the "feel" of a dream but rather that of waking experience. Melville's dream (or daydream) of a nihilistic clerk, on the other hand, allows itself a lesser degree of secondary elaboration. The result is a narrative which, though it takes place in the world of business instead of a dark and solitary room, has much more the "feel" of a dream.

Dreams, to be sure, are dreams and stories, stories. Yet every literary form "imitates," at some remove, a preliterary mode of experience. Our view of the conventions of a given work may be too limited if we take it as being only one of a large and amorphous class of roughly similar literary works. On the contrary, our sense of the given work is sharpened if we think of it in its context of other works that we may agree to call novels and romance but that, in a narrower sense, adapt to a highly specific literary purpose some of the impulses and structures of dream. To link Mary Shelley's book with Kafka's work does, inadvertently, dignify and make it more apparently modern, but it also makes its assumptions and conventions more clear and more aesthetically justifiable.

So *Frankenstein*, like early Gothic before it, like Kafka after it, and like a multitude of works of various periods, such as Melville's *Bartleby*, makes itself out of dream images told, but not fully elaborated, into rational and sequential art. The result is a narrative vehicle which allows a large measure of self-exposure, terror, pathos, and psychic pain to coexist with much absurdity, apparent ineptitude, silliness, and the risk that the whole enterprise will be brushed aside by the reader as making no claims on his mature scrutiny.

III

Rescued from the ice, Victor Frankenstein consents to tell his story to Walton. "Prepare to hear of occurrences which are usually deemed marvellous," he says. "Were we among the tamer scenes of nature, I might fear to encounter your unbelief, perhaps your ridicule; but many things will appear possible in these wild and mysterious regions, which would provoke the laughter of those unacquainted with the ever-varied powers of nature" (p. 30). Precisely: we, of course, are not in the Arctic ice fields when we read Mary Shelley's book but settled quietly at home. That Frankenstein's revelations do not provoke laughter from Walton is due not only to Walton's physical situation, his fervent seriousness and the consequent seriousness of the style, but also to his sharing the psychological stress of Frankenstein, a dreamer condemned to tell his dreams, unable to "elaborate" them into coherent rationality, knowing that the telling of the narratives that issue from his wishes and fears will expose him, try our patience, make himself at times into a low-comic butt rather than the hero he imagines himself to be.

Even before he encounters Frankenstein Walton is unable to supply the waking mind's reasons for the dream-like voyage he so obsessively undertakes. "I shall satiate my ardent curiosity with the sight of a part of the world never before visited, and may tread a land never before imprinted by the foot of man. These are my enticements, and they are sufficient to induce me to commence this laborious voyage with the joy a child feels when he embarks in a little boat, with his holiday mates, on an expedition of discovery up his native river" (p. 16). Walton's learning and his heroic passions coexist with a child-like, prerational fantasy life; the images of his inner life are unabashedly *un*transformed by the conscious mind, leaving him exposed and unsteady, our response to him uncertain. His greatest anxiety, on starting out, is that he has no friend, a startling confession of his human and dream-like image of his own self in society. Why he has no intimate friend, and what difference it now makes that he does not, are difficult to explain, which is to say that the primal imagery once again is only partly transformed by the logic of the waking narrative. As with Frankenstein's creation of the Monster, no reader laughs at Walton's analogy of his voyage with a child's expedition or his complaint of friendlessness. But, in retrospect, one realizes how exposed he has left himself, and how absurd, a polar explorer seen as little boy lost.

Victor's own narration moves quickly into his quest for knowledge and scientific mastery in a sequence that partakes of the structure and tone of the frame comments of Walton. At the age of thirteen Victor comes across a volume of Cornelius Agrippa, which fascinates him, although his father pronounces it "sad trash" (p. 39). Undeterred, he procures the works of Paracelsus and Albertus Magnus, which he reads with delight and enthusiasm. In due course, he leaves for the university at Ingolstadt, where he seeks out Professor Krempe, a crabbed and ugly little man, to whom he discloses his interest in natural philosophy. What has he read? asks Professor Krempe. It is like a dream and a joke. We wait for the line. Paracelsus and Albertus Magnus, poor Frankenstein replies. The professor erupts. "'Every minute . . . every instant that you have wasted on those books is utterly and entirely lost. You have burdened your memory with exploded systems and useless names. Good God! in what desert land have you lived, where no one was kind enough to inform you that these fancies, which you have so greedily imbibed, are a thousand years old, and as musty as they are ancient? I little expected, in this enlightened and scientific age, to find a disciple of Albertus Magnus and Paracelsus. My dear sir, you must begin your studies entirely anew'" (p. 46).

It is funny and not funny, the poor fool who has given years of his life to the wrong books. Its analogue in dream life is the nightmare of all travelers, to be in a country for which one's phrase book is in the wrong language and all one's well-meaning attempts at civility only offend the locals because one has mastered the wrong customs. Nothing in the logic of Mary Shelley's narrative could have compelled her to imagine ritual humiliations for Victor Frankenstein in his progress toward scientific mastery, nothing except the feeling that it was somehow right to invest his learning both with nightmare inefficacy and comic failure.

The Monster is created and abandoned. William is murdered; Justine is tried, convicted, and executed. Victor endures it all as if entranced, immobilized, guilty of both murders because he is guilty of having made and abandoned their murderer; he is obliged, furthermore, to tell it all to us. After a time, Frankenstein and his Monster are reunited and the Monster begins his own narration. He describes his "infancy," his solitary misery, and his first terrifying experience with people. He soon begins to observe the De Lacey family, from whom he learns their manners and customs, their wishes and fears, their language and their very moral sensibilities.

It is an extraordinary posture he assumes, hunched unseen in the shed near the De Laceys' cottage for some months, rarely venturing forth, his eye fixed on a chink in the wall of the cottage. It is, in fact, an act of prolonged voyeurism, in which the whole of his consciousness is filled with his view of, and his speculations on, the people who move in and out of that visual frame. The events within that visual frame have, necessarily, a hallucinatory aspect. "Through this crevice a small room was visible, whitewashed and clean, but very bare of furniture. In one corner, near a small fire, sat an old man, leaning his head on his hands in a disconsolate attitude. The young girl was occupied in arranging the cottage; but presently she took something out a drawer, which employed her hands, and she sat down beside the old man, who, taking up an instrument, began to play, and to produce sounds sweeter than the voice of the thrush or the nightingale" (p. 108). Again, the passage gives a double effect, of psychic intensity in the reading of it and of faint ridiculousness when it is remembered, the immobilized inefficacy of the Monster, the suggestion of perversity in an act of voyeurism extended through an entire winter, the helplessness of the teller, who must relate his absurd experience.

Victor's promise to the Monster—that he make him a mate—proves impossible for him to keep and he gives up the enterprise, tearing up the partly assembled limbs, gathering up the pieces and carrying them away so as not to frighten the peasants. It is a scene filled with diffuse anxiety and ritual frustration, comic in retrospect, the retrospective comedy defusing the anxiety with which the scene is charged. Then follows a passage as haunting and powerful as any in the book, in which Victor, swept ashore in Ireland, is greeted with surliness and hostility, surrounded by a menacing crowd, and led off to a scowling magistrate, protesting his innocence of some unnamed crime. The crime of which he is ultimately accused is the murder of Clerval, whose corpse he agonizedly recognizes. Ineffectual again, inarticulate, impotent, he sinks into convulsions and a long delirious fever. He describes his revival. "But I was doomed to live; and, in two months, found myself as awaking from a dream, in a prison, stretched out on a wretched bed, surrounded by gaolers, turnkeys, bolts, and all the miserable apparatus of a dungeon" (p. 177). This scene powerfully reminds the modern reader of Kafka and Joseph K. The relation between *The Trial* and *Frankenstein* thus becomes one of those Eliotesque or Borgesian situations in which a recent work inadvertently enlarges and complicates our understanding of a previous work. We cannot now will ourselves to be innocent of Kafka; and so Frankenstein's guilt must seem more awesome and mysterious because we can only read through our experience of Kafka. Furthermore, Frankenstein in that scene must suggest the additional parallel, that Joseph K., guilty of nothing yet guilty as charged, moved Kafka to laughter.

As Frankenstein is released from prison and the book works toward its close, he himself conflates his dreams with his waking life: "The past appeared to me in the light of a frightful dream; yet the vessel in which I was, and the wind that blew me from the detested shores of Ireland, and the sea which surrounded me, told me too forcibly that I was deceived by no vision" (p. 183); "during the day I was sustained and inspirited by the hope of night; for in sleep I saw my friends, my wife, and my beloved country" (p. 204). Elizabeth is murdered on their wedding night, and, resolute for the first time since he created the Monster, Frankenstein swears revenge. He kneels and calls on the ministers of vengeance to aid him in "my work," an invocation that is answered by a resounding laughter that seems to be at once the Monster's reply and a comic reverberation.

No reader of *Frankenstein* needs to be reminded of how the end of Victor's narration to Walton becomes a kind of surrealism before its time. It is the supreme chase scene of the fiction of the first half of the nineteenth century, acted out on an Arctic terrain that becomes a lunar landscape, the ice fields of the mind.

But now, when I appeared almost within grasp of my foe, my hopes were suddenly extinguished, and I lost all traces of him more utterly than I had ever done before. A ground sea was heard; the thunder of its progress, as the waters rolled and swelled beneath me, became every moment more ominous and terrific. I pressed on, but in vain. The wind arose; the sea roared; and, as with the mighty shock of an earthquake, it split, and cracked with a tremendous and overwhelming sound. The work was soon finished: in a few minutes a tumultuous sea rolled between me and my enemy, and I was left drifting on a scattered piece of ice, that was continually lessening, and thus preparing for me a hideous death. [Pp. 207–208]

The episode is so terrible because it is so preposterous, the action gradually speeding forward like a movie projector out of control, the pursuer become victim, the final humiliation, the last bad dream, and the last ritual defeat. Adrift on a frozen sea, Frankenstein is rescued and invited to tell his tale, a many-sided invitation which asks at one and the same time, What high mimetic horrors brought you to that frozen sea? and, What low mimetic ineptitude caused you to be adrift on an ice floe in the Arctic Ocean?

IV

I suggested earlier that the rhythms of *Frankenstein*, especially its stylized alterations of movement and inertia, are very pertinent to our ambivalent response to the book. Every artistic effect in *Frankenstein* bears some relation to certain primal patterns of imagery and narration. So it is with the book's rhythms. Those rhythms are, indeed, the central formal means by which the primal psychological impulses out of which the novel obviously grew are given fictional expression.

Passages of stasis in literary works often have the capacity to move us at some basic psychological level. Although most of our lives is lived in stasis—sleeping, eating, reading, sitting at a desk—the image of a character immobilized for any period of time is a disturbing one, haunting, problematic, potentially comic. The first book of *Gulliver's Travels* is rich and intricate, but surely the most affecting moment is the image of Gulliver immobilized, tied down on the beach. Bartleby, once again, also serves as an example of the ambivalent and psychologically potent effects of an immobilized character. It is a literary possibility carried to its farthest extreme in *Oblomov*.

A heightened sense of motion is, in a converse way, equally capable of evoking a strange and potent psychological response. A kinship between literary and dream images is obvious. Our most affecting dreams tend to be dreams of motion. We chase or are chased. We fall. We enter rooms. We arrive in strange towns. We swim, drive, fly. As for prose fiction, some of the most pointless and terrible moments in *Candide* are those passages in which the movement accelerates and the characters move in a kind of unwilling and farcical dance. It is a rhythm that Conrad was aware of; the storm scenes of his middle period are often invested with both a farcical excess of human movement and a horrifying hallucinatory power.

Frankenstein is, in some ways, a remarkably static book. The reader who expects a continuous and demonic energy will surely be disappointed by the amount of talk, those comparatively flat passages, sometimes lasting for many pages, where the suspense is dissipated and somebody explains. But the novel also contains some of the most memorable scenes of movement in all of prose fiction, each conspicuously dream-like. And those passages of stasis in *Frankenstein* are filled with a patterned and highly charged diction of movement, so that even when the characters are physically at rest, they often talk as if they were still in motion.

Here, for example, is Victor in motion:

It was completely dark when I arrived in the environs of Geneva; the gates of the town were already shut; and I was obliged to pass the night at Secheron, a village at the distance of half a league from the city. The sky was serene; and, as I was unable to rest, I resolved to visit the spot where my poor William had been murdered. As I could not pass through the town, I was obliged to cross the lake in a boat to arrive at Plainpalais. During this short voyage I saw the lightnings playing on the summit of Mont Blanc in the most beautiful figures. The storm appeared to approach rapidly; and, on landing, I ascended a low hill, that I might observe its progress. It advanced; the heavens were clouded, and I soon felt the rain coming slowly in large drops, but its violence quickly increased. [P. 75]

It is an odd and affecting night scene, the solitary journey against a background of the gathering storm, as good an example as any of the dream-telling quality that permeates the book. But if we contrast this with passages in which no physical movement occurs, even in such periods of stasis, the verbs, the metaphors dead and alive, the whole stylistic texture evoke movement. In the fourth chapter, for example, Frankenstein begins his studies and describes his path to knowledge, his rapid progress, his pursuit of discoveries, going as far as others have gone before him, arriving at a point, being on the brink, being led to examine, arriving at the summit, obliterating his steps, finding a passage, leading Walton on, being borne onwards like a hurricane, pursuing his undertaking, pursuing nature to her hiding place, being urged forward by a resistless impulse, and so on.

The Monster, with a totally different stylistic range, also moves, and we see his account, and others', of his movement. When he and his creator end their conversation, the Monster leaves: "I saw him descend the mountain with greater speed than the flight of an eagle, and quickly lost him among the undulations of the sea of ice" (p. 148). And elsewhere, "I would have seized him; but he eluded me, and quitted the house with precipitation. In a few moments I saw him in his boat, which shot across the waters with an arrowy swiftness, and was soon lost amidst the waves" (p. 168).

Like his creator, the Monster's diction, when he describes himself, is full of movement; it characteristically alternates between tranquillity and action, real or imagined. "All, save I, were at rest or in enjoyment. I, like the arch-fiend, bore a hell within me; and, finding myself unsympathised with, wished to tear up the trees, spread havoc and destruction around me, and then to have sat down and enjoyed the ruin" (p. 136). Or, a few paragraphs later, "These thoughts calmed me, and in the afternoon I sank into a profound sleep; but the fever of my blood did not allow me to be visited by peaceful dreams. The horrible scene of the preceding day was for ever acting before my eyes; the females were flying, and the enraged Felix tearing me from his father's feet" (p. 137). Basically gentle but endlessly menaced, betrayed, and provoked, the Monster moves, in his meditative self-narration, from stasis to violence.

The Monster, of course, walks, not only from town to town but through the regions of the earth. Frankenstein not only walks; he rides, in a chaise, for example, and a cabriolet. Above all, he rides in boats. The passage in which he approaches Geneva alone in a boat was quoted above. Later he describes the period after the conviction of Justine. "Often, after the rest of the family had retired for the night, I took the boat, and passed many hours upon the water. Sometimes, with my sails set, I was carried by the wind; and sometimes, after rowing into the middle of the lake, I left the boat to pursue its own course, and gave way to my own miserable reflections" (p. 91). Frankenstein meets his creature, hears his narration, and returns to Geneva, where again he passes time in a "little boat." "At these moments I took refuge in the most perfect solitude. I passed whole days on the lake alone in a little boat, watching the clouds, and listening to the rippling of the waves, silent and listless" (p. 150). A few pages later, he voyages down the Rhine with Clerval, in the same mood of passive lassitude. He undertakes, then abandons, the construction of a mate for the Monster, and then moves toward the scene described earlier as especially Kafkaesque: the landing on the Irish shore, the accusation of a nonspecific crime. The transition to that encounter is, again, by a solitary passage by boat, with the clouds, the sky, the wind, and the overwhelming passivity. Freed from prison, he leaves Ireland for Havre-de-Grace. "It was midnight. I lay on the deck, looking at the stars, and listening to the dashing of the waves" (p. 183). On the day of his wedding, he and Elizabeth travel—by boat—with the same incantatory and obsessive effects: the wind, the mountains in the background, the waves, the hypnotic motion of the boat. From that point to the end of the book, the pursuit is as much by sea as by land; and however purposeful the pursuit, something of the dream-like quality of passage by ship is never entirely lost.

What unites all of these modes of action—the Monster moving as if flying, Frankenstein pursuing truth by a vast family of travel metaphors, the monster driven to violence, Frankenstein carried along in his little boats—is a common appearance of automation, both characters acting not out of deliberation and will but helplessly, out of energies they cannot control. Victor's characteristic movements in his boats are not propulsion. He rarely seems to row, or sail; rather, he drifts. The Monster, portrayed in films as slow and awkward, in the book moves with superhuman speed, without the appearance of exertion. Both figures see themselves, and each other, as if they were figures in a dream. And both act out for us the archetypal situation of Bergsonian comic theory. They are automata, mechanized people, puppets, examples, as the operative phrase is customarily translated from Bergson, of "something mechanical encrusted on the living."[7] The phrase, though perhaps oversimple, aptly suggests a last comic aspect of Mary Shelley's serious book.

The characters see themselves at moments of crisis as being without will, drifting, or impelled. Nothing, to them, could be more serious than this helplessness. And, as we read, nothing to us could be more appalling, the figures of both Frankenstein and his Monster being enormously full of potentiality of mind and body. Yet as the book recedes in the mind, the images of the two puppets remain, one of them drifting in a little boat, the other gliding up and down the Alps, both of them automata yet each moving at a different rate, like two clocks with pendulums of different lengths.

The perils of writing about how something happens to be funny are inescapable; the critical argument collapses for the reader who cannot agree that the book in question is, in fact, comic. The professional critics of *Frankenstein*, over the years, have treated the book as seriously as Mary Shelley did. But the common reader has responded to it, at least in the last three decades, with an uneasy awareness of the capacity of the book to arouse an extraordinarily wide range of responses, one of which is amusement. It is a situation that calls for a healthy Johnsonian respect for the common reader. One might imagine a debate between a century and a half of solemn professional critical response, on the one hand, and, on the other, a single "common reader." Our common reader, let us say, responds to the scene in which Frankenstein, mortally ill, starved, with only one dog left to pull him, asks Walton, just before he freezes into that block of ice, "Before I come aboard your vessel . . . will you please have the kindness to inform me whither you are bound?" It is the quintessential scene juxtaposing stasis and motion, characteristic of the dream-like narration. And it will strike the common reader, as anyone knows who has taught the book, as

7. *Comedy: An Essay on Comedy by George Meredith and Laughter by Henri Bergson*, introduction by Wylie Sypher (Garden City, N.Y., 1956), p. 84.

oddly amusing, a reaction that is as honest, as true to the text, and as deserving of respect as the accumulated reactions of the critical tradition.

To describe the comic power contained in *Frankenstein* is not at all irreverent. There is a tradition within which *Frankenstein* unselfconsciously stands on its own, a rich and eclectic mode that remains undisturbed by the coexistence of mythic seriousness, psychic authority, and laughter.

PART
FIVE

THE VISUAL
PROGENY:

Drama and Film

XI

The Stage and Film Children
of *Frankenstein*: A Survey

ALBERT J. LAVALLEY

M OST OF US FIRST became acquainted with Frankenstein and his
terrifying creation not through the pages of Mary Shelley's
1818 novel but through our childhood Saturday afternoons at the
movies or leisurely sessions before the family television set. By the
time we read the novel the images from various films are so firmly
imprinted on our minds that it is almost impossible not to filter the
events and images of the book through the more familiar ones of
the films. We are apt to distort the novel to fit a familiar mold, miss
what is fresh or unfamiliar in it, and react with discomfort and
disappointment.

Even in their worst moments, for example, the classic Frankenstein films were never so rhetorical and loftily mannered as the
language of the novel. And familiar settings, characters, and actions are missing. Where is Frankenstein's marvelous laboratory?
What has happened to the big creation scene? The book gives us a
cryptic account of the Monster's "birth," so brief as to leave us won-
dering how it was done. And where in the creature of the book are
the familiar lineaments of Boris Karloff? Though this creature is
hideous enough, he is intelligent, articulate, quick to learn, and, as
Philip Stevick rightly stresses above, extremely fleet in his movements; he is no lumbering, shuffling, grunting monster mired in
the primitive. Where are Fritz and Ygor and Doctor Praetorius?
And Maria, the little girl drowned in the lake?

It may take time for us to adapt to these losses and to discover
that the book has its own peculiar power, a strength and vision
often quite similar to that of the best *Frankenstein* films—and more
rich and terrifying than any of them. By the time we have read the

243

Monster's painful tale of yearning and rejection, in chapters 11 through 16, we can have little doubt that we have encountered something complex and disturbing. Though the events in these chapters may vary from those in the films, they also supply the closest moments of proximity between film and book. These chapters offer images that often become the source of cinematic incidents expressing similar themes and carrying similar emotions. It is here that the spirit of the book and the classic films most nearly match: they share a vision of man as victim and outcast, innately good and open to the joys of nature and human society, but cut off from positive emotional responses and severed from society, a tormented and pitiful creature. Novel and films conceive the Monster differently, but in each he carries the burden of similar conflicts: endowed with superhuman strength, he is also highly vulnerable, the crucible in which the struggle of joy and suffering, sympathy and revenge, passivity and destructiveness most clearly is worked out. Moreover, every stage and film version preserves the bold outline of the novel's principal action, the creation of an artificial man.

If, in their focus on the Monster, the stage and film versions are faithful to the core of Mary Shelley's novel by evoking the same fascination and same mixture of terror and sympathy with which we behold this primal being, they also threaten to simplify the book's complexities. The multiple points of view furnished by the narrative are removed when we "see" the Monster with our own eyes, rather than through those of Victor or Walton or Felix. Though visualization is a powerful tool and one shot of the Monster slowly looking around can evoke deep fears, the range of associations nowhere seems as rich as that of the book. What is more, unlike the novel itself, most of the films insist on distance and dissociation. The Monster is usually mute or semiarticulate, lacking the "powers of eloquence and persuasion" that, in the novel, defy or compensate for his hideousness. In the film or on the stage that hideousness tends to dominate; as a result Victor has no real bond with his creation and is rarely as ambivalent about him as he is in the novel. The parallels between his increasing desolation and that of the Monster are not underscored, and the melodramatic style of acting first introduced by Colin Clive further prevents an identification with the inner torments of the scientist. No *Doppelgänger* can be suggested when his hysteria and nervousness are set against the

Monster's quite distinct sufferings, when no Walton exists to provide a common denominator.

This simplification in the approach to the book's two central characters and to their relation is usually accompanied by a similar simplification in plotting. Though each of the *Frankenstein* films retains the basic cycle of creation and destruction, and though the so-called "classic" ones—James Whale's 1931 *Frankenstein* and his 1935 *The Bride of Frankenstein*—are quite closely connected to the novel, none of them truly follows the full complexities of the plot. The whimsical way in which characters are shuffled, renamed, and modified (even in the two "classic" films) may well seem perverse and maddening to someone who knows the novel. Why, for instance, does Victor become Henry Frankenstein in the classic films? Has he absorbed the personality of Henry Clerval, his friend? Is Henry a more acceptable name than Victor? Or is this just the perpetuation of accident and confusion from various stage traditions? Why is the older De Lacey deprived of Agatha and Felix, and hence of a scene that has strong visual possibilities?

It is of course useless to quibble about such matters. The baroque plot variations that can be mustered from the core of creation and destruction become the *raison d'être* of a *Frankenstein* film and the source of its own distinct pleasure. Moreover, despite the mutilations of the novel, many of its complexities can somehow be at least implied or suggested in the most powerful visual moments of the film. *Frankenstein* has always been viewed by the playwright or the screenwriter as a mythic text, an occasion for the writer to let loose his own fantasies or to stage what he feels is dramatically effective, to remain true to the central core of the myth, and often to let it interact with fears and tensions of the current time: e.g., certain threats of technology in the 1930s in *The Bride of Frankenstein* or the problem of "identity" (connected with organ transplants) in the late 1960s in *Frankenstein Must Be Destroyed*.

There are also good reasons—inherent in the structure, language, and manner of the novel—for such license. But beyond these there are historical, social, and theatrical explanations for recent modifications, and there are clear lines of transmission from the nineteenth-century stage presentations to the films. Certain events from the book *do* occur again and again and in a similar way; still others recur with varying modifications. There is always a creation scene, a wedding night scene or an abduction of the bride, and a scene of fiery destruction. Other scenes never appear; we never see Justine and the locket that betrayed her, we never meet Walton, and no one has ever seen the Monster read *Paradise Lost* or Plutarch. To recognize how certain key images, themes, and events are handed down and why they are modified, I will here group the *Frankenstein* productions in the popular arts of the theatre and film into historical segments.

I. Nineteenth-century Theatrical Presentations

The most surprising fact we learn about this area from Donald F. Glut's superb and perhaps obsessive collection of Frankenstein information, *The Frankenstein Legend*, is the almost immediate popularity of *Frankenstein* on the stage. In the 1820s, even before Mary Shelley's authorship was widely known, there were several productions playing simultaneously in London. The type and range of these productions are interesting for the future Frankenstein adaptations: they point to inherent problems in dramatizing the novel— changes that were necessarily made in transferring it from the realm of Gothic literature to a more melodramatic popular theatre —and to some common solutions. In tone, they seem to resemble our own classic Frankenstein films, aspects of the Gothic and the wondrous freely mingling with a more popular and moralistic kind of melodrama.

One of them, *Presumption; or The Fate of Frankenstein* (1823), by Richard Brinsley Peake, was to serve as a basic transcription of the novel for the stage and a source for further elaboration. As the title indicates, the moral world that surrounds the hero is more conventional than Mary Shelley's "Modern Prometheus." Like almost all the stage and film presentations to follow, *Presumption* was far less openly daring in its morality than the novel (something Terence Fisher and Peter Cushing claim to have corrected in the Hammer series). As in the classic *Frankenstein* films, the Monster seems to have stolen the show, with Thomas Potter Cooke becoming the Karloff of his day, playing the role some 365 times, and gaining the warm approbation of Mary Shelley herself. Two other plays of the 1820s about which less is known sound like the comic variations of our own time, the spoofs at the end of the Universal series, like *Abbot and Costello Meet Frankenstein* (1948), or the recent Mel Brooks parody, *Young Frankenstein* (1974). One was called *Frankenstitch*, wherein Frankenstein was a tailor sewing dead bodies together; the other was called *Frank-n-steam*.

From the beginning it was clear that the novel posed certain problems to dramatization. No dramatist would want to duplicate its structure of flashbacks, but would instead try to find a chronologically linear plot. Nor could any dramatist really allow the novel's vast range of scenes. The wondrous thus had to be contained within a tighter arrangement of space and time, even though popular theater of the period relished more scene transitions than modern theater. Some condensation was necessary, and the common solution was to look for key scenes that could be highly charged dramatically and around which other scenes could be arranged. Usually these were the creation scene, the bridal night, and the destruction scene. Much of the abstract and philosophical language had to go, as well as the probing into the psyches of Victor and the Monster. These were to some extent rendered in the action, but in other respects they simply slipped away to be replaced by an elaboration of more melodramatic actions, a whole cycle of elaborate pursuits, abductions, and chases. The fragments of *Presumption* that Glut quotes show that a surprisingly large amount of elaborately stylized language was maintained. But while Victor declaims during the creation scene it is in a more conventionally moralistic manner; nor is his declamation as central as the action of the Monster's awakening and the music that orchestrates it step by step. While his speech occupies a large amount of space on the page, in practice it most likely served as a kind of obligato effect on the dominant of the Monster's coming to consciousness.

Despite the problem the book posed for the stage, in many respects it was clearly suited to the theater of the day, which relished melodrama and romance and wondrous excess. In the book when the Monster confronts his creator he approaches Victor while he is sleeping and looks plaintively at him, stretching out his hand as if to detain him; Victor wakens from his dream, sees him, shows his repugnance, and flees. In *Presumption*, much as in the later films, the stress is on action: the Monster and Victor square off as instant antagonists. Victor not only repents of what he has done, but draws a sword and tries to kill the Monster. The Monster snaps the sword in two and smashes down a door after Victor has locked him in a room. Of such spectacular action would later films be made.

Visualizing the Monster also posed a number of serious problems—matters of technique and of meaning and emphasis. First, how to do it? The physical description Mary Shelley gives us is very brief:

How can I describe my emotions at this catastrophe, or how delineate the wretch whom with such infinite pains and care I had endeavoured to form? His limbs were in proportion, and I had selected his features as beautiful. Beautiful!—Great God! His yellow skin scarcely covered the work of muscles and arteries beneath; his hair was of a lustrous black, and flowing; his teeth of a pearly whiteness; but these luxuriances only formed a more horrid contrast with his watery eyes, that seemed almost of the same color as the dun-white sockets in which they were set, his shrivelled complexion, and straight black lips. [P. 52, Rieger edition]

We later learn that the Monster is about eight feet high, able to scale mountain walls and to endure the sharpest cold. But the emphasis is always on his hideousness—a hideousness that the stage and film productions have always tried to exploit.

In the novel, however, that hideousness terrifies us because it is so indefinite. We do not really see the Monster's ugliness; we are reminded of it by its effect on others. Each reader's imagination provides details taken from private dreads. Mary Shelley is capable of producing terror through mere suggestion. When Victor decides that he must destroy the half-formed female monster in his island laboratory, the setting is deliberately hazy: "I sat one evening in my laboratory; the sun had set, and the moon was just rising from the sea. I had not sufficient light for my employment." It is in this penumbra that Victor sees, "by the light of the moon, the daemon at the casement. A ghastly grin wrinkled his lips as he gazed on me, where I sat fulfilling the task which he had allotted to me." The scene is reminiscent, not only of many a Romantic poem in which the "casement" acts as a threshold between two separate realities, but also of the climax of Henry James's "The Turn of the Screw." Is the Monster outside the window real, or is it merely a phantasm concocted by a diseased and tormented imagination? The answer is irrelevant. The "ghastly grin" terrifies us *because* it terrifies Victor. To represent such a scene on stage or in film is to destroy the suspension of disbelief, the cooperation of our own willing powers of fantasy and phantom-building. The novel strongly suggests that our notions of beauty are questionable, that an apparent monster may be moved by emotions like our own. The physical representation on the stage or in the film, however, obviously discourages such ambivalences. Almost any visualizing of the Monster makes him the focal point and a point that is perforce primarily physical. The book may gradually present us with a fully formed human psyche whose feelings, yearnings, and logic are often more profound than those who reject its outward husk, but the stage and film must fix that outward appearance from the very start. At best the makeup artist can suggest some rudimentary humanity and basic yearnings trying to free themselves from a deformed body.

The melodramatic theater of the nineteenth century, with its emphasis on the physical realization of the marvelous, was willing to settle for a compromise, one that stressed the oddity of the creature yet did not wholly deny him humanity and sympathy. From accounts of the play, Cooke's makeup appears to have been more clown-like than monstrous, more exciting and amusing than terrifying: yellow and green greasepaint on his face, black lips, unkempt hair, exposed blue legs. Such an appearance may have made him more accessible, but it must also have made him a figure of grotesquerie upstaging the conventionally clad actors and inevitably preventing any rich themes of interiority from emerging. Cooke did summon forth some of the pitifulness and depths of suffering in the creature, but, consistent with the style of his makeup and the theater of the day, his Monster, like Karloff's, did not talk but only grunted. As we shall see, the problem of makeup in dramatizing *Frankenstein* would remain both an occasion for drama and spectacle and a barrier against the deeper themes of the novel.

Beyond the problems occasioned by the makeup, the exigencies of popular melodrama simplified even further the complicated effects and problems of the novel. There was no time to dawdle over the Monster's education at the De Lacey household; he was simplified to a creature of brute primitive force and emotions. Similarly, in the more moralistic and simplified world of melodrama, Victor Frankenstein was assimilated to the myth of the godless and "presumptive" scientist, tampering with nature's secrets. While this suggestion is hardly absent from Mary Shelley's novel, it is not emphasized. Victor's actions escape conventional moralizing, but the title *Presumption* here neatly boxes them in. (Nevertheless, the performance of the play was vigorously protested as atheistic, probably on the reputation of the novel.)

The makeup and the melodramatic simplifications of *Presumption* obviously placed it on the edge of comedy and ripe for parody. The assistant Fritz—the classic servant figure of popular comedy—was born in *Presumption*, and the production quickly spawned the two burlesques *Frankenstitch* and *Frank-n-steam*. In its highly condensed melodramatic rendering of the plot, *Presumption* clearly foreshadows the classic films: a key creation scene, blind De Lacey consoling the creature, then turning on him along with Frankenstein, the Monster's revenge of Frankenstein's rejection by kidnapping Elizabeth, a pursuit up the mountains, destruction of both through an avalanche triggered by a bullet from Frankenstein's gun. Other adaptations during the century follow the same paths towards comedy or parody or even more excessive melodrama. In *The Man and the Monster* (1826), by H. M. Milner, the Monster burns down a house, is chased by a posse into the mountains, and finally plunges into the mouth of a volcano. In *The Model Man* (1887), Fred Leslie played a comic Monster with a burlesque hat and a monocle singing "Love in the Orchestra," a clear forerunner to Peter Boyle's "Putting on the Ritz" in *Young Frankenstein*. Furthermore, his creator was a woman—perhaps a forerunner to the transsexual Frank-n-furter of *The Rocky Horror Show* (1973).

II. Monsters in Film before the Universal *Frankenstein* of 1931

Two American silent *Frankenstein* films predate the Universal series, the Edison one-reel *Frankenstein* of 1910 and the five-reel *Life Without Soul* of 1915. Neither of these had much impact on the later Universal films, though both conformed to the highly moralistic melodrama of nineteenth-century theatrical presentations. In one surviving still (see illustration 4) of the Edison film, Charles Ogle's bizarre makeup is more terrifying than that of any of the stage Frankensteins. Though it has little relation to the Karloff makeup and more in common with that of the stage, its elaborate grotesquerie seems to signal an understanding that the movies can be more wild and dreamlike than the stage. In the surviving scenario of the movie, almost all the action centers on two scenes, both

The EDISON
KINETOGRAM

VOL. 1   LONDON, APRIL 15, 1910   No. 1

SCENE FROM

FRANKENSTEIN

FILM No. 6604

EDISON FILMS TO BE RELEASED
FROM MAY 11 TO 18 INCLUSIVE

4. The first Frankenstein Monster in film.
Charles Ogle in the single surviving still of
the 1910 one-reel Edison *Frankenstein*.

intensely cinematic: the creation, performed in a cauldron of seething chemicals, and the destruction, wherein Frankenstein finds the Monster as his own reflection in a mirror and gradually banishes him. The latter, of course, suggests those late-Victorian fantasies, *Dr. Jekyll and Mr. Hyde* and *Dorian Gray*, rather than *Frankenstein*, although the fusion of Frankenstein's and the Monster's reflected faces at least acknowledges the kinship between creator and creation, ignored before. Victorian, too, is the overlay of sexuality—a feature that was to persist in later films, notably in Hammer Films *Frankenstein Created Woman* (1966) and in pornographic and semi-pornographic films such as Russ Meyer's *Kiss Me Quick* (1963) and the French production of *Frankenstein Chérie* (1967). In Ogle's silent movie, the Monster vanishes when Frankenstein's love for his wife finds "freedom from impurity." "The creation of an evil mind is overcome by love and disappears," a title asserts, with dubious Victorian moral certitude. Yet eroticism, still covert in this early film, would not disappear at all, but return more fully in future fantasies.

Terror, however, continued to be the predominant mode in American films. The later Universal films (examined in the next section) thus owed much to the psychology of terror so brilliantly exploited in a trio of German films, *The Cabinet of Dr. Caligari* (1920), *The Golem* (1920), and *Metropolis* (1926). *The Golem* is clearly the closest in theme to the Frankenstein story. Mary Shelley may well have been familiar with the medieval legends of the artificial man who becomes both a protector to the Jews and a possible scourge. Paul Wegener's second film of the legend (with himself as the Golem) is based on Gustav Meyrink's novel. Here, Rabbi Löw models his artificial man from clay—hence his chalky, muddy look, and his lack of distinctive human features. Animated by a star of David in the legend, but, oddly, only by a star in the film, the Golem protects the Jewish ghetto from destruction by a tyrannical king but becomes violent when the planets change their course. The rabbi (no Frankenstein) disarms the Golem by removing the star, but a wily servant, jealous of the affection shown by the rabbi's daughter Miriam for the king's courtier, reanimates him. Violence ensues. The Golem hurls the courtier from a roof and abducts Miriam. He hovers over her in a manner reminiscent of the pose struck by Cesare in *Dr. Caligari* over the body of Jane (see illustrations 5 and 6); Miriam and Jane, in turn, resemble the prostrate

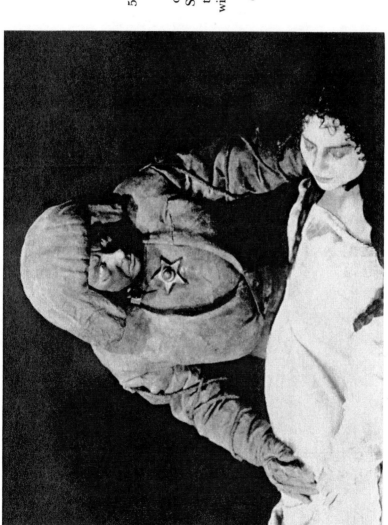

5. *The Golem* (1920). The Golem (Paul Wegener) hovers over Miriam (Lydia Salmonova) much in the way that Cesare will hover over Jane in *The Cabinet of Dr. Caligari* (figure 6).

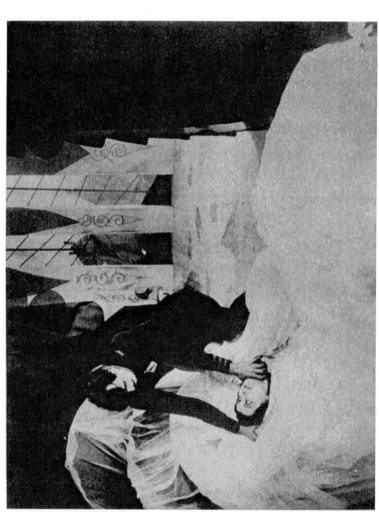

6. *The Cabinet of Dr. Caligari* (1920). Cesare (Conrad Veidt) hovers over Jane (Lil Dagover), whose prostration will be emulated by Elizabeth in Whale's *Frankenstein* (figure 7).

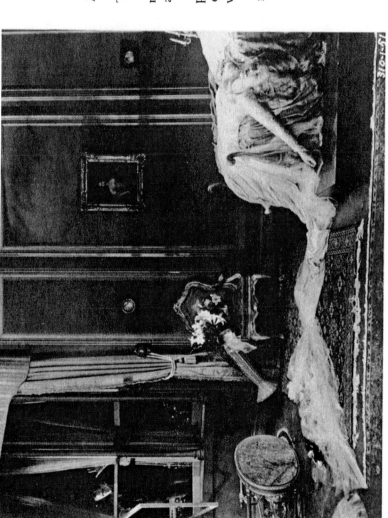

7. James Whale's *Frankenstein*, Universal Pictures (1931). The posture of Elizabeth (Mae Clarke) recalls that of Miriam and Jane (see figures 5 and 6); Karloff's peering Monster may owe more to Victor's vision in the Orkneys in Mary Shelley's novel: "I saw, by the light of the moon, the daemon at the casement."

Elizabeth in Whale's *Frankenstein* (see illustration 7). Once again, the outer frame of terror contains unmistakable erotic components. It is significant that the Golem should be disarmed for the second time by the fearlessness of a small child. The little girl (the prototype for the more tragically fearless child in Whale's *Frankenstein*) quietly removes the star that has become a badge of adult passion (see illustration 16).

The Golem significantly anticipates the Universal Frankenstein films in two other respects. Like *The Cabinet of Dr. Caligari* and the 1925 *The Phantom of the Opera*, it distinctly influenced the appearance that was to be assumed by the most famous impersonator of the Monster—Boris Karloff. And, like *Metropolis*, it helped to establish certain visual features, by now indelibly associated with *Frankenstein* in the twentieth-century popular imagination.

The physical similarities between Karloff's Monster (illustration 8) and Conrad Veidt's Cesare in *Caligari* and Lon Chaney's Phantom are perhaps more readily apparent than his resemblance to Wegener's Golem. Jack Pierce, the makeup man for Universal, obviously drew on Chaney's unmasked Phantom (see illustration 9) in depicting the Monster: in both instances, the gaunt visage and elongated and distorted features are simultaneously terrifying and human. The long face and darkened eyes and mouth of Conrad Veidt's Cesare are just as clearly precursors to Karloff's death-like glaze and darkened eyes and lips (see illustration 10). The similarity goes further. Cesare moves quickly across the rooftops with his victim, but when he approaches her he moves in a slow trance-like fashion. It is this retarded motion—by now the hallmark of any amateur comedian who wants to impersonate "Frankenstein"—that Karloff's Monster owes above all to Wegener's bulky Golem, shuffling forward in a jerky, robot-like way. Commanded, the Golem can be useful; out of control, he is capable of firing buildings, creating social chaos, the sexual abduction of fainting women. Like Karloff's Monster (and, indeed, like Mary Shelley's original), Wegener's Golem is an uneasy blend of primitive innocence and destructive rage.

The scene of the Golem's awakening strongly resembles what has rightly been considered to be one of the most powerful moments of the later film (see illustration 11). Still, the scenario for the Monster's creation is more directly indebted to Lang's *Metropolis*, in

8. Karloff's face in James Whale's *The Bride of Frankenstein*, Universal Pictures (1935). The makeup bears comparison with both Lon Chaney's Phantom (figure 9) and Veidt's Cesare (figure 10).

9. Lon Chaney as the unmasked Phantom
in *The Phantom of the Opera* (1925).

which the vast and well-equipped laboratory, pulsing with electricity, is dramatically essential for Rotwang's creation of a robot. The visual spectacle was irresistible, and Whale imitated it in the creation scene of *Frankenstein* only to surpass it with almost outrageous excess in *The Bride*, where wild music (as in the 1823 stage production of *Presumption*) rises in a crescendo as the body likewise rises on its slab toward the hole in the roof. Whale was aware, of course, that *Frankenstein* was a story set in a pre-electrical age. Yet his awareness, too, of the thunderstorm from which Mary Shelley has Victor learn his first lesson in "electricity" permitted him to adapt the scene from *Metropolis* to his own aims. The raising of the platform, the elaborate machinery, the laboratory's electrical vials

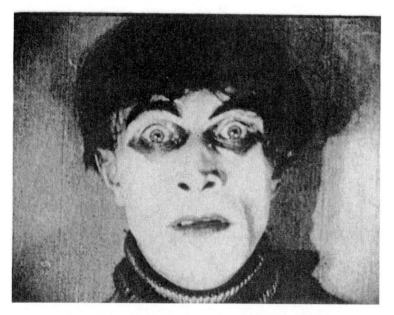

10. Conrad Veidt as Cesare in *The Cabinet
of Dr. Caligari* (1920). A precursor of
Karloff's Monster?

(see illustration 12) became a ritual scene of dark and sinister splendor to be retained by future interpreters of the novel.

Ironically, the rich visual suggestiveness of German expressionist cinema only helped to remove later Frankenstein films further from their novelistic source. Although the Golem legend may actually have influenced Mary Shelley's own conception of the Monster and its creator, Wegener's film, like *Dr. Caligari* and *Metropolis*, also provided Whale and later directors with elements that were either foreign to Mary Shelley's novel or secondary. No icy Arctic wastes, but the pulsating laboratory, no Rousseauvian monster-child, but a hideous figure of destruction, were now given primary and unequivocal emphasis. Cesare is robot-like, a docile yet murderous puppet of the new figure of the evil scientist-magician who will reappear as Doctor Praetorius (Ernest Thesiger) in *The Bride* and as Polidori (James Mason) in *Frankenstein: The True Story*. The eroticism that was dormant in the novel and merely suggested by

259

11. Ernst Deutsch as the servant Famulus
and Albert Stein as Rabbi Löw try to move
the Golem (Paul Wegener) in a prefigura-
tion of Fritz, Henry, and Karloff's Monster
in the Universal *Frankenstein*.

12. Herman Rosse's spacious
lab and Kenneth Strikfaden's
apparatus are utilized by Henry
Frankenstein (Colin Clive) and
Fritz (Dwight Frye) as they raise
the creature on the platform
before Victor Moritz, a friend
(John Boles), Elizabeth (Mae
Clarke), and Doctor Waldman,
Frakenstein's mentor (Edward
van Sloan) in the classical
Universal *Frankenstein* (1931).

Ogle now became a clearly defined motif, subsidiary only to the importance placed on the Monster's capacity to inspire fear. So strong was *The Golem* as an inspiration and source for later versions of *Frankenstein* that even the sets designed by the famous architect Hans Poelzig became the models for the village in the Universal production of 1931.

III. The Universal "Classics": From *Frankenstein* (1931) to *Abbott and Costello Meet Frankenstein* (1948)

Boris Karloff's appearance and portrayal of the Monster (see illustration 8) remain by far the most memorable feature of James Whale's 1931 *Frankenstein*. It is the image inevitably evoked when we say "Frankenstein" and the image against which we must work when we read Mary Shelley's book. Yet it is also, as we shall see, an image that resurrects the novel's central questions about guilt and innocence.

The origins of that image are far more accidental than one might suspect. Universal Studios had originally planned a simple follow-up to the success achieved by Bela Lugosi in *Dracula*, also made in 1931. Robert Florey was assigned to direct the new film; Lugosi was willing to wear heavy makeup much resembling the Golem's if he were allowed to be the intelligent, talkative creature of Mary Shelley's book. Peggy Webling's stage version, a London success of 1930, had featured Hamilton Deane as a talkative Monster, in the usual greasepaint of the stage. Existing stills show him as most unfrightening. It was assumed that the movie, like *Dracula* (which Deane, by the way, had adapted), would follow the stage play. *The Golem*, however, had already signaled public desire for something more terrifying. Florey acquiesced in providing a script change that would give the Monster a criminal brain, the source presumably for his violence. The word "Neanderthal" frequently occurred in press releases. Lugosi balked and Florey himself was shuttled with Lugosi to a Poe movie, *Murders in the Rue Morgue* (1932).

Young James Whale then entered the scene and chose the relatively unknown Karloff to play the Monster. With makeup man and skilled anatomist Jack Pierce presiding, the trio fashioned the appearance of the Monster. The head was shaped like a lid, since Pierce had read that it was the simplest way to open and recap the brain; surgical scars would attest to the brain operation that the movie would not show. A Neanderthal slope over the eyes, done with putty, suggested the desired lower intelligence. The painted mouth contrasted with the pallor of the death-like flesh in the manner of Cesare in *Caligari* (see illustration 10). A tin forehead covered with putty accented the length and gauntness of the face to which Karloff's removal of some false teeth gave an even more sunken appearance. The famous electrodes in the neck were for the purpose of electrically animating the Monster. Twelve-pound boots and a five-pound back brace and heavy clothes made Karloff look bigger and walk stiffly; any conception of the Monster as fleet, wily, and intelligent disappeared under these accents of the primitive. But despite the forty-eight pounds of impediments Karloff managed to bring considerable emotional range to the creature.

Beyond Karloff's performance and some of the laboratory scenes, the movie has little else to recommend it. Unfortunately, what was retained from Peggy Webling's play were some of its talkiest drawing-room scenes; the picture becomes lifeless whenever the Monster is not present. While Webling's original play had more range than that of the movie—it had included the demand for a bride—by 1927, when it was written, the traditions of theater and staging had changed considerably from those of the nineteenth-century melodramatic spectacle. No writer could conceive the vast number of scene changes that the nineteenth-century stage Frankensteins had indulged, nor the spectacular effects of avalanches and flaming volcanoes. No writer could fail to be influenced by the realistic drawing room tradition of high comedy, the use of a few sets and minimal action. In the Webling version, the older melodramatic tradition appears only fitfully, mainly in the spectacular end when the Monster, having destroyed Frankenstein, awaits death by lightning in the laboratory.

The extreme primitiveness of the creature in this and the following films generated another problem. Monsters must be destroyed, but need their creators be? Rabbi Löw, the creator of the Golem, had acted out of the highest motives both in creating and in destroying his creation. With so primitive a monster it was now just as easy to exculpate Henry—no longer Victor—Frankenstein, and the film has Fritz steal the criminal brain after dropping the normal one. Consequently, Frankenstein's ideas are seen as noble even if he himself seems a bit mad. The 1931 *Frankenstein* thus settles for a moralistic compromise: the doctor is injured but not killed by his creation; he is punished for his *hubris* and he willingly singles himself out to confront the Monster in the burning windmill. Risking death, he finds life. The effect, however, is to snap the bond between creator and creature and to forgo Mary Shelley's bleak end: in the last scene, the traditions of drawing-room comedy are reasserted, the wedding is again planned, and the old baron toasts to the hopes of a new son for the line of Frankenstein. However, there is also the hint—confirmed by later movies—that if the doctor can be so easily resurrected, so can the Monster. Like the basic struggles of life, both are eternal.

Two scenes that are severely cut in existing prints point to material that is deeply disturbing and consonant with the conflicting feelings about the Monster which the book generates. The tormenting of the Monster by Fritz, once with a whip and later with a torch (see illustration 13), has no basis in the book but crystallizes a number of sadistic and violent images of humanity in the novel and heightens our sympathy for this socially innocent creature. The equally innocent encounter with the child captures the wonder, excitement, and innate goodness of the creature in the book (see illustration 14), although his drowning of her seems inexplicable. Unlike the deliberateness of his murder of little William in the novel, it is here a result of accident, stupidity, uncontrolled brute strength. The incident with the child and the flower is probably drawn from *The Golem* (see illustration 15), but it also evokes the momentary compassion for little William in the novel, which paralyzes the Monster before the need for revenge asserts itself. Cut from the final prints are the scenes of the Monster hanging Fritz in revenge and the throwing of the child in the lake after the Monster has exhausted his bunch of daisies. If the scenes had been included, we might have had an even more complicated view of the Monster, one that kept but troubled the notion of an innocent and ignorant victim.

The Bride of Frankenstein, the 1935 sequel, pushes the interpretation of the Monster as an innocent victim even further. Indeed, he seems to kill only when provoked. Other murders—that of a child and a housewife and her husband—occur off-screen and we tend to forget what we have not seen. The weight is all towards his persecution by humanity: e.g., the posse that traps him in the mountains (a scene from one of the nineteenth-century plays) trusses him up on a simulated cross. Closeups of Karloff's suffering and barely comprehending face only point up the prevailing cruelty and heighten our sympathy for the Monster (see illustration 8). In the famous blind man scene, where the Monster finds a "friend" and even learns to say the word, the balance tips towards sentimentality: a tear courses down his cheek. He is clearly more human than his persecutors. As the scene fades, a cross in the background stays eerily illuminated and is the last to fade out. The sound track plays a religious hymn.

The blindness of the rage expressed toward the Monster and his half-human incomprehension of it thus recaptures much of the bleak horror of the book, its indictment of society, and its picture of man's troubled consciousness. In the sequel there is also more of an attempt to humanize Doctor Frankenstein, to make him less the mad scientist. Here the evil Doctor Praetorius absorbs some of his darker raving qualities (see illustration 17). Combined with the pressures of the Monster for a mate, Doctor Praetorius's demands make Frankenstein's troubled mind believable and human—even if Colin Clive's acting does not.

Freed from the confines of Peggy Webling's play, *The Bride of Frankenstein* reasserts the novel's theme of corrupted innocence. Whale even used the preface of the novel for dramatic purposes. Mary Shelley tells Byron and Shelley that all did not end in the fiery windmill, that there was more to come (see illustration 18). This preface allowed the main body of the film to appear as science fiction set in a futuristic Victorian England with newly discovered uses of electricity, scientific laboratories, and a mysterious invention, the telephone, which the tied-up Elizabeth uses to communicate with her husband. It was a setting to recur in many later films, more bi-polar in its opposition of good and evil, God and science, more consonant with our images of the godless scientist out of Huxley and Darwin, more ready for suggestions of lurking evil with its fog-shrouded streets out of Dickens and Stevenson, and finally more blasphemous and clever with its aesthetes, dandies, and experimenters in morality out of Oscar Wilde. As sci-fi, it was futuristic, but for Whale and even perhaps for Terence Fisher, Paul Morrissey, and Christopher Isherwood, it was a past that was directly accessible as a living aesthetic model and ideal.

In many other respects Whale used the book intelligently for important incidents. As in the novel, the Monster sees his reflection

13. An image of sadism: Dwight Frye as Fritz menaces the Monster in the Universal *Franken-stein* (1931).

14. An image of innocence (I): Karloff responds to the innocence of little Maria (Marylin Harris) in the Universal *Frankenstein* (1931).

15. An image of innocence (II): Paul
Wegener as the Golem is disarmed by
Greta Schröder in *The Golem* (1920).

16. Innocence parodied: In *Young Frank-enstein*, 20th Century-Fox (1974), Peter Boyle as the Monster meets Ann Elizabeth Beesley as the Little Girl.

17. *The Bride of Frankenstein*, Universal Pictures (1935). The evil Dr. Praetorius (Ernest Thesiger) plays upon the Monster's innocence as he drugs him.

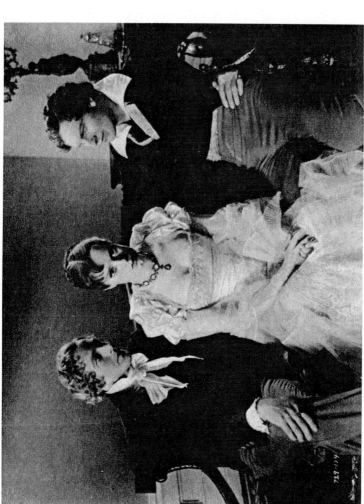

18. The prologue to *The Bride of Franken-stein*, Universal Pictures (1935). Shelley and Byron listen attentively as the demure Mary Shelley (Elsa Lanchester) tells them that there is more to the Frankenstein story than they have so far heard.

in the water, discovers fire at a gypsy camp, and saves a girl from drowning in a stream only to be shot at and wounded by her companions. Finding solace in the household of a blind hermit, he discovers the joys of music and awakens to the wonders of speech, neatly hinting at the education at the De Lacey house. Best of all, he finds a friend from whom he is separated in another cruel moment. Two hunters—Felix figures—disrupt the scene, beat and shoot him while the "De Lacey" hut erupts into flames. Knowing friendship but not having it, the Monster petitions Frankenstein for a mate, which the latter makes under duress. Elizabeth has been abducted by the Monster under the evil commands of Praetorius, and Frankenstein himself is an unwilling victim of forces beyond his control.

The creation of the Monster's mate provides a sequence to rival the creation of the Monster in the first film. Again there is the vast laboratory, designed by Herman Rosse, the electrical equipment devised by Kenneth Strickfaden, but Franz Waxman's music—absent from the first film—and the lifting of the body to the skies is much more elaborate here, as is Whale's extravagant, almost unhinged camera work. Unlike the book, the film has no lonely isle or small hut; all is on the grand scale. Nor is this female counterpart destroyed by its creator. Instead the Monster is rejected by the new creation—the Mary Shelley figure (Elsa Lanchester) of the prologue reincarnated with frightening scars, a wild head of frizzy hair, and a lightning bolt racing through its side (see illustration 19). Death as a release from pain becomes the Monster's wish; he urges Frankenstein to escape to his wife. Of Praetorius and of himself he says, "we belong dead," whereupon he pulls the fatal lever and sets off the explosions that destroy the laboratory. The death wish is obviously true to the novel. It is interesting to note that an early shooting of this scene *did* involve the destruction of Frankenstein as well. In fact, in some of the shots of the exploding laboratory he can be briefly glimpsed. The laboratory could not be rebuilt to rephotograph a saved Frankenstein.

Whale's film is distinctive for its baroque camera work, highly unusual for a studio production in America in the mid-1930s. Though expressionist in tone and lighting, it is much too kinetic and flashy to be so simply labeled. Widely varying angles, tilts, and fast-moving tracking shots all develop a surface of barely controlled hysteria. To this Whale adds a chortling macabre humor, often

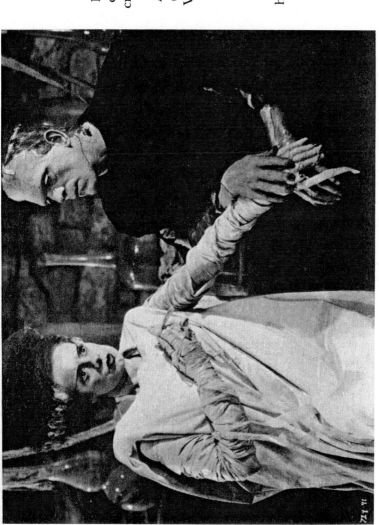

19. The Bride's Rejection: Elsa Lanchester as the newly created monsteress in the Universal *The Bride of Frankenstein* (1935) at last fulfills Victor Frankenstein's prophecy in the novel: "She also might turn with disgust from him . . . ; she might quit him, and he be again alone."

verging on parody or "camp"—as if in acknowledgment of the temptation to parody inherent in any visualizing of the material. In this he both follows the old theater traditions and points ahead to the numerous Universal spin-offs and those of our own day. But his domestication of the terrible is never subversive. Praetorius eating an elegant meal, with wine, on a tombstone, Una O'Connor screeching to the rafters and running scared, Praetorius unveiling his bell jars of little men and mocking kings and queens, even the roughhouse enjoyment of the Monster discovering the pleasure of food—none of these undercuts the true terror and the darker meanings of the myth.

Of all the films, *The Bride* comes closest to Mary Shelley's emphasis on desolation and loneliness. Later versions show a decline, though they provide occasional enjoyable new variations and combinations. Characters like Police Inspector Krogh (Lionel Atwill) in *Son of Frankenstein* (1939), who has lost his arm to the Monster, seem more like figures adrift from *Moby Dick* or *Tiger Shark*. As the basic myths fade, novelty is sought by engrafting other fantasies: *Frankenstein Meets the Wolf Man* (1943). The nadir of myth-making must certainly be the 1965 *Jesse James Meets Frankenstein's Daughter*. And wherever the Frankenstein Monster is found, Dracula is sure to lurk nearby. Universal's *House of Frankenstein* (1944) and *House of Dracula* (1945) seem to be inhabited by both of the monsters, who finally fight it out in *Dracula vs. Frankenstein* (1971). In semipornographic films, such as *House of Bare Mountain* (1962), Dracula and the Monster compete in sexual prowess, to the delight of the young women in a dormitory. It is perhaps no coincidence that the Hammer studio, which produced the cycle examined in the next section, should be even better known for its Dracula films. Rightly or wrongly, the popular imagination has endowed both vampire and Frankenstein Monster with similar appetites. Thus Polidori's *The Vampyre* and Mary Shelley's *Frankenstein*, the presumed products of the same day's imaginings, have been reunited through the filmmaker's fascination with eroticism and aggression.

IV. The Hammer Cycle

After Universal's *Abbott and Costello Meet Frankenstein* (1948), where was there to go? For nine years the Frankenstein Monster lay dormant. In 1957 at Hammer's English studio, it awoke with new force in *The Curse of Frankenstein*, directed by Terence Fisher. Fisher was later to direct several more *Frankenstein* films and the studio produced still others under different directors. Yet when the story of Frankenstein returned to its author's native country (the 1960s also saw a series of Mexican versions, as well as the 1965 Japanese *Furakenshutain tai Baragon*), it underwent a new transformation that distanced it even further from the emphasis that Whale had partially recovered. The pathos of Karloff's Monster is no longer of interest. Cadaverous, repugnant, mummy-like, Christopher Lee's Monster has become a mere prop, an adjunct to the film's emphasis on the necrophiliac activities of the half-criminal, half-pitiful Baron Frankenstein, played by Peter Cushing (see illustration 20). The grisly doings of the laboratory afford a contrast by quick cross-cutting to the elegant, detailed, almost lush Victorian decor. Horror is thus juxtaposed to beauty and elegance, both exalted by the fine color photography. The contrast is well realized and yet it somehow seems more appropriate to the mode of *Dracula*—with its own juxtapositions of musty tombs and lavishly decorated interiors, of mutilated bodies and languid beauties— than to the opposition of Victor and the Monster.

The Hammer *Frankenstein* films featured a good measure of popular and melodramatic bloodiness in their medical details (again, somehow better suited to Count Dracula and the pointed stake and the scarlet gush of blood). Occasional dashes of sexiness, now allowed by an increasingly liberal production code, were also used with deliberate calculation. *Frankenstein Created Woman* (1966; the title itself a teaser to remind the moviegoer of Vadim's popular *And God . . . Created Woman*, with Brigitte Bardot) featured a lovely female monster (played by the former *Playboy* model Susan Denberg) with scarcely a "stitch" on her. The sensationalism is unquestionably distracting. Only in Fisher's *Frankenstein Must Be Destroyed* (1969) does the Monster regain a measure of its former interest, as the brain of a famous scientist uncomfortably inhabits the body of a criminal. In revenge for the transplant, the Monster destroys himself and Frankenstein in the usual fiery finale.

In a remarkably shrewd book on the Hammer films, *The Heritage of Horror, The English Gothic Cinema 1946–1972*, David Pirie claims that these films signal an English reawakening to a venerable Goth-

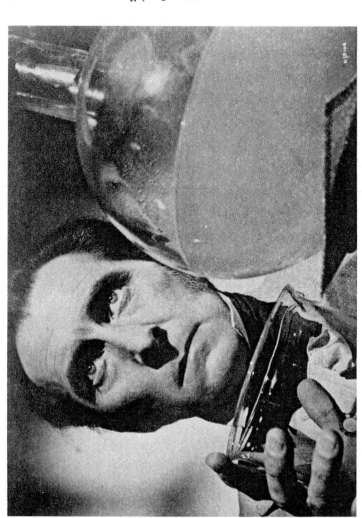

20. Peter Cushing in Terence Fisher's *The Curse of Frankenstein*, Hammer (1957). Doctor Frankenstein has become a Victorian Byronic hero.

ic heritage. For him, Cushing is not just a dabbler in forbidden delights, a Baudelairean or Wildean aesthete, but also a strong cruel man attracted to Selwinism or sadism, a distinctive type found in Gothic literature, in *Melmoth the Wanderer* or *The Monk* or in the personality of Byron himself. The claim may be valid. Still, the *fin de siècle* decadence of the Hammer *Frankenstein* films seems deliberately chosen. Sadism, like eroticism, had always been a component of the Frankenstein films—an intensification of the Monster's (and Victor's) aggressiveness in the novel and of the Monster's desire for a female companion. If the earlier versions of the film stress the cruelty of society (or the tormenting Fritz) yet evoke sympathy for the Monster's plight, the Hammer films go further by suggesting that an obsession with violence and passion is the only possible outlet in a world that is otherwise reduced to meaninglessness and ennui. The viewer is invited to share the malaise of Frankenstein. His Monster is less interesting in itself than as a form of retaliation against a world of surfaces and boredom. Frankenstein thus becomes a version of Camus's Mersault—or at least of Wilde's Dorian Gray and Huysmans' des Esseintes.

It is no coincidence that, between Whale's films and those of Fisher, between Karloff's too-innocent Monster and Cushing's too-knowing Frankenstein, World War Two should have made its impact on the popular mind. The corruption of innocence no longer was a dominant theme. Violence, death by fire, aggression had ceased to terrify by themselves, for they had become a mode of life —existence itself was potentially monstrous. In their sensationalism, the Hammer films stressed—perhaps cynically—aberrations that later productions, notably those of Morrissey-Warhol and Isherwood-Bachardy, would likewise stress. These aberrations, the films suggest, reflect in a distorted fashion the lineaments of a distorted world. Other productions, however, were to adopt a quite different stance. The Living Theater would again return to *Frankenstein* as a political myth by reviving its Rousseauvian (or, at least, Godwinian) metaphoric underpinnings (see Sterrenburg, pp. 148–149, above). And finally, the comic or parodic components, manifested so early in *Frankenstitch*, would also be reasserted to help defuse the anxieties that the Hammer films so morbidly and eagerly tried to stimulate.

v. Recent Interpretations:
The Living Theater's *Frankenstein*,
Frankenstein: The True Story, Andy Warhol's
Frankenstein, Mel Brooks's *Young Frankenstein*,
The Rocky Horror Show, and *The
Rocky Horror Picture Show*

Self-consciousness, already apparent in the Hammer films, is the hallmark of the highly diverse productions discussed in this final section. All draw on a storehouse of common images from novel and film. All assume these images as common knowledge. All therefore are free to pursue their own goals of reworking and reinterpretation. These reinterpretations are political, sociosexual, and parodic; they range from serious to seriocomic to purely comic purposes.

The most serious adaptation of the Frankenstein myth is undoubtedly that performed by the Living Theater during its 1966 tour of Europe, at a time when the group was on the run from tax agents who had shut their loft on 14th Street in New York. The play occurred at a transition point in the group's development from an early fidelity to texts such as Brecht's *Antigone* to the later reliance on improvisation and free form rituals in works like *Paradise Now*. Not as free as the works the group later presented, the production of *Frankenstein* nonetheless was also less scripted and more subject to alterations than the productions that preceded it. As might be expected, the Living Theater saw in the Frankenstein myth a means of asserting its more Rousseauistic leanings, its antipathy to social corruption, its belief in innate human goodness and the universality of cycles of creation and destruction, war and peace. After a series of human horrors of almost every conceivable kind, acted out ritually by the whole company, with each actor as the Frankenstein Monster, Julian Beck as Frankenstein emerged to ask "How can we end human suffering?" The company then proceeded to create a new man, a giant figure assembled by the company with each person acting as a part of the huge body. By the use of a three-tiered set of metal tubes with five boxes on each tier, this act of allegorical significance became possible without unusual acrobatics. The act of creating a new man now suggested a new universal humanity, not merely the Faustian power of the creator.

In act two, with a giant head formed out of electrical tubing at

278

the rear of the set, some of the philosophical ideas of the novel were brought out. In the various boxes, actors represented and mimed special aspects of the individual: love, knowledge, imagination, intuition, ego, death, creativity. Classical myths, dreams, alternate religious traditions were all brought to bear in this search. Mary Shelley's text was not forgotten, though no attempt was made to enact it dramatically. Instead, Stephen Ben Israel as the Monster recited the long passage of his coming to birth and consciousness, his learning experience, and his mistreatment by society. There has clearly never been a more faithful respect shown the Shelley novel. And this must have been the only Frankenstein production where Paracelsus, the model followed by Victor Frankenstein, appeared as an aid—in the company significantly of Sigmund Freud and Norbert Wiener—to create the new man. The last act of the play reflected the Becks' ambivalence about their utopian vision: another new man is created, but only after a harsh prison scene, which seems to suggest that the cycle of creation and destruction is eternal.

The Living Theater's insight into the positive side of Mary Shelley's novel is perhaps the most striking feature of the production. Their interpretation thus explicitly goes beyond even the hopeful political reading of Frankenstein's action that Peter Dale Scott suggests in his essay above. (Another serious political use of the Frankenstein legend occurs in Victor Erice's 1974 Spanish film, *The Spirit of the Beehive*, discussed by William Nestrick below. Erice uses a showing of the original Whale *Frankenstein* in a Spanish village of the early 1940s to comment both on the escapism of the populace and, metaphorically, on the relationship of Franco Spain to the Monster of the film.)

Frankenstein: The True Story (1973) by Christopher Isherwood and Don Bachardy, directed by Jack Smight, was, as its title proclaims, a serious attempt to get away from the melodramatics of terror by accenting the inner torments and the bond between creator and creature. However, like the other films, it preserves only the basic outlines of the myth of creation and destruction. It does examine the relationship of the Monster to Victor (whose name is at last restored), treats the creature as something more than a monster, and covers more of the original events; however, it does not bring these images and actions into line with the book, which, once again, merely acts as an occasion for personal variations.

Like the Hammer films, *The True Story* is set in Victorian England and Scotland—filmed in elegant color, stately in pace, and heavily doused with *fin de siècle* aestheticism and decadence. Perhaps its most ingenious—and I suppose aesthetically witty—suggestion is the reading of the novel as a *roman à clef* through the use of a prologue like that of *The Bride*. Shelley of course is Victor Frankenstein, Byron a daring Henry Clerval—a doctor who lures Shelley-Frankenstein away from his wife, Mary-Elizabeth, to create a new man. Using Byron-Clerval's brain in the Monster when Clerval dies of an attack, Shelley-Victor partially reincarnates his friend and mentor in the beautiful Monster that emerges. Over these doings hovers an extremely evil Polidori. The rather forlorn outcast of that group during the summer of 1816 on Lake Leman, he is the only figure whose name is not changed. Like Ernest Thesiger in *The Bride*, he is portrayed as a witty and decadent aesthete as well as an evil doctor eager to disrupt the beautiful friendship between Victor and his creature. The grim electrical death of Polidori high on a ship's mast provides a grisly melodramatic climax. Later, the creature kills Elizabeth, who appears glowingly surreal in an icy state of death. In an ending reminiscent of the nineteenth-century *Man and the Monster*, Victor and his creature perish in an avalanche released by a shot from Victor's gun. Their death is a *Liebestod*. Strongly homosexual overtones dominate the film and, in the facial decay of the beautiful Monster, one feels more the influence of *Dorian Gray* than of Shelley's novel.

Andy Warhol's Frankenstein (1974), *Young Frankenstein* (1974), and *The Rocky Horror Picture Show* (1975) are outrageous spoofs. The first carries the Hammer images and manner to extremes even Hammer would shy away from. Unlike Morrissey's earlier films for Warhol, this one is elegant, marvelously decorated, elaborately measured, almost ostentatious in its pace, which is largely given by slow pans and tracks. Hammer's cross-cutting between the elegance of the Victorian sets and the grisly lab is parodically exaggerated. While Joe Dalessandro as a peasant stud speaking Brooklynese services the baroness (Monique van Vooren), her husband enjoys his female creation in the lab (see illustration 21). In a further perverse twist, Frankenstein (Udo Kier) is the baroness's brother and husband, a suggestion that the novel often hints at in a more innocent way.

The film glories in the perverse: it is sex unto death in the lab,

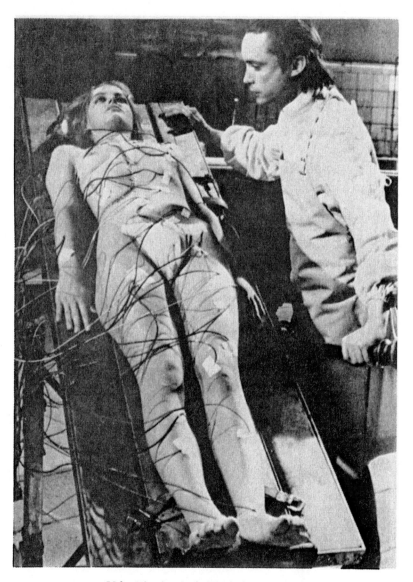

21. Udo Kier in *Andy Warhol's Frankenstein*,
France–Italy (1974), admires his female
monster.

while upstairs in the elegant bedroom the sex seems very boring. As Victor simultaneously makes love to and disembowels his female creature, he solemnly recites to his Fritz-like assistant in a thick German accent, "To know death, you must fuck life in the gall bladder." The whole method of the film is excess, but after the release of laughter something insane and frightening persists. Images are often surreal—a giant pair of shears is used to clip off the head of the victim who will become part of the Monster. His trunk stands up for a while spouting rivers of blood. Both spoofing and paying homage to a failed theatrical experiment of the '50s, the 3D process accentuates the gore, involves us, only to alienate us.

Despite the laughter the film generates, the final effect is that of a grisly kind of beauty, one that shades into horror and death. The final scene with bodies sprawled upon each other in the lab, each done in by a different kind of instrument, recalls the excessive and often ludicrous ends of Jacobean tragedy but also some of the truth in excess that Artaud found in that dramatic form. Toward the end, the creature, freed by his friend, asks only to be killed. And the hero Dalessandro himself is not released by the Frankenstein children who have voyeuristically witnessed the acts of both laboratory and bedroom in silence throughout the film. Together they sharpen the knives to begin the cycle again. *Warhol's Frankenstein* goes beyond mere spoof and parody into dimensions of feeling analogous to those probed by The Theater of the Ridiculous and often sought after by Artaud's prescription for a Theater of Cruelty.

By contrast, Mel Brooks's film *Young Frankenstein* is an unpretentious spoof which lovingly recreates the texture and images of the early *Frankenstein* films in black and white. Its strength is in the wit with which it sends up familiar images. There is no real attempt at reinterpretation, though a viewer is free to do this if he wants. For instance, are we to make anything out of Frankenstein's real bride ending up with the Monster in bed? And Frankenstein in bed with his buxom blonde assistant? The real pleasure is in seeing the old images in a new context: Madeline Kahn with frizzed "Elsa Lanchester" hair, replete with lightning bolt, hissing at Peter Boyle the Monster. Image after image is saluted, then undermined. The scene with the child cut from Whale's film is now fully played out (see illustration 16). When, after the flowers have gone down the well, the girl asks, "What do we do next?" the Monster does a double take into the camera, then lifts her above the well. The scene with the blind hermit is similarly carried to unexpected extremes. As in *The Bride of Frankenstein*, the blind friend offers the Monster food and cigars; yet now scalds him with the soup and sets his finger on fire (see illustration 22).

The Rocky Horror Show (1973) and the less successful film version of it, *The Rocky Horror Picture Show* (1975), fall somewhere between the close parody of *Young Frankenstein* and the more troubling transmutation of *Andy Warhol's Frankenstein*. Here, a bourgeois couple like the duo in *The Old Dark House* must go to a mysterious castle for aid when their car breaks down. The castle contains, however, more than the traditional equipment of horror. Richard O'Brien (a coauthor of the show) as Riff Raff looks like Ygor yet seems more sexually menacing than the familiar figure of the old horror films. The castle's doctor turns out to be "freaky" only in the sexual way. Frank-n-furter is a "transsexual transvestite from Transylvania," a planet where all life is bisexual; gathered with his assorted freaks and grotesques, he stomps and sings his way through the film in a hard rock beat and entirely in drag. During the night, Frank-n-furter reveals his new creation, Rocky Horror, a blond Charles Atlas muscle man and stud whom he has created for his pleasure; he destroys Eddie, a motorcycle tough whom Rocky Horror has replaced, seduces both Janet and Brad, the newlyweds who have come for aid, by impersonating each of them; and finally is himself killed in a battle with the Ygor figure who has destroyed Rocky Horror and wants to return to Transylvania. The intent of the film—if it has one—is presumably to carry the old images into new bi-sexual, "liberated," and often campy dimensions. Rarely does it explore the erotic content of the originals, as the Warhol version frequently does. For all its subversive sexuality, the film of *The Rocky Horror Show* is remarkably free from the disturbing edge these images should suggest. The tone is always outlandishly comic and never really menacing; interest is not in the plot but on how *outré* the next image can be. The big musical numbers dominate the film; the hard rock of Frank-n-furter and his group contrasts with the traditional and heavily parodied romantic duets of Brad and Janet before they visit the castle. The distancing is of course intentional, consistent with the comic, outlandish, and campy tone that is the "liberated" posture of both the movie and its music. *The Rocky Horror Show* comes closest to the music hall

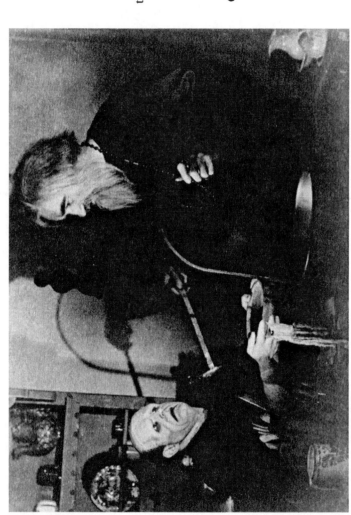

22. Peter Boyle as the Monster begs for soup from Gene Hackman as the Blind Man in Mel Brooks's *Young Frankenstein*, 20th Century-Fox (1974).

numbers of *Young Frankenstein* and really belongs to the venerable tradition of music hall parodies of the nineteenth century. We may recall that in one of them Frankenstein was a woman.

Perhaps such movies signal the end of a cycle. It is hard to see where Frankenstein films can go after such parodies. But the same feeling existed after *Abbot and Costello Meet Frankenstein* in 1948. Though destruction is part of the myth, creator and creature perishing in a final apocalypse, rebirth is also part of it. The figures return because they evoke certain persistently human tensions, desire, and fears: longings for power, innocence, and affection, the threat of ostracism, isolation, and social cruelty, the love for the forbidden, and even a longing for death as a release from pain. In varying degrees, the figures tap these fears and help us interpret them, purge them, and often domesticate and even trivialize them. One feels that the doctor and his Monster will always be reborn. The Isherwood-Bachardy film ends with a witty homage to this principle. After Victor and the Monster have been destroyed in an avalanche, we follow the course of an iceberg traveling south in the spring thaw. To our surprise, as it melts there emerges a wriggling hand.

Bibliographical Note

The best single source for information on this subject is Donald F. Glut's *The Frankenstein Legend* (Metuchen, N.J., 1973). A mine of arcane information, always accurate, but none of it very critically interpreted, it is a product that only someone who has devoted his life to the Monster could assemble. The present article, like almost everything written on this subject, is enormously indebted to it, as well as to Jean-Pierre Bouyxou's *Frankenstein* (Paris, 1969). Also helpful, but far more cursory, are two chapters on stage and film presentations in Radu Florescu's *In Search of Frankenstein* (Boston, 1975). Alan Barbour is responsible for the film chapter here. *Focus on the Horror Film*, edited by Roy Huss and T. J. Ross (Englewood Cliffs, N.J., 1972), contains some interesting theoretical articles on horror films, some contributions on the Frankenstein films, a reprint of the script of the 1910 Edison film, and a detailed shot-by-shot analysis of the creation scene in the *Bride*. Richard Anobile has assembled a shot-by-shot picture script of the Whale *Frankenstein* in the Film Classics Library (New York, 1974). Paul Jensen's article on this film in *Film Comment*, fall 1970, is also very helpful in conjunction with the picture text. Ivan Butler's *Horror in the Cinema* (New York, 1971) and Carlos Clarens's *An Illustrated History of the Horror Film* (New York, 1967) place the films in a general context. David Pirie's *A Heritage of Horror: The English Gothic Cinema, 1946–72* (New York, 1974) concentrates on the Hammer films and has detailed chapters on Terence Fisher and the Frankenstein cycle. Though very specialized, this is a most intelligent and broad-ranging book with interesting connections suggested to Gothic literature. Harry Ringel's lengthy reevaluation of Terence Fisher in *Cinefantastique*, vol. 4, no. 3, is also superb. Pierre Biner's *The Living Theater* (New York, 1972), contains three detailed chapters on the Living Theater's production of *Frankenstein*. Scripts exist for *Frankenstein: The True Story* by Christopher Isherwood and Don Bachardy (New York, 1973), Wiene's *Cabinet of Doctor Caligari* and Lang's *Metropolis* (both in the Simon and Schuster classic scripts series) and *The Golem* in *Masterworks of the German Cinema*, edited by Roger Manvell (New York, 1973). Peggy Webling's play seems to have disappeared from both print and stage; in its stead Samuel French (New York, 1974) distributes an even more drawing-room version, by Tim Kelly, confined to a single set of Frankenstein's study.

Important Frankenstein Productions on Stage and Film

Authors are listed for stage productions, directors for films. The names on either side of the slash are, respectively, those of doctor and creature. The list is by no means comprehensive.

1. Stage Presentations

Presumption; or The Fate of Frankenstein
London 1823—Richard Brinsley Peake
James Wallack / Thomas Potter Cooke

Le Monstre et le Magicien
Paris 1826—Merle and Anthony
London 1826—H. M. Milner

The Model Man (a burlesque)
London 1887—Richard Butler and H. Chane Newton
Nellie Farren / Fred Leslie

286

Frankenstein
London 1930—Peggy Webling
Henry Hallat / Hamilton Dane

The Living Theater's *Frankenstein*
1966
Julian Beck / Stephen Ben Israel and others

The Rocky Horror Show
London 1973—Richard O'Brien and Jim Sharman
Tim Curry / Peter Hinwood

2. Antecedents to Universal

Frankenstein—Edison (J. Searle Darley)
USA 1910, one reel
—— / Charles Ogle

Life Without Soul—Joseph W. Smiley
USA 1915
William Cohill / Percy Darrell Standing

The Golem—Paul Wegener
Germany 1920
Ernst Deutsch / Paul Wegener

The Cabinet of Dr. Caligari—Robert Wiene
Germany 1920
Werner Krauss / Conrad Veidt

Metropolis—Fritz Lang
Germany 1926
Rudolph Klein-Rogg / Brigitte Helm

3. The Universal Films

Frankenstein
USA 1931—James Whale
Colin Clive / Boris Karloff

The Bride of Frankenstein
USA 1935—James Whale
Colin Clive / Boris Karloff

Son of Frankenstein
USA 1939—Rowland V. Lee
Basil Rathbone / Boris Karloff

The Ghost of Frankenstein
USA 1942—Erle C. Kenton
Cedric Hardwick / Lon Chaney, Jr.

Frankenstein Meets the Wolfman
USA 1943—Roy William Neil
————— / Bela Lugosi

House of Frankenstein
USA 1944—Erle C. Kenton
Boris Karloff / Glenn Strange

House of Dracula
USA 1945—Erle C. Kenton
Onslow Stevens / Glenn Strange

Abbott and Costello Meet Frankenstein
USA 1945—Erle C. Kenton
————— / Glenn Strange

4. Hammer Frankenstein Films

The Curse of Frankenstein
England 1957—Terence Fisher
Peter Cushing / Christopher Lee

The Revenge of Frankenstein
England 1958—Terence Fisher
Peter Cushing / Michael Gwynn

The Evil of Frankenstein
England 1964—Freddie Francis
Peter Cushing / Kiwi Kingston

Frankenstein Created Woman
England 1967—Terence Fisher
Peter Cushing / Susan Denberg

Frankenstein Must Be Destroyed
England 1969—Terence Fisher
Peter Cushing / Freddie Jones

The Horrors of Frankenstein
England 1970—Jimmy Sangster
Ralph Bates / David Prowse

Frankenstein and the Monster from Hell
England 1974—Terence Fisher
Peter Cushing / David Prowse

5. Recent Versions

Frankenstein
T.V. film, 1972—USA for ABC
Directed by Glenn Jordan;
scripted by Sam Hall and Richard Landau
Robert Foxworth / Bo Svenson

Frankenstein: The True Story
T. V. Film, Universal 1973
Directed by Jack Smight
Scripted by Christopher Isherwood and Don Bachardy
Leonard Whiting / Michael Sarrazin

Andy Warhol's Frankenstein
France-Italy—1974—Paul Morrissey
Udo Kier / Srdjan Zelonovic

Young Frankenstein
Fox, USA—1974—Mel Brooks
Gene Wilder / Peter Boyle

The Rocky Horror Picture Show
England—1975—Jim Sharman
Tim Curry / Peter Hinwood

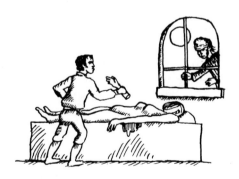

XII

Coming to Life: *Frankenstein* and the Nature of Film Narrative

WILLIAM NESTRICK

I

T HE NARRATIVE MEDIUM that emerged at the turn of this century, the film, achieved the effects and fulfilled the aims of nineteenth-century writers of Romantic fiction. Film gave body to that Fancy which Hawthorne had likened to "an itinerant showman, with a box of pictures on her back." These pictures, according to Hawthorne, needed a magnifying glass to make objects "start out from the canvas with magical deception." Film is the ultimate magical art that fascinated Hawthorne in "The Prophetic Pictures," Gogol in "The Mysterious Portrait," and Wilde in *The Picture of Dorian Gray*. It fulfilled the Romantic desire to magnify a tale and to suggest through chiaroscuro imagery the mysterious influences cast beyond a human object: Golyadkin and William Wilson can meet their doubles before our eyes and Jekyll and Hyde "melt and alter" into one another. The vital principles of variation and movement exploited by early film-makers like Méliès find their special equivalents in those nineteenth-century Romantic fictions devoted to the coming of life of an inanimate object—stories such as E. T. A. Hoffmann's "The Sandman" and, preeminently, Mary Shelley's *Frankenstein*.

Frankenstein is centered on what Victor calls the "miracle" of "bestowing animation upon lifeless matter."[1] Despite the novel's

1. Mary Shelley, *Frankenstein; or, The Modern Prometheus*, ed. James Rieger (Indianapolis, 1974), p. 47; references to this edition will be included in my text. I shall try not to duplicate the bibliographical information contained in Mr. LaValley's essay in this volume except to indicate the special interest for my work of the books by Carlos Clarens, Donald F. Glut, and the *Premier Plan* issue on Frankenstein films. The complete film

much larger cultural and mythological dialectics, it was its emphasis on the magic act of creation that was stressed in early stage productions such as *Le Monstre et le Magicien*, performed in Paris in 1826. Magic and the central relation between maker and Monster have likewise continued to make the novel appealing to film-makers fascinated by the independence of their own animated and self-expressive artworks. If Victor follows in the footsteps of Albertus Magnus, Paracelsus, and Cornelius Agrippa to learn about the "raising of ghosts or devils" (p. 34) the first filmmakers also saw themselves in the role of magician, debased in the nineteenth century to the theatrical showman. The pioneer Méliès, called the Magician of the Screen and King of Fantasmagoria, accidentally brought about a metamorphosis such as the artist-alchemists had always promised. In 1898, while photographing the traffic outside the Paris Opera, Méliès's camera jammed; he continued cranking, with the result that some of the elements in the scene changed between frames:

In projecting the film, just at the point where the break had occurred, I suddenly saw a bus changed into a hearse, and men changed into women.... Three days later, I performed the first metamorphoses of men into women and the first sudden disappearances which had, in the beginning, a great success.

Méliès appropriately titled his film *Magie Diabolique*. Like Victor, he had succeeded in "raising ghosts or devils." The optical principle on which he relied (based on the eye's retention and superimposition of one image on the next) had actually been used in three earlier nineteenth-century toys—the Zoetrope or Wheel of Life, the Thaumatrope or Wheel of Wonder, and the Phenakistiscope or Trick-viewer.[2] Those names represent the conception of his magic open to the filmmaker who chooses as a subject the metamorphic myth of "coming to life"—magic as supernatural, realistic, or illusionistic.

The special way in which the medium of the film engages this

---

script and stills of individual shots from the James Whale *Frankenstein* are available in the edition by Richard J. Anobile (New York, 1974) for the Film Classics Library.

2. For a discussion and illustrations of many of these early inventions, see Martin Quigley, *Magic Shadows* (New York, 1960).

myth of animation can be seen in its persistent return to the literary source of *Frankenstein*. Horror films may vulgarize the inevitable warnings about scientists going too far by usurping God's place. But the myth also offers a cautionary example for the animating artist. Seen in terms of Romantic concepts of the imagination, Victor's creation renders him the artist *maudit* and his wretch a *chef d'oeuvre manqué*. The creature's size is due not to superhuman aspiration but quite simply to his maker's lack of skill. Worse still, the creature represents, just as much as Pegasus, the product of fancy as opposed to the "esemplastic" imagination. He is constructed mechanically. Victor Frankenstein as Pygmalion makes, not a statue, but a machine. It resembles the image Coleridge chose to characterize the "hybrid" plays of Beaumont and Fletcher, who pieced together their works "just as a man might put together a quarter of an orange, a quarter of an apple, and the like of a lemon and a pomegranate, and make it look like one round diverse-coloured fruit."

Although the creature is the product of the mechanical powers of association, its creator is not a mad scientist but an imaginative one. Victor's early interest in natural philosophy is motivated by "the dreams of forgotten alchemists." Dr. Waldman wins Victor to the study of modern chemistry by echoing the magical terms in which the ancient models expressed their aims: the modern philosophers, he tells Victor,

have indeed performed miracles. They penetrate into the recesses of nature and show how she works in her hiding-places. . . . They have acquired new and almost unlimited powers; they can command the thunders of heaven, mimic the earthquake, and even mock the invisible world with its own shadows. [P. 42]

This kind of language reintegrates the imaginative act with the scientific one, reasserts the reality of the subjective, imaginative responses of human consciousness to the phenomenal world that scientists analyze as purely objective. In fusing the artist, scientist, and magician, Mary Shelley performed fictionally what Gaston Bachelard has examined critically in studying the poetic treatment of the Aristotelian elements in the nineteenth century after scientists had abandoned them as unreal categories.

A comparison between Mary Shelley's description of how her vision of the story came to her and the narration of the same event in the novel reveals a further variation of the taboos violated in Frankenstein's creation:

I saw the hideous phantasm of a man stretched out, and then, on the working of some powerful engine, show signs of life, and stir with an uneasy, half-vital motion. Frightful must it be, for supremely frightful would be the effect of any human endeavour to mock the stupendous mechanism of the Creator of the world. His success would terrify the artist; he would rush away from his odious handywork, horror-stricken. He would hope that, left to itself, the slight spark of life which he had communicated would fade; that this thing, which had received such imperfect animation, would subside into dead matter. . . . He sleeps; but he is awakened; he opens his eyes; behold the horrid thing stands at his bedside, opening his curtains, and looking on him with yellow, watery, but speculative eyes. [Introduction to the Third Edition (1831), p. 228]

When this chilling moment is reached in the novel, Mary Shelley develops it with supplementary material that puts the creation into relationship with another set of cultural values:

I slept indeed, but I was disturbed by the wildest dreams. I thought I saw Elizabeth, in the bloom of health, walking in the streets of Ingolstadt. Delighted and surprised, I embraced her; but as I imprinted the first kiss on her lips, they became livid with the hue of death; her features appeared to change, and I thought that I held the corpse of my dead mother in my arms; a shroud enveloped her form, and I saw the grave-worms crawling in the folds of the flannel. I started from my sleep with horror; a cold dew covered my forehead, my teeth chattered, and every limb became convulsed; when, by the dim and yellow light of the moon, as it forced its way through the window-shutters, I beheld the wretch—the miserable monster whom I had created. He held up the curtain of the bed; and his eyes, if eyes they may be called, were fixed on me. . . .
Oh! no mortal could support the horror of that countenance. A mummy again endued with animation could not be so hideous as that wretch. [P. 53]

The metamorphosis of the carnal into the charnel, from Elizabeth to the mother's corpse and, finally, to the "wretch," connects the mother's death and the scientific experiment. Victor's desire to create a new species that would bless him as its creator involves a creation from dead matter: he wishes to "renew life where death had apparently devoted the body to corruption" (p. 49). What Victor does is not simply to create life but rather to recreate life from the dead, to preserve and restore the dead. His guiltiness in this creation expresses its forbiddenness:

I collected bones from charnel houses and disturbed, with profane fingers, the tremendous secrets of the human frame. In a solitary chamber, or rather cell, at the top of the house, and separated from all the other apartments by a gallery and staircase, I kept my workshop of filthy creation. [P. 50]

Victor's experiment is therefore two-sided: it is unnatural as creation (fatherhood without motherhood) and it is unnatural as preservation and restoration of the dead. An examination of the novel shows a constant structuring around alternatives to biological reproduction: friendship between siblings, friendship between men, adoptions.

Once Victor's failures in creation and preservation have been recognized it becomes possible to see that the culturally valued mode of creation and preservation is *art* itself. Coleridge provides a useful clue when, in his letters, he explains how a poem can offer an image of truth by converting a series into a circular whole: "Now what the Globe is in Geography, *miniaturing* in order to manifest the Truth, such is a Poem to that Image of God."[3] The emblem for art, the shorthand hieroglyphic for the abridgment of nature, is, as Claude Levi-Strauss also suggests, the miniature. And Mary Shelley provides just this counter image to the Monster's gigantism in the miniature portraits of Victor's mother and brother.

What makes the case of *Frankenstein* especially interesting is the way the extended series of films derived from it perpetuates the structural relationships in the myth. In *Frankenstein* the filmmaker finds a story that offers a narrative analogy to film itself. The connection will become apparent if we remember the title of Walter Benjamin's brilliant essay, which defines film as "The Work of Art in the Age of Mechanical Reproduction." The film is the animation of the machine, a continuous life created by the persistence of vision in combination with a machine casting light through individual photographs flashed separately upon the screen. Since "life" in film is movement, the word that bridges the worlds of film and man is

3. *Collected Letters of Samuel Taylor Coleridge*, ed. Earl Leslie Griggs (Oxford, 1959), IV:956. I am grateful to Peter Manning for acquainting me with this passage.

"animation"—the basic principle by which motion is imparted to the picture.

In the seventeenth century, the word had been richly suggestive. Animation was the act by which God made man, the informing of an animal body with a soul. Milton wrote of Male and Female Light "Which two great sexes animate the world" (*Paradise Lost*, VIII. 151). But by the nineteenth century the word had lost much of this primal and cosmic sense and came to mean mere vivacity, the appearance of life rather than life itself. For Mary Shelley, though, it is a key word, the center of her myth, a word that occurs in three of the passages quoted so far. By the end of the century, the word recovers a limited meaning in the new medium, where it undergoes an even stricter limitation to the subspecies of film known as the animated film, the cartoon—as if all films were not animated.

The persistence of the Frankenstein myth in film not only reiterates cultural values about reproduction, creation, and preservation, attempts through myth to keep human species and monstrous machines separate, but also displays a continued ambivalence toward film itself. Whereas narratives that do not involve the machine can easily disguise the medium, the narration that brings the machine or doll to life also confronts its own violations of sanctions against such reproduction. Sometimes the mechanical medium is allowed to wind down or shift gears so that we can see the machine; sometimes the motif of "coming to life" reasserts the possibility that the medium can bridge the polarities of technology and human nature and art.

II

The immediate and memorable differences between Mary Shelley's Monster and the Karloff Monster in James Whale's *Frankenstein* are his unbalanced walk and his speechlessness. He seems subhuman rather than superhuman. As Albert J. LaValley notes in the previous essay, several stage versions introduced speechlessness but kept the rapidity of movement attributed to him in the novel. Enacting the novel on stage or screen makes the audience *face* his physical aspect, a reversal of the way the reading audience enters into the creature's highly articulate monologue.

The Karloff Monster's imperfections are largely his lack of skills: he is the oversized child who has not acquired the ability to walk smoothly and with balance or to make himself understood except with grunts. Seeing this grotesque adult without these skills is somehow a terrifying reminder that our adulthood depends on our acquiring them. The sense of his towering height is created not just with platform shoes but by photographing him from below, the way that adults appear to be even taller to children because of their angle of vision. A product of art, the Monster remains innocent of the arts by which we identify our adult and fully human nature.

The placement of the camera, which recreates a child's perspective of an adult figure, is also the perspective by which the adult sees movies, the inferior position of audience to a screen that magnifies the human beyond life-size. And if we remember that Whale's film was released in the Christmas season of 1931, only a few years after *The Jazz Singer* brought sound and a few days after the silent *Ben Hur* was rereleased with music and sound effects, we can see that this screen is haunted by a figure who embodies an earlier form of the film itself, the stage at which the movies had not learned to talk.

It has been noted that Charlie Chaplin's Tramp has a walk that objectifies the way people appear to walk in silent films when the camera was handcranked and the speed varied so as to cause people to appear to walk fast. But the Monster's walk is the alternative possibility: the cranking that causes the movement to slow down. Whereas Chaplin's jaunty gait keeps his back slightly behind the walk, the Monster tilts forward as if he were getting ahead of his legs. The Monster, then, is a vestigial embodiment of the film conceived as having its own childhood, growth, adulthood and education. These metaphors of human development are falsely attributed to film history, but, conversely, the recognition of skills —speech, walking (the lack of which makes an adult a monstrous child)—asks the price of our feeling that these skills are not the real we, but mechanical excrescences. Whale's *Frankenstein* encourages us to feel that being human is being the creature of cultural forms imposed *ab extra*. For a moment we do not belong to ourselves and experience ourselves as "tailored" creations.

At the end of Whale's *Frankenstein*, when the Monster and his creator are trapped in a windmill, a series of shots is taken through the rotating spokes of gears. In this moment, poised between pursuit and escape, the two figures seem to look at and see each other for the first time. Photographed in analogous shots and positions, diametrically opposite each other, Victor confronts a barely perceived alter ego; for a moment, he can acknowledge this thing of darkness his. The only movement in this recognition scene, which appears preternaturally outside time, is the movement of the gears. This recognition comes about through the medium of film itself, and *this* recognition is for the medium retrospection: the principle of the zoetrope—that wheel of life—slowed down for the moment of consciousness of an opposite and primitive self, a moment possible only through the intercession of the machine. Soon, this image is ritualistically purged, as the villagers, hunters now with primitive torches, set fire to the windmill, *that* primitive source of energy substituted for the laboratory. The Monster is returned to elemental nature.

Our ability to recognize Mary Shelley's myth in this film, which omits or changes so much of the novel, means that the dialectical oppositions of the myth are not mutilated. The film creates two visual worlds: one, the region of mechanical reproduction, the laboratory; the other, the world associated with natural human reproduction. The laboratory is the place of manufacture, where Henry talks of making the creature with his own hands, and where the Monster comes to life by moving his hand. The center of the other world is Lucy: long shots situate her in a huge family manor; close-ups illuminate her face with candlelight. To her world belong the arts of civilization, ceremony, nature, and the church. The camera registers the fine texture of her lace, the microscopic craft as opposed to the Monster's magnified and crude stitching. When she prevails and Henry quits his laboratory to be nursed back to health, the film shows them seated in a garden, a *locus amoenus*, so light-filled as to seem overexposed. We hear the birds singing as Henry says, "It's like Heaven—being with you again." The marriage of cultured arts and nature is observed in the objects about them—the coffee service, the Russian wolfhound, the cigarette, Lucy's pearls. The refinement of detail created by a civilized society is rendered through the help of natural light, the leaves in the trees, and the textured fabric of Lucy's hat.

Whale's film also offers visual alternatives to Frankenstein's preservation of the dead. The wedding scene begins with a close-up of a bell jar under which are preserved not only the orange blossoms of Henry's parents' wedding, but also miniature portraits of the couple. After offering a wish that in thirty years a youngster of

Henry's will carry on the tradition, the Baron proposes a toast in wine laid down by Henry's great-grandfather, another reminder of the culture that preserves and enriches the materials nature provides. Even the burgomaster's reference to Henry as "a fine young man, the image of his father" reiterates the sense of perpetuation through biological and natural process.

The curious transference of the name "Frankenstein" from creator to creature has perpetuated the very dialectic of the myth. Film sequels become offspring; the Monster half of the narrative parodies the kinship terms—the bride of Frankenstein, the son of Frankenstein. *The Bride of Frankenstein*, again directed by James Whale, ostensibly refers to the wife of the scientist, but the climax to that film is the creation of a mate for the Monster—a wild-eyed creature played by Elsa Lanchester sporting a Nefertiti-inspired permanent wave. As the bride stands between her two makers, Dr. Frankenstein and a new figure, Dr. Praetorius, who hold out her surgical–wedding gown, Dr. Praetorius announces, "The Bride of Frankenstein," thus incorporating into the film the popular confusion of the names.

Dr. Praetorius, the new scientist figure, further varies the theme of alternative forms of reproduction with his parody of the divine injunction, "Be fruitful and multiply." To create a man-made race upon the earth, Praetorius identifies his principle of life, the "culture" from seed. His artificial process, modeled on the dictum "Follow nature," promises a new world of gods and monsters, and his monsters, things to be shown, must *be* shown in a new way. Unlike Karloff's mechanical and primitive grotesquerie, Praetorius's creatures are perfect miniatures—all kept in glass jars, specimens of his "black magic." Cinematically, what is interesting is that these figures, because of miniaturization, become parodic and comic. Products of seed cultures, they also represent for an American audience, outmoded, overcivilized, or fairytale aspects of Old World culture: a king and queen, a ballerina, an archbishop, a devil. Tinkling music suggests their doll-like quality—we think of Coppelia and Hoffmann—and as a result of speeding up the sound-reproducing instrument their voices are unnaturally high, ringing like bells through the glass. They are human beings as dolls, reduced through a technical process of superimposition (multiple exposure either in the camera or in optical printing). Dr. Praetorius' black magic is simply James Whale's camera trickery. The film thus returns to another of its origins, the illusionism of the phenakisti-scope and Méliès.

III

James Whale's manipulation of the image through optical pro-cesses is an assertion of cinematic art, and the effect is, paradoxical-ly, to weaken his role as magician. But his action may serve as a reminder that to criticize cinematically is to deal with the total screen image, the artist's framed picture. Hermann Warm, one of the designers of *The Cabinet of Dr. Caligari*, once announced, "Films must be drawings brought to life." That film, which figured both helpfully and dangerously in causing film to be regarded as "art," includes the narrative motif that Warm restated in cinematic terms. At one point, Dr. Caligari "brings to life" the somnambulist Cesare. Bringing to life here is essentially the reverse of hypnotism, which is an inducement to sleep. Caligari, though offering himself as theatrical wonder-maker, essentially wishes to extend his control and power into the world beyond the barrier that separates per-former and spectator. Cesare, the somnambulist, is the Munch-like, spectral, poster-figure brought to life (see illustration 10). But he is more than a drawing; he is a vertical walking shadow, the nature of film itself, whose murderous action on his audience is photographed as shadow. Between Caligari's puppet-like move-ment and Cesare's faun-like ballet, we see the extremes of human and inhuman motion. The very two-dimensionality of the stagey sets helps us see the movement that is the "dynamization" of the screen space.[4] By the painterly distortion of perspectives and the discontinuity of planes we are able to *see* the continuity of human space and movement, especially in the movement from rear to front, the "depth" that movement can create. The most famous shot in the film, as Cesare carries the heroine across the rooftops, a jagged movement across virtually the entire screen image, finally places him against a glowing horizon line where he stands out in his true being as silhouette brought to life.[5]

4. Erwin Panowsky defines the "unique and specific possibilities of the film medium as "dynamization of space" and the "spatialization of time."
5. For an extended development of these ideas and the relationship of film to plastic arts, see my *The Cabinet of Dr. Caligari: Notes and Analysis* (New York, 1976).

In their simplest form, films as "drawings brought to life" would be the translation of the narrative elements in a picture into a continuous linear structure in time. In *Laughter in the Dark* Vladimir Nabokov imagines a character who actually hopes to have "some well-known pictures, preferably of the Dutch School, perfectly reproduced on the screen in vivid colors and then brought to life." This desire to extend the world of art into life is a hilarious but understandable response to the magical possibilities of film, an obvious extension of popular entertainments of the nineteenth century.

In 1935, an American film called *Dante's Inferno* appeared, set in an amusement park where a kindly old man nicknamed "The Professor" unprofitably runs an exhibit of Dante's *Inferno*. His barker, played by Spencer Tracy, persuades him that people must be entertained, and replaces the small exhibit of paintings and relics of the figures in the *Inferno* with a show, a three-dimensional model of the Inferno (see illustration 23). The visual mode here is clearly theatrical, a stage set through which the audience passes. But at the climax to the film, the Professor, in a hospital, suggests that the barker-now-big-businessman actually read the poem, and he holds out the book as the camera moves in on—not Dante's *Inferno*—but Gustave Doré's. As the illustration fills the screen it dissolves into "the real thing." It comes to life as "the terrifying picture of those who lived ruthlessly" promised by the Professor (see illustration 24). The film thus progresses from painted Inferno, through stage Inferno, to film Inferno, and thereby manages to project its "morality play" beyond the realistic narrative. In the sequence of Infernos, the film comes into its own in opposition to the drawing or stage set. It puts to special narrative use the understanding of how a film brings to life through the total movement of the framed images. The film appeared around the time that Josef von Sternberg was showing his own, far greater understanding of that same principle; as he put it,

the greatest art in motion picture photography is to be able to give life to the dead space that exists between the lens and the subject before it. Smoke, rain, fog, dust, and steam can emotionalize empty space, and so can the movement of the camera.[6]

6. *Fun in a Chinese Laundry* (New York, 1965), p. 326.

23. H. Lackman's *Dante's Inferno*, Fox (1935), courtesy of the Museum of Modern Art. "The Professor" conducts a tour of his amusement park exhibit of the Inferno. The grotesque statues of the damned call attention to the essentially static quality of this version.

24. The dramatic luminosity of this Doré-inspired vision of the Inferno acts as a foil to the conventionally theatric fires of the earlier amusement park scenery (figure 23). The figures are now dwarfed by the monumental landscape. (*Dante's Inferno*, Fox [1935], courtesy of the Museum of Modern Art.)

IV

The way an image represents the narrative motif of coming to life determines how it relates to magical or realistic thinking. Since the film itself is fundamentally a "bringing to life" through technology and the machine, the mode of representation can also reveal the director's own attitude to the medium. Thus, a figure may come to life by technological manipulation of the screen image in an optical process—for example, it is probable that a transformation from skeleton to flesh described in a script for a now-lost silent *Frankenstein* was done through superimposition. The figure may also come to life by nontechnological means, simply by having the human actor start to move, such as Cesare or Karloff's monster. In this second case, different states must be implied by narrative means: a shift from death to life or from sleep to somnambulism is caused by some external directing force. The various treatments of the motif thus follow the three conceptions of the illusionary nature of movement evident in the three nineteenth-century optical toys mentioned earlier.

The mechanical means by which the medium reproduces animation, however, go beyond the movement in the frames. The movement between shots is created through editing. Editing reassembles separate shots into an illusion of continuity. It is a mechanical stitchwork, a piecing together that becomes another cinematic equivalent of the Frankenstein Monster, that product of its creator's mechanical fancy, the faculty that, in Coleridge's words, "has no other counters to play with, but fixities and definites."

The analogy between film editing and Victor Frankenstein's suturing persists in the history of film and film theory. From Dziga Vertov's own montages to contemporary ideas about "suturing reality" filmmakers have subordinated the camera's power of reproduction to its power to piece together a new creation. As early as 1923 Vertov insisted that the camera was more than a mere copier. In words strikingly similar to Victor Frankenstein's he described himself as a creator who could improve on nature herself by recombining fragments:

I am an eye. I have created a man more perfect than Adam; I create thousands of different people in accordance with previously prepared plans and charts.
I am an eye.

I take the most agile hands of one. The fastest and most graceful legs of another. From a third person I take the handsomest and the most expressive face, and by editing I create an entirely new perfect man.[7]

Near the end of his manifesto Vertov extends his audience the invitation, "Please come into life."

Vertov's own film, *The Man with the Movie Camera*, shows how Kino Pravda can bring an audience to life in his special sense. Every "trick" of the moving picture is there, but always justified by bringing freshness to the commonplace. When the motif of coming to life occurs in this film, it does so with a difference. Through single-frame photography, Vertov animates the movie camera itself. It stretches itself out on a tripod, turns, and scrambles away. Such trickery implies the presence of an absence—the magic of moving an inanimate object suggests its human operator, the man with the movie camera. Vertov's "entirely new perfect man" comes to life only when the film is a unified organism, and such a unity is conferred by the consciousness of a human editor making connections and continuities.

The paradoxes of the cutter's hand splicing together pieces to create a new, hybrid, superior form of life are familiar to a literary audience; they can be found in *A Winter's Tale*, Polixenes' answer to Perdita's complaints about the gillyflowers.

> This is an art
> Which does mend nature—change it rather—but
> The art itself is nature.

And it is just this passage that Eisenstein uses as an epigraph for his essay, "The Structure of the Film." In line with his epigraph, Eisenstein declares,

A work of art—an art-ificial work—is built on those same laws by which non-artistic phenomena—the "organic" phenomena of nature are constructed.[8]

The work imitates not only the law of structure in natural organic phenomena but also the pathos of the spectator:

7. "Kinoks-Revolution," in "The Writings of Dziga Vertov," *Film Culture* no. 25 (1962): 52–53.
8. Eisenstein, "The Structure of the Film," *Film Form* (New York, 1949), pp. 152–78.

the laws of (the work's) construction are simultaneously the laws governing those who perceive the work.... Each spectator feels himself organically related, fused, united with a work of such a type.

The vital element in the film is the affective action in the audience. The kinetic quality of the film is the moving, that pathos experienced by the spectator. Eisenstein, like Shakespeare, recognized the weight in those verbs—the art that does *mend*, or rather *change* nature. Shakespeare's resolution of his tale is not the pastoral sheepshearing scene but an act of magic, as Paulina says to the "almost transported" Leontes,

> If you can behold it,
> I'll make the statue move indeed, descend
> And take you by the hand. But then you'll think—
> Which I protest against—I am assisted
> By wicked powers.
>
> . . . .
> It is required
> You do awake your faith.
>
> . . . .
> Music! Awake her, strike.

Shakespeare keeps the balance between the magical and religious meanings and the rational and natural explanations available to the audience, and in the special quality of the magic act (bringing the statue to life) where the only magic may be an act of "awaking"— awaking the faith of the spectator, awaking as a means of redeeming life from death.

Eisenstein's theory of pathos involves the transported spectator as well:

Pathos shows its affect—when the spectator is compelled to jump from his seat.... When his eyes are compelled to shine with delight, before gushing tears of delight.... In brief—when the spectator is forced to go out of himself.

The affective and kinetic structure of a film, then, is from stasis to ekstasis—literally, standing out or going out of oneself, a departing from one's ordinary condition. The narrative motif of coming to life is perhaps the basic prototype of the guides Eisenstein could offer the spectator. Departing from one's ordinary condition, a transposition in the mode of being, suggests the discontinuity that is part of the film's nature and is now in harmony with the structure of pathos itself.

In bringing her statue to life, Paulina keeps hesitating to call her work magic. A film director who sees his magical art as reasserting the real unity between the artificial and the natural and who views his leaps into opposition as essentially an awakening to reality may wish, like Prospero, to cast off the role of magician. Ingmar Bergman writes about his own initiation into film, when he received, at ten years of age, a film projector and a piece of film: "It showed a girl lying asleep in a meadow, who woke up and stretched out her arms, then disappeared to the right." The banality and brevity of the footage should not disguise the presence even here of the magical motif of coming to life:

This little rickety machine was my first conjuring set. And even today I am really a conjurer, since cinematography is based on deception of the human eye. I have worked it out that if I see a film which has a running time of one hour, I sit through twenty-seven minutes of complete darkness—the blankness between frames. When I show a film I am guilty of deceit. I use an apparatus which is constructed to take advantage of a certain human weakness, an apparatus with which I can sway an audience in a highly emotional manner. . . . Thus I am either an impostor or, when the audience is willing to be taken in, a conjurer. I perform conjuring tricks with [an] apparatus so expensive and so wonderful that any entertainer in history would have given anything to have it! [9]

In his film *The Face*, released in the United States as *The Magician*, Bergman offers every variation of the magician as wondermaker, illusionist, and life-giver. The film opens with Vogler's Magnetic Health Theatre silhouetted skeletally against the horizon. Vogler himself is the stage magician, but he is accompanied by a witch-like crone who performs superstitious acts and ceremonies. Vogler explains his superiority to this kind of supernatural world when he tells her, "Your tricks are out of date—they can't be explained." In Vogler, Bergman presents the magician-illusionist, the trickster whose magic is technique but who suffers because his audiences want answers and belief beyond his magic. The point at which the magician and moviemaker touch is made explicit in the dialogue:

9. Ingmar Bergman, *Four Screenplays* (New York, 1960), pp. xiv, xv.

"We use apparatus, mirrors, projection, not magic, and not fraud." Vogler's projective apparatus is the Laterna Magica, and the only magic it performs is to superimpose and replace a human image with a death's head. The film proves the filmmaker's power to create illusion with the willing cooperation of the audience that Bergman attributed to the conjurer. *The Face* tells at least four different stories in differing cinematic modes. These violent swings from terror to burlesque, using every alienation effect possible, still do not defeat the willingness of the audience to enter in, to be compelled and terrified, with the least narrative continuity, to create continuous affecting fictions with the barest sequence of discontinuous shots.

In his remarkable series of films since 1966, Bergman continually tries to let the spectator see the apparatus, the presence of the illusionist and the machine, in order to see the wonder of the collaboration. The beginning and end of *Persona* are shots of projection equipment, the beginning is the light of the arc-lamp, and the conclusion of the narrative intersperses shots of the camera photographing earlier scenes. The title sequence shows us a series of dead bodies; one of them suddenly opens her eyes—however, this coming to life is done with a jump cut—in one frame the eyes are closed, in the next (the cut) they are open. It is Méliès' Paris Opera transformation returned to the realistic film. But then a child's body begins to stretch and move. Coming to life parallels the act of awaking. The leap into opposition (eyes closed, eyes open; death, life) is not felt to be wholly unlike the child's natural awakening. The intrusions of the apparatus to awake the movie viewer to the filmic illusion occur in a narrative about the gradual interinanimation of two women, the transference of one psyche to another. But even such violent reminders of film life cannot overcome the effect of the scenes of transference, where the gray areas of the psyche are shown by such a lack of photographic contrast that the two women virtually dissolve into shades and into each other.

Bergman's attempts to demystify the magician end by proving the impossibility of this act. Exposing the illusionist and his tricks also exposes the cooperative fiction-making power of the audience. Bergman's act restores this power to the audience. In his later films he continues to reduce most austerely his narrative motifs, and yet the audience greets the reduced motifs with endless elaboration.

Still, our relief at returning to "fiction" is evidence of the inter-subjectivity, the agreement that the director's fiction has a correspondence to our sense of reality, both what we "half create and what perceive."

V

The importance of *Frankenstein* to film has always been more than the history of the film versions of the novel. Since the sixties, the most avant garde filmmakers have returned to the myth as homage, as allusion, as model for their own relationship to film. In a compelling gesture, Karloff's Monster gropes towards the light that shines on him and is then cut off by Dr. Frankenstein's shutter. This reaching for the light is a reminder that the Monster's life comes from the sky and the film's indication, of which Mary Shelley would have approved, that the Monster has a potential for good. The most extreme form of abstract film is a reduction to cinematic elements: projected light alternating with darkness. The flicker film appears as a quintessential purification and refinement of film to its elemental nature and returns us to the stroboscopic effects of the early cinematic toys that analyzed movement. In Tony Conrad's first film, *The Flicker*, his alternation of black and white (transparent) frames abstracts from all movies the principle involved when we go to the "flicks." [10] His second film explores further the perceptual responses to intermittent presentations of light (all that remains of the film is a section showing video "snow"), and the title of *that* film is *The Eye of Count Flickerstein* (1966), with a nod to Universal's coupling of *Dracula* and *Frankenstein*. Whereas one might expect the technique of the flicker film to remain within the realm of pure cinema, the effects are quite the opposite: although we may "know" in some sense that we are seeing only frequencies of light, Conrad presents us with hallucinatory experiences in which the screen shape seems to change, grow larger, recede; there seem to be horizontal movements, afterimages of color, and so on. The flicker film does not remain in the Romantic heterocosm but breaks out to affect the perceiving spectators.

Flickerstein, flicker film. Frankenstein, Frank Film. For Frank

10. For further information on the flicker film, see Robert Russell and Cecile Starr, *Experimental Animation* (New York, 1976).

Mouris, "coming to life" can only be done frankly in a film that parades its mechanism. *Frank Film* (1973) exemplifies the last stage of organicity in Eisenstein's theory, the stage at which the author's breath infuses the life. At the same time that the film manages to be frank about its film nature, it manages to be Frank as well. It transforms the self into another mode of being. This leap is a transformation of the self into product. The screen images are collages, images built out of images, images cut from advertisements for a consumer audience. A stop-frame process animates these inanimate photographs and designs. The sequences are responses to two sound tracks, each with its own principle of continuity: one sound track is an autobiographical narrative, a life story; the other is a word association, an association that is formal insofar as it is alliterative and at the same time both a mechanical aspect of the human mind and one of its deepest projections. The animation process, visual squeeze, changing the image between frames, allows us to see to the limit of our visionary power, the single frame, the fragmentation of films. But in the sweeps of books and tires across the screen we are also allowed, through multiple exposures, to see the persistence of vision, the vestigial hauntings of imagery. One process of this film, by which the inanimate objects are given a fairy-like twinkling life, is called "pixillation," and we may remember that Coleridge defined pixies as "Fancy's children." The images of the self are the images of mechanical reproduction, and it is at the moment when Frank decides to rebuild himself that our prime image of mechanical reproduction, the Frankenstein Monster, reappears, now reproduced in a photograph. (One of the key words in the alliterative sound track is "fantasy," and the seizure on the image of the Frankenstein Monster is a way of acknowledging that the frankness of the film is very much bound up with the overflow of powerful fantasies even in the most banal products; an iconographical allusion to Warhol in the animation of the soup can acknowledges this side of pop art.)[11] The rebuilding as filmmaker is

11. An interesting variant of the connection between technology and fantasy (as opposed to simple camera realism) can be found in a statement by the still photographer Benno Friedman, who explains the origins of his own mutilated and tinted pictures: "A continuous interest/fascination with the sensual/sexual/erotic bringing me from time to time into the theaters of Times Square. In watching the movies, becoming aware that the turn-off was in the excessive reality of the situation. Realizing that photo-

the leap into another form of being, and the point when Frank can turn himself into the movie, to become Frank Film. But the film manages to remain wonderfully human despite the despairing images with which we can build ourselves; the final humanity here is the voice, scrawny, accented, self-ironic, libidinous, and shy, with resonances in its very flaws, that finally convinces us of the animator's individuality that breathes the unity into the film and with a sigh of relief ends it.

Everything in the film points to the discovery of the self through the animation of the saved magazine images. Deciding what one is going to be (a filmmaker) is an act of self-creation, an act not possible without a sense of the imagistic givens that are redeemed in the "other" world. It is interesting as a corroboration of this interdependence of *Frank Film* and Frank Film to discover that the film was made as a substitute for a live-action autobiographical film which was not working out:

I wanted my collages to have liveliness. And their moment came. My wife Caroline and I were stalled in the filming of my autobiographical film; the footage was disappointing. It was mostly live-action, so it was undeniably me—but it wasn't *really* me. So we decided that I should just use my cutout images, and by the time they were shot and Tony Schwartz added his genius to the soundtrack, it really *was* me, *Frank Film*.[12]

Frank Mouris shifts from architecture to art because "you can do the thing entirely yourself." Despite the credits at the conclusion of *Frank Film*, the animated film *would* appear to be the form in which the individual most completely controls his work. But the film, certainly the live-action film, is admittedly a corporate–committee product. Mouris understands the self-as-collage, the hypnotic power of synthetic images, but it was only appropriate that the Fac-

---

graphing directly from the screen was perhaps a method for reintroducing mystery. I photographed in the theater, which probably destroyed/invaded the fantasies of everyone else with each rifle shot from my Nikon. From being bored at the movies, I became turned on in my darkroom. The technical manipulation and general chicken-scratching this photograph (and almost all my photographs) was subjected to is the unswerving dedication to the dream/visions of the late Dr. Frankenstein" (*Esquire*, February 1976, p. 113).

12. "Frank on the *Frank Film*: Animation and Other Obsessions," *Film Library Quarterly* VIII, no. 1 (1974): 45.

tory recognize the paradoxes in film-as-autobiography increasingly practiced by Fellini and Bergman for the working out of personal problems in a universal-international medium. *Warhol's Frankenstein* (1974), directed by Paul Morrissey, belongs to this category of the self-defining film. An *auteur* like Warhol, fully in the tradition of self-negation, can find in the Frankenstein-film a reverse-autobiographical product. In an interview with Paul Gardner in *The New York Times* (July 14, 1974), Paul Morrissey states that in filming *Frankenstein* he "thought it might be a kind of exorcism for Andy and all the people who are crippled and haunted by some nut case" (a reference to the attack on Warhol by Valerie Solanas in 1968). Shortly after the attack, Leticia Kent interviewed Warhol:

"It's sort of awful, looking in the mirror and seeing all those scars. . . . The scars are really very beautiful.
"Since I was shot," Warhol went on, hypnotized by the central idea of his own resurrection, "everything is such a dream to me."[13]

After five hours on the operating table, he had returned to life, as Gardner states, "glued together."

In the same interview with Kent, Warhol had played with the meanings now assigned to "real" and "fake"; the choice of the composite Frankenstein to define the self belongs to this transvaluation and interchange between personal and synthetic. To be true to Warhol's self, the film has to make a special comment on the technology of the medium itself, and its method is to choose the technological novelty of the 3D process—a novelty that was, in fact, a re-novelty, bringing back the short-lived process of the early fifties. In those days, the process was advertised as "Natural Vision." Warhol recalls the artificial aspect of such technology. Every step taken toward (seemingly) increasing the film's "realistic" representation has the effect of undermining the sense of what *is* real in the film and of transferring our measurement of what is real back to the Whale–Karloff *Frankenstein*. To take one case (also stressed above by Albert LaValley): the accents of the cast, largely composed of German actors, seem like an incredible "put on," parodies of the accents supplied to mad scientists in countless Hollywood films. There are English accents in the Whale *Frankenstein*, but these belong to the Old World atmosphere of barons and peasants and

13. "Andy Warhol: 'I Thought Everyone Was Kidding,'" *The Village Voice*, September 12, 1968, p. 38.

burgomeisters. Probably the biggest laugh in *Warhol's Frankenstein* comes when the virile young peasant, picked up for the aristocratic woman's pleasure, opens his mouth and we hear the authentic New York accent of Joe Dalessandro. The improvised dialogue, the true accents of the players, all have their claims to heightened reality or authenticity, but here, pasted together in a composite conglomeration, they all become equally fake.

Once the film has unmasked Natural Vision as artificial process and converted realism into theatricality, it can proceed to dissolve the moral distinctions between natural and unnatural acts and act out the incestuous and homosexual fantasies latent in the original novel. In making his film "leap" into life through optical illusion of three-dimensionality and in choosing the myth of Frankenstein, Warhol gives a climactic embodiment to his own film career with its parody of the star system, its hostile and loving relationship to popular art; for his *Frankenstein* is a magnification and literalization of the very idea of the fetish (from the Latin *factitius*, artificial), the projection into an inanimate object of magical power. Having so overprojected this fetishism, the film can deal openly with the superhuman sexuality that the earlier *Frankenstein* films disguise. (Mel Brooks, in *Young Frankenstein*, which recreates the black and white world of the Whale films and includes images photographed from the original laboratory set, makes similar jokes about the Monster's "equipment" and technique.)

The films by Warhol–Morrissey and Brooks parody *Frankenstein* by asking impertinent questions excluded from the overt content of the Whale film. A remarkable Spanish film, *The Spirit of the Beehive*, also proceeds by questioning, this time more profoundly, that earlier film. In the opening sequence, a truck enters a Castilian town and a traveling movie show is set up in a hall; the film projected is the Whale *Frankenstein*. Victor Erice thus frames the Whale film in the world. The camera scans the audience, village people, mostly women and children, while the sound track reproduces warnings about scientists who go too far. The philosophical and religious mythology of the film appears humorously remote as a cautionary tale, yet the faces watch intently.

Erice's film is about the exemplary value of the *Frankenstein* film and the community created by its mythic thinking (the beehive of the title is the explicit and iconographically traditional symbol for this community). When the two girls (Isabel and Ana), with whom the film is primarily concerned, return home from the show, they continue to meditate on the film's implications—the younger one, aged eight, asking a set of questions that the earlier film encourages us *not* to ask: why did the Monster kill the girl and why did the villagers kill the Monster? The first question reveals the fascination of the involved spectator and displays the narrative's facile moral absolutes to justify the destruction of the Monster; the second question acknowledges the scapegoat mentality expressed so hysterically in the pursuit of a Monster whose murder of a child does not vitiate his own claim for human compassion.

The older sister's answer to both questions is simple: "They didn't kill him or the little girl . . . because in the movies everything is a lie." Erice's film occupies an unusual place between the self-reflexive film and the demystifying film; it explores what happens when the myth of the Monster is taken seriously. Ana will continue to reenact the scene in which little Maria gives the Monster flowers only to be killed by him; Isabel (and the audience) observe Ana acting out the flower scene in pantomime by a well where Isabel has declared the spirit of the Monster to dwell. Once the spirit of the Monster has been asserted to be manifest in different forms, the way is open for the political, religious, and psychological reinterpretation of the myth, as Ana befriends and feeds a military deserter (or refugee); the betrayal of this man by Ana's father leads to her decision to commit suicide by eating a poison mushroom; her choice, however, results in a hallucination—a reenactment, this time "in life," in color, of the Monster's encounter with Maria. Erice's camera recomposes the individual shots and the general sequence. The child's decision to die has fulfilled itself in a cinematic epiphany where she can act out in the visual terms of Whale's *Frankenstein* her understanding of the kind of preparedness to sacrifice that she had sensed in her question about Maria's death. At the same time, the film converts the hunting of the Monster into the search with dogs and torches for the missing Ana.

Whereas the film seems a finely perceived realization of two children's experience of a movie and their metamorphosis of their own world when apprehended in a movie's terms, the climax enters into the child's vision and into a fantastic theatricality. At the opening of the film, Erice includes in the frame the introductory section from the Universal film where Van Sloan, appearing before a stage curtain, warns the audience about what is going to be presented and tells them not to take it too seriously. Again, the introduction seems remote, a theatrical frame transcended by the Whale film as the narration proper begins and by the Erice film by the framing within the frame of this black and white narrative. The immediate cut after this semiserious warning is to a huge close-up of a man in protective gear stunning bees with smoke. The close-up is startling. It magnifies the previous shot's proportions and is reminiscent of those science-fiction horror films in which special garments are worn to protect against radiation or poisons. After this initial shock, the image is contextualized: we are able to identify the threatening figure as a beekeeper. But the moviegoer is also allowed to see a technique used in horror films such as the Universal series—the bee burner that spreads particles so that rays of sunshine can be photographed. The film that so clearly opens with a split between film (the Whale *Frankenstein*) and reality (Erice's narrative) thus moves to reconcile the two. As Ana's action seems redemptive in a religious sense, so Erice's film recombines the sense of cinematic myth and imaginative reality. It is not simply demystification when the filmmaker reincorporates the bee resin-mist into his own film or brings the Monster back to life in a hallucinatory sequence.

To take another example, the two girls perform the old experiment of putting their ears to the rails to hear an approaching train. Thematically, the scene is connected with the need for evidence of things unseen, the faith in the "espíritu" (spirit), a word applied to the Monster and to the hive itself. But when Ana puts her head on the track, the shot is derived from all the melodramatic films where the heroine is threatened with being tied to the rails before an oncoming train. Photographed in close-up from the side, the girl's head on the tracks seems to betoken impending danger; her gesture seems suicidal, even sacrificial. The position also suggests one from which heads on pillows are photographed and hence serves as another reminder of the "sleep as an image of death" theme that has been quoted earlier in the film.

This proximity, even continuity, between two worlds, sleep and death, the melodramatic film and the realistic film, receives its most potent statement in the scene in which Isabel plays dead. Ana confronts her sister's death as an act of the Monster, and then, in a position and a shot composition reminiscent of the train rail sequence, she listens for Isabel's heartbeat. It is hard (I think impossible) not to join in the testing of Isabel's death state; in this case the evidence is reversed so that we must watch Ana to translate for us the heartbeat that we cannot hear. What is remarkable is that the shot of Ana's listening is held so long that we become uncomfortable and are likely to entertain the idea that the girl is really dead. Like the cut from Van Sloan's reminder not to take *Frankenstein* too seriously to the terrifying shot of the beekeeper-monster, Erice moves us to take seriously what we begin in the expectation of game-playing and macabre humor. Because we expect Ana to be satisfied easily about Isabel's heartbeat, we are disoriented by a shot that is unnecessarily long and, consequently, build up alternative fictions of death and reanimation.

The Spirit of the Beehive and *Warhol's Frankenstein* reanimate the myth of Frankenstein for the seventies with the ironic recognition that the Whale film is the strongest evidence of the film as heterocosm, as a completed and fixed other world. From opposite directions, the two films break through the sealing-off process to reanimate the movie tradition itself by variously expanding the scope of the Whale film. The potency of that mechanical Monster becomes their way to investigate the compelling power of the screen. With all the ambivalence toward creation through the images of reproduced nature, they offer, by means of optical illusion, inherent in the nature of film, to make Adam's dream come true and, through ever greater consciousness of film technology, to make us wake to the paradoxical status of film life.

Appendix

"Face to Face":
Of Man-Apes, Monsters, and Readers

$\int$ CIENCE in *Frankenstein* is, of course, pseudo-science. Though Victor Frankenstein begins his studies in natural science by reading Pliny and Buffon, the "sudden light" that breaks in on his later research—"a light so brilliant and wondrous, yet so simple"[1] —is never identified. The carefully documented scientific background given to Lydgate in *Middlemarch* is clearly unnecessary in a romance like *Frankenstein*. It is surprising, therefore, to find that a central strategy used in Mary Shelley's novel should also be attempted forty-five years later by a genuine scientist—indeed, by the defender of nineteenth-century evolutionary biology, T. H. Huxley himself.

In *Man's Place in Nature* (1863) Huxley relentlessly brings his civilized readers "face to face" with "blurred copies" of themselves,[2] a succession of seemingly alien monsters. And, like Mary Shelley, though for purely scientific reasons, he uses these deformed "copies" of human beings to force their presumed "originals" into an act of kinship that will involve a humiliation of their pride. If Mary Shelley's Monster spares its creator from contemplation of its hideousness by placing his "hated hand" before Victor's eyes (*F*, p. 96), Huxley is not so considerate. In the printed version of his 1863 lectures, Huxley forces image after image upon the startled reader's eyes: he invites us to behold a 1744 drawing of a mandrill with a human face (see illustration 25) and presents us with a gallery of monstrous anthropomorpha in a woodcut from the work of Linnæus's student Hoppius (see illustration 26). Nor does Huxley limit himself to archaic drawings. Holding that chimerical creatures seen in "half-waking" dreams can presage "reality," Huxley

1. *Frankenstein; or, The Modern Prometheus*, ed. James Rieger (Indianapolis, 1974), p. 47. Cited hereafter as *F* in the text.
2. *Man's Place in Nature and Other Anthropological Essays* (New York, Authorized Edition, 1896), p. 80. Cited hereafter as *MPN* in the text.

25. William Smith's figure of the "Mandrill" (1744), reproduced in T. H. Huxley's *Man's Place in Nature* (1863).

examines early accounts of "creatures approaching man more nearly than [Centaurs and Satyrs] in essential structure, and yet as thoroughly brutal as the goat's or horse's half of the mythical compound" (*MPN*, p. 1). Turning to *Purchas his Pilgrimage*, the same text on which Coleridge claimed to have based his dream-vision in "Kubla Khan," Huxley traces Purchas's allusions to the African experiences of Andrew Battell, "my neere neighbour," to Battell's own 1625 account of his encounter with "two kinds of monsters, which are common in these woods, and very dangerous." Battell's description of the "greatest of these monsters," called Pongo, is enlisted by Huxley:

This Pongo is in all proportion like a man; but that he is more like a giant in stature than a man; for he is very tall, and hath a man's face, hollow-eyed, with long haire [sic] upon his browes. [P. 5]

Huxley's monster-show seems a harmless entertainment. Yet his purpose, still concealed, is satirical and aggressive. Huxley subtly relies on accounts of half-factual and half-legendary creatures to prepare the ground for his later proof of the relation between humans and apes. Linnæus's "Homo Caudatus" (deemed at the

26. The Anthropomorpha of Linnæus (in
Man's Place in Nature [1863]).

time "a third species of man") and "Satyrus sylvestris" or Edwards's
"Man of the Woods" are, of course, chimerical classifications made
by seventeenth- and eighteenth-century naturalists who had not yet
recognized the distinguishing characteristics of "Chimpanzee, Gib-
bon, and Orang." As late as 1798, Huxley notes, the "Pongo" found
by the German officer Von Wurmb in 1781 was mistaken for "a
fourth and colossal species of man-like Ape," since all specimens
previously observed were "small of stature . . . ; while Wurmb's
Pongo was a monster twice their size, of vast strength and fierce-
ness, and very brutal in expression" (pp. 26–27).

Huxley's satire, however, is directed less at the misconceptions of
late-eighteenth-century naturalists on whose colossal "men of the
woods" Mary Shelley quite possibly drew in conceiving her vegetar-
ian creature (who promises to go to the tropical forests of South
America). Instead, Huxley's target is a nineteenth-century audience
unwilling to face their Yahoo cousins. Despite erroneous classifications, mythologizing, and misidentifications, the earlier naturalists
had acknowledged what pious Victorians would desperately try to
deny: kinship with these monstrous anthropoids. Huxley wants his
readers to acknowledge that kinship—a kinship, however, that is
not the emotional affinity that Mary Shelley's huge monster demands from Victor, Walton, and the reader, but a relation based
on incontrovertable scientific fact.

Despite this difference in intention, however, there is a startling

27. From Huxley's *Man's Place in Nature*:
"The Gorilla (after Wolff)."

similarity in the strategies used in *Frankenstein* and *Man's Place in Nature*. Just as Mary Shelley first renders Victor's horrified reaction to the Monster to distance us from a creature whose humanity will only later become apparent, so Huxley, too, at first pretends that no involvement is needed in our spectatorship of what purports to be merely an amusing Victorian freak show. It is only after we have been instructed about the true habits and lineaments of the orang-utan (see illustration 28) and have been stared back at, like a spec-

28. From Huxley's *Man's Place in Nature*:
"An adult male Orang-Utan, after Müller
and Schlegel."

tator at a zoo, by it and by a gorilla (who then, in a further bit of
Huxleian irony, turns its posterior towards us [see illustration 29]),
that Huxley finally sees fit to announce his true purpose:

Brought face to face with these blurred copies of himself, the least
thoughtful of men is conscious of a certain shock, due perhaps, not
so much to disgust at the aspect of what looks like an insulting cari-

cature, as to the awakening of a sudden and profound mistrust of time-honoured theories and strong-rooted prejudices regarding his own position in nature, and his relations to the under-world of life. [Pp. 80–81]

Huxley's language mocks by its very guardedness: "a *certain* shock" hardly does justice to the jolt that he has so carefully charged for sudden release. We *have*, for eighty pages, been amused with blurred copies of ourselves, only to be shown relentlessly from now on that it is we—"erect and featherless bipeds" that we are (p. 95)— who are copies of the monster-apes we have kept at a distance. It is only now, in Huxley's very act of denial ("due perhaps, *not* so much to disgust") that we recognize the "insulting caricature." The caricature has been intentional. And it was meant to disgust us, to shock us into an unpleasant recognition.

Victor Frankenstein's own disgusted reaction to the Monster's outstretched hand is a denial not allowed in *Man's Place in Nature*. Victor flees his creation; Huxley's reader cannot evade his affinity with the so-called "brutes." No Victor-like imprecations ("Abhorred monster!" "Devil!") can help Huxley's Victorian audience resist their relation to life's "under-world" (the word recalls that other, more Romantic, term for primal kinship that Wordsworth had called "nature's unambitious underwood"). Huxley's mirror reflects inescapable truths: despite their Victorian frocks and Victorian crinolines, humans *are* apes.

Frankenstein's Monster, too, offers an identity that readers cannot escape. To be sure, Mary Shelley proceeds far more circumspectly in forcing us to identify with that other denizen of the underworld of life. In her fable, monster-hood is more dangerous a classification than in Huxley's scientific world of fact. It carries personal fears and guilts that do not enter Huxley's calm insistence on our true place in the scheme of nature. Still, the novel's endurance surely owes much to the shock with which reader after reader is forced to acknowledge the Monster as kin. Huxley insists that "the attempt to draw a psychical distinction" between ourselves and apes is as "futile" as the attempt to erect a "structural line of demarcation" (p. 152). His remark also applies to *Frankenstein*. The "psychical" barrier Victor erects is broken as soon as we overhear the Monster's pained eloquence.

Like Huxley's grotesque man-apes, Shelley's Monster is physically ugly, alien to all human notions of beauty. Huxley cites William Smith's 1744 description of the mandrill with obvious satisfaction:

The head is monstrously big, and the face broad and flat, without any other hair but the eyebrows; the nose very small, the mouth wide, and the lips thin. The face, which is covered by a white skin, is monstrously ugly, being all over wrinkled as with old age; the teeth broad and yellow; the hands have no more hair than the face, but the same white skin, though all the rest of the body is covered with long black hair, like a bear. They never go upon all-fours, like apes; but cry, when vexed or teased, just like children. [Pp. 15–16]

Compare this description with Shelley's more memorable account of the "un-human features" that so unsettle Victor Frankenstein:

His yellow skin scarcely covered the work of muscles and arteries beneath; his hair was of lustrous black, and flowing; his teeth of a pearly whiteness; but these luxuriances only formed a more horrid contrast with his watery eyes, that seemed almost as the dun white sockets in which they were set,[3] his shrivelled complexion, [and] straight black lips. [P. 52]

Allowing for the transposition of yellow and white (face and teeth), the two descriptions are remarkably similar. Had Mary Shelley seen Smith's drawing (see illustration 25), which, unlike the verbal description, shows the deep sockets of the mandrill's eyes? Such speculations can be carried to absurd extremes: did she possibly see Smith's work as a child? Did his remark about the mandrill's crying "when vexed or teased" remain engraved in her mind? The questions are fruitless (or, as Huxley would add, unscientific). It would be equally fruitless to point to some common impulse binding Mary Shelley and T. H. Huxley in their efforts to force us into an admission of affinity with ugly and alien creatures. The psychobiographer may wish to point to a common aggressive impulse or to dwell on Mary's and Huxley's isolation at crucial and formative stages of their life. The psychology I wish to stress, however, is that of their readers.

Both Mary Shelley and Huxley force their readers into coming "face to face" with alien and deformed features that they must recognize in themselves before they are restored to their identities

3. Battell's description of the "Pongo" monster also stresses its "dunnish colour" (*MPN*, p. 5).

as civilized men and women. Just as the reader of *Heart of Darkness* must, through Marlow, see a self-reflection in Kurtz's "horror," so must the reader of both Mary Shelley's fantasy and Thomas Henry Huxley's scientific treatise admit a kinship with primal forces that lie outside the realm of the observances of civilization. In each case, that recognition is restorative. Huxley concludes *Man's Place in Nature* by asking rhetorically, "Where, then, must we look for primæval Man?" Future human fossils, he predicts, will produce a lost link, the "remains of a human being intermediary between Man and Apes" (*MPN*, p. 205). In the mythic reality of *Frankenstein*, however, the mediator Huxley seeks to complete his literal search has already been fully identified. Unlike Huxley's missing link, the Monster is a metaphor. Its "remains" not only lie charred somewhere near the North Pole, but also within the consciousness of each reader who has come "face to face" with its vivid anxieties and anger—of each viewer, even, who has seen Karloff scowl and grimace, and stumble. Where, then, must we look for *this* primeval being? Obviously, within ourselves.

U. C. K.

29. From Huxley's *Man's Place in Nature*: "Gorilla walking (after Wolff)."

Contributors

PETER BROOKS is professor of French and Comparative Literature at Yale University. He is the author of *The Novel of Worldliness* (1969) and *The Melodramatic Imagination* (1976), and has published widely on French, English, and American fiction.

KATE ELLIS is associate professor of English at Livingston College, Rutgers University. She has published on various aspects of women's literature and is now concluding a book on the masculine and feminine tradition in Gothic fiction.

ANDREW GRIFFIN is associate professor of English at the University of California, Berkeley. He has published essays on Wordsworth and on Mill and is presently completing studies of Dickens' *Great Expectations* and of Wordsworth's approach to narrative.

U. C. KNOEPFLMACHER, professor of English at Berkeley, currently holds a visiting appointment at Princeton University. He is the co-editor, with G. B. Tennyson, of *Nature and the Victorian Imagination* (1977) and has written books on George Eliot and on the Victorian novel.

ALBERT J. LAVALLEY has taught at Yale, Rutgers, Santa Barbara, Santa Cruz, and the California State University at San Francisco. The author of *Carlyle and the Idea of the Modern* (1968), he has edited an anthology of Hitchcock criticism and recently has devoted most of his time to the study of film.

GEORGE LEVINE is professor of English at Livingston College, Rutgers University. The author of *The Boundaries of Fiction* (1968), he has coedited *The Art of Victorian Prose* (1968) and *Mindful Pleasures: Essays on Thomas Pynchon* (1977) and is finishing a book on the monstrous in nineteenth-century fiction.

ELLEN MOERS is professor of English at Brooklyn College, City University of New York. She is the author of *The Dandy* (1960), *The Two Dreisers* (1969), and *Literary Women: The Great Writers* (1976), in which the essay reprinted here originally appeared.

WILLIAM NESTRICK, associate professor of English and head of the Group Major in Film at the University of California, Berkeley, has written on Spenser, Greene, Herbert, Milton, Browning, Faulkner, Fitzgerald, and on various German and American films.

PETER DALE SCOTT, a former member of the Canadian diplomatic service, holds a degree in political theory from McGill University but is now associate professor of English at Berkeley. He has written on subjects ranging from Alcuin to the Vietnam war and at present is supervising the edition of a new volume of his poetry.

LEE STERRENBURG, assistant professor of English at Indiana University, has written articles on Gothic fiction and on the imagery of revolution in nineteenth-century literature. His essay on *Frankenstein* is related to a book in progress, "The Confessional Voice: Politics and Demonism from Mary Shelley to Carlyle."

PHILIP STEVICK is professor of English at Temple University. He has written widely on eighteenth- and twentieth-century fiction and fictional theory. His work includes the anthologies *The Theory of the Novel* (1967) and *Anti-Novel* (1973), as well as an edition of *Clarissa*.

JUDITH WILT is associate professor of English at Boston College and the author of *The Readable People of George Meredith* (1975) and of essays on James, Richardson, and Dickens. She has completed a book on the Gothic in Jane Austen, George Eliot, and D. H. Lawrence.

Select Annotated Bibliography*

1. Relevant works by Mary Shelley

The Letters of Mary W. Shelley, ed. Frederick L. Jones. 2 vols. Norman: University of Oklahoma Press, 1944.

The Journal of Mary W. Shelley, ed. Frederick L. Jones. Norman: University of Oklahoma Press, 1947.

Mary Shelley: Collected Tales and Stories, ed. Charles E. Robinson. Baltimore: Johns Hopkins University Press, 1976.

A carefully edited collection of the short fiction, excluding some falsely attributed in Richard Garnett's edition of the Tales in 1891, and including new ones.

The Last Man, ed. Hugh J. Luke, Jr. Lincoln: University of Nebraska Press, 1965.

The one novel, besides *Frankenstein*, for which serious literary claims have been made. It is much too long and operatic, but is interesting for the light it throws on Mary and Percy Shelley.

Mathilda, ed. Elizabeth Nitchie. Chapel Hill: University of North Carolina Press, 1959.

This short novel, discussed in the present volume by U. C. Knoepflmacher, has important autobiographical implications and is here well edited and introduced.

Frankenstein; or, The Modern Prometheus, ed. M. K. Joseph. London: Oxford University Press, 1969.

The best edition of the 1831 text. Contains useful supplementary materials.

Frankenstein or the Modern Prometheus, ed. James Rieger. Indianapolis: Bobbs-Merrill, 1974.

Perhaps the best edition, based on the 1818 text, with complete notation of all known variations, and useful supplementary materials.

II. Essays and Books about *Frankenstein*

Harold Bloom. "Frankenstein, or the New Prometheus." *Partisan Review* 32 (1965): 611–18. Reprinted in *Ringers in the Tower* (Chicago: University of Chicago Press, 1971), pp. 119–29.

*See also the "Bibliographical Note" on pp. 285–89, above.

Reads *Frankenstein* as "one of the most vivid versions . . . of the Romantic mythology of the self."

Wilfred Cude. "Mary Shelley's Modern Prometheus: A Study in the Ethics of Scientific Creativity." *Dalhousie Review* 52 (1972): 212–25.

Sees *Frankenstein* as a Romantic adaptation of the Prometheus myth.

P. D. Fleck. "Mary Shelley's Notes to Shelley's Poems and *Frankenstein*." *Studies in Romanticism* 6 (1967): 226–54.

Uses evidence of the novel, the poems (and notes to them), and the journals to argue that *Frankenstein* is a critique of Romantic idealism.

Donald F. Glut. *The Frankenstein Legend: A Tribute to Mary Shelley and Boris Karloff*. Metuchen: N.J.: Scarecrow, 1973.

A remarkable and obsessive history of virtually every manifestation of *Frankenstein* in drama, fiction, radio, television—even cereal boxes.

M. A. Goldberg. "Moral and Myth in Mrs. Shelley's Frankenstein." *Keats–Shelley Journal* 8 (1959): 27–38.

Analysis of the theme of isolation in *Frankenstein*; notation of parallels in several other writers by whom Mary was influenced.

R. Glynn Grylls. *Mary Shelley: A Biography*. London: Oxford University Press, 1938.

An interesting biography, especially up to Percy's death; very little criticism of the fiction.

Susan Gubar. "Mother, Maiden and the Marriage of Death: Women Writers and an Ancient Myth." *Women and Men: The Consequences of Power*, ed. Dana V. Hiller and Robin Ann Sheets. Cincinnati: Office of Women's Studies, University of Cincinnati, 1977. The look at the "nurturing sisterhood between mother and daughter" in Mary's verse drama *Proserpine and Midas* has bearings on *Frankenstein*.

J. M. Hill. "Frankenstein and the Physiognomy of Desire." *American Imago* 32 (1975): 332–58.

An interesting psychological reading, seeing the Promethean sin as having "incestuous roots," and the novel as an exploration of the problem of "why or how" we are "to settle for less than our desires demand."

Robert D. Hume. "Gothic Versus Romantic: A Revaluation of the Gothic Novel." *PMLA* 84 (1969): 282–90.

Brief consideration of *Frankenstein* as a Gothic novel treating, characteristically, the Promethean theme.

Gerhard Joseph. "Frankenstein's Dream: The Child as Father of the Monster." *Hartford Studies in Literature* 7 (1975): 97–115.
Frankenstein as a "child's myth," a dramatic enactment, growing from the experience of nightmare, "of Frankenstein's repressed infantile fantasies."

Robert Kiely. *The Romantic Novel in England*. Cambridge, Mass.: Harvard University Press, 1972.
Excellent analysis of *Frankenstein* in the tradition Kiely defines as the "Romantic novel"—not quite the same thing as the Gothic novel.

George Levine. "*Frankenstein* and the Tradition of Realism." *Novel* 7 (1973): 14–30.
Extensive analysis of *Frankenstein* as romance that yet embodies the central concerns and attitudes of later nineteenth-century realistic fiction.

Nelson Lowry, Jr. "Night Thoughts on the Gothic Novel." *Yale Review* 52 (1963): 236–57.
Important consideration of the Gothic as expression of the subversive energies repressed in traditional fiction. In *Frankenstein*, Mary Shelley gives us a symbolic narrative of psychological states.

Mary Graham Lund. "Mary Godwin Shelley and the Monster." *The University of Kansas City Review* 27 (1962): 253–58.
Frankenstein embodies the "tragedy" of the nineteenth century, although Mary Shelley did not really understand what she was creating.

W. H. Lyles. *Mary Shelley: An Annotated Bibliography*. New York: Garland Publishing, 1975.
A careful listing of all the works, including dramas, poems, and stories, and description of most reviews, articles, and books containing materials about Mary Shelley or her works.

Mrs. Julian Marshall. *The Life and Letters of Mary Shelley*. 2 vols. London: Richard Bentley and Son, 1889.
A sound, decorous, nineteenth-century "life and letters."

Irving Massey. *The Gaping Pig*. Berkeley: University of California Press, 1976.
In a larger study of "metamorphosis" in literature, *Frankenstein* is read almost as an allegory of solipsism—both Victor and his mon-

ster being without any relationships except the half-struggle with each other that allows Victor to remain "permanently exempt from the necessity of developing his self-awareness."

Milton A. Mays. "*Frankenstein*, Mary Shelley's Black Theodicy." *Southern Humanities Review* 3 (1969): 146–53.
The use of *Paradise Lost* and the Faust myth in the novel shows a world in which injustice predominates.

Masao Miyoshi. *The Divided Self: A Perspective on the Literature of the Victorians*. New York: New York University Press, 1969, pp. 79–89.
The *Doppelgänger* motif as it reflects fundamental nineteenth-century dualisms.

Elizabeth Nitchie. *Mary Shelley: Author of Frankenstein*. New Brunswick, N.J.: Rutgers University Press, 1963.
A critical biography with much useful factual information and a sensible perspective on the quality of Mary's writing.

Sylvia Norman. "Mary Wollstonecraft Shelley." *Shelley and His Circle*. Vol. 3. Cambridge, Mass.: Harvard University Press, 1970, pp. 397–422.
Brief biographical study; sound literary judgments.

Robert M. Philmus. *Into the Unknown. The Evolution of Science Fiction from Francis Godwin to H. G. Wells*. Berkeley: University of California Press, 1970, pp. 82–90.
Frankenstein as a version of the Faust myth.

Burton R. Pollin. "Philosophical and Literary Sources of *Frankenstein*." Comparative Literature 17 (1965): 97–108.
The influence of the writings of Godwin, Milton, Ovid, Locke, and several others, on *Frankenstein*.

James Rieger. "Dr. Polidori and the Genesis of *Frankenstein*." *The Mutiny Within: The Heresies of Percy Bysshe Shelley*. New York: Braziller, 1967.
A correction of Mary Shelley's 1831 introduction to the novel and a discussion of Polidori's relation to Mary.

Christopher Small. *Mary Shelley's "Frankenstein": Tracing the Myth*. Pittsburgh: University of Pittsburgh Press, 1973. Originally, *Ariel Like a Harpy: Shelley, Mary, and Frankenstein*.
The novel in juxtaposition to Godwin, to Shelley's *Prometheus Unbound*, and to later works in which technology becomes monstrous.

Muriel Spark. *Child of Light: A Reassessment of Mary Shelley*. Hadleigh, Essex: Tower Bridge Publications, 1951.

Half biographical, half concerned with approaches to *Frankenstein* and other fictions. Includes abridgment of *The Last Man*. One of the first to identify the *Doppelgänger* motif in *Frankenstein*.

L. J. Swingle. "Frankenstein's Monster and its Romantic Relatives: Problems of Knowledge in English Romanticism." *Texas Studies in Literature and Language* 15 (1973): 51–56.
Thematic connection of *Frankenstein* with the work of the great Romantic poets, especially Wordsworth and Keats.

Martin Tropp. *Mary Shelley's Monster.* New York: Houghton Mifflin, 1977.
A light but lucidly written reading of *Frankenstein* as "dream," and a delightful analysis of the Frankenstein films, with a listing.

William A. Walling. *Mary Shelley.* New York: Twayne Publisher, 1972.
Excellent brief study of Mary and her works.

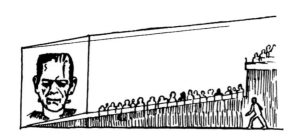

Index

3121